MGM

This is the first comprehensive history of MGM from its origins in 1905 to the present. Following a straightforward chronology corresponding to specific periods of film industry history, each chapter describes how successive managements adjusted their production strategies and business practices in response to evolving industrial and market conditions.

As the production subsidiary of the Loew's Inc. theatre chain, MGM spent lavishly on its pictures and injected them with plenty of star power. The practice helped sustain MGM's preeminent position during the heyday of Hollywood. But MGM was a conservative company and watched as other studios innovated with sound and widescreen, adjusted to television, and welcomed independent producers. By the 1960s, the company, sans its theatre chain, was in decline and was ripe for a takeover. A defining moment occurred in 1969, when Kirk Kerkorian, a Las Vegas entrepreneur, made a successful bid for the company. There followed a tumultuous thirty-six-year period when Kerkorian bought and sold MGM three times. Meanwhile, MGM never regained its former status and has functioned as a second-tier company to this day.

Focusing on MGM's top talent – such as Louis B. Mayer, Irving Thalberg, David O. Selznick, and Arthur Freed; directors King Vidor and Vincente Minnelli; and stars of the screen Greta Garbo, Judy Garland, Clark Gable, and Mickey Rooney – and award-winning films, this book highlights the studio's artistic achievements and status within the industry.

Tino Balio is Professor Emeritus of Film in the Department of Communication Arts at the University of Wisconsin–Madison. He is the author of numerous books and articles on the American film industry, most recently *Hollywood in the New Millennium*, London: BFI Palgrave, 2013.

Routledge Hollywood Centenary

Series Editors: Yannis Tzioumakis and Gary Needham

The eleven-year period 2012–2023 marks the centennial anniversary of all seven Hollywood major studios: Universal, Paramount, 20th Century Fox, Warner Bros. Columbia, Disney, and MGM. Originally self-run organizations operating within a clearly defined film industry, from the sixties onwards these companies have become divisions of various conglomerates during a long period of corporate consolidation and, more recently, of media convergence driven by the advent of digital technology and changes in distribution and consumption. The Routledge Hollywood Centenary book series provides a detailed and authoritative history of these long-standing organizations, aiming to chart their hundred-year development and their transition from film studios to divisions of global entertainment conglomerates.

Each individual volume examines in detail the evolution of the major Hollywood players over the course of a hundred-year period. With some of the studios having been divisions of conglomerates for more than fifty years and as they have continued to evolve under changing corporate ownership and increasing media convergence, the Routledge Hollywood Centenary volumes assess how this evolution, and its periodization, impacts our understanding of Hollywood film history. From the 'studio' to the 'post-studio' era, from 'Classical Hollywood' to 'Conglomerate Hollywood', through changes in ownership and management regimes, and through collaborations with ever changing clusters of talent each Hollywood studio has been a major contributor to the ways in which American cinema acquired a particular identity at different historical junctures. The Routledge Hollywood Centenary series volumes examine in detail how each studio has put an indelible stamp on American cinema and beyond.

MGM
Tino Balio

For more information about the series, please visit: www.routledge.com/ The-Routledge-Hollywood-Centenary-Series/book-series/RHC

MGM

Tino Balio

Routledge
Taylor & Francis Group

LONDON AND NEW YORK

First published 2018
by Routledge
2 Park Square, Milton Park, Abingdon, Oxon OX14 4RN

and by Routledge
711 Third Avenue, New York, NY 10017

Routledge is an imprint of the Taylor & Francis Group, an informa business

British Library Cataloguing-in-Publication Data
A catalogue record for this book is available from the British Library

Library of Congress Cataloging-in-Publication Data
A catalog record for this book has been requested

ISBN: 978-1-138-91364-6 (hbk)
ISBN: 978-1-138-91366-0 (pbk)
ISBN: 978-1-315-69129-9 (ebk)

Typeset in Bembo
by Apex CoVantage, LLC

CONTENTS

FIGURES

Images provided with permission from the Wisconsin Center for Film and Theater Research

SERIES EDITORS' PREFACE

The eleven-year period 2012–2023 marks the centennial anniversary of all seven Hollywood major studios: Universal, Paramount, 20th Century Fox, Warner Bros. Columbia, Disney, and MGM. Originally self-run organizations operating within a clearly defined film industry, from the sixties onward, these companies have become divisions of various conglomerates during a long period of corporate consolidation and, more recently, of media convergence driven by the advent of digital technology and changes in media distribution and consumption. The Routledge Hollywood Centenary book series provides a detailed and authoritative history of these long-standing organizations, aiming to chart their hundred-year development and their transition from film studios to divisions of global entertainment conglomerates.

The genesis of this series goes back to 2011, when we became aware that 2012 would mark the centennial anniversary of Universal and Paramount. At that point we began to envisage a book series that would account for the 100-year histories of the Hollywood studios, with a view to chart their evolution over the decades and explore the reasons for their radical transformation. As scholars whose work has been focusing primarily on American cinema, we were fully aware that these companies have received constant attention by the academic community as part of a huge variety of topics and through the prism of a multitude of methodological approaches. However, we were also aware that the number of detailed, book-length studies that focused entirely and exclusively on individual studios was very small – miniscule if one searched for scholarly works that tried to account for the entirety of a studio's history.

The reasons behind the absence of such studies are several. Arguably the most significant is the paucity of archival sources that would help scholars to construct the histories of the Hollywood majors with authority and conviction. Although some corporate records are available for the earlier incarnations of these companies – which of course has led to the publication of foundational histories that detail their operations in the so-called studio era – such records do not exist for the more recent decades of the studios' history or, if they exist, they are largely inaccessible to film scholars. Of course, the absence of corporate records can be compensated to a substantial extent by the presence of different sources (the trade and popular press, the personal papers of various industry professionals associated with individual studios), but access to these requires resources that are not always readily available to scholars.

A second significant reason for the absence of comprehensive accounts that focus exclusively on the major Hollywood players is the increasing conglomeration of the film industry, which saw the former studios being subsumed within labyrinthine structures as divisions of 'filmed entertainment units' or 'motion picture groups.' This has made it increasingly difficult for scholars to approach them conceptually in recent decades. While film historians who examined the Hollywood studios in the 'classical' era could focus on what were clearly defined companies within an easily demarcated film industry, this is not the case for scholars interested in the more recent iterations of these companies as parts of increasingly 'postclassical,' converged media industries. Indeed, such efforts would require separating the film division not only from the corporate parent but also from a number of sister companies and other subsidiaries that might operate in the same market but have different mandates in terms of the kinds of media products they produce and/or distribute.

Indeed, this particular problem has been at the core of the rationale for this series. Having noticed that a significant amount of recent scholarly work on Hollywood film and media has been 'collapsing' the names (and identities) of particular film divisions of entertainment conglomerates to the ones of their corporate parents, we sought to redress the balance by commissioning volumes in which authors have the space to make these distinctions clearly. Even though the extent to which such distinctions can be made might differ from film division to film division and from corporate parent to corporate parent, the focus of each volume on one Hollywood major allows authors to delve into such matters with more emphasis and discuss the extent to which it is possible to isolate the film division from its sister companies and corporate parent.

With individual volumes having the space to examine in detail the evolution of the major Hollywood players over the course of a hundred-year-long period, another key objective of the series is to tackle issues around the periodization of Hollywood cinema. With some of the studios having been divisions of conglomerates for more than fifty years and as they have continued to evolve under changing corporate ownership and increasing media convergence, the Routledge Hollywood Centenary volumes are interested in exploring how this evolution impacts our understanding of Hollywood film history. From the 'studio' to the 'poststudio' era, from 'Classical Hollywood' to 'Conglomerate Hollywood,' through changes in ownership and management regimes, and through collaborations with ever-changing clusters of talent, each Hollywood studio has been a major contributor to the ways in which American cinema acquired a particular identity at different historical junctures. With each volume proposing a new periodization of the history of each studio, the Routledge Hollywood Centenary series as a whole aims to make a strong statement in terms of how Hollywood cinema can be periodized and, effectively, understood.

To materialize this vision, as editors, we approached eminent scholars with a very significant work in the field of American film history, especially the history of the major Hollywood studios, as authors of these volumes. Our rationale was that such experienced authors would be able to bring to their respective projects a strong foundation from which they would then be able to move to areas and directions that have been hitherto underresearched. Indeed, we have encouraged authors to use part of their earlier work as a stepping stone for the construction of these centennial histories and even consider revising that work if their new projects necessitated such a decision. Furthermore, and besides asking authors to ensure that their accounts covered some key areas common to all these companies (emergence/establishment of each company; house style in the studio era; place within the studio system; response to the Paramount Decree; links to the television industry; life within the conglomerate structure; impact of media convergence; and a few others), we have not tried to impose any singular approach to these studies and the ways they are constructed and presented. On the contrary, we have actively encouraged authors to approach each studio in the way they thought is the most appropriate, including the proposed periodization of their respective histories. We also recruited an advisory board that provided significant support to the series, with its members reading proposals and reviewing manuscripts, to ensure that the series produced film histories of the highest quality. Finally, Routledge was instrumental in providing authors with a very generous period from the commissioning of each volume to manuscript submission, which has also contributed to the efforts of both authors and editors to produce the best possible work on the subject.

We hope that these volumes will become the key points of reference for all scholars interested in the history of the major Hollywood studios and American cinema more broadly.

Yannis Tzioumakis and Gary Needham
Routledge Hollywood Centenary series editors

Advisory board:
Warren Buckland, *Oxford Brookes University*
Peter Kramer, *University of East Anglia*
Paul McDonald, *King's College, London*
Eileen Meehan, *University of Illinois at Urbana-Champaign*
Thomas Schatz, *University of Texas at Austin*
Janet Staiger, *University of Texas at Austin*
Janet Wasko, *University of Oregon*
Justin Wyatt, *University of Rhode Island*

INTRODUCTION

During its heyday, from around 1930 to 1950, Metro-Goldwyn-Mayer was the uncontested leader of the American film industry. Filmgoers identified it as the studio with 'more stars than there are in heaven.' Even in its declining years, the MGM motto and Leo the Lion logo signified the glory days of Hollywood. Writing the history of MGM poses a problem. MGM's corporate records and production files are not available to researchers. What remains of these materials is not known. The *New York Times* reported on 24 March 1987 that Lorimar Telepictures accidentally destroyed Louis B. Mayer's correspondence and other materials after it took over the studio from Ted Turner. A treasure trove of film history had been lost. Writing my two-volume history of United Artists, I had access to primary sources. The first, *United Artists: The Company Built by the Stars* (1975), was based on the corporate records of the company from 1919 to 1951, which were donated to the Wisconsin Center for Film and Theater Research in 1969 while I was its director. The second, *United Artists: The Company That Changed the Film Industry* (1987), was based on the corporate records of the company that were made available to me by the company after UA was acquired by MGM. These records were stored uncatalogued in a warehouse the size of an airplane hangar in Meadowlands, New Jersey. I spent much time searching for proverbial needles in the haystack. The correspondence, memos, contracts, and financial ledgers I uncovered along with interviews with company personnel (including one with company founder Charlie Chaplin for the first book) obviously provided me with insights into UA's operations that I could not have otherwise obtained.

Without primary sources, it's still possible to write an authoritative history of a Hollywood studio, as I hope to demonstrate, by taking advantage of the considerable databases available online. Complete runs of the *New York Times* (www.nytimes.com) and *Weekly* and *Daily Variety* (www.variety.com) are available to subscribers. Extensive runs of *Los Angeles Times* and other newspapers are available to patrons of a university research library in ProQuest Historical Newspapers (www.proquest.com). Relevant academic articles and electronic books can be gleaned from JSTOR (www.jstor.org), and recent news content and public records can be found in the LexisNexis database (www.lexisnexis.org). The latter two databases are freely available to researchers at colleges and universities, public libraries, and other institutions. And then there is Lantern (www.lantern.mediahist. org), an open-access database containing collections of classic media periodicals in the public domain. The Hollywood Studio System Collection, for example, contains extensive runs of trade periodicals such as *Variety*, *Motion Picture Herald*, *Motion Picture News*, and *Film Daily* and influential fan magazines such as *Photoplay*, *Modern Screen*, and *Screenland*.

To get a sense of the reception of MGM's pictures, I have relied mainly on the reviews appearing in *Variety* and the *New York Times*. As a leading trade publication, *Variety*'s reviews were directed to exhibitors and assessed the box-office potential of new releases, among other things. *Variety*'s staff reviewers were invariably on target. As a leading national newspaper, the *New York Times*'s film critics reviewed all of MGM's top releases when they received their New York premiere. The reviews, especially those by Bosley Crowther, were likely to set the tone for the national release. The reviews are available online as indicated and in the following print editions: *Variety Film Reviews* (New York: Garland, 1983–) and *The New York Times Film Reviews* (New York: *New York Times*, 1913–). (Quotations from the two sources are cited in-text as *VFR* and *NYTFR*, respectively. Quotations of reviews from other sources are cited as bibliographic entries.)

Financial information about MGM can be found in the trade press, the *New York Times*, and in the Eddie Mannix Ledger. As publicly held companies, Loew's and later MGM issued fully audited quarterly and annual reports regarding profit or loss. These were reported in the press. During the period when MGM was a Loew's subsidiary, the reports often broke out MGM's contribution to the Loew's bottom line.

How Loew's Inc. managed its books is not generally known, but this much is understood. As a fully integrated company during the era of the studio system, Loew's was involved in the exhibition, distribution, and production of motion pictures. In addition, Loew's controlled three music publishing companies, a radio station, two artists' booking services, and other businesses. Each division of the company and its subsidiaries generated profits, but rentals from motion pictures comprised the largest source of revenue. For example, as *Fortune* magazine pointed out, of the $122.7 million in gross revenues that Loew's took in in 1938, around $75 million came from film rentals, as did some $7 million of its $10 million profits ('Loew's Inc.' 1939: 287). At the exhibition level, Loew's controlled around 125 theaters in the United States and Canada and 28 theaters abroad. More than half were owned outright, and the others were either controlled, leased, or managed through subsidiaries. To fill the playing time of its theaters, Loew's booked selected pictures from the other majors in addition to MGM's. The majors owned theater chains in different parts of the country mostly and played each other's films to achieve national coverage. The Loew's box office paid the overhead expenses of the theaters, the funded debt to purchase the chain, film rentals, leasing costs, and other expenses.

At the distribution level, Metro-Goldwyn-Mayer Distributing Corporation released all MGM's pictures in the domestic market exclusively; in foreign markets it sometimes released locally produced pictures as well to conform to quota laws. In all cases, MGM Distributing levied a distribution fee. The proceeds paid the print and advertising costs for the pictures and the expense of operating a worldwide sales organization. At the production level, Metro-Goldwyn-Mayer turned out as many as fifty pictures a year. MGM's producers, stars, directors, and other creative personnel were under long-term contracts. In building a budget for a picture, the studio apportioned a part of their salaries to the project. These were the above-the-line costs. The respective production departments also factored in the material and labor costs for sets, costumes, and so forth – the below-the-line costs. Then the studio tacked on an overhead charge to help cover the administration and ancillary services of operating a physical plant.

The Eddie Mannix Ledger is a remarkable document that lists every film MGM produced between 1924 and 1962 along with each film's production cost, domestic and foreign earnings, and profit or loss. The domestic and foreign earnings for each film represented the distribution gross and not box-office returns. The box-office gross is a good measure of a film's popularity. But the distribution gross is a better indicator of a film's relative profitability. The distribution gross is the total amount collected from exhibitors in the form of film rentals, and it is this figure that goes to pay off the distribution fees, prints, and advertising expenses and the negative cost of a motion picture. Mannix was the long-time general manager of the studio and Louis B. Mayer's right-hand man. The Ledger was discovered in the materials Howard Strickling, MGM's veteran publicity chief, had donated to the Margaret Herrick Library of the Academy of Motion Picture Arts and Sciences. Why the Ledger was compiled is not known, but there is no reason to doubt its accuracy. H. Mark Glancy analyzed the figures in an article entitled 'MGM Film Grosses: 1924–1948: The Eddie Mannix Ledger,' which was published in the *Historical Journal of Film, Radio & Television* in 1992. His Appendix 1, 'The Top Ten Films of each season, based on their total earnings followed by other films mentioned in the text,' was a godsend by revealing the performance of MGM's highest-grossing pictures each season (which went summer to summer) and by providing an insight into MGM's production strategies during its heyday. (Distribution grosses for MGM's releases from 1949 to 1962 are taken from individual Wikipedia articles about the films that cited the Mannix Ledger in the Herrick.) As Glancy pointed out, during the thirties and forties, B movies pretty much covered the studio's overhead by generating small but predictable returns each year. Big-budget pictures had the best chance of generating the greatest returns, but often as not they lost money because of high production costs. The industry average for such films was about one out of three. Blockbusters had the corollary function of burnishing MGM's reputation as a prestige studio. (Unless cited otherwise, the production costs, domestic and foreign earnings, and profit or loss for individual MGM pictures are taken from the Ledger.)

A vast amount of information about MGM and Hollywood is now easily accessible to researchers, but the task remains how to frame the information into a coherent narrative. I have attempted to write a comprehensive history of MGM from its origins in 1905 to 2015. The published research by Douglas Gomery (1986), Thomas Schatz (1997), Mark Vieira (2009), Scott Eyman (2005), and Bosley Crowther (1957) helped me lay the groundwork. My history follows a straight forward chronology corresponding to specific periods of film industry history. Within each chapter, I describe how successive managements adjusted their business and production strategies in response to evolving industrial and market conditions.

Chapter 1 describes MGM's prehistory – the rise of Marcus Loew's theater empire leading up to the founding of MGM on 17 April 1924. The merger of Metro Pictures, Goldwyn Pictures, and the Louis B. Mayer Company climaxed an effort by Marcus Loew to acquire a dependable source of films for his theaters during a period of rapid industry consolidation. Marcus Loew rose from poverty on Manhattan's Lower East Side to build Loew's, Inc., one of the most profitable motion picture theater chains in the United States by the twenties. But its position was threatened by the likes of Adolph Zukor, another industry pioneer, who had built a fully integrated motion picture empire containing many of the top stars in the business. Metro and Goldwyn were on shaky grounds at the time of the merger, but Loew had the good sense to bring in Mayer and his production chief Irving Thalberg to run the new studio. Marcus Loew died in 1927; he was succeeded by Nicholas Schenck, his second in command, who ruled the Loew's empire for the next thirty years.

Chapter 2, covering the period before sound, describes Mayer's and Thalberg's success in building the studio. They accomplished what they set out to do in a remarkably short period of time by producing a full roster of pictures. The generous profit-sharing agreement with Loew's gave Mayer, Thalberg, and their partner J. Robert Rubin plenty of incentive to succeed. Mayer cobbled together elements from the three studios to create a smoothly running operation that rivaled Zukor's Famous Players-Lasky and Fox Films within a year. Thalberg placed his stamp on the central producer system by reining in maverick directors, by building a star roster to rival any in the industry, and by producing a remarkable series of hits, among them: Victor Seastrom's *He Who Gets Slapped* (1924) starring Lon Chaney; Fred Niblo's *Ben-Hur* (1925) starring Ramon Novarro; King Vidor's *The Big Parade* (1925) starring John Gilbert and *La Boheme* (1926) starring Lillian Gish; Erich von Stroheim's *The Merry Widow* (1925) starring Mae Murray; Clarence Brown's *Flesh and the Devil* (1926) starring John Gilbert and Greta Garbo; and Harry Beaumont's *Our Dancing Daughters* (1928) starring Joan Crawford. MGM ended the silent period in a comfortable position.

Chapter 3 covers the advent of the talkies. MGM adopted a wait-and-see attitude during the conversion, but once Nick Schenck gave the go-ahead, MGM moved rapidly to adopt the new technology. The merger movement had run its course by 1930, and the industry took on a structure that characterized it for the next twenty years. Loew's Inc. and four other vertically integrated companies would dominate the industry, while three smaller companies played supporting roles. For a while, Loew's Inc. had been merged with Fox Films. Unknown to Mayer and Thalberg, in 1929 William Fox had acquired the Loew's stock belonging to the family and estate of Marcus Loew and from Nicholas Schenck and other Loew's executives. But the deal collapsed after the Wall Street crash and an intervention from the Hoover White House. During the early thirties, Thalberg turned out a remarkable mix of pictures: prestige films such as Clarence Brown's *Anna Christie* (1930), Edmund Goulding's *Grand Hotel* (1932), and Richard Boleslawski's *Rasputin and the Empress* (1933); fallen-woman films such as Robert Z. Leonard's *The Divorcee* (1930) and *Susan Lenox (Her Fall and Rise)* (1931) and Victor Fleming's *Red Dust* (1932); sentimental comedies such as George W. Hill's *Min and Bill* (1930); social-problem films such as George W. Hill's *The Big House* (1930); and horror pictures such as Tod Browning's *Freaks* (1932). The pictures were studded with such stars as Greta Garbo, Joan Crawford, John, Ethel, and Lionel Barrymore, Norma Shearer, Clark Gable, Jean Harlow, Marie Dressler, and Wallace Beery. MGM's distinctive house style was created by art director Cedric Gibbons, costume designer Adrian, and cinematographer William Daniels, among others. MGM's premier status was reflected in the top-ten polls in the press, in the number of Academy Awards it received, and in the box office.

Chapter 4 describes Thalberg's legacy. Thalberg's health broke at the end of 1932. While he convalesced, Mayer decentralized production. Mayer assumed all the administrative duties, formed a production unit for his son-in-law David O. Selznick to produce prestige pictures, and then upgraded Thalberg's associate producers by giving them responsibility for their own films and by giving them screen credit as producers. The shift from the central producer system to the producer-unit system was an industry-wide phenomenon. It was designed to increase the number of creative inputs into production and to more efficiently monitor costs. Until his premature death in 1936, Thalberg functioned as a special-projects producer. His projects included Sidney Franklin's *The Barretts of Wimpole Street* (1934) starring Norma Shearer, Fredric March, and Charles Laughton; Ernst Lubitsch's *The Merry Widow* (1934), a remake of the Franz Lehar operetta starring Jeanette MacDonald and Maurice Chevalier; Frank Lloyd's *Mutiny on the Bounty* (1935) starring Charles Laughton, Clark Gable, and Franchot Tone; and George Cukor's *Romeo and Juliet* (1936) starring Norma Shearer and Leslie Howard. Even after his death, Thalberg continued to cast a long shadow over MGM with the films he had in development. They were assigned to select producers and helped sustain MGM's reputation for 'polished elegant craftsmanship.' Loew's survived the Depression unscathed, the only major to do so. The rise of labor militancy threatened the entrenched studio system during the Depression, but had little effect. MGM ended the thirties on a high note by releasing David O. Selznick's *Gone With the Wind* (1939).

Chapter 5 describes MGM's war effort. The outbreak of World War II closed foreign markets to Hollywood. However, conditions at home had improved. Employment was up, and the production of consumer durable goods such as automobiles and household appliances had ceased, leaving Americans with disposable income. Movies were the most popular form of entertainment and Hollywood entered a new era of prosperity. The U.S. Justice Department had filed an antitrust suit against the majors in 1938 but postponed the trial for the duration. MGM's bread-and-butter pictures during the war were three long-running B series: Andy Hardy starring Mickey Rooney; Dr. Kildare starring Lionel Barrymore and Lew Ayres; and Maisie starring Ann Sothern. After releasing four of its fading leading ladies in 1942 – Joan Crawford, Norma Shearer, Greta Garbo, and Jeanette MacDonald – MGM replaced them with Katharine Hepburn, Greer Garson, Kathryn Grayson, and Hedy Lamarr. MGM also nurtured a new generation of younger talent, such as Judy Garland, Van Johnson, Robert Walker, Lana Turner, and two precocious child actors, Margaret O'Brien and Elizabeth Taylor. Once the United States entered the war, MGM went full throttle to build morale at home and to support the war effort. War-related themes permeated all of MGM's production trends, the most important of which were American and British home-front dramas, musicals, and family classics. MGM's biggest hit of the decade was William Wyler's *Mrs. Miniver* (1942), a British home-front picture starring Greer Garson and Walter Pidgeon.

Chapter 6 describes the impact of the postwar recession. Things were never the same for Hollywood after the war. Returning servicemen married, had children, and moved to the suburbs. They also enrolled in colleges and universities to take advantage of the G.I. Bill. Moviegoing suffered as a result. Overseas, governments established trade barriers limiting the number of films allowed in and froze the earnings of American companies. At home, the *Paramount* antitrust case had reached the U.S. Supreme Court in 1948, which declared that the five majors had conspired to monopolize motion picture exhibition. The majors as a result entered into consent decrees agreeing to divorce their theater chains, among other things. MGM under Mayer was slow in adjusting to postwar conditions. In 1948, Nicholas Schenck instructed Mayer to find 'a new Thalberg' to revive the studio. He chose Dore Schary, a liberal Democrat, who aspired to inject socially relevant pictures into MGM's roster. The studio system of production went by the boards in the fifties as the industry shifted to independent production, but MGM stood pat with a central producer. Schary and Mayer frequently clashed over the direction of the studio, and in 1951 Nicholas Schenck fired Mayer to give Schary a freer hand. Most of Schary's message pictures lost money. But under his watch, MGM released such hits as Vincente Minnelli's *Father of the Bride* (1950), Mervyn LeRoy's *Quo Vadis* (1951), and Richard Brooks's *Blackboard Jungle* (1955) and a remarkable string of Arthur Freed musicals, among them George Sidney's *Show Boat* (1951), Vincente Minnelli's *An American in Paris* (1951), Stanley Donen and Gene Kelly's *Singin' in the Rain* (1952), and Stanley Donen's *Seven Brides for Seven Brothers* (1954). Nicholas Schenck retired in 1955, a decision that was prompted by the Loew's board, whose members were becoming restless with the slow restructuring of the company. He was replaced by Arthur M. Loew, son of company founder Marcus Loew, in December 1955. Loew considered it an interim appointment and stepped down in 1957. Loew wisely held on to MGM's film library rather than selling it to a television syndicator to make a quick profit. He was replaced by Joseph Vogel, who immediately called for Dore Schary's resignation. In 1957, the studio posted a loss for the first time in its thirty-four-year history. Schary was not entirely to blame; the safety net of B-movie production had been removed from the roster during the rise of commercial television. Schary was replaced by Sol Siegel as production chief. Vogel fended off proxy fights to take control of management and successfully brought the *Paramount* proceedings to a conclusion in 1959. After shedding its theaters, Loew's Inc. took the name of its former studio subsidiary: Metro-Goldwyn-Mayer Inc.

Chapter 7 describes MGM's adjustments to the sixties. Under the Vogel–Siegel management, MGM adopted the Big Picture production strategy to lure people from their TV sets. The strategy was an outgrowth, in part, of the box-office triumph of William Wyler's remake of *Ben-Hur* (1959). Under the Vogel–Siegel management, MGM finally segued into independent production by offering profit-participation deals first to in-house producers and then to outside producers and directors. The Big Picture production strategy practically sank the company as it released a string of box-office failures, the likes of Anthony Mann's *Cimarron* (1960), Vincente Minnelli's *The Four Horsemen of the Apocalypse* (1961), and, most notoriously, Lewis Milestone's *Mutiny on the Bounty* (1962).

The losses on these films led to another management shakeup. Siegel was replaced by Robert M. Weitman in 1962 and Vogel by Robert H. O'Brien in 1963. Although the O'Brien–Weitman team was responsible for such hits as David Lean's *Doctor Zhivago* (1965) and Stanley Kubrick's *2001: A Space Odyssey* (1968), they failed to placate Philip J. Levin, a major shareholder who spearheaded two unsuccessful proxy fights to oust them in 1966 and 1967. Levin ultimately sold his stake in MGM to Edgar M. Bronfman, the thirty-eight-year-old president of Joseph E. Seagram & Sons, who moved up to chairman of the board in 1969. MGM's earnings were off in 1969, which led to O'Brien's ouster. The board replaced him with Louis F. Polk, Jr., a thirty-eight-year-old former financial vice president of General Mills, Inc. He was the first chief executive of a major studio to be brought in from outside the industry. He served only a few months in that position until Kirk Kerkorian, a Las Vegas hotel developer and entrepreneur, bought a controlling stake in the company in October 1969.

Chapters 8 and 9 describe the buying and selling of MGM by Kirk Kerkorian. Kerkorian was not a builder like Steve Ross at Time Warner or Lew Wasserman at MCA or Rupert Murdoch at News Corp.; he was primarily an investor and a shrewd one at that and had the knack of almost always buying low and selling high, whether it was airlines, studios, or casinos. Kerkorian bought and sold MGM three times. He bought MGM the first time in 1969 when the company was going downhill fast at the start of a three-year recession. To turn the company around,

Kerkorian hired James Aubrey Jr., the controversial president of CBS-TV known as 'the boy wizard.' Aubrey saved MGM from disaster by selling off assets – Judy Garland's ruby red slippers included – by downsizing, and by withdrawing from distribution. However, his track record as production head was abysmal. Aubrey resigned in 1973, leaving MGM a second-tier motion picture company, dependent on the risky business of motion picture production for most of its income.

In 1980, Kerkorian split its production and casino units into separate companies, Metro-Goldwyn-Mayer Film Co. and MGM Grand Hotels, Inc. To head the film unit, Kerkorian chose David Begelman, the rehabilitated former head of Columbia Pictures who had been convicted of forgery and embezzlement. Next, he recaptured its distribution by acquiring United Artists from Transamerica Corporation for $185 million in 1981 and formed a new company, MGM/UA Entertainment Company. Begelman's expensive slate of pictures scheduled for 1981 turned out to be flops, and he was ousted in mid-1982. Burdened with debt from the purchase of United Artists and from a continual string of box-office failures, Kerkorian sold MGM/UA to Atlanta broadcaster Ted Turner for $1.5 billion in 1985.

Chapter 9 describes the aftermath of Turner's takeover. Turner and not Kerkorian, as many have alleged, was responsible for dismantling the company. Turner was desperate to acquire the MGM library for his WTBS superstation. After failing to come up with the money to complete his buyout in 1986, he sold the studio with its back lot, Irving Thalberg Building, Metrocolor Film Laboratory, and twenty-four sound stages to Lorimar-Telepictures, a TV producer and syndicator.

Sans a studio, the new MGM/UA Communications Co. was a revolving door of production chiefs who turned out far more misses than hits. But MGM, which still owned the MGM logo and United Artists film library, retained its allure and attracted some unsavory characters, chief among them Giancarlo Parretti. Kerkorian was happy to take his money, and in 1990, he sold MGM a second time to the Italian financier, who merged MGM/UA Communications with his Pathé Communications Group, to form MGM–Pathé Communications. Parretti set out to loot the studio, and it wasn't long before Crédit Lyonnais, his principal creditor, foreclosed. The French bank had five years to dispose of MGM under U.S. banking laws. To recoup its investment, the bank poured more money into the studio to kick start production – it even revived United Artists – and prepare it for auction. But the effort fell short, and Crédit Lyonnais lost any hope of recouping all of its $2.5 billion investment in the studio.

After putting up the studio for auction in 1996, Kirk Kerkorian's $1.3 billion bid won out. Buying MGM a third time, Kerkorian then acquired the Orion Pictures, Samuel Goldwyn Pictures, and PolyGram Filmed Entertainment film libraries to create the world's largest film vault and overhauled MGM's management yet again in an attempt to remake MGM into a Hollywood major. The latter task Kerkorian gave to Alex Yemenidjian, a casino executive and senior executive at Kerkorian's Tracinda Corp. Yemenidjian scaled back production, milked MGM's film library for every dollar, and repositioned United Artist Films as a specialty unit under Bingham Ray. But the effort was futile. As a second-tier company, MGM had no separate 'profit centers' to even out the risks of motion picture production. The James Bond films, which came with the United Artists acquisition, righted the ship more than once. Kerkorian held talks to acquire or merge with other companies, but when his bid to acquire Vivendi Universal fell short, he began to look for an 'exit strategy' to cash out.

In Chapter 10, MGM ends up a hybrid. In 2005, Kerkorian sold MGM a third time to a consortium of investors led by Sony Corporation of America in a leveraged buyout for $5 billion. Sony wanted MGM's library of 4,000 films to help its Blu-ray technology win the high-definition-format war. Rather than purchasing MGM outright, Sony took on Comcast and a number of hedge funds as equity partners and submitted the winning bid for the studio. At the conclusion of the buyout in September, Metro-Goldwyn-Mayer became a private company. To take ownership of MGM, the consortium formed MGM Holdings, Inc. on 11 February 2005.

The new owners dismantled MGM's movie business and fired most of MGM's staff. Sony focused on selling MGM's DVD films and television shows in the home entertainment market and on cofinancing and coproducing new motion pictures for the company, such as future installments of the James Bond franchise, to keep the library relevant to retailers. However, MGM's majority investors became dissatisfied with Sony's distribution of MGM's DVDs in 2005 and hired Harry E. Sloan, a high-flying entrepreneur and former Lionsgate board member, to take charge. But the company was hobbled by $3.5 billion in debt from the 2005 buyout, production had nearly ground to a halt, and DVD sales, the most profitable side of MGM's business, had plunged as consumers switched to new technologies. In 2009, Sloan was replaced Stephen F. Cooper, who had nurtured Krispy Kreme's revival after its 2001 bankruptcy. MGM's creditors refused to restructure MGM's long-term debt and allow it to continue with its current business model. MGM, as result, filed for Chapter 11 bankruptcy in 2010. MGM emerged from bankruptcy in December 2010 with a new management team headed by Spyglass partners Gary Barber and Roger Birnbaum. After investing $1.3 billion in the company in 2005, the hedge funds saw their entire stake in the company wiped out. Barber and Birnbaum's restructuring succeeded. MGM ended up a hybrid – a company with a historic brand that owns a treasure trove of films containing mostly non-MGM titles and earns the lion's share of its revenue distributing reality television shows. It is a far cry from the glory days of Louis B. Mayer and Irving Thalberg.

1

MARCUS LOEW AND THE FOUNDING OF METRO-GOLDWYN-MAYER (1905–24)

Marcus Loew's is a rags-to-riches story, like those of Adolph Zukor, Samuel Gold-wyn, Louis B. Mayer, and other the founders of the American film industry. Loew was born on 8 May 1870 in a slum on New York's Lower East Side. His father, a Jewish waiter, had immigrated to the United States from Vienna a few years earlier and had married a German widow with two children. Marcus was one of five children. At age 6, he was selling newspapers in the early morning in front of a saloon on Hester Street. Three years later, he left school to find his way in the world. After pulling maps in a printing plant for 35 cents a day and teaming up with a man with a hand printing press to publish a weekly throwaway paper called *The East Side Advertiser*, he wound up in the fur business at age 16 working for a wholesaler on lower Broadway. He was made general superintendent after six months, but naturally, he wanted to go it alone, and with $63 in cash in his pocket, he became an independent fur broker. But Loew was unable to keep up with the fashions, and within a year he was bankrupt.

'He emerged from bankruptcy with unpaid debts amounting to $1,800, which seemed an enormous sum to him then,' recounted his obituary ('Marcus Loew' 1927). 'Going back to work for others, he became a fur salesman, and, by carefully saving, got together enough to pay off the $1,800 which, he insisted, he still owed his creditors, although, having been through bankruptcy, he was not legally responsible to them.' This story would be recounted in various versions in the trade and popular press and became a centerpiece of the Marcus Loew myth. Loew had another go at the fur business and barely escaped bankruptcy a second time when the fur trade collapsed. After Loew paid off his debts, he was left with $7. Now he had a wife to support, having married Caroline Rosenheim in 1894. Loew's fortunes improved when he was hired by Herman Baehr, an expert furrier, who knew how 'to buy [furs], to cut them, to manufacture the garments. Loew knew how to sell,' said Crowther (1957: 22).

FIGURE 1.1 Marcus Loew

People's Vaudeville Company

Loew moved into show business by chance. One day, while looking over some apartments as investments to protect him from the volatile fur trade, he happened to meet David Warfield, an up-and-coming stage actor, who too was looking at apartments. From this chance encounter in 1899, they became business associates and close friends. Warfield had witnessed the carloads of pennies being collected by a penny arcade called the Automatic One-Cent Vaudeville and convinced Loew to try to buy into the venture. Warfield was starring in a hit Broadway play, *The Music Master*, and had money to invest. The arcade was located in Union Square, the heart of the city's entertainment district, and contained more than one hundred peep-hole machines – mostly phonographs, mutoscopes, and penny-in-the-slot machines that delivered peanuts, candy, and the like. The men behind the operation were two fur dealers who were branching out – Adolph Zukor and his partner Morris Kohn – and a Buffalo merchant, Mitchell H. Mark. Warfield and Loew made their pitch to the group in 1903, and it was accepted. With the new cash infusion, they formed the Automatic Vaudeville Company in 1904 and set out to open new arcades in Newark, Philadelphia, and Boston.

Within a year, Loew and Warfield struck out on their own to form People's Vaudeville Company. They opened their first penny arcade in January 1905 on Twenty-Third Street, near Seventh Avenue. This was the beginning of Loew's theater empire. He was 35. The same year, Marcus Loew hired the man who would become the financial mastermind behind the company, David Bernstein. As reported in the *New York Times* ('David Bernstein' 1945), 'in 1905, Mr. Bernstein, then 23, answered a "want ad" of the Marcus Loew People's Vaudeville Company requesting the services of a young bookkeeper. He found that the job demanded knowledge of corporation accounting, of which he knew little.' Bernstein, who was raised in Utica, had dropped out of school at age 18 and was a clerk in a dry goods store. People's Vaudeville hired him at a salary of $14 a week with the understanding that he had to report in three days. In the interval, he taught himself corporation accounting. In 1910, Bernstein was made general manager of Marcus Loew's operations and, two years later, vice president, treasurer, and board member of the company. At the time of his death in 1945, the *New York Times* stated, 'His skillful guidance had enabled the company to weather the financial storms that had threatened the industry during the last thirty years.'

Loew soon opened four more arcades in the city. 'These got along fine for a few months,' he said, 'and then they all took a decided turn for the worse. In fact, we lost all our money and as much more as I could raise . . . Luck finally changed six months later, when I opened my first moving picture show in a room over my last penny arcade in Cincinnati,' one of his stops on his selling trips ('A Motion Picture Show Magnate' 1911: 324). He named it the Penny Hippodrome. As reported in *Moving Picture World* (Judson 1917: 78), 'Someone told him about a motion-picture show across the Ohio River at Covington, and he went over to see it. The proprietor was the ticket seller, gateman and operator.' The man 'would sell tickets till he got his lobby filled, then he would open the gate and let them into the theatre, close the gate again and repeat the process until the theatre was full, and then he would begin projecting the pictures.' He was paid $75 a week, and 'Loew thought he could do as well.' The following Sunday, Loew opened his nickelodeon with a [Pathé] comedy called *Hot Chestnuts* and a few other shorts. Nearly 5,000 people paid their nickels to see the cheap show. The following week, business picked up even more. After returning to New York, Loew removed the penny machines from his arcades and converted them into nickelodeons. In six months, 'we had forty other places going, all store shows, and all doing a land-office business,' he said.

Motion picture exhibition expanded prodigiously beginning in 1905. Thousands of nickelodeon theaters were springing up all over the country, particularly in urban, industrial cities with large immigrant populations. It was an ease-of-entry business. After renting a storefront, restaurant, or amusement parlor, a newcomer needed only a projector – easily purchased – a supply of films – now readily available from Edison, Biograph, Vitagraph, and other studios – and some chairs, a piano, and perhaps a gaudy sign outside to lure in the customers. Programs lasted fifteen to twenty minutes. The industrial workweek was declining, albeit slowly, and workers now had some leisure time for entertainment. The circus, burlesque, legitimate theater, vaudeville, billiard parlors, and saloons prospered along with the movies, but a five- or ten-cent nicklelodeon ticket provided a special inducement.

Small-time vaudeville

By 1907, Loew sensed that the nickelodeon craze had peaked and started unloading theaters. In the bigger cities, the market had become saturated. Nickelodeon operators, as a result, had to compete harder to attract customers. And securing more and better films for their programs proved difficult. Although American film producers had adopted mass production techniques, they were simply unable to keep up with the demand. Loew found a way to survive by converting his houses to small-time vaudeville. As the name implies, small-time vaudeville was a second-tier version of big-time vaudeville. Big-time vaudeville was dominated by a few powerful circuits such as Keith-Albee, Proctor, and others. Both tiers presented a mix of short films and variety acts, but big-time paid higher prices for the top acts and presented national celebrities in purpose-built houses to a better-class clientele. Big-time programs played twice a day, while small-time played three times daily or on a continual basis.

Loew's first dedicated movie theatre was a boarded-up burlesque house in Brooklyn, known as Watson's Cozy Corner. Loew purchased it in 1907 for a song and had it fumigated physically and then morally by booking an Italian stock company. 'To give it a new standing,' Loew said, 'I engaged an Italian tragedian, Antonio Miori, and kept him there for six months in Shakespearian plays. Then I entered upon my original plan and changed it into a moving picture and vaudeville theatre,' which he renamed the Royal. The first year, Loew made a profit of $63,000. 'It was undoubtedly the combination of moving pictures and vaudeville that did the trick,' he said ('A Motion Picture Show Magnate' 1911: 324).

Loew's goal thereafter was 'to provide a high-class entertainment to a great number of people at the same time at a nominal price' (Judson 1917: 78). He could do this by spreading the cost of the best shows among as many patrons as possible. Loew adopted a 10–15–25 cents admission scale; big-time circuits charged twenty-five cents to a dollar. 'The Loew policy of vaudeville and pictures, no matter what kind of vaudeville or what kind of pictures that were made in those days, commenced to do business,' said *Variety* ('Expansion' 1919: 12). 'In fact the Loew houses seemed to do business from the moment he opened their doors.'

In search of bargains, Loew leased older houses in out-of-the-way places at first. With the proceeds, he constructed new theaters in the better parts of town. To jump-start the box office, he would give away thousands of passes through department stores and other places of business. Whenever he encountered competition from a big-time house that lowered its ticket prices to compete directly with a Loew house, Loew spent more to acquire better acts and was willing to sit tight until business improved. By the summer of 1909, People's Vaudeville operated a popular-priced vaudeville circuit covering a large part of the East. In New York alone, he had twelve houses.

The brothers Schenck

Meanwhile, in 1906, Marcus Loew became associated with two more individuals who would play key roles in his growing theater empire, Nicholas and Joseph Schenck. The brothers were born in Rybinsk, Russia, and had immigrated to the United States as young boys with their parents and brother in 1893. They sold newspapers and did odd jobs to get by. At nights, they slept behind a drugstore where their older brother worked as a pharmacist. In 1905, they invested in a beer concession called the Old Barrel at the Fort George Amusement Park. The park was located in Upper Manhattan and had a spectacular view of the Harlem River. The park consisted mainly of a loose and disorganized strip of sideshows when the Schencks bought in, but the park had potential. It stood on the highest point of Manhattan and caught summer breezes. And it could be easily reached from most parts of the city by trolley for a nickel. The Old Barrel was a spectacular success, and with the proceeds, they constructed a new summer park on the premises called Paradise Park in 1906. 'Paradise Park is plainly designed to attract the poor class of patronage,' said *Variety* ('Summer Parks' 1906: 12). 'The chief attractions are the music hall giving a vaudeville bill of nine acts and a dance hall.' Admission to the park was free; revenue was derived from the sale of concessions, which cost five cents.

The decade prior to World War I spawned more than 400 amusement parks around the country, and the Schencks had gotten in on the ground floor. Marcus Loew was a steady visitor to Paradise Park and had befriended the brothers. After the first season's receipts came in, he agreed to loan them money to add several thrill rides to the park. After the second season's receipts came in, Loew invited the Schencks to join him in the People's Vaudeville venture. 'Thus the brothers were joined in a 20-year association with Loew until his death in September, 1927,' said *Variety* ('Nick Schenck' 1969: 4). Nick Schenck 'remained at Loew's side to the end as chief lieutenant in charge of theatre operations' and Joe Schenck as 'head of the various Loew talent booking offices' before going into independent production in 1919.

Loew's Consolidated Enterprises

In a bid to raise additional capital, Loew and his partners agreed to pool their assets and form a new corporation, Loew's Consolidated Enterprises, in February 1910. It was capitalized at $1.5 million and acquired the assets of People's Vaudeville (Crowther 1957: 32). Marcus Loew assumed the presidency, Adolph Zukor was elected treasurer, and Nick Schenck secretary. (Marcus Loew and Adolph Zukor had become friends and had previously cooperated on some joint ventures.) A large block of the Loew's Consolidated stock was sold to Broadway producers Lee and Jacob Shubert, who were building the largest chain of legitimate houses in the country. Having rented two idle New York houses to Loew's People's Vaudeville in 1909, they had acquired a taste for small-time vaudeville and wanted in. Loew now had sufficient capital to expand throughout New York City and beyond. In October 1910, he opened the National Theater in the Bronx, which served for a time as his flagship theater, and acquired control of the lucrative Harlem Casino. By the 1910–11 season, he owned a circuit of forty small-time vaudeville theaters, stretching from Chicago to New England. Loew's next move was to purchase the William Morris independent vaudeville circuit in March 1911. The circuit included the American and Plaza theaters in New York and houses in Chicago, St. Louis, and Cincinnati. After the buyout, Loew moved his headquarters to the American Theatre on Eighth Avenue between Forty-First and Forty-Second Streets.

To assure a steady supply of vaudeville acts, Loew formed the Marcus Loew Booking Agency in 1910 with Joseph Schenck as manager. To assure a steady supply of films for his theaters, Loew formed the People's Film Exchange in 1910 with David Bernstein as manager. People's Film was a state's rights exchange that distributed single reelers. In both cases, Loew cut out the middleman and collected the booking fees and film rentals. The film exchange did not last long, however. In 1911, Loew sold the exchange to General Film Company, the new distribution arm of Motion Picture Patents Company, which was maneuvering to take over the industry. Loew, like other state's rights distributors, had little choice in the matter. Either they sold out to General Film or faced the threat of having their entire film supply cut off.

Loew's Theatrical Enterprises

In 1911, Loew reorganized a second time and formed Loew's Theatrical Enterprises. It was capitalized at $5 million and took over the assets of Loew's Consolidated (Gomery 1986: 53). Zukor resigned from the company in 1912. He saw the future of the business in feature films and moved into film production by forming Famous Players in Famous Plays. Loew did not follow Adolph Zukor into motion picture production at this point. Rather, he expanded his theatre circuit to reach the Pacific coast. He did this in August 1914 by acquiring the Sullivan & Considine Theatrical Syndicate, which comprised around thirty houses in the Midwest and Far West. Loew bought out the circuit for a reported $4 million, and for a while, Loew's chain comprised around a hundred theaters that stretched coast to coast. Formed in 1906, Sullivan & Considine operated both theaters and a booking agency in New York to supply a steady stream of acts to the expanding circuit. Charlie Chaplin, Will Rogers, Marie Dressler, and Albini the Magician had gotten their start playing the circuit. However, the deal went sour nearly at once, and Loew returned the houses to Sullivan & Considine in April 1915 after having lost $500,000 in the venture. Loew's brand of small-time vaudeville did not take off in these theaters.

The Loew's circuit for the time being was confined to the East. Small-time vaudeville had been good to Marcus Loew. In a little more than ten years, he had become a wealthy man and had won the attention and respect of the financial community. As the *Los Angeles Times* opined, 'He has demonstrated how a man can win a fortune quickly and still honestly, and the strangest part of his career is that he has built up this huge fortune with nickels, dimes and quarters'('Facts about Marcus Loew' 1914).

The rise of Famous Players-Lasky

But Loew dared not stand pat. The film business was changing, in no small measure due to Adolph Zukor. Zukor's Famous Players in Famous Plays had become a resounding success after the release of the French import *Queen Elizabeth* (Desfontaines and Mercanton) starring Sarah Bernhardt in 1912. Zukor then teamed up with Daniel Frohman, a big theatrical producer, and signed up Broadway stars to perform feature film versions of their Broadway hits. In 1916, he staged a coup and took control of Paramount Pictures, the national feature film distributor founded by W. W. Hodkinson, and merged Paramount with his Famous Players and the Jesse L. Lasky Feature Play Company to form Famous Players-Lasky Corporation. When Zukor completed his consolidations and acquisitions in December 1917, he had created the largest motion picture company in the world. Zukor maintained a strategic hold on the market by signing most of the biggest stars in the industry, among them Mary Pickford, Douglas Fairbanks, Gloria Swanson, and William S. Hart. He then implemented the next stage of his thinking by raising film rentals. By using the distribution practice of block booking, which is to say on an all-or-nothing basis, Zukor guaranteed that his pictures would be rented to exhibitors on his terms.

Loew played Adolph Zukor's *Queen Elizabeth* but did not start booking feature films in a significant way until 1914. He was a cautious man and waited until feature films were more than a passing fad. Once the decision was made to adopt feature films, Loew treated them like a vaudeville act, which is to say, they travelled his circuit, playing three days in each house before moving on to the next. Some houses offered small-time vaudeville, others straight vaudeville or straight films. Whenever a feature played a Loew's house, one act was left out of the vaudeville mix and therefore cost the theatre nothing to book the picture. By 1915, feature films had become the industry standard.

Exhibitors rebelled against the imperious Zukor in 1917 by forming the First National Exhibitors Circuit. The brainchild of Los Angeles exhibitor Thomas Tally, First National was an alliance of twenty-six important exhibitors who owned more than 100 first-run theaters in all parts of the country. Capitalizing on their considerable buying power, First National captured many of the biggest box-office names, such as Mary Pickford and Charlie Chaplin. It did so by putting up financing, allowing the stars to produce their own pictures. In return, First National acquired the rights to distribute them through its franchisees. Within a year, First National had secured a steady supply of outstanding pictures for its franchise holders, who by then controlled nearly 200 first-run houses in the largest metropolitan areas. First National had become an aggressive opponent.

First National's control of the biggest first-run theaters posed an ominous threat to Zukor. Their proximity to large concentrations of population meant they received the bulk of the business. Without access to such houses, no picture could earn a profit. Zukor, as a result, went into the theatre business. With the backing of Kuhn, Loeb, and Company, Zukor went on a buying spree in 1919, acquiring chain after chain of theaters, some of which had formerly been allied to First National. By adding exhibition to its production-distribution arms, Famous Players-Lasky had become fully integrated and a force to be reckoned with.

Regardless of how the battle between Famous Players-Lasky and First National played out, Loew saw his bargaining power diminished. He chose not to hook up with First National, and although Zukor remained a close friend (Zukor's daughter married Loew's elder son, Arthur, in 1920), he was at a competitive disadvantage. Reverting to an all-vaudeville policy for his theaters made no sense given the increasing popularity of feature films. Loew therefore decided to go into production.

Loew's Inc.

To raise the money, Loew reorganized a third time by forming Loew's Inc. on 18 October 1919 and issuing 700,000 shares of common stock. Of this amount, 380,000 shares were retained by Loew and his partners in Loew's Theatrical Enterprises; 160,000 shares were retained by Liberty Securities Corporation and Van Embrugh & Atterbury, the banks that oversaw the financial reorganization; and 160,000 were offered to the public ('Loew Interests' 1919). Loew's Inc., which was listed on the New York Stock Exchange in 1920, had on its board Charles E. Danforth of Van Embrugh & Atterbury; Harvey Gibson, president of Liberty National Bank; W. C. Durant, president of General Motors; Daniel Pomeroy, vice president of Bankers Trust; James Perkins, another New York Banker; and Lee

Schubert, the Broadway theatre magnate. Loew was now ready to go into production, but he would not start afresh. Rather, he looked to buy a going concern. That was Metro Pictures Corporation, which he acquired in 1920.

Metro Pictures Corporation

Metro Pictures Corporation, with offices at 1465 Broadway, was owned by eighteen film exchanges located around the country. It was incorporated on 5 March 1915 out of the remains of the Alco Film Corporation, a distribution company founded in 1914 by Al Lichtman, a former field manager for Adolph Zukor's Famous Players. Alco was modeled after W. W. Hodkinson's Paramount Pictures but designed to service small exhibitors with a steady supply of features. Like Paramount, Alco provided production financing up front to producers in return for the distribution rights to their pictures for a fee. The financing came from a coalition of state's rights buyers who put up their film rentals in advance. Alco floundered within a year, 'torn by internal disagreement,' said Schmidt (1982: 47).

Alco's disgruntled exchange men led by Richard A. Rowland, a former Paramount franchisee from Pittsburgh, reorganized the company. The Metro board comprised Rowland, president; Joe Engel, treasurer; and James Clarke, secretary. Louis B. Mayer, who owned the Alco film exchange in Boston and a theater chain covering much of the Northeast, was soon named vice president. J. Robert Rubin, who later became a member of 'the Mayer group,' served as counsel to the company during its reorganization. Rubin was born in Syracuse, New York, in 1882 and had a law degree from Syracuse University. Coming to New York in 1906, he worked for a law firm for a while and as an assistant district attorney before joining Alco.

Metro planned on releasing one feature a week. It initially secured its films from four minor producers – Rolfe Photoplays, Quality Pictures Corporation, Popular Plays & Players, and Columbia Pictures Corporation (not the current Columbia Pictures). They were located in the New York area with the exception of Quality, which had its backlot in Hollywood. Metro's first release was R. A. Rolfe's *Satan Sanderson* (1915) starring Orrin Johnson of Broadway fame on 29 March 1915. Rowland soon signed some of the biggest stars in the business, among them Ethel and Lionel Barrymore, Alla Nazimova, Francis X. Bushman, Olga Petrova, Margarite Snow, and Mary Miles Minter. 'By July 1915, Metro was an industry-wide sensation,' said Schmidt (1982: 47). 'During one week in July all but one theater on Broadway was showing a Metro feature.' To stay competitive in a rapidly expanding industry, Metro reincorporated in 1917 and used the proceeds to purchase its production companies outright and centralize production under its own banner in Hollywood.

By 1918, however, it was not clear that Metro could keep pace. Louis B. Mayer left the company to produce films on his own, some of Metro's exchanges were failing, and the price of producing feature films had gone up. The star system was a big burden, which led Rowland to proclaim in 1919 that 'motion pictures must cease to be a game and become a business.' He wanted to supplant the star system. Metro, he said, 'would thenceforth decline from "competitive bidding for billion-dollar stars" and devote its energies to making big pictures based on "play value and excellence of production"'('Star System' 1919: 53). But Metro was reduced to producing cheap 'program' pictures costing around $15,000 to $20,000 each. 'This was a perilous policy, since such pictures could not get booking in the better theaters,' as Crowther noted (1957: 51). By 1919, the better theaters that drew the largest crowds were being taken over by Famous Players-Lasky and First National. Already overextended, Metro remained on the sidelines without theaters.

Marcus Loew had the theaters but not the reliable supply of films he craved. He was therefore receptive to a deal proposed by Rowland and Metro counsel J. Robert Rubin to acquire a half interest in Metro, but Loew, sensing a bargain, wanted the entire company. Loew acquired Metro in January 1920 for $3.1 million. But actually Loew's Inc. paid nothing out of pocket for the company. Metro's stockholders received $1.5 million of Loew's stock and $1.6 million in cash (Crowther 1957: 52). To raise the cash, Loew simply deducted the revenue generated by the distribution fee charged to Metro's foreign releases and transferred the money to his company's books. Loew had acquired a Hollywood studio, a lineup of actors, directors, writers, and cameramen, and a network of exchanges around the country. Rowland continued as president after the takeover; as did Rubin as counsel.

The deal turned out better than expected. On 6 March 1921, Metro released Rex Ingram's *The Four Horsemen of the Apocalypse* (1921) starring Rudolph Valentino.

FIGURE 1.2 Rudolph Valentino dancing the tango in Rex Ingram's *The Four Horsemen of the Apocalypse* (1921)

FIGURE 1.3 Loew's corporate headquarters, 1540 Broadway, New York

It premiered in New York at the Lyric Theater on a reserved-seat basis and broke the house record. In development at the time of the Metro buyout, *The Four Horsemen* was based on the Vicente Blasco Ibáñez's war romance and adapted for the screen by June Mathis, the head of Metro's scenario department. It was Mathis who convinced the studio to cast an aspiring actor by the name of Rudolph Valentino to play the part of Julio. The film was epic in every respect. The first 'million-dollar picture,' as Metro called it, took six months to complete. 'Upwards of 12,000 persons were engaged in the undertaking,' reported the *Los Angeles Times*. 'An entire French village, capable of housing 6000 souls, was put up and destroyed . . . more than 500,000 feet of raw film were exposed in the taking of the picture; fourteen cameramen were employed to "shoot" the big scenes from every angle, and Rex Ingram, at times had fourteen directors assisting him' ('Some Statistics' 1923). *Variety* called the picture 'a masterpiece of motography' and accorded Rex Ingram 'a place alongside [D. W.] Griffith,' adding, 'his production is to the picture of today what *The Birth of a Nation* was' (*VFR*, 18 February 1921). *Four Horsemen* turned Valentino into a superstar as a 'Latin lover,' inspired a tango craze, and grossed $5 million worldwide; thus Loew 'got a production company for nothing and made a profit,' as *Variety* put it ('Leo's 20th' 1944: 104).

Although Marcus Loew had acquired a film studio, he still considered himself a theater man. With its newest infusion of capital, Loew's Inc. went on a building spree, and on 29 August 1921, it opened the Loew's State Theater (designed by classicist Thomas Lamb) on Broadway at Forth-Fifth Street in the heart of the theater district. The 3,200-seat combination film and vaudeville palace cost $6 million to build and was part of a sixteen-story office building Loew's constructed to serve as its new corporate headquarters. Loew's State was the 127th theater in the chain. Most were located in the East. Greater New York had the largest concentration with thirty-four. The Metropolitan in Brooklyn had a seating capacity of 4,000; the average was around 2,000. Some showed just movies, others vaudeville and movies. Loew's State was not the last theater on the construction agenda. The plan was to open a new one every week for the next two months. In line with the company's conservative bent, reported *Film Daily* ('Loew's Doubles Net' 1927: 9), the majority of the new houses were financed by local capital so that the company's actual outlay was comparatively small.

Rex Ingram went on to make *The Conquering Power* (1921), which costarred Rudolph Valentino and Alice Terry, his wife; *The Prisoner of Zenda* (1922), which costarred Alice Terry and Ramon Novarro, his newest find; and *The Arab* (1924), which again costarred Terry and Novarro. *The Arab* was shot in North Africa and was designed to rival Valentino's *The Sheik* (Melford, 1921), produced by Famous Players-Lasky. Metro also released two Buster Keaton starrers, *The Saphead* (1920) and *The Three Ages* (1923); two Mae Murray hits directed by Robert Z. Leonard, *Fascination* (1922) and *Peacock Alley* (1922); and a hit by child star Jackie Coogan, *Long Live the King* (Schertzinger, 1922). But most of Metro's pictures were second rate. As Richard Koszarski (1990: 80) put it, 'The acquisition of Metro was not to be the answer to Loew's problems.'

Goldwyn Pictures Corporation

In 1924, Marcus Loew was presented with another deal too good to pass up – Goldwyn Pictures. It was proposed by Lee Shubert, a trusted friend and a Loew's board member. Goldwyn Pictures was formed by Samuel Goldfish in 1916 in partnership with Broadway producers Edgar and Archibald Selwyn and Arthur Hopkins and the playwright Margaret Mayo, who was Edgar Selwyn's wife. After his marriage to Blanche Lasky in 1910, Goldfish and Jesse Lasky became infatuated with the movies and with all the nickels and dimes they collected. In 1913, they pooled their resources and formed the Jesse L. Lasky Feature Play Company in partnership with Cecil B. DeMille and Arthur Friend. They made it big the first time out by producing *The Squaw Man* (1914), a Western starring Dustin Farnum. It was codirected by Oscar Apfel and Cecil B. DeMille and shot in Los Angeles, a first. The Jesse L. Lasky Feature Play Company became one of the most successful early film producers and in 1916 it merged with Zukor's Famous Players to form Famous Players-Lasky. Goldfish became the new board chairman and Zukor the president. But Goldfish was unwilling to share authority with Zukor and, at Zukor's instigation, Goldfish was voted out of the company.

Goldfish had a passion for quality. After forming Goldwyn Pictures, he set out to produce features from the Selwyns' play library. To make them, he leased the Solax Studio in Fort Lee, New Jersey, and released his first picture, *Polly of the Circus* (Horan and Hollywood) starring Mae Marsh in September 1917. In 1918, he moved west and took over the old Triangle Pictures lot in Culver City, California. His talent roster now included playwrights Bayard Veiller, Avery Hopwood, and Margaret Mayo; stage and opera stars Maxine Elliott, Mary Garden, and Geraldine Farrar; and designers Robert Edmund Jones, Hugo Ballin, and Everett Shinn. In 1918, Goldfish petitioned the courts to allow him to take the company name as his own. 'Since the name was copyrighted, it was necessary to get the company's consent. Goldfish as president, consented,' said Crowther (1957: 65). Goldwyn's stars could not compete with newcomers like Mary Pickford, Charles Chaplin, Douglas Fairbanks, Norma Talmadge, or Mary Miles Minter. He therefore conducted an experiment to make story value the supreme element in a film by forming a special unit in his company called Eminent Authors in 1919. He signed many of the established writers of the day such as Rex Beach, Gouverneur Morris, Mary Roberts Rinehart, and Rupert Hughes and gave them carte blanche to translate literature into film.

Eminent Authors films were stodgy, but the publicity surrounding the venture attracted the interest of the Shuberts. In 1919, Lee Shubert and the playwright A. H. Woods approached Goldwyn and proposed the name of a man who was a genius for raising money – Frank Joseph Godsol. Godsol had made millions from his business dealings with France during World War I. Goldwyn took the bait and appointed Godsol, Shubert, and Woods to the board. *Variety* described Godsol as 'probably the first of the fiscal wheeler-dealers who have frequently controlled giant film organizations without the slightest aptitude of production or showmanship' ('Nick Schenck' 1969). Godsol induced Goldwyn to bring the du Ponts – H. F. du Pont and Eugene E. du Pont – and the Chase Bank and the Central Union Trust into the company to establish a pool for corporate expansion. With the infusion, Goldwyn purchased and overhauled the Triangle studio in Culver City and opened the new Capitol Theatre at Broadway and Fiftieth Street in Manhattan, the largest in the country. But the Thomas Lamb–designed theater did not solve Goldwyn's problems. The battle for theaters was in full force, and studios the size of Goldwyn had to work to line up first-run houses. Moreover, Goldwyn's Eminent Authors had become a costly failure. Goldwyn's quest for quality did little to endear him to his backers, and in March 1922, the board, led by the du Ponts, ousted Goldwyn as president of the company. With the settlement, Goldwyn went into independent production.

Godsol took over as president, but after the coup, the company went downhill. Godsol bolstered the production lineup by forming a joint distribution venture with William Randolph Hearst's Cosmopolitan Productions in 1923. The newspaper tycoon had set up Cosmopolitan in 1918 especially for the popular comedienne Marion Davies. Godsol also hired June Mathis away from Famous Player-Lasky as scenario editor, signed up top-notch directors such as Marshall Neilan, King Vidor, and Erich von Stroheim, and launched two ambitious projects, *Ben Hur* and *Greed*. But films were becoming more expensive to produce, and Goldwyn did not have the financial wherewithal to fill the pipeline. Goldwyn's stock dropped from 22 in the spring of 1923 to 8¼ by year's end (Crowther 1957: 70).

Goldwyn Pictures was ripe for the taking. It comprised the large Goldwyn (ex-Triangle) Studio complex in Culver City; distribution rights to Hearst's Cosmopolitan pictures; the services of directors Marshall Neilan, King Vidor, Charles Brabin, Victor Seastrom, and Erich von Stroheim; stars Blanche Sweet, Conrad Nagel, Aileen Pringle, Renée Adorée, and William Haines; and New York's Capitol Theatre. The deal would also include the talents and skills of production manager J. J. Cohn, art director Cedric Gibbons, and advertising and publicity chief Howard Dietz, the man who created the Goldwyn lion logo and the *Ars Gratia Artis* motto.

Louis B. Mayer Productions

Marcus Loew was about ready to sign when he realized he needed an experienced movie man to oversee his new Hollywood operations. He and Nick Schenck were theater men and knew little about the tricky business of making movies. He found the person – Louis B. Mayer. 'Compared to Zukor, Fox, Loew, the Schencks and Carl Laemmle, Mayer was an upstart newcomer, but one with ability to recognize trends and talent,' said *Variety* ('Nick Schenck' 1969). Louis B. Mayer was born in Minsk, Russia, sometime around 1882. He was one of five children, and his given name was Lazar. The family fled the pogroms of Czarist Russia when he was 2 and ended up in St. John, New Brunswick. His father Jacob worked as a junk collector, and Louis followed in his steps. At age 19, he searched for a better life and moved to Boston. He worked for a local scrap dealer, married a butcher's daughter, Margaret Shenberg, on 14 June 1904, and had two daughters. He continued to sell junk, and by 1907, he was basically broke.

Mayer entered the film business in 1907 by leasing a vacant burlesque house in Haverhill, Massachusetts, the Gem, and converting it into a nickelodeon. Mayer got the owner to come down by half. After cleaning up the place, he opened it with a new name, the Orpheum, on 28 November 1907 and presented a mixed program of short films and vaudeville acts. His theater was an immediate hit with the Haverhill millworkers. Mayer renovated other houses and built new ones. Before long, Mayer and his partner, Nathan Gordon, owned a theater chain covering much of the Northeast.

In 1914, Mayer and Gordon went into distribution and acquired a film exchange in Boston to handle feature films. They made a fortune by purchasing the New England distribution rights to D. W. Griffith's *Birth of a Nation* in 1915. As a partner in Metro Pictures, Mayer was content handling the studio's pictures through his exchange at first, but he soon became interested in production. He helped produce a Francis X. Bushman serial, and in 1917, he lured Anita Stewart away from Vitagraph with the intention of forming a separate unit at Metro to produce her films. There was just one problem: Stewart's contract was still in force, and Vitagraph threatened to sue if Metro distributed her pictures. Fearing that Metro would go the way of Alco if it lost the suit, Rowland acquiesced. His decision created a breach in their relationship, and Mayer resigned to form Louis B. Mayer Productions in 1918. Rubin, his partner, stayed on as Metro counsel.

To raise capital, Mayer planned on selling his theater chain, which now numbered around fifty houses. Mayer moved to Hollywood and leased parts of the William Selig Studio in downtown Los Angeles to begin production and arranged distribution through First National. Mayer's director roster included George Loan Tucker, Lois Weber, Marshall Neilan, and John M. Stahl. Mayer had finally acquired the services of Anita Stewart after buying out her contract from Vitagraph. Mayer's first Anita Stewart film, *Virtuous Wives* (Tucker 1918), was shot in a Brooklyn studio and opened at the Strand in New York on 29 December 1918. Afterward, her pictures were the major prop of Louis B. Mayer Productions; otherwise he was just limping from one picture to the next. Clearly, Mayer had to rely on more than Anita Stewart to carry the company. The star system was in full force. It began with Adolph Zukor, like much else, and peaked in 1919, when four of the biggest stars in the industry – actors Mary Pickford, Charlie Chaplin, Douglas Fairbanks, and director D. W. Griffith – formed United Artists.

To take charge of his studio, Mayer hired Irving Thalberg away from Carl Laemmle's Universal Pictures on 15 February 1923, at a salary of $500 a week (Eyman 2005: 69). Irving Grant Thalberg was born on 30 May 1899 in Brooklyn, the son of middle-class German immigrants. He was diagnosed with a congenital heart defect, and his doctors predicted that he would not live beyond 20 or 30 at best. He graduated from Boys' High School in Brooklyn but decided to forego the rigors of college because of this illness. Instead, he took evening classes at New York University and at business schools. He became proficient in Spanish, dictation, and speed typing. After a few office jobs, Thalberg secured work as an office boy at Universal's New York office at age 18. There he caught the attention of Carl Laemmle, Universal's founder and chief, who made Thalberg his private secretary.

During film screenings, Thalberg took notes for Laemmle and would proffer suggestions to improve the new films when asked. In 1919, after two years on the job, Thalberg accompanied Laemmle on a business trip to Universal City in the San Fernando Valley. When Laemmle returned to New York, he left Thalberg behind with instructions to help reorganize an underperforming and mismanaged studio. Thalberg immediately asserted his administrative skills and took over as general manager of the studio in 1920 at age 21, with a salary of $450 a week (Vieira 2009: 8). To turn out a full season of features and shorts on schedule, Thalberg was determined to center control of production in the front office, away from directors.

Thalberg was now being referred to in the press as 'the boy wonder.' He earned this reputation, in part, by firing Erich von Stroheim from *Merry-Go-Round* (1923) midway through production because he had reneged on his commitment to stay on schedule and within budget. 'With this bold act,' said Vieira (2009: 12), 'Thalberg established the precedent of the omnipotent producer. In a few years it would change the structure of Hollywood filmmaking, shifting power from directors such as Stroheim, D. W. Griffith, and Rex Ingram to producers such as B. P. Schulberg, Darryl Zanuck, and Sol Wurtzel.' 'For the time being,' he added, 'its significance was that of a David-and-Goliath story. A frail, untutored youth had bested a powerful, worldly man. It was incredible that Thalberg should dare to do this, let alone succeed.' After shepherding through *The Hunchback of Notre Dame* (Worsley, 1923) starring Lon Chaney, Universal's biggest hit to date, Thalberg expected Laemmle to honor his request for a modest pay hike to $500 a week from the $450 he had been earning the previous three years, but Laemmle refused, citing economy measures, a thoughtless decision that led to Thalberg's exodus.

The MGM merger

The merger of Metro Pictures, Goldwyn Pictures, and the Louis B. Mayer Company was completed on 17 April 1924 – one of the largest mergers in the history of the American film industry. No money changed hands; the merger was effected by a simple exchange of stock. Loew's new subsidiary was called Metro-Goldwyn Pictures. It was headed by Louis B. Mayer, vice president and head of studio operations; Irving Thalberg, second vice president and supervisor of production; and J. Robert Rubin, secretary. The 'Mayer group,' as it was called, was put under a personal-service contract for three years, with options. To start, Mayer received $1,500 a week, Thalberg $650, and Rubin $600 (Crowther 1957: 81). In addition, the group participated in a profit-sharing agreement. They were to receive 20 percent of the profits of all the pictures the studio produced. (A picture's profits were to be calculated after the payment of all production and distribution costs and the withholding of sufficient monies to pay an annual dividend of at least $2 a share on the common stock.) The profits were to be divided among the Mayer group according to a partnership arrangement as follows, reported Crowther: Mayer was to receive 53 percent, Rubin 27 percent, and Thalberg 20 percent. It underestimated Thalberg's worth.

FIGURE 1.4 Louis B. Mayer presiding over the formal dedication of the Metro-Goldwyn studio on 26 April 1924

Mayer agreed to produce a minimum of fifteen pictures over two years. If he failed to deliver, the personal-service contracts would be voided. Mayer would sign all the contracts with stars, directors, and writers, but no contract could be made without the approval of the Loew's head office. Metro-Goldwyn adopted Goldwyn's lion production logo and Howard Dietz's *Ars Gratia Artis* motto. Its pictures were first introduced in the title cards as 'Louis B. Mayer Presents,' but the introduction was dropped in 1925, and the name was changed to Metro-Goldwyn-Mayer to better reflect Louis B. Mayer's stature in the company. But the movie title cards always reminded audiences that MGM was 'Controlled by Loew's, Inc.' The formal dedication of the Metro-Goldwyn studio took place in Culver City on 26 April 1924. 'Neither Loew nor Nick Schenck was present,' said Crowther (1957: 83), 'a pointed reminder of the actual proprietors of the studio.'

A final detail needed to be dealt with to complete the merger – distribution. As part of the deal, Loew's combined Metro's and Goldwyn's film exchanges to create Metro-Goldwyn-Mayer Distributing Corporation and appointed James R. Grainger to run it as general manager. The combined exchanges were located in the thirty-three key cities across the U.S. and Canada distributors used to achieve national distribution. Grainger resigned after one year to join Fox Films and was replaced by Felix F. Feist, who held the position for eleven years until his death in 1936. Howard Dietz, the former Goldwyn publicity chief, was named director of MGM advertising, exploitation, and publicity, and Arthur Loew, Marcus Loew's son, was head of MGM's foreign department.

In 1925, Nick Schenck and his brother Joe, who was then chairman of United Artists, proposed merging MGM's distribution subsidiary with United Artists. United Artists was formed in 1919 by Mary Pickford, Charlie Chaplin, Douglas Fairbanks, and D. W. Griffith as a distribution company for top-ranked independent producers. After turning independent, the UA founders had formed their own production companies and put up the financing to make their films. Forming United Artists gave them control over how their pictures would be promoted and sold to exhibitors. UA also helped out with the financing by collecting film rentals for their pictures in advance of release – exhibitors were that eager to book their pictures. By 1925, UA had released such hits as Pickford's *Pollyanna* (1920), Chaplin's *The Gold Rush* (1925), Fairbanks's *The Thief of Bagdad* (1924), and Griffith's *Broken Blossoms* (1919).

Nick may have had misgivings about the quality of MGM's future product and wanted access to UA's star lineups. And Joe no doubt wanted stronger distribution for UA's pictures, many of which he was now personally producing, and easy access to the Loew circuit. But the plan went nowhere. Charlie Chaplin was against it, and his partners acquiesced. Chaplin had little respect for MGM, which he referred to at the time as 'three weak sisters' (Balio 1976: 61).

By 1927, Loew's 'had achieved much of what it set out to do three short years earlier,' reported the *New York Times*. Loew's profits had improved steadily after the merger, from $2.9 million in 1925 to $4.7 million in 1926 to $6.7 million

FIGURE 1.5 Loew's salesmen mapping plans to sell the next season's roster

in 1927. In 1927, MGM contributed a net profit of $2.9 million to the Loew's bottom line, 'making it the most successful film company in the industry' ('Corporation Profits' 1928).

The consolidation of the industry was in full force and was on the verge of converting to sound. Marcus Loew would not be a witness to the new era; he died of heart disease on 5 September 1927 at age 57. On the day of his funeral, which was held in Cypress Hills, New York, all the Loew theaters closed for the day. As reported by the *Los Angeles Times* ('Last Rites' 1927), the memorial service at the Culver City studio 'marked one of the most impressive events ever carried out in a screen studio, as 2,000 prayed and the studio flag was lowered to half mast.' Dr. [Edgar F.] Magnin, in a touching tribute, referred to the life of Marcus Loew as 'the greatest drama in the history of the screen industry he did so much to develop.'

Loew had battled his way up from poverty. At the time of his death, his company owned or controlled 144 theaters, a major motion picture studio, and other enterprises that were capitalized at $100 million, and Marcus Loew's estate was valued anywhere from $35 million to $50 million ('Marcus Loew Dies' 1927). Nick Schenck, who had had administrative charge of the company the previous three years when Loew was in failing health, was elected president; Arthur Loew was elected first vice president to succeed Schenck; and J. Robert Rubin, MGM general counsel, was chosen to take Arthur Loew's place on the board of directors.

2

BUILDING A PRESTIGE STUDIO (1924–28)

Setting up shop

Taking charge, Mayer upped the ante by announcing plans to make fifty pictures the first season. Mayer and Thalberg had been producing around a dozen pictures a year. Now, they geared up to release one feature a week. Mayer revamped the Culver City studio and ordered the construction of four new stages, three administrative buildings, and a prop building to enlarge the wardrobe and furniture departments. 'Although now large in size,' said the *Los Angeles Times* ('Millions' 1924), 'the studio will become the largest and most complete film producing plant in the world through the expansion.' To organize the various studio departments into an efficient assembly line, Mayer retained J. J. Cohn from the Goldwyn Company as production manager. Cohn's job was to keep MGM films on or under budget. To help trumpet MGM's stars, Mayer hired Pete Smith, a former press agent, to head the studio's publicity department.

As vice president and head of studio operations, Louis B. Mayer became the public face of the studio. As top man, he set company policy, approved production budgets, hired and fired, negotiated contracts, and served as the studio liaison with the Loew's home office, among other duties. Mayer's inner circle comprised Eddie Mannix, comptroller, and Benny Thau, casting office head. Mannix had worked for the Schenck brothers in various managerial capacities since the Palisades Park days. Nicholas Schenck appointed him comptroller of the studio, but he was soon moved up to studio manager. He later oversaw the construction of MGM's new sound stages and became an expert in industrial relations. Benny Thau had worked as a booker for the Loew's vaudeville circuit before Mayer appointed him head of MGM's casting office in 1927. Mid-level managers took care of the myriad business affairs of operating a studio plant, including payroll, security, industrial relations, maintenance, and food services.

As second vice president and supervisor of production, Irving Thalberg's job was to construct the studio's annual roster. His responsibilities as a prototypical central producer will be discussed in more detail in the following chapter. MGM, like the other majors, produced a wide variety of pictures every season. Most were produced in the low- and mid-budget range and contained second-tier players. Such pictures paid the overhead; profits came from the studio's prestige pictures, which were based on well-known properties and showcased the studio's top stars and directors. Thalberg personally supervised the big-budget pictures and delegated the others to his production supervisors. Thalberg followed the entertainment trends and chose the properties for the studio's stars and directors. He then oversaw the development of the scenario. He did this assisted by studio writers with the goal of tailoring the scenario to a star's image and playing to the strengths of the director. He also made sure his scripts contained proven audience ingredients. Thalberg treated the finished film as raw material. His philosophy was 'Movies aren't made, they're remade' (Thomas 2000: 117). No big-budget picture would be released until it was subjected to a sneak preview. Thalberg and his entourage would typically travel by private trolley directly from the studio to a neighborhood theater in Pasadena, Glendale, or Pomona and observe an audience's reaction to the screening. If an audience did not like something or failed to respond in the appropriate way, he did not hesitate to have parts of the picture reshot. The sets for the movie would not be dismantled until it passed muster. It was a costly process, but Thalberg believed that the process could make a good picture even better. The record bore him out, but for all his efforts, he never himself took a screen credit.

To fill out the production roster, Thalberg initially relied on three production supervisors, Harry Rapf, Hunt Stromberg, and Bernard Hyman. Rapf had just finished a three-year stint at Warner Bros., where he developed the profitable *Rin-Tin-Tin* series. Before that, he did a stint at Mayer's studio, where he produced a popular series based on Elinor Glyn romance novels. Hunt Stromberg started out as a publicity director for Goldwyn Pictures and as a production assistant to Thomas Ince before going into independent production in partnership with Charles R. Rogers in 1921. Hunt Stromberg Productions produced a series of Bull Montana comedies, Harry Carey Westerns, and Priscilla Dean pictures, which were distributed by Producers Distributing Corporation (not to be confused with the Poverty Row PDC). Bernard Hyman, a Yale University graduate, had once worked for Thalberg at Universal as a screenwriter. Rapf was placed in charge of the lower-budget pictures and oversaw Norma Shearer comedies and Lon Chaney thrillers; Hunt Stromberg specialized in action and adventure films; and Bernard Hyman supervised the bread-and-butter Aileen Pringle/Lew Cody and Karl Dane/George K. Arthur comedies.

MGM's combined star roster included Ramon Novarro, Jackie Coogan, Mae Murray, and Buster Keaton from Metro; Marion Davies, Conrad Nagel, Blanche Sweet, John Gilbert, Eleanor Boardman, and William Haines from Goldwyn; and Norma Shearer, Hedda Hopper, Renée Adorée, and Lon Chaney from Mayer's company. MGM originally served only as a distributor for Coogan, Keaton,

Marion Davies, and Mae Murray, who had their own independent production companies. None of these players had made it to any 'top ten' lists. It was too early for MGM to claim that it had 'more stars than there are in heaven.' Clearly, its roster needed bolstering.

The combined director roster included King Vidor, Marshall Neilan, Monta Bell, Fred Niblo, John Stahl, Erich von Stroheim, Robert Z. Leonard, Frank Borzage, Rex Ingram, Victor Schertzinger, and Victor Seastrom. Because of MGM's large production commitment, Thalberg intended to control all facets of production. 'For directors who played by the rules – directors such as King Vidor and Clarence Brown,' said Koszarski (1990: 83), MGM 'offered unprecedented material support and the fabulous distribution potential of the Loew's chain. . . . For the favored few,' he added, 'a measure of artistic freedom could be achieved, but it was clear from the beginning that it was the executive office that would have the last word at MGM, an attitude underscored by Thalberg's increasing reliance on a producer system by the end of the silent period.'

MGM's Scenario Department was headed by an aspiring writer named Robert Harris. Harry Carr (1924) described the department as follows: 'Carey Wilson and Waldemar Young are veteran screen writers. As also are Bess Meredyth, John Lynch, Albert Shelby Le Vino, Agnes Christine Johnston, Monte M. Katterjohn and Alice D. G. Miller. Charleton Andrews is the author of several opera books and lyrics. Adela Rogers St. John is a short-story writer of distinction. Bela Sekely is a Hungarian literary man who is employed at the studio as a critic. This, with [the novelist] Elinor Glyn, is beyond doubt the most imposing array of writing talent that any studio has ever gathered together.' The roster would soon be embellished by Lenore Coffee, Dorothy Farnum, Joe Farnham, John Colton, Frances Marion, and Albert Lewin.

MGM's distinctive look was largely the creation of Cedric Gibbons, the studio's star art director. Gibbons, a holdover from the Goldwyn Company, oversaw the construction of a vast assortment of permanent sets on the studio's back lot – a village, several town squares, city streets, a park, and a waterfront, among others. He also set up some of the finest ancillary departments in Hollywood, such as a scene painting shop, models and miniatures, and special effects. In one way or another, Cedric Gibbons's art department affected the work of 70 percent of the studio's 4,500 workers. He had a clause inserted in his contract stipulating that his credit would appear on every picture the studio produced, a stipulation that the studio respected with few exceptions until his retirement in 1956, said Heisner (1990: 61–2). Gibbons personally approved every set that was built. To complement MGM's opulent and sophisticated house style, Gibbons imposed on MGM's pictures a consistency of style and mood; settings were bathed in brilliant high-key lighting that created a soft gray-white glossy look. In practice this meant that Gibbons supervised the lighting of all the large, important sets but left the lighting of close-ups entirely to the judgment of the cinematographer.

In 1928, MGM discovered a costume designer who could stand beside Gibbons, Gilbert Adrian. Adrian trained at the Parsons School of Fine and Applied Art in

Paris and worked on Broadway designing costumes for Irving Berlin's Music Box Revues and George White's Scandals before moving to Hollywood. At the invitation of Natacha Rambova, Rudolph Valentino's art-director wife, he designed the costumes for Valentino's *The Eagle* (Brown, 1925). He then went to work for Cecil B. DeMille, where he did the costumes for *The Volga Boatman* (1926) and *The King of Kings* (1927), among others. When Louis B. Mayer gave DeMille a three-picture contract in 1928, Adrian came with him. After producing three flops in a row, DeMille departed the studio, but Adrian stayed behind to become MGM's chief costume designer until 1941. His screen credit read 'Gowns by Adrian.' Adrian designed the costumes for more than 250 pictures, period and modern alike. By the time he left the studio, 178 people worked in the wardrobe building. More than anything, his costumes helped define the 'look' of MGM's top female stars, in particular, Greta Garbo, Joan Crawford, and Norma Shearer. As Bingen (2011: 34) said, 'He displayed a unique ability to design costumes that reflected the individuality of the characters in each film again and again.'

The launch

Reining in directors

'In the company's first months, Mayer and Thalberg had their authority tested several times by their most prestigious directors,' said Eyman (2005: 96). 'They lost one test and won the rest.' The directors were Erich von Stroheim, Rex Ingram, and Marshall Neilan. All three had films ready for release. In the case of von Stroheim's *Greed* (1924), MGM had inherited a completed film from Goldwyn, albeit a film too long to be released commercially. Frank Godsol had signed von Stroheim to a three-picture contract in 1922, which gave him considerable freedom to make them with the proviso that they stay within ninety minutes. For his first project, von Stroheim chose *Greed*, which was based on Frank Norris's naturalistic novel, *McTeague*, published in 1899. *Greed* starred Gibson Gowland as McTeague, Zazu Pitts as Trina, and Jean Hersholt as Marcus. Von Stroheim shot the picture on locations in San Francisco and Death Valley over nine months and ran up a bill of nearly half a million dollars, spectacular if not unprecedented at the time.

Von Stroheim's original version lasted nine and a half hours. MGM inherited a version about half as long after von Stroheim himself cut it down to a more workable length, with the intention of having it shown in two parts on successive nights. Thalberg thought it was still too long to be shown commercially, and after von Stroheim refused to make further cuts, Thalberg removed the picture from his control and gave it to June Mathis, MGM's story editor, for further editing. The final version, two and a half hours long, opened in New York at the Cosmopolitan Theatre on 4 December 1924 and was a box-office failure. *Variety* summed it up by saying, *Greed* 'will never get a cent at the box office commensurate with the time and money put into the picture,' adding, 'nothing more morbid and senseless from a commercial picture standpoint has been seen on the screen in a long time . . . It came as a distinct shock to those viewing it' (*VFR*, 10 December 1924).

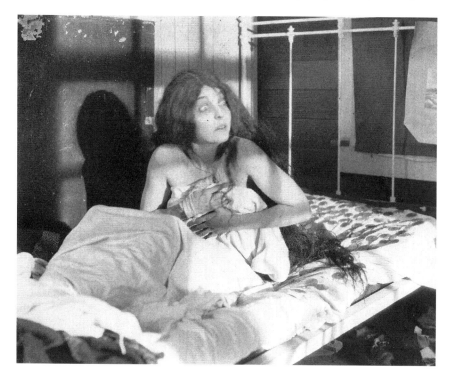

FIGURE 2.1 Zazu Pitts in Erich von Stroheim's *Greed* (1924)

But in an addendum to the review, *Variety* noted that MGM had contemplated releasing the longer version in two parts but decided against it. It further noted that when MGM ordered the film cut from twenty-six reels to ten, the final release print was no longer von Stroheim's *Greed* but the cutter's *Greed*. 'On the trade side no one can know just what was cut out. They see only what was left in. Whose judgment is to be preferred, the director's or the cutter's?' It added, 'because no American picture was ever shown before in two sections of the length of 26 reels is no positive reason why it couldn't be done' (*VFR*, 10 December 1924). MGM took over von Stroheim's contract after the merger. He made one further film for the company, *The Merry Widow* (1925), before succeeding in getting a release.

Ingram's *The Arab* (1924) starred Ramon Novarro and Alice Terry and was shot in North Africa. Casting Novarro in the lead was Ingram's attempt to create a new Latin lover like Rudolph Valentino. Ingram was disaffected with Hollywood and wanted to keep his distance from meddling studio executives. Moreover, he had resented the fact that he had been passed over as director for *Ben-Hur*. Matters came to a head when he read that *The Arab* was going to be released as a 'Louis B. Mayer Presents . . . a Metro-Goldwyn Picture.' He demanded that Mayer's name be taken out and that his picture be presented as a 'Rex Ingram Production for Metro Gold-wyn.' Nick Schenck stepped in and persuaded Mayer to go along with Ingram's demands. Ingram had been a favorite of Marcus Loew and Schenck ever since *Four Horsemen*. Mayer understood this and saw no point in antagonizing his new bosses. Ingram was then given a new contract that allowed him to set up his operations at the Victorine Studio in Nice. As Barton (2014: 138) stated, 'It was a coup that only a director of Rex's stature could have pulled off. Difficult as the Irishman was, he made pictures that spelled prestige and income in equal measures.' Ingram had come up with the money on his own to acquire the studio. Loew's agreed to put up money for renovations but charged the expense to his next pictures.

The Arab premiered in New York at the Capitol on 23 July 1924 to mixed reviews. (After the MGM merger, Thomas Lamb's Capitol Theatre became the flagship house of the Loew's chain, a position it retained until the sixties.) *Variety* called the picture 'the finest sheik film of them all. *The Arab* is a compliment to the screen, a verification of the sterling repute of director Rex Ingram. As a sheik Ramon Novarro is the acme. Surrounded as he is by genuine men of the desert . . . he seems as bona fide as the Arabs themselves' (*VFR*, 16, July, 1924). Mordaunt Hall described it as 'Desert Humbug' (*NYTFR*, 14 July 1924).

After setting up in Nice, Ingram reported directly to Nick Schenck and not to Mayer or Thalberg and made the following pictures before the inevitable split occurred: *Mare Nostrum* (1926), *The Magician* (1926), and *The Garden of Allah* (1927), all of which starred his wife, Alice Terry.

Marshall Neilan was one of Mayer's first hires after the merger. He was married to Blanche Sweet and had his own independent production company. He was best known for having directed Mary Pickford in some of her greatest films. Neilan's contract for MGM called for him to direct a series of pictures starring his wife. *Tess of the d'Ubervilles* (1924), his first entry, was based on the Thomas Hardy novel and starred Blanche Sweet and Conrad Nagel. Neilan shot much of it in 'Hardy Country' in the south of England to give it an authentic look. Neilan followed Hardy's story complete with its tragic ending – Tess is hanged after killing the man who raped her. Mayer thought that the audience would be turned off by the ending and insisted that Neilan prepare a 'happy' ending. Neilan insisted that the film should be shown to preview audiences with both endings to gauge the reaction. Although the preview audiences preferred the tragic ending, Mayer stood his ground and insisted that exhibitors be given the choice of endings. The picture opened in New York at the Capitol on 27 July 1924 with the tragic ending. Mordaunt Hall said, 'Those who are not afraid of a tragic ending, who are interested in a classic story told in a really artistic way on the screen and acted with great sincerity, will appreciate this pictorial effort. It is the life of yesteryear, and it is grim' (*NYTFR*, 28 July 1924).

Harriette Underhill (1924) said, 'While a few pictures may have been ruined by a morbid ending, thousands have been the victims of the happy ending. But Mr. Neilan has displayed imagination as well as rare good taste and good sense in leaving the tale just where he has left it.' Neilan made two more pictures for MGM before he succeeded in getting a release from his contract on 10 April 1925. Miss Sweet remained behind.

Ben-Hur

Mayer and Thalberg's biggest headache was *Ben-Hur*, another Goldwyn holdover. The production was in shambles. June Mathis, the scenarist and supervisor, Charles Brabin, the director, and George Walsh, the star, had set up production in Rome, but had accomplished little. Mayer and Thalberg might have considered shelving the picture since MGM had yet to invest any money in it. But *Ben-Hur* was too valuable to abandon. Published in 1880, General Lew Wallace's *Ben-Hur: A Tale of the Christ* sold nearly as many copies as *Uncle Tom's Cabin*; the stage version produced by the Klaw & Erlanger theatrical syndicate opened on Broadway in 1899 and had toured the country as a roadshow for twenty-two seasons. Goldwyn absurdly agreed to pay Klaw & Erlanger 50 percent of the gross for the movie's rights and had invested heavily in the picture before MGM took over (Eyman 2005: 99).

Mayer and Thalberg scrapped much of what had already been shot and relocated the production to Culver City. Marcus Loew had gone to Rome in December 1924 'to take up the tangled threads of *Ben-Hur*, long in production,' said *Variety* ('Niblo' 1925: 117) and personally broke the news to Mathis, Brabin, and Walsh that they were being replaced. Mathis was replaced by Bess Meredyth and Carey Wilson, Brabin by Fred Niblo, and Walsh by Ramon Novarro. Marcus Loew thought the production could remain in Italy, but Mayer and Thalberg disagreed and Loew assented.

FIGURE 2.2 Ramon Novarro in Fred Niblo's *Ben-Hur* (1925)

MGM built a new Circus Maximus on a 45-acre tract outside the Culver City studio for the chariot race. In full view of some of Hollywood's invited elite, including Mary Pickford and Douglas Fairbanks, Niblo used a battery of forty-two cameras to shoot the race that was cheered by thousands of extras in the crowd scenes. *Ben-Hur* premiered at the George M. Cohan Theater in New York on 30 December 1925 as a roadshow. (The roadshow was a form of motion picture exhibition that emulated the live theater. Such a picture would be booked in a prominent legitimate house and presented twice daily, at scheduled performances. The presentation was divided like a play into two 'acts' with an intermission in between, and, during the silent period, accompanied by a symphony orchestra that played a full score. Tickets were sold in advance on a reserved-seat basis at two dollars top. MGM would use this technique to launch its most prestigious releases.) Francis X. Bushman as Messala and Mary McAvoy as Esther shared top billing with Novarro. MGM billed it as 'The $4,000,000 Picture,' the costliest ever, but *Variety* ('Inside Stuff' 1926: 10) stated that the actual figure was probably closer to $7.5 million. *Variety* called *Ben-Hur* 'the greatest achievement accomplished on the screen. When produced as a play the great Chariot Race scene was relied on to carry the play,' it noted. 'On the screen it isn't the Chariot Race or the great battle scene between the fleet of Rome and the pirate galleys of Gothar . . . that carry the great thrills. It is the heart interest that has been inculcated into the silent presentation of Gen. Lew Wallace's tremendous play' (*VFR*, 6 January 1926).

Ben-Hur played as a roadshow attraction in selected legitimate theaters around the country for nearly two years before it went into general release in October 1927. It was a tremendous hit. As H. Mark Glancy (1992: 131) pointed out, 'at a time when domestic earnings of $1,000,000 and foreign earnings of $500,000 were the benchmark of a box-office hit, *Ben Hur* had a domestic gross of $4,359,000 and a foreign gross of $5,027,000. The foreign gross was particularly impressive; it would not be matched for another 25 years.' But because of the high production costs, the picture initially lost a considerable sum. Nonetheless, *Ben-Hur* became MGM's first great public-relations triumph, establishing an image for the company of grandiose productions that persisted for years.

He Who Gets Slapped

MGM's first production of its own and its first release was Victor Seastrom's *He Who Gets Slapped* (1924), a prestige picture based on Leonid Andreyev's expressionist play that was presented by the Theatre Guild in 1922. Seastrom and Carey Wilson adapted the script. To play the tragic clown HE, Thalberg signed the character actor Lon Chaney, a master of makeup and body distortion who had made it big as the crazed and grotesque bell ringer in *The Hunchback of Notre Dame* (1923) for Universal. Norma Shearer and John Gilbert, who had both worked for Mayer before the merger, supplied the love interest. Shearer was just starting out; Gilbert was a veteran with eighty pictures to his credit.

FIGURE 2.3 Lon Chaney in Victor Seastrom's *He Who Gets Slapped* (1924)

In *He*, Chaney played a brilliant scientist whose research and wife are stolen from him by his mentor. A ruined man, he flees to the circus and becomes a clown. In his act, he is slapped by his fellow clowns whenever he attempts to speak, all to the howling laughter of the audience – a symbolic reenactment of his personal and public humiliation. The film opened on 9 November 1924 at the Capitol Theatre. Mordaunt Hall said, 'Mr. Seastrom has directed this dramatic story with all the genius of a Chaplin or a Lubitsch' (*NYTFR*, 10 November, 1924). *Variety* described Chaney 'as possibly the greatest character of the screen. In this role he displays an understanding of character beyond anything he has done heretofore' (*VFR*, 12 November 1924). *He Who Gets Slapped* was named one of the top ten pictures of the year by the *New York Times*, *Los Angeles Times*, and fan magazines. Produced at a cost of $170,000, *He Who Gests Slapped* turned in a nice profit of $350,000 to rank number one on the studio's roster for 1924–25. MGM was off to an auspicious start.

Seastrom went on to direct two Lillian Gish pictures for MGM, *The Scarlet Letter* (1926) and *The Wind* (1928), before returning to Sweden in 1930. Chaney burnished his reputation as 'The Man of a Thousand Faces' in sixteen silent MGM pictures. Tod Browning directed many of the best, among them, *The Unholy Three* (1925), *London after Midnight* (1927), and *The Unknown* (1927). John Gilbert went on to become MGM's top leading man. He made three additional pictures the first season, Monta Bell's *The Snob* (1924) and King Vidor's *His Hour* (1924) and *Wife of the Centaur* (1924). Edwin Schallert (1924) said of the latter, 'The feature is really another episode in the amorous adventures of Gilbert as screen hero, which, by this time ought to be sufficiently ample to make up an attractive Christmas book for the flapper fan.' Gilbert 'is holding his place magnificently, it would seem, as the busiest Don Juan of the season, and *Wife of the Centaur* will in all probability enhance his popularity.' Gilbert's biggest hit was King Vidor's *The Big Parade* (1925). Afterward, he sustained his reputation playing opposite Greta Garbo. In 1928, MGM signed him to a contract that paid him $250,000 a picture, 'the richest deal for a contract actor in Hollywood,' said Eyman (2005: 147).

Norma Shearer made a dozen more silent pictures for MGM, among them Monta Bell's *Pretty Ladies* (1925), *Upstage* (1926), and *After Midnight* (1927). Gavin Lambert (1990: 53) said the pictures Shearer and Bell made together 'show Norma at her most original and free as a silent film actress . . . He extended her technique, tapped her humor and inventiveness, encouraged her to be intimate with the camera, discouraged theatrical poses.' He further remarked that her roles were so varied, 'she never creates a fixed star image.' In 1925, Shearer received a new contract that paid her $1,000 a week, rising to $5,000 over the next five years (Lambert 1990: 57).

In Thalberg's eyes, Norma Shearer had ranked second only to Greta Garbo. As a reward, he cast her in her first prestige picture opposite Ramon Novarro, *The Student Prince* (1927), an operetta directed by Ernst Lubitsch. Edwin Schallert (1927) said, 'There can be no question about the charm of the Lubitsch interpretation. He has imbued *The Student Prince* with a heart-touching enchantment.' Ramon Novarro as the young Crown Prince Karl, he said, 'is splendid. I do not know of any performance that he has ever given that equals this.' Norma Shearer as Kathi the ebullient barmaid, he thought, was miscast. The picture was a temporary setback. Shearer and Thalberg married in September 1927, and afterward, she assumed the title 'Queen of the MGM' lot.

Independent productions

Pictures from MGM's independent producers rounded out the first season. Mae Murray made *Mademoiselle Midnight* (1924) and *Circe, the Enchantress* (1924), both directed by Robert Z. Leonard, her husband. They were produced by Tiffany Pictures, which Murray and Leonard set up at Metro Pictures in 1921. (Tiffany is not to be confused with the Poverty Row studio of the same name.) Murray was known as 'The Girl with the Bee Stung Lips' and played mostly vamp roles. Her first two MGM entries were profitable and did not depart from the formula. Murray and Leonard divorced in 1924, and their production company dissolved, after which MGM signed her to a contract.

Buster Keaton made *The Navigator* (1924) and *Seven Chances* (1925). They were produced by Buster Keaton Productions, which was headed by Joseph M. Schenck, Nick Schenck's brother. Joe Schenck went into independent production after he departed Loew's and set up production units for Norma Talmadge, his wife, and for Buster Keaton, his brother-in-law, who was married to Norma's sister, Natalie. Schenck gave Keaton full supervisory control over his pictures. Keaton's first two MGM entries were hits. *Variety* called *The Navigator* 'a laugh getter' and added, 'Columbus Day at the Capitol saw a house jammed to the doors. Though the laughs came late in the footage they were there nonetheless, with the audience giving every indication of being well satisfied' (*VFR*, 15 October 1924). Keaton delivered two more pictures the second season, *Go West* (1925) and *Battling Butler* (1926). Afterward, Keaton joined up with Joe Schenck at United Artists, where Schenck had been functioning as chairman of the board since 1924. Keaton made three pictures for United Artists, *The General* (1927), *College* (1927), and *Steamboat Bill Jr.* (1928). Although scholars would later describe them as masterpieces, they were not profitable. As a result, Joseph Schenck closed down Keaton's company and convinced him to return to MGM as a contract player.

Jackie Coogan made *Little Robinson Crusoe* (1924) and *The Rag Man* (1925) directed by Edward Cline. Jackie Coogan's pictures were produced by Jackie Coogan Productions, which his father set up after Jackie became a star playing a lovable street gamin in Charlie Chaplin's *The Kid* (1921). As *Variety* said of *The Rag Man*, 'The return to battered cap, sweater and long trousers shows that Jackie, naturally enough, has grown considerably since the days he first became the world's favorite youngster. He is still small enough to be entirely winsome and appealing, and there appears a new boyishness about him that ingratiates' (*VFR*, 4 March 1925). MGM agreed and signed him to a new contract in 1925. After making Edward Cline's *Old Clothes* (1925) and Archie Mayo's *Johnny Get Your Hair Cut* (1927), Coogan's popularity began to wane as he grew into adolescence. MGM took over his production company in 1927 in an attempt to sustain his career but failed to find the right formula to do it.

Marion Davies, the most important holdover, made *Yolanda* (1924), directed by Robert G. Vignola, and *Janice Meredith* (1924), directed by E. Mason Hopper. They were produced by Hearst's Cosmopolitan Productions. Hearst's distribution contract with Goldwyn was still in force after the merger. *Yolanda*, a lavish costume picture set in fifteenth-century France, was made at Hearst's Cosmopolitan Studio in New York and was a sequel of sorts to Vignola's *When Knighthood Was in Flower* (1922), which made Davies a star. *Yolanda* conformed to Hearst's formula 'of placing Marion in a context of history heavily romanticized and rendered "human" mainly through Marion's infectious personality,' said Guiles (1972: 11).

Hearst's losses on these pictures convinced him to get out of independent production. In March 1925, he entered into a production pact with MGM calling for MGM to finance six Cosmopolitan pictures a year based on stories from Hearst's *Cosmopolitan* magazine. Hearst retained the right to select the stories and was given full production control. Profits were to be split fifty-fifty. Davies was to be paid $10,000 a week, $6,000 from MGM and $4,000 from Hearst, making her the highest-paid star on the lot (Eyman 2005: 114). Mayer agreed to these stiff terms, with the knowledge that Hearst's newspapers would heavily promote Davies' and MGM's pictures. After the deal closed, Hearst shuttered his New York studio and moved his production operation to Culver City, where he built a fourteen-room 'bungalow' on the studio lot.

Marion Davies hit her stride in 1925. After marching through 'pompous and pampered roles' in *Knighthood* and *Yolanda*, 'her real comedy talent was discovered,' said Chamberlin (1930: 87). 'She forthwith branded the gay hoyden, and the real Marion Davies was introduced.' Davies delivered three pictures the second season, George Hill's *Zander the Great* (1925), Monta Bell's *Lights of Old Broadway* (1925), and Sidney Franklin's *Beverly of Graustark* (1926). In *Zander the Great*, Davies 'gives a portrayal filled with gorgeous comedy and rich in pathos. It's a performance that will endear her to the public and place her in the rank of the Gishes, the Pickfords and Colleen Moore,' said *Photoplay* ('Shadow Stage' 1925: 50). After starring in a few duds in 1927, she closed out the silent period by making two big hits, King Vidor's *The Patsy* (1928) and *Show People* (1928). As Guiles (1972: 209) said, 'they are not so much farce as they are comedies of manners – the manners of socially ambitious middle-class America in *The Patsy* and the bizarre manners of Hollywood folk in *Show People*.'

The first full season

To promote MGM's upcoming 1925–26 roster, Howard Dietz ('Transcontinental Trip' 1925: 40), MGM's publicity and advertising director, launched 'the greatest single exploitation stunt in the history of motion pictures,' as he put it. MGM sent 'America's First Trackless Train' cross-country beginning in May 1925 to promote the next season's lineup. The train was motor driven and traveled by highway complete with locomotive tender, a Pullman car, and an observation platform. The crew headed by Eddie Bonns, the exploitation manager of MGM's distribution arm, passed out advertising material and MGM buttons in front of local theaters from town to town. 'The Trackless Train's 3,000 mile trip across the continent to the west coast will establish Metro-Goldwyn pictures first in the minds of millions of people who will be directly reached by this astonishing medium of exploitation,' said Dietz by way of understatement. By 1928, the train had toured the U.S. three times and had been sent to England, Europe, South America, and Australia.

The Merry Widow

MGM had three big pictures lined up for its first full season, Erich von Stroheim's *The Merry Widow* (1925), King Vidor's *The Big Parade* (1925), and Rex Ingram's *Mare Nostrum* (1926). MGM had taken over von Stroheim's contract after the merger and selected Franz Lehar's operetta *The Merry Widow* for his first MGM project, with Mae Murray as the Widow and John Gilbert as Prince Danilo. Von Stroheim was allowed to write the scenario and, as *Variety* noted, had 'taken manifold liberties with the original writing to insert a sex angle that consumes the first 50 minutes' (*VFR*, 2 September 1925). Von Stroheim fought with Mae Murray, John Gilbert, and Louis B. Mayer during production, but finish the picture he did. Thalberg insisted on cutting some of the offensive material from

FIGURE 2.4 John Gilbert and Mae Murray in Erich von Stroheim's *The Merry Widow* (1925)

the completed film, 'Whereupon, von Stroheim agreed to waive his right to edit the picture if he be relieved of his contract. He was,' said Crowther (1957: 90). 'And with that he took his departure from Metro-Goldwyn and Mayer.'

The Merry Widow premiered on 26 August 1925 at Loew's elegant new Embassy Theatre on Times Square as a roadshow. The audience was composed of 'society people, film magnates, novelists and stage and screen favorites,' reported Mordaunt Hall. Von Stroheim, he said, 'is to be credited with having elicited from Mae Murray the best acting she has done in the last few years. She is well made up and always effective, especially when she appears in her gorgeous gowns' (*NYTFR*, 30 August 1925). *The Merry Widow* earned a profit of $758,000 and gave Murray a new contract and a boost in salary. Murray's next pictures reverted to the old formulas and kept her fans happy. The critics, however, had had enough. Her decline began in 1926 with Dimitri Buchowetzki's *Valencia* (1926), which was built around the popular song 'Valencia,' and 'the current rage for Spanish shawls for evening wear,' reported *Film Daily* ('Valencia' 1927: 9). *Photoplay* ('Shadow Stage' 1927: 55) said, 'Frankly, one of the worst films of the year. No story and bad acting.' Harriette Underhill (1926) said, '*Valencia* is, from beginning to end, the most artificial picture we ever saw . . . and this includes Miss Murray's transformation, the sets, the acting, the story, and the direction.' Murray's next pictures fared little better. She had grown tired of her roles and retreated to Europe. Soon after, she and MGM agreed to go their separate ways.

The Big Parade

After making a pair of 'sex dramas' starring John Gilbert and Aileen Pringle – *His Hour* (1924) and *Wife of the Centaur* (1924) – Vidor asked Thalberg to let him make 'an honest war picture.' They chose *The Big Parade* and cast John Gilbert and Renée Adorée in the leads. The picture was inspired by the hit Broadway antiwar play *What Price Glory?* by Laurence Stallings and Maxwell Anderson. It was adapted by Vidor and Harry Behn from an autobiographical novel by Laurence Stallings describing his wartime experiences. *The Big Parade* told the story of three doughboys, each from different walks in life, who are swept up by patriotic fervor during World War I and join the army. The soldiers were played by John Gilbert as Jim, a rich man's idle son; Tom O'Brien as Bull, a bartender from the Bowery; and Karl Dane as Slim, an ironworker and riveter. As Franklin (1959: 65) noted, 'For John Gilbert, the film marked a complete about-face from his usual role as a handsome but colorless romantic idol.' 'Minus the moustache that had become his trade mark, and in drab khaki uniform,' he said, Gilbert 'proved to the doubting MGM executives that he was a genuinely fine actor and not just a handsome profile.' Gilbert and Adorée, the French actress, provided the love interest in the first section before the outfit is sent to the front. As noted by *Variety*, Vidor 'knew that he would have to show the horrors of war, and therefore worked his story out in such a manner that it had plenty of comedy relief and a love sequence' in the beginning (*VFR*, 11 November 1925).

Vidor (1935) later described his intent as a filmmaker thus: 'I have always felt that in a motion picture one must appeal to the heart rather than to the head.'

FIGURE 2.5 John Gilbert and Renée Adorée in King Vidor's *The Big Parade* (1925)

Take for example, 'the scene in *The Big Parade* where poor Renée Adorée ran after John Gilbert as his army truck was taking him away to the front.' She was shown 'grasping at his arms, his coat-sleeves, his trouser legs, his shoes, as she gradually saw him slipping out of her life. It was a scene designed to "jerk a tear," and it did it.' When Mayer showed rushes of the scene to Jeff McCarthy, the man who handled the record-breaking *Birth of a Nation* and *Ben-Hur* roadshow tours, they saw an epic in the making. Print in hand, Mayer went to New York and convinced Nicholas Schenck to increase the budget. Vidor then restaged the mobilization sequence in Texas and shot other scenes Mayer had wanted.

The Big Parade premiered as a roadshow at Grauman's Chinese in Hollywood on 5 November 1925. Two weeks later, it opened in New York as a roadshow at the Astor and played there for nearly two years. (Jeff McCarthy managed the roadshow tour.) Mordaunt Hall called it 'An eloquent pictorial epic of the World War . . . a subject so compelling and realistic that one feels impelled to approach a review of it with all the respect it deserves, for as a motion picture it is something beyond the fondest dreams of most people.' The thunderous belching of guns follows on the heels of a delightful romance between a Yankee doughboy and a fascinating French farm girl,' he noted. 'There are humor, sadness and love, and the suspense is maintained so well that blasé men last night actually were hoping that a German machine gun would not "get" one of the three buddies in this story' (*NYTFR*, 20 November 1925). *The Big Parade* earned a $3.5 million profit and transformed John Gilbert and Renée Adorée into major stars. 'The Big Parade* made the reputation of both King Vidor and the studio, also giving Metro-Goldwyn-Mayer a rock-solid financial footing that would last for more than twenty years,' said Eyman (2005: 112). He added, *The Big Parade* also 'confirmed to Thalberg and Mayer that their theories of filmmaking were correct, that a film wasn't finished until they thought it was, and that spending money on the right things was a good way to make more money.'

The Mayer group salary adjustment

The Mayer group had proven its worth. Metro-Goldwyn-Mayer now ranked up there with Famous Players-Lasky and Fox Films. As a reward, they received a boost in salary in late 1925: Mayer's to $2,500 from $1,500, Thalberg's to $2,000 from $650, and Rubin's to $1,000 from $600. In addition, they received a guarantee that the profit-sharing arrangement would never fall below $500,000 (Crowther 1957: 119). The salary adjustment kept the Mayer group happy for just one year, said Crowther: 'In the fall of 1926, Mayer told Schenck that they would lose Thalberg unless some better arrangement for compensation was made. So this time Thalberg's salary was jumped to $4,000 a week and it was guaranteed that his personal compensation from salary and percentages would not fall below $400,000 annually.' He was 27. The package was an acknowledgement of his value to MGM and Loew's.

Mare Nostrum

Coming up next on the 1925–26 roster was Rex Ingram's *Mare Nostrum* (1926), MGM's most expensive picture of the year. It was based on the Vicente Blasco Ibáñez novel about German submarine warfare during the war and starred Alice Terry as a German spy and Antonio Moreno as a Spanish sea captain who deserts his home for her. MGM released it as a roadshow at the Criterion in New York on 15 February 1926.

'Few will deny that [Ingram] has turned out a picturesque gem. Barcelona, Pompeii, Naples, Marseilles – they're all there "in the flesh," and it's pretty work,' said *Variety* (*VFR*, 17 February 1926). 'But landscapes can't and don't make a picture which runs just five minutes short of two hours in actual reelage . . . [A]s it stands it's unquestionably draggy.' 'Besides which,' *Variety* added, 'it's a gruesome tale without a solid laugh during the entire telling.' Mordaunt Hall agreed. He described the opening night's audience being left 'slightly dazed by the weird delivery of the film . . . Mr. Ingram goes about the unfolding of this narrative with a dislike of haste. He seems to tell you that you must gaze upon his story as he tells it or not at all.' 'This production does not do justice to the talent of the man who made *The Four Horsemen of the Apocalypse* and *Scaramouche*,' he added. (*NYTFR*, 16 February 1926). *Mare Nostrum*, the most expensive picture of the season, was also the biggest loser – $67,000.

Ingram made two more pictures for MGM, *The Magician* (1926) and *The Garden of Allah* (1927), before the inevitable break occurred. Both pictures were panned by the critics. *Variety* (*VFR*, 27 October 1926) said of *The Magician*, a thriller based on the Somerset Maugham novel, that Ingram had turned out 'a very slow moving, draggy picture that has but a single thrill.' The *Variety* reviewer went on to suggest that Ingram might want to return to the United States 'to keep pace with the development of the screen technique in adapting and directing.' Ingram had one more picture to make on his contract and Mayer insisted that he make it in Culver City, where he could be supervised. Ingram refused, naturally, which led to his exit from the studio. Gone was the last of MGM's maverick directors.

Bolstering the star roster

Lillian Gish

MGM added star power to its roster in 1925–26 season by signing Lillian Gish, the great D. W. Griffith heroine, and Greta Garbo, a promising young actress from Sweden. Signing Lillian Gish 'was a coup which attested to the rise in the studio's prestige, for Miss Gish had a place in the world of movies comparable to that in the theater of a Sarah Bernhardt or an Eleanora Duse,' said Crowther (1957: 107). MGM paid her a top salary of $800,000 for six pictures and gave her consultation rights on stories, directors, and cast (Eyman 2005: 124). Gish made five pictures for MGM, King Vidor's *La Boheme* (1926), Victor Seastrom's *The Scarlet Letter* (1926) and *The Wind* (1928), John Robertson's *Annie Laurie* (1927), and Fred Niblo's *The Enemy* (1927).

Miss Gish, now 33, eschewed the innocent and wistful waifs of her Griffith pictures and chose more mature roles based on literary adaptations. For her first

FIGURE 2.6 Lillian Gish and John Gilbert in King Vidor's *La Boheme* (1926)

picture, she selected *La Bohème*. Having admired *The Big Parade*, Gish wanted King Vidor to direct, John Gilbert to play her lover Rodolphe, and Renée Adorée her friend Musette. Copyright issues prevented MGM from using plot elements from the Puccini opera, which meant that screenwriter Fred De Gresac had to turn to Puccini's source, Henri Murger's 1851 novel, *Scènes de la vie de bohème*, about struggling young artists in nineteenth-century Paris. Copyright issues also prevented MGM from using Puccini's music for accompaniment. Instead, it used a serviceable musical score composed by William Axt. *La Bohème* premiered in New York at the Embassy Theater on 24 February 1926. Mordaunt Hall called it 'a photoplay of exquisite beauty, an effort that constantly stirs the emotions, and the performances of the principals, Lillian Gish and John Gilbert, are unrivaled in a romance of this type' (*NYTFR*, 25 February 1926). Edwin Schallert (1926) gave a more qualified judgement, saying, 'Some of the potentially loveliest scenes have been spoiled by the too frantic efforts of Miss Gish to give them lightness.' 'She is anything but a reposeful personality in the picture as a whole, and the closing scene is the most impressive in some ways because it is the quietest,' he said. 'There is not the least doubt in the world that Miss Gish dies beautifully,' he added, 'and that is worth the ardent picturegoers' time to witness with what splendid appealingness she performs this undoubtedly taxing feat. The scene is by all odds one of her finest.' But fan magazines gave top acting honors to John Gilbert. 'Mr. Gilbert is the perfect *Rodolphe*,' said *Motion Picture Magazine* (Reid and Smith 1926: 63–4). 'We are getting tired of praising Mr. Gilbert, but what can we do about it? He runs away with the picture; he makes the production. Here is acting so exuberant, so filled with human emotions, so gay, colorful and live, that it fairly burns up the celluloid.' *La Bohème* was Gish's biggest MGM success, turning a profit of $377,000.

Gish's choice of the Nathaniel Hawthorne classic for her second picture would raise the hackles of the censors, Mayer cautioned, but after Gish wrote personal letters to church leaders and women's groups seeking their opinions, she was told they trusted her judgment in handling the controversial adultery element. To play opposite her Hester Prynne as the Reverend Dimmesdale, Mayer proposed Lars Hanson, the young Swede he had admired in Mauritz Stiller's *The Saga of Gösta Berling* (1924). Frances Marion adapted the novel without violating the spirit of the work. As the *Motion Picture News* ('Scarlet Letter' 1926: 681) stated, 'Gratitude . . . for not making the ending an inconsistently happy one.' *The Scarlet Letter* premiered in New York at the Central Theater on 9 August 1926 as a roadshow. Miss Gish's acting continued to receive mixed reviews from the daily press, but the carping was passé. Miss Gish had 'abandoned the greater portion of . . . repetitious mannerisms and emerged a great artist,' said *Motion Picture Magazine* ('Picture Parade' 1926: 63). Norbert Lusk in *Picture-Play Magazine* (Lusk 1926: 60) noted, 'There is one scene in which Hester is taken from the prison to the scaffold where a scarlet A for adultery is to be sewn upon her gown. She walks down an aisle cleared for her in the crowd, her baby in her arms.' 'We do not ever remember seeing anything more poignantly sensitive than Miss Gish's conception of this scene,' he said. 'She is not a broken creature . . . There is a shadow of disdain upon her face . . . she suggests the queen being mobbed by commoners who can never really destroy her because she possesses something far beyond them.' *Variety* stated that Lars Hanson in his American debut handled his role 'with a great deal of finesse. He is certain to be a popular favorite with the women after this picture.' Seastrom's direction, it said, was as 'pretty near perfect and the composition in some of the scenes bespeaks the highest art in picture photography' (*VFR*, 11 August 1926). Although the picture lacked the dimensions of a roadshow in *Variety*'s opinion, it nonetheless earned $296,000 and became MGM's second-biggest moneymaker of 1926.

Greta Garbo

Louis B. Mayer discovered Greta Garbo in Berlin at an invited screening of Mauritz Stiller's *Saga of Gösta Berling* (1924). He was on a talent hunt in Europe after checking in on the *Ben-Hur* production in Rome. Garbo, age 19, had a small part, but 'the magic in her face' impressed Mayer. To get Garbo, Mayer had to offer a contract to Stiller as well. Stiller had been managing her career ever since he discovered her in training at the Royal Dramatic Theatre in Stockholm. Garbo signed with MGM on 26 August 1925. She was given a standard three-year contract starting out at $400 a week. Garbo's first picture for MGM, Monta Bell's *The Torrent* (1926), was produced by Hearst's Cosmopolitan Productions, which owned the rights to the underlying property by the Spanish author, Vicente Blasco Ibáñez. It told the story of a poor Spanish peasant girl who becomes a *prima donna*. Said *Variety*, 'Greta Garbo, making her American debut as a screen star, might just as well be hailed right here as the find of the year,' said *Variety*. 'This girl has everything, with looks, acting ability, and personality. When one is a Scandinavian and can put over a Latin characterization with sufficient power to make it most convincing, need there be any more said regarding her ability?' (*VFR*, 24 February 1926). *The Torrent* was produced for $250,000 and earned a modest profit of $126,000.

Her second picture, Fred Niblo's *The Temptress* (1926), was based on another Ibáñez story and was also produced by Cosmopolitan. She played a femme fatale opposite another Latin lover, Antonio Moreno. Mauritz Stiller was originally supposed to direct the picture, but he was unaccustomed to and unwilling to conform to the ways of the studio system and was replaced by Niblo, the director who helped rescue *Ben-Hur*. Thalberg scrapped everything Stiller had shot and started afresh. '*The Temptress* boasts no highly original plot,' said the *Los Angeles Times* ('The Temptress' 1926: 16). 'Basically, it is merely the story of the siren, caught in her own snare, who is willing to sacrifice everything – even her own life – for the man she idolizes. But with Miss Garbo as the heroine, the old story becomes fresh and intensely interesting.' *The Temptress* cost $669,000 to produce. Although it grossed nearly $1 million at the box office worldwide, the picture ended up with a $43,000 loss.

Garbo's third picture, Clarence Brown's *Flesh and the Devil* (1926), made her a star. It was based on the Hermann Sudermann novel *The Undying Past* and adapted by Benjamin F. Glazer. Garbo had second billing playing a vamp opposite John Gilbert in his usual 'Great Lover' role. The love scenes in the film made the biggest splash. Richard Watts, Jr. (1927: E3) said, 'Never before has John Gilbert been so intense in his portrayal of a man in love. Never before has a woman so

FIGURE 2.7 Greta Garbo and John Gilbert in Clarence Brown's *Flesh and the Devil* (1926)

alluring, with a seductive grace that is far more potent than mere beauty, appeared on the screen. Greta Garbo is the epitome of pulchritude. If you miss seeing *Flesh and the Devil*, we do not believe there ever will be another picture like this.' *Variety* said, 'Here is a picture that is the "pay-off" when it comes to filming love scenes. There are three in this picture that will make anyone fidget in their seats and their hair to rise on end – an' that ain't all. It's a picture with a great kick, a great cast, and great direction.' It added, 'If they don't star this girl after this picture, Metro-Goldwyn doesn't know what it is missing. Miss Garbo properly handled and given the right material will be as great a money asset as Theda Bara was to Fox in years past' (*VFR*, 12 January 1927). The picture generated a nice profit of $466,000.

Certainly the most famous star–cinematographer collaboration of the era was between MGM's Greta Garbo and William Daniels. Working with Garbo on her first picture, Daniels was able to capture Greta Garbo's unique features, and after Garbo became a star, she had it written into her contract that the cinematographer on all her pictures must be Daniels. Garbo made twenty of her twenty-five American films with Daniels.

By the time she made *Flesh and the Devil*, Garbo realized her true worth to the studio and demanded an immediate raise to $5,000 a week. She was currently making $600 a week (Walker 1980: 65). To press her case, Garbo had hired a shrewd business manager named Harry Edington and returned to Sweden for seven months until her terms were met. Cal York (1927: 29) stated that 'Miss Garbo is precipitating a show-down on the rights of producers and stars. Where is the dividing line between right and wrong in questions of this kind?' he asked. The box-office returns of *Flesh and the Devil* broke the impasse. 'They were sensational enough to make the studio consider it better to yield to Garbo and make another fortune than resist her demands and lose one,' said Alexander Walker (1980: 69). Mayer gave her a new contract on 1 June 1927 back-dated to 1 January, a week before the opening of *Flesh and the Devil*. She would now get $2,000 a week the first year, going up in steps to $6,000 a week in year five. 'It was a remarkable contract' said Walker. Garbo had made only three films and had been in Hollywood for two years, yet she had 'held the most powerful company there to virtual ransom.'

A full-service studio

After setting up feature film production, MGM conformed to industry norms by becoming a full-service studio. An evening's entertainment at the movies now also included a selection of short films, such as cartoons, newsreels, travelogues, and comedies. Shorts were included in the feature film packages that were sold to exhibitors as part of a trade practice known as block booking and were in high demand in many areas. In many situations, exhibitors presented live vaudeville acts and elaborate stage presentations as part of the evening's program. But booking a regular supply of fresh acts to provide the needed variety was often difficult. Shorts were a good alternative.

MGM Shorts Department

Nick Schenck organized MGM's Shorts Department in February 1927 and hired Fred C. Quimby to run it. Quimby had formerly worked for Fox in the same capacity. Quimby operated out of New York and was involved strictly in sales. While Mayer and Thalberg concentrated on producing feature films, Loew's turned to outside producers for its shorts. The first deals were struck with the Hearst organization and with Hal Roach Studios in 1927 and were personally negotiated by Nick Schenck. The Hearst organization agreed to produce 104 newsreels a year under the name *MGM News*. They were to cover local, national, and international events. Hearst had been producing a newsreel service for Universal called *International Newsreel*. *MGM News* would be a separate venture. Roach agreed to supply MGM with forty shorts the first year, ten each from the popular Our Gang, Charley Chase, Max Davidson, and All-Star series. MGM, in turn, agreed to advance production financing and to split the profits. Under the terms of the deal, Roach was to be the sole producer of short comedies for the company. Roach had been releasing his pictures through Pathé, but MGM's offer was too good to resist. The partnership lasted more than a decade.

Hal Roach shorts

Hal Roach Studios was one of the top independent studios specializing in short comedies. It was located on eighteen acres in Culver City, about a mile down Washington Boulevard from MGM, and employed more than 600 people. Roach started in the movies in 1912 'as a $5-a-day cowboy extra,' said Peter Flint (1992). 'He rose quickly, working variously as a minor actor, cameraman, writer and assistant director, and he became a director and producer within two years.' In short time, he had a roster of great comedians that included Harold Lloyd, Will Rogers, Harry Langdon, and Charley Chase.

The Our Gang series originated in 1922 and was supervised and directed by Robert McGowan. The original cast comprised 'Mickey Daniels, freckled; Jackie Condon, tousle-haired and irrepressible; Jay R. Smith, skinny; Joe Cobb, fat; 'Sunshine' Sammy, colored; Jack Daniels, tough guy; and Johnny Downs, typical American boy,' said the *New York Times* ('Rounding Up' 1938). There was a complete turnover of the cast every three or four years. The members were replaced one at a time as they grew up. Roach produced 168 Our Gang shorts for MGM from 1922 to 1938, and it became the most popular juvenile series ever filmed.

Charley Chase started out at the Roach studio as a director under his real name, Charley Parrott. A former vaudevillian, Parrott had played bit roles at Mack Sennett's Keystone Studios in support of such rising stars as Charlie Chaplin and Fatty Arbuckle before turning to directing. Hal Roach hired him in 1920 to direct Snub Pollard comedies. After Roach's top star Harold Lloyd left the studio in 1923, Roach had the hunch that Parrott could replace him. Parrott took up the challenge, changed his name to Charley Chase, and developed his own comedy series in which he both acted and directed. Chase made single reelers at first, which were crafted in collaboration with the young director Leo McCarey. They were so well received by exhibitors and the public that Roach upgraded the series to two reels, which became the standard length of the series for more than a decade. His first picture for MGM release was *Sting of Stings* (1927). Within a year, Chase became Roach's top money maker. Max Davidson, a popular ethnic Jewish comedian, had been on Roach's star roster earlier in the twenties. In 1927, he was given his own series, but it lasted only one season. His portrayal of Jewish stereotypes was found offensive, and Nick Schenck wanted it cancelled.

The All-Star series was designed as a training ground for Roach's roster of contract players, among them Stan Laurel, Jimmy Finlayson, Viola Richard, Martha Sleeper, Oliver Hardy, and Lupe Velez. Out of this series grew one of Hollywood's most beloved comedy teams. Stan Laurel and Oliver Hardy had been with Roach for several years and had appeared in several films together, but they were not billed as a team until *Duck Soup* in 1927. After starring in the All-Star pictures the first season, Roach featured them in a series of their own as Laurel and Hardy and scheduled ten two-reelers for the 1928–29 season. During the silent period, Laurel and Hardy's biggest hits were *Battle of the Century* (Bruckman, 1927), *Two Tars* (Parrott, 1928), and *Big Business* (Horne and McCarey, 1928).

Tim McCoy Westerns

MGM added a Western series to its roster in 1926 for the first and only time. The series starred Tim McCoy, who made sixteen historical Westerns at MGM between 1926 and 1929. They were supervised by Larry Weingarten, Harry Rapf's new assistant. Several were based on original stories by Peter B. Kyne, and the best of the series were directed by W. S. Van Dyke. Pauline Starke, Louise Lorraine, Dorothy Janis, Polly Ann Young, Joan Crawford, and other MGM starlets supplied the love interest. (Weingarten started out in public relations and as a salesman and general manager of a production company specializing in biblical stories.) 'The purpose of these films was manifold,' said Everson (1992: 110). 'They provided useful second features for Metro's own "A" features in the slowly growing double-bill market, and they were big enough in size to play single bill in the action houses. They also were useful training grounds for new directors.'

McCoy was an authentic cowboy. Born in Saginaw, Michigan, in 1891, he went out west in 1909 and found work on cattle ranches in Wyoming. He enlisted in the Army when the United States entered World War I and rose to the rank of lieutenant colonel. After the war, he was tapped by Governor Bob Carry to serve as adjutant general of Wyoming. Intrigued with the Indian way of life, he befriended Indian River Reservation Indians and even mastered their sign language. In 1922, he resigned from the post and took a job as a technical advisor on Famous Players-Lasky's Western epic, *The Covered Wagon* (Cruze, 1923). His task was to find five hundred Indians to work as extras for the picture. After the release of *The Covered Wagon*, Paramount no longer needed him. He was about to return to his ranch when MGM approached him to take a screen test and was quickly offered a contract.

McCoy 'was a good actor and a striking figure of a man,' said Everson (1992: 112). McCoy 'always believed that the story – and where possible, an adherence to the facts – mattered more than action.' His films, as a result, 'contained less physical action than those of major Western stars . . . However, nobody was his equal at entering a saloon, letting the swinging doors flap behind him, and then cowing the entire room by flashing his steely eyes.' MGM's ads in the trade press promoting its stars gave McCoy equal billing with John Gilbert, Greta Garbo, Norma Shearer, and other big names and called his historical Westerns 'epics.' They were shot on location and featured authentic Indians, but *Covered Wagon*s they were not. McCoy's pictures were made on the cheap. *Sioux Blood* (1928–29), which was shot in Glacier National Park, cost $41,000 and 'was the cheapest film MGM ever made,' said Glancy (1992: 132). Nonetheless, they were all profitable. The talkies killed the series, and 'MGM never had consistent success with westerns again.'

An era closes

Garbo's return

After Garbo returned from Sweden to resume work, 'Thalberg decreed that henceforth Garbo would play a young but worldly-wise woman who is married to (or kept by) an older man. She discovers love for the first time with an inexperienced younger man, and for him she must give up everything, perhaps even her life', (Vieira 2009: 71). Garbo's fans could not get enough of her movies. She made eight more silent pictures over the next two years, and all made money. Her leading men were John Gilbert, Lars Hanson, Conrad Nagel, Lewis Stone, Nils Asther, and Lew Ayers.

'It was her films with Gilbert . . . that made her MGM's most lucrative female star of the silent era,' said Glancy (1992: 132). Garbo made two more silent pictures with Gilbert, Edmund Goulding's *Love* (1927) and Clarence Brown's *A Woman of Affairs* (1928). *Love* (1927) was based on Tolstoy's *Anna Karenina*. John Gilbert played Vronsky, the man for whom she gave up everything. 'Miss Garbo's singularly fine acting as Anna held the audience in unusual silence,' reported Mordaunt Hall. 'It can be said that Miss Garbo is ably supported by John Gilbert, but throughout this photodrama it is the portrait of Anna that is the absorbing feature. Other characterizations and even the story take second place when compared to the work of this Nordic player.' 'Miss Garbo is elusive,' he added. 'Her heavy lidded eyes, the cold whiteness of her face and her svelte figure compel interest in her actions. Sometimes she reminds one of a blonde Mona Lisa and on other occasions she is gentle and lovely' (*NYTFR*, 30 November 1927). The film grossed $1.67 million in rentals and earned a profit of $571,000, the second most profitable picture of the 1927–28 season behind *The Big Parade*.

A Woman of Affairs (1928) was based on Michael Arlen's controversial bestseller *The Green Hat*. 'In it, Arlen created a new type of heroine,' said the *New York Times* ('Michael Arlen' 1956). 'His Iris March was a modern woman who met men on their own ground rather than behind the etiquette of femininity.' Because the property alluded to homosexuality and venereal disease, it was banned by the Hays Office (the film industry's trade organization otherwise known as the Motion Picture Producers and Distributors of America, headed by Will Hays). To get a clearance, MGM had to change the title and the names of the characters and refrain from making any mention of the original version in the program or in the advertising. *Variety* described Garbo's femme fatale role as: 'the best thing she has ever done. But the kick is out of the material, and, worse yet, John Gilbert, idol of the flappers, has an utterly blah role.' 'At this performance (the second of the Saturday opening), whole groups of women customers audibly expressed their discontent with the proceedings,' it reported. But 'Miss Garbo saves an unfortunate situation throughout by a subtle something in her playing that suggests just the exotic note that is essential to the whole theme and story. Without her eloquent acting the picture would go to pieces' (*VFR*, 23 January 1929).

Garbo's 'eloquent acting' saved more than one second-rate property the studio chose for her. Garbo made her last silent picture in 1929, Jacques Feyder's *The Kiss*, based on an original story by Feyder. Tazelaar's review (1929) in the *New York Herald Tribune* noted, 'Greta Garbo once again lends her glamourous personality to a story scarcely worth it . . . As always her performance is a haunting, beautiful, imaginative one; moving, despite its limitations in plot.' *The Kiss* was also MGM's last silent picture.

Gish's decline

Gish's career declined after her success in *La Boheme* and *The Scarlet Letter*. The problem was that both Gish and Thalberg failed to find a successful formula to sustain her career. Gish had the right of approval over script and director in consultation with Irving Thalberg. 'The arrangement was perfect because Irving was a brilliant producer and we never disagreed,' recalled Gish (1987). In its ads, MGM hyped *Annie Laurie* (1927), her next picture, as follows: 'It is – confidentially – a rather different type of Lillian Gish vehicle. For one thing it is pitched in a key of merriment, and while it ranges to a strong, rugged climax, it might well be classified as a story that touches the sunny, rather than the seamy, side of life.'

It was based on an old Scottish song and told a story about two warring clans. It was directed by John Robertson and costarred Norman Kerry. Mordaunt Hall stated that *Annie Laurie* was 'unconvincing in actions and atmosphere.' For example, 'Scots have invariably a touch of color about their physiognomies. Miss Gish, looking like a hothouse plant, is not suited to roles where she has to dash over crags to light beacons after being injured' (*NYTFR*, 22 May 1927). MGM invested a lot of money in *Annie Laurie*, but it lost $264,000.

After the returns were in, Thalberg asked Gish to take a reduction in salary. She acquiesced, although she wondered if MGM wanted to drop her altogether. Thalberg then gave the go-ahead to two projects she proposed, *The Wind*, based on a novel by Dorothy Scarborough, and *The Enemy*, based on an antiwar play by Channing Pollock. For *The Wind*, Gish chose Frances Marion to adapt the scenario, Victor Seastrom to direct, and Lars Hanson to costar. *The Wind* was shot mostly on location in the Mojave Desert near Bakersfield. As Gish remembered it (1987), 'the daytime summer temperature was never below 113 degrees and usually about 120 degrees. Film coating melted from its celluloid base, and film could not be developed, so it had to be packed in ice and rushed to Los Angeles.' When MGM sales executives viewed a rough cut, they didn't quite know how to handle it. 'The picture was an unrelenting view of the effects of a brutal desert environment on a delicate young woman unable to cope with it. The wind forces her into an unwanted marriage, brings about her meeting with a man who later rapes her and helps drive her to kill him,' said Gish. MGM invited a group of prominent exhibitors to preview the picture and they detested it, especially the ending. 'In the original version, the attack and murder derange the woman and she dazedly wanders into a violent sandstorm – to her death,' said Gish (1987). MGM ordered Seastrom to shoot a happy ending, and a revised version of the film was ready for release by July 1927. But the studio shelved it for more than a year.

Meanwhile, *The Enemy*, directed by Fred Niblo, opened at the Astor on 27 December 1927 as a roadshow. The setting was Vienna during the war. Gish played Pauli Arndt, daughter of a pacifist, whose young husband is taken from her the morning after her marriage. Pauli is left behind and suffers the deprivation of war. When she sees 'her baby starving for lack of money to buy it food,' she enters a brothel to try to save it. 'It is hard to see how this screen version . . . can exert a strong pull from the public,' said *Variety*. 'The subject matter is not timely, and in the transition from stage to screen the adapters have created mayhem and a little arson upon the material they worked with,' adding, 'Lillian Gish doesn't register in this sort of stuff. You have to be pretty naïve to accept Lillian as a creature of sin without an involuntary twitch at the corner of the mouth' (*VFR*, 11 January 1928). Mordaunt Hall described the picture as having 'a great deal of shrieking and shouting . . . Its comedy is preposterous and Fred Niblo's dull direction does not enhance its entertaining value . . . Lillian Gish gives a charming performance, but her acting is always reminiscent of her past work' (*NYTFR*, 1 January 1928). The picture earned a modest profit of $96,000.

The Wind opened at the Capitol on 4 November 1928 unheralded. *Variety* ('Lillian Gish' 1928: 4) reported that *The Wind* was being sold as a western and in the promotion materials little mention was being made of Gish. 'Salesmen . . . find it hard to sell Gish products to exhibitors,' it explained. Earlier, *Variety* had stated in its review, 'Some stories are just naturally poison for screen purposes and Miss Scarborough's novel here shows itself a conspicuous example . . . It is a sad, heartrending duty to report . . . that Miss Gish, in some of her most dramatic moments, drew laughter instead of tears from a Sunday afternoon audiences composed mainly of New Yorkers' (*VFR*, 7 November 1928). The picture posted a loss of $87,000. After the two failures, both MGM and Miss Gish had had enough, and MGM let her go.

Keaton's return

Buster Keaton returned to MGM in January 1928, but only as a contract player. The move was engineered by his producer and brother-in-law, Joseph Schenck. As noted earlier, Keaton's pictures at United Artists had not done well, and Schenck could no longer afford to finance them now that Keaton was facing the uncertainties of sound. Keaton had both Nick and Joe Schenck's assurance that he could make the kinds of pictures he liked with the resources of MGM. But his contract gave him consultation rights on his stories, and little else. MGM needed a star comedian to fill out its roster and was willing to sign Keaton for $3,000 a week for two pictures a year plus a profit participation, which he would share with Schenck. The deal made Keaton one of the highest-paid actors on the lot, reported Eyman (2005: 165).

MGM's comedy roster comprised two popular teams – Karl Dane/George K. Arthur and Polly Moran/Marie Dressler. Both made low-budget pictures targeted at low-brow tastes. Dane/Arthur was the brainchild of Harry Rapf, who recognized Karl Dane's comic potential as Slim, the tobacco-chewing doughboy in *The Big Parade*. Dane was a husky six feet three inches, while Arthur was a small fry and effeminate. They first appeared together in *Rookies* (1927) directed by Sam Wood. Mordaunt Hall: 'Any doubt regarding the success of this combination was quickly dispelled yesterday afternoon when an audience greeted the gestures and

FIGURE 2.8 Buster Keaton in Edward Sedgwick's *The Cameraman* (1928)

expressions of these two players with gales of laughter' (*NYTFR*, 25 April 1927). *Rookies* turned a nice profit ($255,000) and launched a series.

Polly Moran and Marie Dressler first appeared together in George W. Hill's *The Callahans and the Murphys* (1927), about two feuding Irish families living in a tenement. Frances Marion had come up with the idea. After reading Kathleen Norris's rough-and-tumble novel, she persuaded Thalberg to hire Dressler, her dear friend, to play Mrs. Callahan. Mordaunt Hall said the picture was 'played for loud laughs . . . Veering from the recent vogue of Irish–Jew burlesque, it is all Irish and, as might be expected, full of fights and broad slapstick' (*NYTFR*, 12 July 1927). The picture was a success initially, but Irish-American groups protested the broad caricature of their ethnic group as drunkards, and the picture was withdrawn. MGM took a $44,000 loss on the picture, but it had found another winning comic team. Moran and Dressler's next silent, Jack Conway's *Bringing Up Father* (1928), was based on a comic strip in the Hearst papers and took in a profit of $83,000. The team made it into the talkies; Marie Dressler also worked on her own and became a great and beloved Hollywood star.

Keaton made two silent pictures for MGM, *The Cameraman* (1928) and *Spite Marriage* (1929). They were directed by Edward Sedgwick and placed under the supervision of Lawrence Weingarten. In *The Cameraman*, Keaton plays Luke Shannon, a street photographer who takes tintype portraits of passerby. He spots a beautiful woman who is part of a gaggle of MGM newsreel cameramen and devises a way to land a job with them to be close to her. Part of the movie was shot on location in New York City, and Keaton was allowed to depart from the script at times to improvise his gags. *Variety* wrote, 'The same old stencil about a boob that does everything wrong and cashes in finally through sheer accident. The familiar pattern has been dressed up with some bright gags and several sequences where the laughs come thick and fast. All in all, it will probably deliver general satisfaction' (*VFR*, 27 September 1928). The picture grossed $797,000 – Keaton's highest returns to date – and turned in a profit of $67,000.

Spite Marriage did even better, grossing $901,000 and turning in a profit of $197,000. Mordaunt Hall said, 'Words can hardly tell of the relief it was to look at Mr. Keaton's imaginative but silly silent antics in his latest farce, *Spite Marriage.*' 'There were waves of laughter from top to bottom of the house,' he reported. 'Mr. Keaton's Mohican-like visage stands him in good stead, for he can do crack-brained things and yet make people happy' (*NYTFR*, 25 March 1929). As will be discussed in the next chapter, MGM's investment in Buster Keaton made Keaton rich, but at a cost to Keaton the artist.

Joan Crawford's flapper

MGM added another star to its roster in 1928, Joan Crawford. Crawford had been a contract player at the studio since 1925 after Harry Rapf saw her in the chorus of *Passing Show* on Broadway under the name of Lucille LeSueur. After reading the serialization of the Josephine Lovett story *Our Dancing Daughters* in the Hearst newspapers and hearing that Cosmopolitan was going to produce the movie, Crawford pleaded with Thalberg to cast her in the lead. Thalberg acquiesced and chose Anita Page and Dorothy Sebastian in support. As 'Dangerous Diana' Medford, Crawford played a 'flapper, wild on the surface, a girl who shakes her windblown bob and dances herself into a frenzy while the saxes shriek and the trombones wail, a girl drunk on her own youth and vitality,' said Vieira (2009: 84). Three days into the opening run at the Capitol Theater in New York, 'they were five deep behind the last row with standees to the door on one side of the lobby,' reported *Variety* (*VFR*, 10 October 1928). The picture was a big hit. Produced on a modest budget, it earned a gross of $1,099,000 and a profit of $304,000.

MGM next cast her in Jack Conway's *Our Modern Maidens* (1929) and Harry Beaumont's *Our Blushing Brides* (1930). Crawford was again teamed with Anita Page and Dorothy Sebastian. *Our Modern Maidens* was based on another Josephine Lovett story, which *Variety* described as 'juvenile and silly, but the sort of silliness the more youthful fans gobble up by the carload.' It was released in September 1929 as a silent well into the talkies, but that didn't matter. As *Variety* said, 'Miss Crawford's fans won't be disappointed, even a little bit. She wears her clothes as she always does and gives them the limit in a half-clad dance at one of her house parties. Her pantomime is far-fetched, but vivid' (*VFR*, 11 September 1929). It turned a profit of $248,000. *Our Blushing Brides* (1930), an all-talkie and the most

FIGURE 2.9   Joan Crawford in Harry Beaumont's *Our Dancing Daughters* (1928)

expensive picture of the trio, turned in the highest profit – $412,000. *Film Daily* ('Our Blushing Brides' 1930: 10) described it as 'another of those pretty screen stories made for the shop-girl vote . . . A lot of the film is given up to fashion displays of lingerie, with the girls behind the counter also acting as models – and all for 20 bucks a week.' As will be discussed in the following chapter, Crawford segued from a flapper to a shop girl, a formula that sustained her career for much of the 1930s.

Crawford's trilogy of carefree youth in the jazz age had a distinctive look. Cedric Gibbons had attended the landmark Paris Exposition des Arts Decoratifs et Industriels Modernes in 1925 and had come under the influence of Art Deco and Art Moderne. He first introduced these modernistic styles in the Crawford pictures. The designs for these pictures, said Carey (1981: 80), 'were drawn in accordance with what he called his philosophy of the uncluttered – they were clean, functional and often highly stylized, a look that was to cause a major revolution in movie decor.' Since modernism became associated with luxury, glamour, and affluence, it became the perfect visual style to complement Thalberg's urban strategy of producing pictures based on contemporary sources and themes.

Mayer and Thalberg accomplished what they set out to do in a remarkably short period of time – create a major motion picture studio. The generous profit-sharing agreement with Loew's gave the Mayer group plenty of incentive to succeed. Marcus Loew was astute in choosing Mayer to run the merged studios.

Mayer cobbled together elements from the three studios to create a smoothly running operation that rivaled Famous Players-Lasky and Fox Films within a year. His achievement is even more impressive given the rapid consolidation of the industry that was taking place. Taking charge of production, Irving Thalberg reined in maverick directors and consolidated production in the front office with him at the helm. Although maverick directors had been responsible for producing Hollywood's most memorable films, Thalberg demonstrated his considerable moviemaking talents by building a formidable star roster, by spending strategically on production, and by crafting many of the finest pictures that defined the silent film era and that stamped MGM as a prestige studio.

3

MGM ACCORDING TO IRVING THALBERG (1929–32)

The talkies arrive

Nick Schenck, Irving Thalberg, and Louis B. Mayer were not about to be dragooned into the talkies. As late as December 1928, Schenck was criticizing the industry for its hasty conversion: 'The novelty of sound has upset all reason,' he said. 'Sound has been applied indiscriminately whether it belonged or not. Everywhere the cry is for "talkies" regardless of subject matter. Certain properties lend themselves to dialogue,' he said, 'but they are not many and there you have the root of the trouble. Hysteria on the part of exhibitors who envision fortunes accruing through sound has reached the studios via sales departments and the pressure from the field' (Crafton 1997: 206). In setting up the MGM production slate for the 1927–28 season, talking pictures found no place.

The technology to successfully synchronize silent motion pictures with sound had finally been perfected by 1924. The technology required the invention of many complex components – the microphone, the amplifier, speakers, and the like – and took the resources of an outside firm – the Western Electric laboratory and manufacturing arm of American Telephone & Telegraph – to create such a system. But prudent studio chiefs were not about to tamper with a flourishing business. Producers had extensive inventories of silent films. Their studios were designed for the production of only such pictures, and theaters throughout the country were built and equipped for them. Actors in whom producers had made huge investments were trained in making silents. To convert to sound would involve not only scrapping millions but investing corresponding amounts in sound equipment. Yet within three years, the conversion to the talkies was so sweeping that a silent picture could not be found anywhere except in small towns.

Warner Bros. and Fox Films, two mid-tier studios, took the plunge first and developed separate strategies to fortify their positions in the business. Warner Bros.

cultivated an audience using Western Electric's sound-on-disk technology marketed under the name Vitaphone and produced shorts performed by stage, opera, and vaudeville stars and features with synchronized musical accompaniment. Warner Bros. lacked a theater chain, and its future was in doubt. Such films would be attractive to independent theaters, enabling them to compete with downtown movie palaces, which presented a mixed program of live acts followed by a main feature, which was accompanied by either an organ or a full-sized pit orchestra. Fox differentiated itself from Warner Bros. by innovating a sound on film technology under the name Movietone to produce newsreels and features to accomplish a similar end. Implementing the strategies progressed slowly. Loew's and the other majors waited on the sidelines to see if sound was just a passing fad. In February 1927, they signed the Big Five Agreement to act in concert if they were to make the conversion.

The transition began with the premiere of *Don Juan* (Crosland, 1926) at the Warners' Theatre in New York on 6 August 1926. It starred John Barrymore and had a synchronized musical score played by the New York Philharmonic. It was the eight Vitaphone preludes on the program that caused the greatest stir. Will Hays, the president of the Motion Picture Producers and Distributors Association, introduced the program. The New York Philharmonic under the direction of Henry Hadley led off with the Overture to *Tannhauser*, followed by distinguished concert and operatic stars Mischa Elman, Marion Talley, Efrem Zimbalist, and Anna Case, among others. 'A marvelous device known as the Vitaphone, which synchronizes sound with motion pictures, stirred a distinguished audience in Warners' Theatre to unusual enthusiasm,' reported Mordaunt Hall. 'The natural reproduction of voices, the tonal qualities of musical instruments and the timing of the sound to the movements of the lips of singers and the actions of musicians being present was almost uncanny.' 'The future of this new contrivance,' he said, 'is boundless, for inhabitants of small and remote places will have the opportunity of listening to and seeing grand opera as it is given in New York' (*NYTFR*, 7 August 1926).

Fox Movietone scored it big in May 1927 with a newsreel showing Charles Lindbergh's takeoff from Roosevelt field, Long Island, to begin his solo transatlantic flight. 'Not only did one hear the whirring of the airplane's motor,' said Hall (1927), 'but one also heard the cheers of the throng that saw the fearless young flyer take off on his dash to the French capital.' To gather news, Fox stationed Movietone sound trucks with camera crews in various parts of the country and in Europe to record football games, political events, scenic views, and other subjects. In December 1927, Fox initiated a weekly all-sound newsreel edition; the following year, it was twice a week.

The Big Five and lesser companies reached a decision to convert to sound in May 1928; afterward, the switchover proceeded rapidly and smoothly. The public had welcomed the talkies enthusiastically and unequivocally, which seemed to justify the enormous expenditures required to wire the nation's theaters and to convert Hollywood's studios to sound. Looking back over 1929, Waller (1930: 87) reported that in New York City, the talkies had 'driven legit shows to the side streets and [had] given filmdom a command of Broadway with an array of pictures unexcelled numerically and in quality.'

MGM converts to sound

Once Loew's made the decision, Schenck embarked on a crash program in June 1928 to wire the entire Loew chain. The company then leased the Cosmopolitan Studio in New York to begin producing *Metro Movietone Acts*, sound shorts featuring vaudeville, opera, and legit headliners, to accompany its silent releases. They were produced under the supervision of Major Edward Bowes, the managing director of the Capitol Theatre, Loew's flagship house. Hal Roach converted to sound as well in 1928 and his Laurel & Hardy, Our Gang, Charlie Chase, and All Star series remained favorites throughout the early thirties. Hearst converted to sound in 1929 and continued supplying MGM with its popular newsreel service under a new name, *Hearst Metrotone News*. MGM closed the Cosmopolitan studio facility in 1929 and resumed short film production in Culver City. The early short film lineup included *Novelty Group*, a showcase for MGM contract players; *All Barkie Dogville Comedies*, which featured trained dogs dressed up to parody MGM stars in current release and voiced by actors; *Around the World with Burton Holmes*, a travelogue series featuring the famed travel lecturer; and *Pete Smith Specialties*, a comedy series featuring MGM's studio publicist, who added sarcastic narration to silent sports and fishing footage. During the 1930–31 season, MGM ventured into the animation field by releasing *Flip the Frog* cartoons, which were independently produced by ex-Disney staffer Ub Iwerks.

MGM added twenty-two new sound stages to its Culver City studio. They were designed with the help of Verne O. Knudson, a UCLA physics professor, and other academics and constructed under the supervision of Eddie Mannix. The man who provided MGM with the technical know-how to make talking films was Douglas Shearer, the head of MGM's new Sound Department. Shearer had followed his sister Norma to Hollywood from his native Montreal in 1925 and broke into moviemaking by accident. With his engineering training and interest in sound technology, he convinced the studio to conduct an experiment to promote his sister's newest picture, *A Slave of Fashion* (Henley, 1925). The experiment involved Los Angeles radio station KFI, which simultaneously broadcast Norma Shearer's and Lew Cody's narration to radio receivers in fifteen theaters on the West Coast showing Shearer's promotion short. The experiment was conducted in August 1925 and was 'an undisputable success,' according to *Radio Age* ('Radio' 1925). But Radio Cinema, as it was called, was a technological dead end. Taking charge of the Sound Department, Shearer supervised the installation of state-of-the-art Western Electric sound equipment in the studio and became involved 'in virtually every aspect of the motion picture's technical evolution following the coming of sound,' such as improved traveling microphones, blimped cameras, and mixing processes, said Lafferty (no date).

To produce talking pictures, MGM 'engaged scores of stage and musical celebrities, players, writers and directors,' reported Nick Schenck (1929: 145). They included lyricists and composers Irving Berlin, Vincent Youmans, Herb Nacio Brown, Arthur Freed, Herbert Stothart, and Dr. William Axt; actors Charles Bickford, Basil Rathbone, Roland Young, Charles King, George Marion, Kay Johnson, and Cliff Edwards; writers Edwin Justus Mayer, Willard Mack, Laurence Stallings, Crane Wilber, John Howard Lawson, and Gladys Unger; and directors Bayard Veiller, Edgar Selwyn, Gus Edwards, and Edgar MacGregor.

Two years after the premiere of Warner Bros.' *Don Juan* (1926) and nearly a year after *The Jazz Singer* (Crosland, 1927), MGM finally released its first picture with sound, *White Shadows in the South Seas* (1928), a large-scale scenic shot in the Marquesas Islands which told a somber story about the impact of greedy white traders on the indigenous people of the Pacific. To direct it, Thalberg had originally hired Robert Flaherty, the famous documentary filmmaker who had made *Nanook of the North* (1922). But Flaherty was unaccustomed to commercial filmmaking and its rigid schedules and quit soon after production started. W. S. Van Dyke, who had been assigned as his assistant, completed the picture. Douglas Shearer hastily added synchronized music, a theme song, and special effects to the completed film. The sound quality left much to be desired, but as Glancy (1992: 133) has noted, the novelty of sound had 'an enormous drawing power over audiences, particularly in the domestic market. *White Shadows in the South Seas* earned a higher gross than many of MGM's top silent releases.'

FIGURE 3.1 Bessie Love, Charles King, and Anita Page in Harry Beaumont's *The Broadway Melody* (1929)

During the 1928–29 season, MGM released eighteen of its fifty-three pictures with sound of some sort. Many of these were simply silent films with added sound effects. MGM had a lot of catching up to do. MGM's first season included three notable pictures, *The Broadway Melody* (1929) a musical, *The Trial of Mary Dugan*, a trial film, and *Madame X*, a drama. *The Broadway Melody* was MGM's first all-sound picture. It was a backstage musical directed by Harry Beaumont, with an original score by Nacio Herb Brown and Arthur Freed. Promoted as ALL TALKING! ALL SINGING! ALL DANCING! *Broadway Melody* used songs both within a story and as part of a Broadway show being performed. The hit songs by Brown and Freed included 'You Were Meant for Me,' 'Truthful Parson Brown,' and the title song, 'Broadway Melody.' The story by Edmund Goulding contained in pristine simplicity the main elements of the cycle – backstage romances, wisecracking chorines, an imperious impresario, a dilettante backer, and big-hearted moments. Charles King played a song-and-dance-man and Bessie Love and Anita Page were two sisters from the Midwest who tried to break into show business. The picture premiered at Grauman's Chinese in Los Angeles on 1 February 1929 and played as a roadshow for nearly a year during its initial release to become the top money earner of the season. The picture also won an Academy Award for Best Picture and set the pattern for all the show business pictures to follow.

Bayard Veiller's *The Trial of Mary Dugan* (1929) was MGM's first all-dialogue dramatic film. It starred Norma Shearer making her talking picture debut and was a trial film based on Veiller's Broadway hit of 1927. 'The trial film genre seemed tailor-made for the talkies because it was set-confined, dialogue driven, and easily adapted from the abundant theater source material available,' noted Crafton (1997: 286). Shearer played a chorus girl charged with murdering her wealthy lover. In court, she is defended by her brother, played by Raymond Hackett. The cast also included Lewis Stone and H. B. Warner – all stage veterans. Shearer had no previous stage experience. Thalberg, as a result, had the cast rehearse the play for two weeks and then perform it before a studio audience as a test before placing it into production. The picture premiered in New York on 28 March 1929 at the Embassy. 'For Norma Shearer this picture is a vindication and a triumph,' said Lusk (1929). 'The former because it validates her claim to stardom in the minds of some of us for the first time, and the latter,' he said, 'because in her first talking picture she skillfully combines the techniques of both stage and screen and emerges as a compelling actress of greater individuality than she ever revealed in silent pictures.'

MGM scored an even greater triumph with the release of *Madame X* (1929), a melodrama starring Ruth Chatterton. It was based on Alexandre Bisson's 1908 play that originally starred Sarah Bernhardt in the title role. Goldwyn Pictures had made a silent film version of the play in 1920 starring Pauline Frederick. To transform it into a talkie, Thalberg selected Lionel Barrymore to direct, his first such assignment, and Willard Mack to write the dialogue. Miss Chatterton played a fallen woman who kills a blackmailer to shield her son from discovering what his mother had become. At her murder trial, she is defended by a lawyer, her son, who does not know her true identity. *Madame X* premiered in New York on 24 April 1929 at the Sam Harris Theatre, a legitimate house, as a roadshow. *Madame X* was 'the first talkie to register largely with the American public,' said Merrick (1931). 'We already had some good talkies . . . but the world in general regarded the talking picture as an experiment which might, at any moment, be relegated to the dust bin. Ruth Chatterton's art as shown in *Madame X* revealed to the public a possibility in the talking pictures which nothing else had shown them.' The picture was another box-office hit and won Lionel Barrymore an Oscar nomination as Best Director.

By the 1929–30 season, MGM released nearly all its pictures with sound. The biggest hit of the season was Charles F. Reisner's *Hollywood Revue of 1929*. During the conversion to sound, producers used the revue to showcase stars and contract players. They performed comic sketches, gaudy musical numbers, acrobatics, and even short dramas and were presented in a variety format, each introduced by a master of ceremonies. Big dance numbers might be photographed in two-strip Technicolor. *Hollywood Revue* featured contract players Marion Davies, John Gilbert, Norma Shearer, William Haines, Joan Crawford, Bessie Love, Charles King, Marie Dressler, Gus Edwards, Polly Moran, Buster Keaton, and others and debuted Nacio Herb Brown and Arthur Freed's show biz classic, 'Singin' in the Rain.' Conrad Nagel and Jack Benny served as masters of ceremonies. Mordaunt Hall said, 'A light-hearted piece of work is this production. It trots gaily along from beginning to end with a wonderful fund of amusement and its clever and lavish staging is enhanced by imaginative camera work . . . All the stellar lights in this gleeful series of shadows share and share alike. They all contribute unfailingly to the arousing of smiles, chuckles and laughter' (*NYTFR* 15 August 1929).

The Fox–Loew's merger

By being the first to innovate, Warner Bros. and Fox Films earned extraordinary profits, which were used to solidify their positions in the top echelon of the industry. Warner Bros. acquired a theater chain 500 strong, an important music publisher, and a major Hollywood studio with an international presence – First National – among other properties.

Fox Films attained major status by building Movietone City, an all-sound studio facility near Beverly Hills in 1928, and buying up theaters, among them the 6,000-seat Roxy in New York and Grauman's Chinese in Los Angeles. But in an audacious move, William Fox acquired a controlling interest in Loew's Inc. on 28 February 1929. The merger created the largest motion picture company in the industry. To acquire Loew's, Fox purchased a large block of Loew's common stock held by the estate and family of Marcus Loew and by Nicholas Schenck and other Loew's executives. Fox paid $125 a share for a stock that was selling at around $80 at the time (Gomery 1986: 56). Fox secured the financing from AT&T and Halsey, Stuart & Company. Nicholas Schenck and David Bernstein brokered the deal and received $9 million as a bonus for their efforts. Fox had cleared the deal with Washington with the assurance that 'the two producing units brought together by the merger would remain completely independent and would in no manner be under the same control,' reported the *New York Times* ('Fox and Warners' 1929).

The Fox merger was negotiated in complete secrecy. Mayer, Thalberg, and Rubin – the Mayer group – learned of it only after it was publicly announced on 3 March 1929. They were understandably outraged, not only because they believed that Schenck had sold out the company but also because Schenck and Bernstein had pocketed a $9 million bonus on top of the profits from the sale. But there was nothing they could do about it. Their employment contracts remained in force, and Schenck assured them that Fox would not interfere with the management of MGM. Nonetheless, whatever bonds of trust that existed between the Loew's home office and the Culver City studio were severely tested by the deal. In fact, they may have been broken.

In the summer of 1929, Fox was seriously injured in an automobile accident and was incapacitated for months. By the time he recovered, the stock market had crashed, and his vast, highly leveraged empire had started to crumble. A month later, the Justice Department under the new Herbert Hoover administration filed an antitrust suit under the Clayton Act to dissolve the merger. Fox was forced to sequester the Loew's stock with federal court-appointed trustees, and the merger, as a result, was placed on hold. Louis B. Mayer was a close friend of the president and may have 'let a word drop here and there of his distinct disapproval and suspicions of the legality of the Fox deal,' said Crowther (1957: 160). To cover his margin calls, Fox was forced to sell off personal assets to General Theatres Equipment, Inc., based in Chicago, for an estimated $18 million in 1930 ('Fox Out of Films' 1930). As a condition of the buyout, Fox was forced to relinquish control of the company he had founded in 1915. The antitrust suit was settled in 1931, and Fox Film was ordered to divest itself of its Loew's shares. They reverted to a holding company organized by the Chase Bank and were eventually sold in the open market.

Making it into the talkies

During the 1929–30 season, Greta Garbo, Joan Crawford, William Haines, Ramon Novarro, Marion Davies, and Buster Keaton all made it into the talkies. Greta Garbo's debut was the most eagerly anticipated. MGM delayed her talkie debut as long as possible, thinking that her Swedish accent would prove fatal. Thalberg found the perfect vehicle in Eugene O'Neill's *Anna Christie*, a naturalistic drama about a waterfront prostitute that won a Pulitzer Prize in 1921.

The picture was directed by Clarence Brown and featured Charles Bickford, George F. Marion, and Marie Dressler. In one sense, *Anna Christie* departed from the typical Garbo vehicle in that 'Garbo wore only the drabbest of clothes amid the most sordid surroundings' (*VFR*, 19 March 1930); in another sense, it continued

FIGURE 3.2 Greta Garbo in Clarence Brown's *Anna Christie* (1930)

her established pattern. Garbo played a poor farm girl who runs away from drudgery, becomes a prostitute, falls for a seaman, loses him when she tells him of her past, but wins him back in the end. Garbo's accent sounded natural in the role because the heroine was also Swedish. Moreover, the adaptation built up suspense by delaying her entrance until well over thirty minutes into the film. And when she said her first lines, 'Gimme a whiskey. Chinger ale on the side. An' don't be stingy, babee,' audiences applauded. *Anna Christie* premiered in New York on 14 March 1930 at the Capitol Theatre. It received rave reviews. 'The triumph of Miss Greta Garbo in the complicated medium of the talking films is . . . the most exciting event in recent screen annals,' said Richard Watts Jr. (1930). 'No player has had to face and overwhelm one-third the handicaps that Miss Garbo encountered in her audible debut; and because she managed her problems so completely, her success becomes almost complete.'

Joan Crawford easily made it to the talkies in Jack Conway's *Untamed* (1929), a drama that showcased her singing and dancing. Marion Davies made her debut in Robert Z. Leonard's *Marianne* (1929), a musical comedy in which she showed 'no hint of her legendary stuttering,' reported Crafton (1997: 319). William Haines sustained his reputation as a young wisecracker who wins the girl just before the fadeout in the Clarence Brown comedy *Navy Blues* (1929). Ramon Novarro, MGM's 'Latin Lover,' made it into the talkies going against type in Sidney Franklin's

Devil May Care (1929), a musical that showcased Novarro the singer, a talent he had previously revealed singing 'Pagan Love Song' in *The Pagan* (1929).

Buster Keaton's transition was the most unfortunate. He made his talking debut in *Free and Easy* (1930). As a contract player, he had little input into the choice of properties or his supporting cast. Keaton's slapstick comedy relied on pantomime and improvisation on the set, but at MGM, his gags were created by others. *Free and Easy* was produced by Lawrence Weingarten. Edward Sedgwick directed it, and a team of writers comprising Richard Schayer, Paul Dickey, and Al Boasberghe concocted a backstage Hollywood studio story set within a musical revue framework. Keaton was teamed with Anita Page and Robert Montgomery to provide the love interest. 'Some of Keaton's old spark remains,' said Crafton (1997: 321), 'but not enough to distract critics from his strained performance.' *Film Daily* ('Free' 1930: 11) stated, 'Here he is the king playing in a musical comedy extravaganza, and the stuff falls pretty flat. Buster seems out of his element, for his well known pantomimic ability is sacrificed to the new school of articulate gagging.' Keaton hated the picture, but it turned a small profit.

Keaton went on to make six more talking pictures for MGM. All, save one, were directed by Edward Sedgwick. Keaton continued playing a 'dumb mugg' in stories provided him by a 'flock of writers,' said *Variety*. The laughs were 'derived from a few situations which the story may have included but which are funniest because of Keaton and his support. Slapstickish always, a couple sequences nevertheless bring in several hearty laughs' (*VFR*, 17 November 1931). In his last three pictures for MGM – *The Passionate Plumber* (1932), *Speak Easily* (1932), and *What, No Beer?* (1933) – he was teamed with Jimmy Durante. 'Durante's aggressive, verbal style of comedy virtually wiped Keaton's understated deadpan humor off the screen,' said Dooley (1979: 395). Unlike his United Artists pictures, all his MGM talkers made money. Thalberg's formulas made Keaton a rich man, but as an artist, he was demoralized. In addition, Keaton was beset by personal problems and missed days of shooting because of his drinking. Since such behavior drove his films over budget, MGM let his contract lapse in 1933.

Two by Vidor

During the transition to sound, MGM released two remarkable films, King Vidor's *The Crowd* (1928) and *Hallelujah!* (1929). Both were personal projects films that Thalberg allowed him to make following the enormous box-office success of *The Big Parade*.

The Crowd

The Crowd was released in the 1928 season, the peak year of the silent period. It was inspired by German Expressionism. Vidor proposed the project about an American Everyman to Thalberg in 1927. Thalberg went along with it after some persuading, but Mayer was against the whole thing. *The Crowd* was based on an

FIGURE 3.3 James Murray and Eleanor Boardman in King Vidor's *The Crowd* (1928)

original story coauthored by Vidor and John V. A. Weaver about a young couple struggling against the anonymity of a big city. After many drafts, the project was placed into production with a budget of $551,000, one of the highest of the season, with Eleanor Boardman and James Murray in the leads. It was seven months in the making, with parts shot in New York, Pittsburgh, and Niagara Falls.

The Crowd opened in New York at the Capitol Theatre on 19 February 1928 to respectful reviews. MGM hyped it as *The Big Parade* of peacetime. Reviewers generally admired Vidor's courage in making such a movie, but the public did not go along. *Variety* called it 'A drab actionless story of ungodly length and apparently telling nothing . . . King Vidor, the director, has interjected a little of everything, including freaky photography and hokum, the latter taking in a bit of comedy, but it fades into the monotonous and deadly detail of it all' (*VFR*, 22 February 1928). After playing at the Capitol for one week at popular prices, MGM changed tactics and moved the picture to the Astor for a special run as a roadshow to target a more sophisticated audience. In both versions, the picture ended with a question mark, and the audience is left to wonder what's in store for the hero.

MGM had doubts about the picture's commercial prospects from the start and directed Vidor to shoot an alternative optimistic ending for exhibitors. As Robert

E. Sherwood (1928: 24) described it, 'The picture ends with the hero on the crest of a wave; he is successfully coining advertising slogans and money.' But to no avail; the picture ended up playing mostly in neighborhood houses. But *The Crowd* was by no means a flop; it grossed nearly $1 million worldwide and earned a profit of $69,000. Louis B. Mayer stood firm in his opposition to the picture and voted against it at the Academy Awards.

Hallelujah!

MGM publicity described *Hallelujah!* as 'the first epic film dealing with the lives of those "brethren" below the Mason-Dixon Line torn between the flesh and the devil.' It opened in New York on 20 August 1929, a week after *Hollywood Review*, at two theaters, the Embassy as a roadshow and at the Lafayette 'all colored' theater in Harlem. Vidor wrote the story, which, he said, was 'based on events with which I was familiar as a boy at home in Texas' ('Another' 1929). It told the story of a 'colored boy, indirectly responsible for his young brother's death in a gaming house brawl, who becomes a negro revivalist, of his devotion to his ideals and of his craving for a seductive "yeller girl."' Nick Schenck doubted that white theater owners in the South would play the picture, but Vidor wanted to do something different and forewent his salary to get MGM's approval. *Hallelujah!* cost a nominal $320,000 and contained an all-Black cast – they were unknowns, whom Vidor found mostly in Harlem. Daniel Haynes as Zeke the poor cotton farmer had played a role in *Show Boat* on Broadway, and Nina Mae Kinney as Chick the vamp, had performed in the chorus of *Blackbirds* on Broadway. Vidor shot the exteriors of the picture silent on location in Tennessee and Arkansas. Back in Culver City, he shot the interiors and dubbed in the dialogue and sound effects. Vidor infused *Hallelujah!* with spirituals and folk songs performed by the Dixie Jubilee Singers and with blues and jazz numbers (including two songs by Irving Berlin) performed by Kinney and Victoria Spivey. The film also contained some big scenes in cabarets, revival meetings, baptisms in the river, and others. *Variety* described the picture as Vidor's 'greatest work' but was more guarded about its box-office pull. 'Will *Hallelujah* have any common denominator for the everyday white person detached from the liberal movement that centers in New York City? . . . There is nothing in it to attract the flappers or superficial lunch-goers who flock to a matinee after a morning's shopping in town' (*VFR*, 28 August 1929).

The first slate of sound films

MGM released its first full slate of sound films in 1930–31. MGM's last silent film, Greta Garbo's *The Kiss* (1929), premiered in New York on 15 November 1929. *The Kiss*, besides being MGM's and Garbo's last silent, turned out to be Hollywood's last silent. 'Before anyone could say "Okay for sound,"' said Vieira, 'an era had ended' (2009: 106). No one at the home office was complaining; Loew's had posted a profit of $14.6 million in 1930 and had more than caught up with the leaders (Gomery 1986: 52). At the Academy Awards in 1930, Douglas Shearer won the first Academy Award for Sound Recording for his work on *The Big House* (1930) directed by George Hill. (At the same Awards ceremony, Norma Shearer won the Best Actress Oscar for *The Divorcee*.) Produced by Hearst's Cosmopolitan Productions, *The Big House* was inspired by accounts of actual prison riots in 1929 and starred Chester Morris, Wallace Beery, and Lewis Stone. Frances Marion wrote the screenplay and won an Oscar for her efforts. It premiered in New York on 24 June 1930 at the Astor Theatre. Purporting to present a realistic portrait of prison life, *The Big House* depicted the processing of inmates, their mealtimes, and routines in the yard. The picture also introduced what were to become prison stereotypes: the hardened criminal, the semi-hysterical weakling victimized by both guards and fellow prisoners, the informer, the ineffectual warden, the vicious guard, and the strong-willed leader. And true to form, the climax of the picture presented a thrilling revolt, which graphically depicted how officials used hand grenades, barrages, stench bombs, tractor attacks, and other means 'to deal with foolhardy prisoners. . . . Prison life on the half-shell,' said *Variety* (*VFR*, 2 July 1930).

    The Big House was the first of fourteen Oscars awarded to Douglas Shearer. '"Sound . . . Douglas Shearer" on a Metro movie was as familiar as Leo the Lion's Roar,' said Thomas (1971). 'A credit such as Shearer's . . . was more than mere assurance of a certain technical excellence. It was, by virtue of its very inevitability,

FIGURE 3.4 Wallace Beery, Robert Montgomery, and Chester Morris in George Hill's *The Big House* (1930)

a kind of subliminal guarantee that there was a continuity and permanence in the pleasurable escapism of going to the movies, especially MGM's glossy productions.' Lon Chaney, the last MGM star to make a talkie, made his debut in Jack Conway's *The Unholy Three* (1930), a remake of his 1925 silent hit. Chaney delayed his debut until he was able to master the five distinctive dialects he would be using in the picture. As 'The Man of a Thousand Faces,' 'he had secured most of his facial distortions by holding foreign substances of divers shapes and sizes in his mouth,' reported the *New York Times* ('Lon Chaney's' 1930). For this reason, skeptics thought that MGM would be forced to use doubles to record his voices. As a publicity gimmick, Chaney had a Los Angeles notary issue a signed affidavit stating that all the voices in the picture were his, including the parrot's. Chaney was also holding out for a substantial bonus. A compromise was reached, and Chaney signed a five-picture contract to make five talkies based on his silent successes. *The Unholy Three* was a hit, but as *Variety* said, 'Its main asset is that it is the first Chaney talker with Chaney talking. Fans probably will be attracted to the Chaney lure. Otherwise it's about an average release in box office possibilities' (*VFR*, 9 July 1930). Chaney, who had been suffering from throat cancer, died a month after the picture's release.

MGM's top silent stars had made the transition, but not all endured, as we have seen with Buster Keaton. Another casualty was John Gilbert, whose failure was problematic. Gilbert had been given a new contract in 1928, when he contemplated moving to United Artists. Nick Schenck negotiated the deal without consulting Mayer or Thalberg. He did not want to lose a valuable star just as he was negotiating the sale of the company to William Fox. The new contract required Gilbert to make only two pictures a year for three years, and he was to be paid the princely sum of $250,000 for each one (Crafton 1997: 506). All of Gilbert's talking pictures lost money. Gilbert's voice was not a factor; part of the problem was Gilbert's high salary which made it difficult to recoup costs. Another was MGM's strange choice of properties for its star. Gilbert's first talkie, Fred Niblo's *Redemption* (1930), had been completed in 1929 but then shelved for a year. *Variety* described the picture as 'Dull, sluggish, agonizing. Hardly a redeeming aspect. Even the photography, editing and other taken-for-granted items are under standard . . . . *Redemption* is unworthy of first runs, regardless of John Gilbert' (*VFR*, 7 May 1930). As Vieira (2009: 121) put it, 'The question was why the film was released at all. If the studio had hoped to redeem Gilbert, this was not the vehicle. His voice, in spite of journalistic jibes, was not high-pitched.' Afterward, Gilbert's career never recovered. Gilbert didn't help matters by drinking heavily, by marrying and divorcing, and by generating bad publicity. His fans had turned on him. At the conclusion of his contract in 1933, he was let go. However, at Greta Garbo's insistence, he returned to play opposite her in *Queen Christina* (1933).

Buster Keaton's fade-out had much to do with his drinking and personal problems, as discussed. William Haines and Ramon Novarro were victims of changing audience tastes. In Novarro's case, he had made a comeback in Greta Garbo's *Mata Hari* (1932), directed by George Fitzmaurice. As Mata Hari, Garbo played a German who poses as a courtesan and seduces Russian officers to secure enemy secrets. Her method was 'to get 'em in the bedroom and keep them interested, while an assistant operative snatches the papers,' said *Variety* (*VFR*, 5 January 1932). Novarro played one such victim. *Mata Hari* was one of Garbo's biggest box-office hits and won Novarro a new contract, but afterward, his allure faded, and MGM released him in 1935.

Marion Davies made nearly a dozen talkies for MGM under the Cosmopolitan banner. Davies was a gifted comedienne and still had her fans, but she never really clicked in sound. Most of her pictures lost money, due in part to her high salary and Hearst's meddling, but MGM was happy to foot the bills in return for free publicity from Hearst's newspapers. Hearst insisted that Davies be given more sophisticated roles to sustain her career, but most of the best properties were seemingly going to Norma Shearer, Irving Thalberg's wife. The matter came to a head in 1934, when Thalberg refused to assign her the leading roles in *The Barretts of Wimpole Street* and *Marie Antoinette*. They had already been chosen for Shearer. Moreover, Thalberg and Mayer thought the roles totally inappropriate for her, given her screen persona. As a gesture of goodwill, Shearer offered to give her *Marie Antoinette*, but Mayer would give his okay only if Hearst picked up the tab for the film. Hearst was hard hit by the Depression and could not afford to do it, which Mayer knew. Feeling the insult, Hearst and Davies departed for Warner Bros.

Industry adjustments

Foreign distribution

The talkies impeded foreign distribution at first since spoken dialogue seemingly introduced an impenetrable language barrier. Moreover, theaters overseas were slow to convert to sound. To service these theaters, American distributors used subtitling. To service theaters wired for sound, Hollywood initially produced multiple-language films for different markets using native casts. Paramount made the biggest commitment to multiple-language films by setting up production at Joinville Studios outside Paris in 1929 under Robert Kane. MGM adopted a different practice, preferring instead to produce foreign-language talkies in Culver City. Hal Roach adopted the practice as well for his comedies. MGM hired more than sixty international writers, directors, and actors to make its multilinguals. The unit was supervised by Al Lewin.

By the end of 1931, dubbing supplanted foreign-language versions as the accepted practice in international trade. But dubbing was considered unfair competition in France and Germany, which passed laws barring the entry of films dubbed outside their borders. American film companies therefore constructed dubbing studios in these countries and elsewhere. MGM's first dubbed films were *Trader Horn* (1931) in France and *Min and Bill* (1930) in Italy. By the mid-thirties, American films were dubbed into practically all languages of the world and restored foreign distribution to its former profit levels.

Motion picture censorship

Since its founding in 1922, the Motion Picture Producers and Distributors of America, the 'Hays Office,' had forestalled cries for federal censorship of the movies by assuring civic, educational, and religious groups that the industry could regulate itself. In 1927, the MPPDA adopted a code of self-censorship entitled 'Don'ts and Be Carefuls.' The Don'ts comprised things that could not be shown on the screen, such as white slavery, miscegenation, and disrespect of the clergy; the 'Be Carefuls' comprised the handling of subjects such as international relations, murder techniques, first-night scenes, and use of drugs. The document was distilled from the specific rejections and deletions made by state censorship boards. Jason Joy, the head of the MPPDA's Studio Relations Department, administered the code. Will Hays asked for voluntary compliance from the film industry because an enforcement machinery was thought to be repugnant to producers.

But when Hollywood turned to Broadway for suitable material for their talkies, the censorship battle resumed. As Maltby (2003) noted, 'Throughout the 1920s Broadway had been castigated for its "realism" and "sophistication," particularly in its representation of sexual mores and improprieties.' 'With the coming of sound, and Hollywood's increasing adaptation of Broadway plays,' he said, 'provincial morality perceived that the threat had moved much closer to home. Broadway's dubious dialogue and "sophisticated" plot material was now playing on Main Street for the children to see and hear.'

Hollywood now took social reformers more seriously to avert trouble. In 1929, Hays formed another committee, chaired by Thalberg, to come up with a new code. 'This time, it had a strong dose of Catholic conscience,' said Crafton (1997: 472). Martin Quigley, a committee member and the publisher of *Exhibitor's Herald-World*, took the initiative and enlisted the assistance of Father Daniel A. Lord, a Jesuit priest who had been technical advisor on Cecil B. DeMille's *King of Kings* (1927). Lord presented his version of the new code to Hollywood leaders in February 1930. Although Thalberg and other producers had differences with Lord's moralistic document, the 'Code to Govern the Making of Talking, Synchronized and Silent Motion Pictures' was adopted by MPPDA members on 31 March 1930. Initially, the studios voluntarily submitted their scripts to the Studio Relations Department for vetting and were responsible for implementing the letter and spirit of the Code, but after a raft of gangster and fallen-women films hit the market, code procedures were considerably tightened.

In 1934, the majors responded to the crusade to clean up the movies led by the Catholic Legion of Decency by installing Joseph I. Breen, a devout Catholic, as the head of the Production Code Administration, the revamped Studio Relations Department. MPPDA members were now required to submit all scripts and completed films to Breen's department for vetting. Breen's findings were subject to review only on appeal to the presidents of MPPDA companies. Now a picture would have to receive a seal of approval before it could be exhibited in a theater belonging to the majors. Any member violating this rule was subject to a $25,000

fine, it was announced. But as Maltby (2003) points out, 'There was no funda-
mental shift of Code policy in July 1934.' 'The apparent changes brought about
by the negotiations with the Legion of Decency were in fact mainly cosmetic,
and had much more to do with the movies appearing to make a public act of
recantation than with substantive changes in the practice of self-regulation.'

Thalberg: 'His brain is the camera'

In a company profile of MGM published in December 1932, *Fortune* magazine
could comfortably state, 'For the past five years, Metro-Goldwyn-Mayer has made
the best and most successful moving pictures in the United States. No one in
Hollywood would dream of contradicting this flat statement' ('Metro' 1932: 257).
The man responsible for MGM's producing success was Irving Thalberg. Describing his function as a central producer, the magazine said, 'His brain is the camera
which photographs dozens of scripts in a week and decides which of them, if
any, shall be turned over to MGM's twenty-seven departments to be made into a
moving picture.' It attributed Thalberg's track record in part to 'heavy but saga-
cious spending' which imparted 'a certain common denominator of goodness' in
MGM's pictures. But 'It is easier to state what this goodness is *not* than what it
is,' it added ('Metro' 1932: 268). It was not innovation – MGM was the last major
studio to convert to sound. It was not superior direction – 'Probably no MGM
director is as gifted as Ernst Lubitsch or Josef von Sternberg' at Paramount. And
it was not 'superior writing – MGM has the largest literary staff in Hollywood,'
but its superiority was 'debatable.' It was the acting in its pictures that provided
a 'clue to MGM's preeminence. . . . No one will deny that the MGM roster
exudes more personality than any other in Hollywood,' *Fortune* concluded.

As regards Louis B. Mayer, *Fortune* described him as 'probably the most dignified personage in Hollywood.' After turning over production to the young Thalberg,
Mayer 'probably does not spend more than half his time on matters pertaining to
MGM,' it said ('Metro' 1932: 265). His other time was being spent mainly on
promoting Republican causes. The article had identified a sore spot for Thalberg.
Given his heavy work load, Thalberg had resented the profit-sharing arrangement
in the Mayer group, which gave Mayer the largest cut of the profits. After Thalberg aired his feelings to Nick Schenck in early 1932, Mayer agreed to reduce
his share by 5½ percent so that both would be receiving equal 37½ percent shares.
Schenck, in addition, agreed to give Thalberg three months off each year and an
option to purchase 100,000 shares of Loew's stock at a bargain price. After making further adjustments to the Mayer group contract, it was extended to December
1938 (Eyman 2005: 171–72).

Thalberg's production supervisors were now being referred to as associate
producers, and like Thalberg, they worked without screen credit. *Fortune* listed
eight – Hunt Stromberg, Al Lewin, Bernard Hyman, Bernie Fineman, Eddie Mannix, Larry Weingarten, Harry Rapf, and the late Paul Bern. They were soon joined
by Walter Wanger, who had recently departed Paramount. Functioning as Thalberg's

FIGURE 3.5 Irving Thalberg

surrogates, associate producers oversaw two or three pictures simultaneously and stayed with a picture from start to finish. Describing the associate producer's job, *Fortune* said, 'Without being able in most cases to act, write, or direct, they are supposed to know more about writing than either the director or the star, more about directing than the star or the writer' ('Metro' 1932: 261).

MGM's A-list directors included George Cukor, Sidney Franklin, Clarence Brown, W. S. Van Dyke, King Vidor, Edmund Goulding, Mervyn LeRoy, Jack Conway, Victor Fleming, George Hill, Robert Z. Leonard, and Rouben Mamoulian. These were the directors that made it to *Film Daily's* annual top ten and were the ones MGM entrusted with its top stars. But their status under Thalberg remained fixed. Their job was 'solely to get out on the stage and direct the actors, put them through the traces that are called for in the script,' said David O. Selznick (1972: 24).

MGM's Story Department was now headed by Samuel Marx. He took over from Robert Harris in 1930 when Harris left to pursue his writing. MGM's readers in the Story Department covered the entertainment and cultural scenes in New York, Los Angeles, and Europe and reviewed countless novels, plays, stories, and original scripts in search of suitable properties for MGM's stars. Under Marx, the department soon had under contract some of the most famous American and British novelists, playwrights, and journalists, among them Ben Hecht, Charles MacArthur, Anita Loos, S. N. Behrman, Sidney Howard, F. Scott Fitzgerald, William Faulkner, Aldous Huxley, Dorothy Parker, Christopher Isherwood, Herman Mankiewicz, and George S. Kaufman to name a few. Thalberg never expected these big names to write finished screenplays alone. He looked to them for words, ideas, and ingredients that could be incorporated into a finished shooting script. Shooting scripts typically went through several stages of development and often required fixes by writer-specialists before they were greenlighted. This procedure was followed at all the major studios. But Thalberg took the practice to another level. As *Fortune* pointed out, 'as many as ten of MGM's staff of writers may be set to work simultaneously, in groups of two or three, on the same story. There are said to be unproduced stories in MGM's files which cost $1,000,000' ('Metro' 1932: 258).

The Music Department was headed by Martin Broones, a composer of musical comedies. During the conversion to sound, MGM added sixty-three composers, arrangers, and musical directors to its staff, reported Russell (1929: 55). Two names would endure, songwriter Arthur Freed and composer Herbert Stothart. Freed continued to write lyrics mostly in partnership with composer Nacio Herb Brown. In 1939, he was made a producer and soon headed his own unit to make musicals. And that he did. Freed went on to produce some of Hollywood's greatest musicals. Stothart was hired by MGM in 1929 to compose the music for *The Rogue Song* (1930), an operetta starring Metropolitan Opera star Lawrence Tibbett. Stothart had spent twelve years on Broadway composing the music and serving as music director for a string of hit shows, such as *Wildflower*, in collaboration with Vincent Youmans; *Rose Marie*, with Rudolf Friml; *Song of the Flame*, with George Gershwin; *Good Boy*, with Kalmar and Ruby; and *Golden Dawn*, with Oscar Hammerstein.

Stothart became MGM's foremost composer after *The Rogue Song*. For the next twenty years, he composed, arranged, adapted, and conducted scores for more than one hundred MGM pictures. During the thirties, they included such top prestige pictures as *Treasure Island* (1934), *The Barretts of Wimpole Street* (1934), *David Copperfield* (1935), *A Tale of Two Cities* (1935), *Camille* (1937), *Marie Antoinette* (1938), the Nelson Eddy-Jeanette MacDonald operettas, and *The Wizard of Oz* (1939) for which he won an Oscar.

MGM's publicity department was headed by Pete Smith. In 1934, he turned to producing shorts for the studio and was replaced by Howard Strickling. Strickling had joined Metro's publicity department in 1919 and became Pete Smith's assistant after the merger. He remained department head until his retirement in 1969. Howard Dietz's advertising and publicity department in the New York home office was an arm of Metro-Goldwyn-Mayer Distributing and was responsible for creating advertising and promotion campaigns for new releases. Strickling's department was responsible for promoting MGM's stars and publicizing upcoming releases. The department also handled front-office news concerning such matters as the hiring and firing of key studio personnel, the acquiring of important properties, and the financial affairs of the company. A suicide, a messy divorce, or a scandal turned Strickling's job into public relations with the goal of protecting the image of the studio or of salvaging the reputation of a star. Working under Strickling were unit reporters who covered the big pictures and publicists who were assigned to individual stars. Unit reporters prepared plot synopses and special-interest stories about MGM's stars and forthcoming productions for use by newspapers, fan magazines, and general-interest magazines. Publicists promoted the studio's top stars and sometimes even handled their private financial affairs. Other sections of the department supplied fashion layouts for fan magazines and planted tidbits with gossip columnists such as Louella Parsons, Sheila Graham, and Hedda Hopper. The still photography department supplied the images.

Top stars of the 1930–33 seasons

With the largest and most prestigious stable of stars in Hollywood, MGM produced nearly a third of the top-grossing films every year during the thirties. Taking maximum advantage of MGM's talent pool, Irving Thalberg instituted a 'galactic' system of casting a picture that teamed two or more stars to increase its box-office power. He instituted the practice making his prestige pictures. Beginning in 1931, *Motion Picture Herald* conducted an annual exhibitors' poll to determine the ten best box-office draws. During the first half of the decade, the polls indicated that so-called down-to-earth stars were the most popular. At MGM, they were Marie Dressler and Wallace Beery. Marie Dressler ranked number one in the polls for 1932 and 1933. MGM's reigning leading ladies on the list were Greta Garbo, Norma Shearer, and Joan Crawford.

Thalberg was constantly replenishing his talent pool and had added two big names, Clark Gable and Jean Harlow. Clark Gable, MGM's first big male star of the era, represented a new type. Unlike the Latin lovers and suave lotharios of the twenties, Gable was a man's man and a sexy one at that. Gable was born in Cadiz, Ohio, in 1901 and had built a fledgling career on Broadway during the twenties playing villains. In 1930, his agent, Minna Wallis, landed him a part in the Los Angeles premiere of John Wexley's *The Last Mile*, a prison melodrama about 'the sensational fight for freedom of six men who were sentenced to be hanged.' Gable was singled out for his performance, which got him parts at RKO and Warner Bros. before MGM cast him in a minor role in *The Easiest Way*, a fallen-woman film starring Constance Bennett in 1930. At the preview, 'Gable electrified the audience,' reported Marx (1975: 157), and convinced Thalberg to sign him to a contract. Afterward, MGM type cast him as a tough guy playing rough with Norma Shearer in *A Free Soul* (1931), Joan Crawford in *Possessed* (1931), Greta Garbo in *Susan Lenox* (1931), and Jean Harlow in *Red Dust* (1932). In 1932, he made it to *Film Daily*'s Top Ten for the first time, ranking number eight.

Jean Harlow started out as an extra in 1928. She was 17 and unhappily married. Her big break came when Howard Hughes cast her in his talking version of *Hell's Angels* (1930). To spice it up, she played a vamp with blonde hair who said the words, 'Would you be shocked if I changed into something more comfortable?' Hughes had discovered a new sex symbol and signed her to a five-year contract. Hughes's publicity director coined the term 'platinum blonde' for her buildup. In 1931, Hughes loaned her to Columbia to make a picture with Frank Capra but was unhappy with the proposed title and convinced the studio to rename it *Platinum Blonde*. Harlow's acting was often panned by the critics, but Paul Bern saw her potential for comedy and convinced Thalberg to buy out her contract from Hughes in 1932. 'After just a few years at MGM,' said Eyman (2005: 221), 'Harlow had risen to be a wonderfully brash comedian with a specialty in good-hearted floozies, and at least a competent actress.' Miss Harlow's career was cut short in 1937; she died of kidney failure at age 26.

Production trends

Prestige pictures

MGM's signature production trend under Thalberg was the prestige picture, typically a big-budget special based on a presold property, often as not a 'classic,' and tailored for top stars. Prestige pictures played a crucial role in defining the public image of a company and encompassed different genres, production trends, and motion picture styles – Broadway adaptations, musicals, biopics, historical dramas, women's films, and even horror films. Regardless of the genre, prestige pictures were injected with plenty of star power, glamorous and elegant trappings, and elaborate special effects. At the exhibition level, MGM's prestige pictures were typically launched in New York at the Astor Theatre as roadshows before they were placed in general release at regular prices.

FIGURE 3.6 Edwina Booth in W. S. Van Dyke's *Trader Horn* (1931)

Trader Horn (1931), directed by W. S. Van Dyke, was an anomaly. It was based on Alfred Aloysius Horn's 1927 best seller describing his adventures as an ivory trader in Africa. It starred Harry Carey in the title role and Edwina Booth, 'the White Goddess' who saves Horn and his partner from the natives. Van Dyke shot much of the picture in the African interior. The cast and crew had to endure harsh conditions, and almost everyone came down with the fever at one time or another. Van Dyke did not attempt to record dialogue. The dialogue sequences were shot in Culver City, and some scenes were reshot on domestic locations. *Variety* called it 'nothing more than an out-and-out lecture tour, as the various herds of animals are described by the voice of Harry Carey, in the title role. . . . Studio has simply interpreted the original novel as it saw fit,' it said, 'lifting a couple of characters therefrom and putting them through a succession of narrow escapes from four-footed enemies and a cannibal tribe.' *Variety*'s verdict: 'Good looking animal picture which will roll up a lot of coin' (*VFR*, 11 February 1931). That it did; *Trader Horn* racked up the highest profit of the 1930–31 season.

Now that pictures could talk, Thalberg initially looked to Broadway to bring 'magic to the screen,' said Vieira (2009: 124). Thalberg's first catch was Helen Hayes, whom the *New York Times* ('Pictures' 1931) described as 'a fixture on the American stage in spite of her youth.' Miss Hayes was married to Charles MacArthur, the MGM screenwriter and playwright, and was probably best known for starring in a revival of Sir James Barrie's *What Every Woman Knows*, which enjoyed a long run on Broadway in 1926. Barrie's play posited that 'every woman knows' she is the invisible power responsible for the successes of the men in her life. For her MGM debut, Thalberg chose *The Sin of Madelon Claudet* (1931), a melodrama directed by Edgar Selwyn. It was based on Edward Knoblock's 1923 play *Lullaby*, about a mother who 'makes all manner of sacrifices so that her illegitimate son may be educated and become a physician.' *The Sin of Madelon Claudet* 'became the overnight sensation of cinema land,' reported Morris (1931: 5) and won two Oscars, including the Best Actress award for Miss Hayes. Thereafter, Miss Hayes 'either suffered or breathed her last' in Clarence Brown's *The Son-Daughter* (1932), an Oriental melodrama, and Victor Fleming's *The White Sister* (1933), a romantic drama. MGM finally relented and agreed to make *What Every Woman Knows*, costarring Brian Aherne with Gregory La Cava directing, in 1934. It received a warm New York welcome but ultimately failed. Hayes later wrote, 'I had high hopes for the movie, but they were dashed when I read the script. Barrie's delicate comedy had been torn apart in the most insensitive way' (quoted in Vieira 2009: 255). Hayes made one more picture for MGM, which also failed, before returning to Broadway.

Thalberg's next catch was Alfred Lunt and Lynn Fontanne, the most glamorous and sophisticated couple of the American stage. He allowed them to make a film

FIGURE 3.7 John, Ethel, and Lionel Barrymore with Tad Alexander in Richard Boleslawski's *Rasputin and the Empress* (1933)

of their choice. They selected *The Guardsman* (1931), Ferenc Molnar's comedy of manners, which they originally performed together for the Theatre Guild in 1924. It premiered in New York at the Astor on 9 September 1931 as a roadshow. Mordaunt Hall (1932a) observed, 'One might hazard that the best picture of the year was *The Guardsman*, which had the great advantage of the talented acting of Mr. Lunt and Miss Fontanne. Even though it may not bring in the shekels that more popular films have done, it is a feather in Metro-Goldwyn-Mayer's cap, for this extremely amusing but utterly implausibly tale has been produced in a suave and clever fashion.' *Variety* was more blunt in its assessment: 'To the sophisticated it is all sublimated high comedy; to the commonality of gum chewers, it will be either a dark mystery or a sacrilege' (*VFR*, 15 September 1931). The picture failed at the box office, which convinced the Lunts to confine their considerable talents to Broadway.

Thalberg's biggest coup was to unite the Royal Family of Broadway – the Barrymores – to make *Rasputin and the Empress* (1932). This marked the only time the siblings appeared together on the screen. Lionel had joined MGM in 1926; John had signed a nonexclusive contract with the studio in 1931; but Ethel, who was regarded as the 'First Lady of the American Theater,' had stayed put. She accepted Thalberg's offer only because she had lost much of her money in the 1929 crash and was playing vaudeville. John, who was billed first, played Prince Chegodieff, Rasputin's assassin; Ethel played the Czarina; and Lionel played the mad monk, Rasputin. Charles Brabin was originally slated to direct, but Ethel hated his slow working method and demanded that he be replaced by Richard Boleslawski, whom she had known from Broadway. Boleslawski was a Polish émigré who founded the influential American Laboratory Theatre in New York in the twenties and introduced the Stanislavsky method of acting to the United States. At the time, he had been on the MGM payroll as a writer after publishing a bestseller in 1932 called *Way of a Lancer*, a memoir about his service in the Russian war of 1917, which saw Czar Nicholas abdicate. Since he probably knew more about the fall of the Romanoffs than anyone else, Thalberg agreed. Charles MacArthur wrote the screenplay.

Rasputin and the Empress premiered in New York at the Astor on 23 December 1932 as a roadshow. It received mixed reviews. Mordaunt Hall called it 'an engrossing and exciting pictorial melodrama' and praised Boleslawski for working out 'his episodes in an impressive fashion' and the Barrymores for giving 'equally fine performances' (*NYTFR*, 24 December 1932). Richard Watts Jr. (1933) pointed out the 'furious inaccuracies' in the picture: 'The picture of the Czar is as falsely sympathetic as that of the monk is savagely vilified,' he said. *Variety* said, *Rasputin and the Empress* 'is not a good picture . . . a long-winded affair, rather vague and aimless and at no time gripping. The inclusion of the three Barrymores . . . is the best showmanship about it, but that's not particularly effective. 'Apart from the general ineptitude of the story, the whole structure lacks conviction and sympathy,' it added (*VFR*, 27 December 1932). The picture was plagued by production delays, which ran up the cost, and became one of the studio's costlier failures.

Thalberg had better luck transforming his wife, Norma Shearer, into 'the screen equivalent of a great lady of the theater.' To begin, Thalberg teamed Shearer with Robert Montgomery in Sidney Franklin's *Private Lives* (1931), an adaptation of Noel Coward's sophisticated comedy, which he designed as a vehicle for himself and Gertrude Lawrence and that had enjoyed long runs the year before in London and in New York. Mordaunt Hall called it 'one of the most intelligent comedies that has come to the screen.' 'Sidney Franklin's direction is excellent,' he added, 'and Norma Shearer as Amanda Prynne gives an alert, sharp portrayal. She appears to have been inspired by the scintillating dialogue, and, taking all things into consideration, it is her outstanding performance in talking pictures' (*NYTFR*, 19 December 1931).

Thalberg then teamed Shearer with Clark Gable in Robert Z. Leonard's *Strange Interlude* (1932), MGM's second adaptation of a Pulitzer Prize–winning drama by Eugene O'Neill. Shearer and Clark Gable repeated the roles Lynn Fontanne and Alfred Lunt created in the original Broadway production of 1928. C. Gardner Sullivan and Bess Meredyth compressed the five-hour play to less than two hours. Shearer played Nina Leeds, a frustrated housewife who is driven by her husband's impotency and by fear of the insanity running in his family to have a child by another man. A case study of Freudian sexuality, the role required her to age from eighteen to her late sixties, during which she has 'a romantic fixation on her father, escapes from it into marriage and motherhood, still feels confined, liberates herself again with an affair, and ends up as a kind of Jocasta to her Oedipal son,' said Lambert (1990: 165). O'Neill's play was experimental for its time, using asides to reveal a character's thoughts and feelings. In the movie, 'Douglas Shearer made the asides plausible with a "voice-over" technique; a prerecorded disk was played on the set so that the actors could adjust their facial expressions to their audible thoughts,' said Vieira (2009: 190).

Strange Interlude premiered in New York at the Astor on 31 August 1932 as a roadshow. Mordaunt Hall said, 'It is one of those very rare pictures in which the intelligent dialogue never elicited so much as a murmur of disapproval, which on a first-night is exceptional. . . . Norma Shearer has given several noteworthy performances in recent motion pictures, but in this present offering she easily excels anything she has done hitherto' (*NYTFR*, 1 September 1932).

Variety said, 'Despite the impressive and stellar investiture, "Interlude" will have tough going when competing in the field, say against Chevalier or a Jean Harlow sex subject, or a Keaton–Durante or Marx or Lloyd type of comedy – that means in the grinds' (*VFR*, 6 September 1932). *Variety* was right; 'the hinterland' was cool to the picture, and it ended up $90,000 in the red.

Thalberg's sorcery worked better for Edmund Goulding's *Grand Hotel* (1932), a multi-character picture based on Vicki Baum's bestseller *Menschem im Hotel.* MGM acquired the motion picture rights to the book with the proviso that the studio would finance a dramatization of the novel on Broadway. William A. Drake did the adaptation, which was produced by Herman Shumlin in 1930 and ran for more than a year on the stage. Drake wrote the screenplay with Frances

FIGURE 3.8 Greta Garbo and John Barrymore in Edmund Goulding's *Grand Hotel* (1932)

Marion (uncredited). The movie opened at the Astor as a roadshow on 12 April 1932. The narrative formula interwove the stories of a cross-section of humanity within a single setting. The all-star cast contained Greta Garbo as the world-weary Russian ballerina Grusinskaya; John Barrymore as the luckless Baron von Geigern; Joan Crawford as the hotel stenographer Flaemmchen; Wallace Beery as the ruthless industrialist Preysing; and Lionel Barrymore as the downtrodden clerk, Kringelein. 'Story is many angled in characters and incidents of sure-fire human appeal,' said *Variety*. 'There is the romantic grip of the actress-nobleman lovers; there is the eternally successful element of the triumph of the under-dog in the figure of Kringelein, the humble bookkeeper doomed to approaching death and determined to spend his remaining days in a splurge of luxury in the Grand Hotel' and 'there is the everlasting Cinderella element in the not-so-good stenographer who at last finds a friend and protector in the dying Kringelein.' 'Given these roles, ordinary players would be good,' it said. 'This group of stars make the play something of a screen epic in a season of mediocre celluloid foot-age' (*VFR*, 19 April 1932).

Variety gave first honors to Lionel Barrymore for an inspired performance as the soon-to-die bookkeeper, 'a character drawn with bold outlines and etched in with a multitude of niceties of detail.' Richard Watts Jr. (1932a) argued for Garbo. Her portrayal 'of the bored and weary dancer, whose ebbing spirits and career are restored when she falls in love with a dashing brigand,' he said, was 'so lovely and exciting . . . so lyric and yet so lively and humorous and human in all of its shifting phases, that those who had predicted that someone else would steal the picture from her must today be feeling pretty much ashamed of themselves.'

Produced at a cost of $700,000, the picture was given roadshow treatment and grossed nearly $2.6 million the first year of its release. It played in more than a hundred cities as a roadshow, 'the first time since the days of *Ben-Hur* and *The Big Parade* that a production has been shown as an attraction on a "two-a-day" basis, on so large a scale,' reported the *New York Times* ('Grand' 1932). Cedric Gibbons's dazzling Art Deco lobby set for the picture, which was designed by unit art director Alexander Toluboff, was a visual delight. *Grand Hotel* won the Academy Award for Best Picture and ranked number one on *Film Daily*'s Top Ten.

Adventure films

Tarzan, the Ape Man (1932), another adventure film directed by W. S. Van Dyke, did just as well as *Trader Horn* and was the top draw of the 1931–32 season. It was based on Edgar Rice Burroughs's novel, *Tarzan and the Apes*, first published in 1912, which had spun off innumerable Tarzan films, books, comic strips, and merchandise. *Variety* implied that MGM made the movie to use up the leftover footage from *Trader Horn*. Regardless, the 'footage was loaded with a wealth of sensational wild animal stuff,' it said (*VFR*, 29 March 1932). *Tarzan* starred newest find Johnnie Weissmuller, a champion swimmer who won five Olympic gold medals and set sixty-seven world records in the twenties. He was working for BVD and endorsing its swimwear line when MGM signed him to a seven-year contract. MGM teamed him with Maureen O'Sullivan, Neil Hamilton, and C. Aubrey Smith. The picture was made in and around Culver City and told a slight story of how Tarzan saves an English trader and his daughter from a band of pigmies while searching for the 'traditional elephants' graveyard where ivory abounds.' *Tarzan* presented adventure of a high order, said *Variety*. It showed Tarzan 'battling singlehandedly and armed only with an inadequate knife, not only with one lion, but with a succession of a panther and two lions, and saved at the last minute from still a third big cat only by the friendly help of an elephant summoned by a call of distress in jungle language.' *Variety* concluded its review by saying, 'Whether the swimming champ will ever find another such outre role to play is the barrier to his career on the screen, but for this production he's a smash' (*VFR*, 29 March 1932).

As it turned out, *Tarzan, the Ape Man* initiated a series of six pictures that lasted until 1942. Johnny Weissmuller and Maureen O'Sullivan became one of MGM's many popular screen couples, and the series remained profitable to the very end. As James Robert Parish (1971: 305) has noted, 'The rather sensuous yet pure romance of Weissmuller's Tarzan and O'Sullivan's Jane set the tone' of the series. The highlights of the Tarzan films, he added 'were always the idyllic swimming sequences with the king of the jungle, his mate, and later Boy.' MGM anticipated that the popularity of the pictures would diminish significantly overseas during the war, where they had always done substantial business, and allowed the option on the Edgar Rice Burroughs story to lapse in 1942. The franchise continued at RKO with Weissmuller in the lead.

Woman's films

The woman's film typically revolved around an adult female protagonist and, as the name implies, was designed to appeal mainly to women. Introduced as a production trend in the twenties, the woman's film was enriched by the talkies, and during the thirties it flourished. In the first half of the decade, the woman's film accounted for more than a quarter of the pictures on *Film Daily*'s Top Ten. They included fallen-women films, maternal melodramas, romantic dramas, Cinderella romances, and gold digger and working-girl pictures. MGM produced more woman's films than any other studio. As a group, they are distinguishable from the output of other studios by their star power and by their special handling. Norma Shearer, Greta Garbo, Joan Crawford, Helen Hayes, and Jean Harlow generated the star power, and MGM's publicity machinery provided the special campaigns and roadshow releases.

After her sensational talking debut as a washed-out prostitute in *Anna Christie*, Garbo invariably played either a vamp who broke men's hearts or a disillusioned woman of the world who falls hopelessly and giddily in love and suffers and sometimes dies when her lover deserts her on hearing of her past. Garbo's fans eagerly anticipated her next talkie, Clarence Brown's *Romance* (1930). It was based on Edward Sheldon's stage hit of 1913 about an Italian opera star with a past who falls in love with a young clergyman, the protégé of her paramour. Critics were concerned with her voice. Could she make it in the talkies? Mordaunt Hall (1930) said that Miss Garbo appeared 'quite at ease in speaking her lines' in *Romance*. 'She is a breath of life in this love story, which, old as it may be in theme really is no more old than love itself. It is quite an affecting picture.'

Thalberg cast her in three pictures in rapid succession in 1931. She played a Parisian artist's model in Clarence Brown's *Inspiration* (1931), a courtesan in *Susan Lenox (Her Fall and Rise)* (1931), and a German spy in George Fitzmaurice's *Mata Hari* (1931). Not until she teamed up with Clark Gable in *Susan Lenox* did her leading man have what fan magazines called 'masculine S.A.' *Susan Lenox* was based on David Graham Phillips's muckraking novel about the real life of women in turn-of-the-century America. After its New York premiere at the Capitol on 16 October 1931, Lusk (1931) reported, 'Even with five shows a day the waiting line is always to be seen far into the night, and is its own answer to so-called hard times and financial depression.' She is paired 'for the first time with an actor who is almost her equal in drawing power and who is virtually her match in acting. The combination of Garbo and Clark Gable is a sensation artistically and financially.'

Garbo had reached her peak as a commercial property playing the role of prima ballerina Grusinskaya in *Grand Hotel*. Thalberg rushed her into *As You Desire Me* (1932) soon after because her five-year contract with the studio expired in June 1932. Garbo wanted a greater say in the choice of her properties, and the negotiations were at a standstill. As Schallert (1932a) noted, 'She is the ace star of the organization. Her pictures cause more of a sensation than any others. They garner huge box-office returns. Consequently, she can afford to wait until the last minute, in the event that she will decide to re-sign.' Garbo departed for Sweden after completing *As You Desire Me*. She planned on staying there until the studio capitulated.

After *The Trial of Mary Dugan*, Norma Shearer specialized in adult romantic dramas playing daring and unconventional ladies. *The Divorcee* (1930), *Let Us Be Gay* (Leonard 1930), and *Strangers May Kiss* (Fitzmaurice 1931) deal with infidelity and, according to Lambert (1990: 137), are 'gift-wrapped in the conventions of the time.' 'Each time she is finally reconciled with her husband, or the man who wants her to settle down and marry him, and each time an "excuse" is made for her infidelities, she feels neglected or misunderstood or the husband is unfaithful first.' 'From Long Island to Paris, Mexico to Madrid,' he said, 'her partying takes Norma back to the Jazz Age; then, weary of pleasure, she accepts the post-Depression verdict of her suitor in *Strangers May Kiss*: "We like to mix our drinks, but we take our women straight."' She received a new seven-year contract in 1931, which called for her to make six pictures over the next two and a half years with a boost in salary.

Sidney Franklin's *Smilin' Through* (1932) took her 'out of the hard brittle world of the modern heroine and returns her to the romantic sphere,' said Schallert (1932b). It was based on the play by Jane Murfin and Jane Cowl, which originally starred Jane Cowl on Broadway in 1919. Miss Shearer had a dual role, her second venture into the unusual in drama after *Strange Interlude*. In the hoop-skirted Victorian-era sequences, she played Moonyeen, who is accidentally murdered by her jilted suitor on her wedding day; in the modern scenes, she played Kathleen, Moonyeen's orphaned niece, who 'finds happiness after considerable woe, with the son of her aunt's assassin.' It costarred Fredric March and Leslie Howard. The picture premiered in New York on 13 October 1932 at the Capitol. *Variety* reported that on the first night, the audience was kept 'spellbound and hushed, saved for the flutter of women's handkerchiefs' (*VFR*, 18 October 1932). *Smilin' Through* became Shearer's biggest hit since *The Trial of Mary Dugan*.

Joan Crawford had segued successfully from flapper to what *Life* magazine called 'the Shopgirl's Dream.' In such films as *Paid* (Wood 1930), *Dance Fools Dance* (1931), *Possessed* (1931), *Grand Hotel* (1932), and *Letty Lynton* (1932), she took on a new persona, 'the image that a legion of admirers came to accept as archetypical. She is the working girl, initially at an economic disadvantage, who uses her sex appeal as a climbing rung on society's ladder to status and success' (Walker 1983: 67–8).

FIGURE 3.9 Robert Montgomery and Joan Crawford in Clarence Brown's *Letty Lynton* (1932)

Harry Beaumont's *Dance Fools Dance* was the first of eight pictures in which Crawford and Clark Gable appeared together, although he received sixth billing. In this riches-to-rags-to-riches story, Crawford starts out a wealthy socialite until her father loses everything on Wall Street and commits suicide. Afterward, she is forced to get a job and winds up a dogged reporter who goes undercover as a cabaret dancer to solve a gangster shooting, unaware that it involved her brother. As Alexander Walker described it, *Dance Fools Dance* was 'an opportunistic amalgam of *Our Dancing Daughters* and *Scarface* and was based on the St. Valentine's Day massacre and the Chicago underworld slaying of a newsman, both offences which are laid at Gable's door.' 'To get the goods on him,' he said, 'Crawford enrolls in the cabaret at his speakeasy – she dances vigorously in a silver mini-skirt, but becomes a "lady" once again by clipping an ankle-length one over it' (1983: 72). *Variety* said, 'This picture will rock the b.o. Few films have emerged from studios with a more mixed up story. But if the story lacks coherency, the situations more than atone for it. Metro has tried here to have Joan Crawford show everything she had. She does . . . She's s.a. from toes to headlights' (*VFR*, 25 March 1931). Walker (1983: 76) said, 'The period between the release of *Paid* and *Dance, Fools, Dance*, roughly the turn of the year 1930–31, can be said to be the time when Crawford consolidated her stardom for the rest of the decade.' She was given a new contract on 7 April 1931 starting at $3,000 per week and rising in steps to $5,000 a week in 1936 (Walker 1983: 76).

In *Grand Hotel*, Crawford had a supporting role. True to type, she played Flaemmchen, a stenographer and aspiring actress who uses her wiles on the ruthless industrialist Preysing, played by Wallace Beery, to advance her career. Hall (1932b) said that Crawford 'holds her own extremely well among the galaxy of stellar performers. She gives vitality to the part, which serves as an excellent contrast to the spiritual Grusinskaya.' *Letty Lynton* directed by Clarence Brown confirmed her new stature as a versatile actress. It was based on a novel by Marie Belloc Lowndes and costarred Robert Montgomery. Miss Crawford played a socialite of questionable morals who poisons one of her ex-lovers and 'is saved from the law when the hero commits perjury by declaring that she had passed the evening with him at the time of the alleged killing.' 'There is no trace of moral disapproval, no suggestion of punishment, no effort to soften the implications of tale,' said Watts (1932b). 'Howard Hughes,' he said, 'whose gangster film, *Scarface*, has been banned both by Will Hays and the state censors for its ethical delinquencies, is likely to be pretty much bewildered when he sees *Letty Lynton*.' Summarizing the New York reception of the movie, Lusk (1932) said, 'The triumph of Joan Crawford is unmarred by a single dissenting voice. She takes her place among the most accomplished actresses by reason of a brilliantly distinguished performance in the best of her starring pictures.' One of Adrian's costumes for the film, Crawford's white ruffled organdy, became all the rage and was widely copied by the fashion industry on New York's Seventh Avenue. Macy's claimed to have sold fifty thousand inexpensive copies of the dress.

By the time Jean Harlow joined MGM in 1932, the fallen-woman cycle had just about run its course. But the studio used the cycle to good advantage by capitalizing on Harlow's flair for comedy. Jack Conway's *Red-Headed Woman* (1932) was Harlow's breakthrough picture. And it was her most provocative. Anita Loos adapted the novel by Katherine Brush. Scheuer (1932) described it 'as frankly honest, audacious and provocative a story of a bad baby as ever hit the abashed screen.' Jean Harlow, he said, had 'miraculously transformed into something resembling an actress.' She 'wheedles, cajoles, pleads, sobs, and even browbeats her way' from stenographer to wife, mistress, and lover. *Red-Headed Woman* was 'extraordinary,' he added, because it told the story without moralizing, which is to say she was not made to suffer for her behavior.

Jean Harlow made headlines of a different sort in 1932, when Paul Bern, her new husband of two months, was found dead from a gunshot wound along with a mysterious suicide note. For a while, Harlow was thought to be implicated in his death. Her next picture, Victor Fleming's *Red Dust* (1932), became her first big box-office hit. She was paired with Clark Gable. He ran a rubber plantation and she played a prostitute in a 'hot-love-in-the-isolated tropics' story, a theme that was repeated by the pair in *China Seas* (1935), which did even better (*VFR*, 8 November 1932). Hall observed that at the opening of *Red Dust*, 'Miss Harlow's presence in the picture apparently attracted a host of other platinum blondes, for on all sides there were in the seats girls with straw-colored hair. Miss Harlow's performance suits the part' (*NYTFR*, 5 November 1932).

She had a memorable part in George Cukor's *Dinner at Eight* (1933) playing the 'petulant, nouveau riche wife' of Wallace Beery (*VFR*, 8 November 1932). Then she was paired again with Clark Gable in Sam Wood's *Hold Your Man* (1933). 'The popularity of the Jean Harlow–Clark Gable combination cannot be questioned,' said Frank Nugent. 'Virtually every seat in the Capitol Theatre was taken a few minutes after its doors were opened yesterday for the first showing.' 'It was a friendly audience,' he added. 'Laughter and applause punctuated the unreeling of the story and there is no explanation for that other than the popularity of Mr. Gable and Miss Harlow. Certainly there was little else about the film to merit such a response' (*NYTFR*, 1 July 1933).

Comedy

Sentimental comedy, or folksy comedy as it was sometimes called, was the popular favorite during the early thirties. Exploited mainly by MGM and Fox, the trend revolved around 'down-to-earth' stars. At MGM, the cycle actually began in the late twenties when Marie Dressler revived her fading silent screen career by teaming up with Polly Moran to make a series of low-budget comedies. Playing plain older women of the type usually described as 'battle-axes,' the two were typically cast as 'friendly enemies' in 'rough-and-tumble' comedies 'addressed to the banana peel sense of humor' and containing a dollop of sentiment. These pictures appealed to 'the mob' and did their best business away from the 'class spots,' said *Variety* (*VFR*, 21 January 1931). Marie Dressler and Polly Moran appeared together in five pictures during the thirties. Among them were three box-office hits, Charles Reisner's *Reducing* (1931) and *Politics* (1931) and Sam Wood's *Prosperity* (1932).

MGM's cycle of sentimental comedies took off when the studio teamed up Dressler with Wallace Beery in George Hill's *Min and Bill* (1930), a vehicle written by Frances Marion and Marion Jackson based on the Lorna Moon play *Dark Star*. Min is 'a hard boiled old gal, landlady of a fishing village inn, catering exclusively to sea rats but acting a lot tougher than she really is,' and Bill, an old salt, is her sweetheart (*VFR*, 26 November 1930). *Min and Bill* became the biggest box-office draw of the year; it also earned Dressler an Oscar for Best Actress. MGM teamed Dressler and Beery a second time in Mervyn LeRoy's *Tugboat Annie* (1933), a sequel of sorts in which Dressler plays 'a game old woman, the captain of a tugboat, who is inordinately proud of her son (the captain of a liner) and has an ineradicable fondness for her husband (the tugboat's chief liability), who [she says] "has never struck me except in self-defense."' Said *Variety*, 'Those who will be irritated or annoyed by the story's hokey, sobby, stale baloney nature are likely to be a very small minority. The average Dressler–Beery fan, of whom there are many, will eat it up as is without asking for Worcester sauce' (*VFR*, 15 August 1933). By herself, Dressler made Clarence Brown's *Emma* (1932), a vehicle designed

FIGURE 3.10 Wallace Beery and Marie Dressler in George Hill's *Min and Bill* (1930)

for her by Frances Marion. In this picture, Dressler is a servant who devotes her life to raising the children of a widower only to see them turn on her in her old age. Miss Dressler died of cancer in 1934, and her passing was deeply mourned by the public.

Wallace Beery made it to the top-ten list every year until 1935. An experienced character actor like Dressler, he sustained a faltering career during the transition to the talkies by playing lovable old rogues with hearts of gold. Given his looks, he had little other choice. He once said, 'Like my dear old friend, Marie Dressler, my mug has been my fortune.' *Min and Bill* also made Beery a star, a position which he solidified by winning an Academy Award for Best Actor in King Vidor's *The Champ* (1931). Beery played a broken-down ex-heavyweight fighter who is training for a comeback, a role written for him by Frances Marion. At his side is his young son, played by child star Jackie Cooper. Using Cooper to good advantage, MGM pulled out all the stops at the conclusion of *The Champ*. Describing the pathos of this scene, *Variety* said, 'the tears are drawn by [Jackie Cooper] alone. The Champ, his father and his idol, dies at the finish. The kid goes into a crying panic. He walks from one sympathizer to another in the dressing room, rejecting each condolence with a scream for the Champ' (*VFR*, 17 November 1931).

Hal Roach had understood early on that Laurel and Hardy were popular enough to succeed in features – features had the potential of generating significantly more revenue than shorts. 'By May 1930, Laurel and Hardy were more popular than many feature film stars. Their short subjects were frequently billed on theater marquees over the feature picture,' reported Skretvedt (1987: 201), who added, 'The problem was how to sustain the comedy for more than twenty minutes?'

Roach produced eleven Laurel and Hardy features for MGM, beginning with *Pardon Us* (1931) directed by James Parrott. Thereafter he released one Laurel and Hardy feature a year until 1935, when he ceased short film production and concentrated exclusively on features, with the exception of the Our Gang series. MGM released the first features at the Capitol, the company's principal New York launching pad. One picture, *Babes in Toyland* (1934), premiered at the prestigious Astor. But most of the pictures were released at the Rialto, a Times Square house noted for its cheap exploitation pictures. This suggested that the Laurel and Hardy pictures released there were destined to play the lower side of double bills.

Roach's first big hit was *The Devil's Brother* (1933), an operetta that featured Broadway baritone Dennis King. Roach personally directed the musical and dramatic sequences. The picture was based on an early-nineteenth-century comic opera, *Fra Diavolo* by Daniel F. Auber, about a 'desperado who robs stage coach passengers and who is wont to appear at social gatherings under the name of the Marquis de San Marco,' said Hall (*NYTFR*, 18 June 1933). Laurel and Hardy are robbed by one of Fra Diavolo's underlings and 'it occurs to them that being a bandit is so simple that they would do well to try it themselves.' He added, 'The shining light of the film is Dennis King, for one never tires of listening to his splendid baritone voice. The only regret is that there is not more of Mr. King's singing and less of the rowdy activities allotted to Messrs Laurel and Hardy.' The picture earned $475,000 in profits, according to Ward (2005: 211).

Roach next delivered two Laurel and Hardy classics, William I. Seiter's *Sons of the Desert* (1933) and Gus Meins and Charles Rogers's *Babes in Toyland*. *Sons of the Desert* was based on a story by Frank Craven and Byron Morgan. 'Let it be said at once that the new Laurel and Hardy enterprise has achieved feature length without benefit of the usual distressing formulae of padding and stretching. It is funny all the way through,' said Andre Sennwald. 'A Quixote and Panza in a nightmare world, where even the act of opening a door is filled with hideous perils, they fumble and stumble in their heartiest manner. At the Rialto spectators are checking their dignity with the doorman; an audience yesterday spluttered, howled and sighed in sweet surrender' (*NYTFR*, 12 January 1934).

Babes in Toyland was loosely based on a Victor Herbert operetta and was adapted by Frank Butler and Nick Grinde. It was released shortly before Christmas at the Astor. The picture earned the best reviews of Laurel and Hardy's career. Andre

FIGURE 3.11 Stan Laurel, Oliver Hardy, and Charley Chase in William I. Seiter's *Sons of the Desert* (1933)

Sennwald said, 'Every youngster in New York ought to find a ticket for *Babes in Toyland* in his Christmas stocking. If he is a good boy he should be permitted to see it twice' (*NYTFR*, 13 December 1934).

Variety, which had disparaged the features as two-reelers stretched to seven reels and was the pair's severest critic, said, 'If Hal Roach aimed at the production of a purely juvenile picture to which children might conceivably drag their elders, he has succeeded . . . He has made a film par excellence for children. It's packed with laughs and thrills and is endowed with that glamour and mysticism which marks juvenile literature' (*VFR*, 18 December 1934). According to Ward (2005: 211), *Sons of the Desert* earned a profit of $300,000, but *Babes in Toyland* barely broke even during its first release because of the film's high production cost.

Laurel and Hardy made six more features beginning in 1935. Perhaps the best of the lot was James W. Horne's *Way Out West* (1937). Margaret Tazelaar (1937) said, 'Its slapstick is right out of low-comedy, pie-throwing days of Mack Sennett, and the piece is nothing more than a string of gags; but, because of an individual style, the two clowns keep the nonsense sustained, and at time yesterday rendered the Rialto's patrons helpless.'

Roach's brand of slapstick comedy, represented by the Laurel and Hardy films, had a tenuous hold on the market. On 16 May 1938, Roach decided to change course. He terminated his eleven-year association with MGM and signed an eight-year distribution agreement with United Artists. The deal allowed him to concentrate more heavily on conventional feature film production. Roach delivered one last Laurel and Hardy picture on his MGM contract, James G. Blystone's *Block-Heads* (1938). *Variety* described it as 'lacking originality as to situation and gags' (*VFR*, 31 August 1938).

Horror films

Stylistically the least realistic of all the production trends and certainly the smallest in terms of quantity, the horror film left an indelible mark on the era. The first phase of the sound horror cycle, known as the classic period, lasted from 1931 to 1936, during which around thirty horror films were produced by the eight majors. MGM had originally responded to the demand for horror films by bringing Lon Chaney and Harry Earles out of retirement to remake their 1925 silent, *The Unholy Three* (Conway 1930), about the feats of a trio of crooks – a transvestite ventriloquist, a dwarf, and a strongman. However, Chaney died one month after the release of the picture, frustrating MGM's plans to produce a series of Chaney remakes.

Reentering the horror market in 1932, MGM produced one of its most unusual efforts, Tod Browning's *Freaks* (1932), probably the most sensational horror picture of the period. Written by Willis Goldbeck and Leon Gordon from a short story, *Spurs* by Todd Robbins, the action takes place in a European touring circus. A 'midget' from the sideshow falls in love with a 'normal' trapeze artist, who marries him with the intent of poisoning him for his money. When the freaks discover her motives, they chase the woman down one stormy night and change her into a legless giant hen. At the end of the picture, she is shown squatting in a pile of sawdust, a sideshow monstrosity like the other freaks. Harry Earles played one of the midget leads and was supported by carnival performers imported from all over the world. Turning the conventions of the horror film around, Browning wanted the audience to respect and sympathize with the so-called 'abnormal' freaks and posed the threat as coming from 'normal' people. *Variety* said that 'As a horror story, in the "Dracula" cycle, it is either too horrible or not horrible enough . . . It is gruesome and uncanny rather than tense, which is where the yarn went off track' (*VFR*, 12 July 1932). Others attacked the picture for being exploitative and tasteless, and after a short run, MGM withdrew it from circulation.

Thalberg's greatest year

In December 1932, the same month that the *Fortune* article appeared extolling Thalberg's producing prowess, Thalberg's health finally broke. He was stricken by influenza, which further weakened his heart. The fear of a heart attack kept him confined to his bed until he was strong enough to mount a recovery. Thalberg took an extended leave and convalesced in Germany during the first half of 1933. During his absence, Nick Schenck and Louis B. Mayer reorganized the studio.

Mark Vieira was rightly impressed with Thalberg's greatest year. 'It was adventurous filmmaking – the most diverse catalogue of entertainment in Hollywood's history.' 'Each project began with a fresh concept,' he said. 'As often as not this concept originated with Thalberg.' Examples: 'An all-star film. Two Barrymores in one film. All three Barrymores in one film. Norma Shearer in an old-fashioned romance. A horror film more horrible than Dracula and Frankenstein combined. A jungle film like *Trader Horn*, directed by Woody Van Dyke, but shot in California.' 'And why not from an Edgar Rice Burroughs novel?' (2009: 169)

4

LOUIS B. MAYER REORGANIZES (1933–39)

Decentralizing production

While Thalberg was out, Louis B. Mayer reorganized the studio. With Nick Schenck's approval, he decentralized motion picture production by instituting the producer-unit system. As the term implies, production was apportioned among autonomous producers to fill the annual roster. Each was responsible for three to six pictures a year. In the process, Thalberg's production supervisors were upgraded to producers and given screen credit for the pictures they developed. The shift to a producer-unit system was an industrywide phenomenon. During the Depression, weaknesses in the central producer system became apparent when it was determined that a single person could not effectively monitor production costs on a regular basis. It was also thought that placing a studio's entire annual output in the hands of one person minimized originality and the exchange of ideas. At MGM, Mayer set up units for Hunt Stromberg, Lawrence Weingarten, Bernard Hyman, Walter Wanger, Lucien Hubbard, David O. Selznick, and Harry Rapf. They were to report directly to Mayer. Thalberg would head his own unit upon his return, but Schenck eliminated Thalberg's position as vice president in charge of production.

Walter Wanger, a newcomer, had been hired as an associate producer by Mayer early in 1932. Dartmouth educated, Wanger had served a seven-year stint as general manager of Paramount's Astoria Studios from 1923 to 1931 and had worked for Harry Cohn at Columbia for a year. At Columbia, he produced a pair of social-problem films, James Cruze's *Washington Merry-Go-Round* (1932) and Frank Capra's *The Bitter Tea of General Yen* (1933). Wanger's stint at MGM was also brief. After producing *Gabriel Over the White House* (1933), a political allegory starring Walter Huston, *Queen Christina* (1933), a biopic starring Greta Garbo, and *Going Hollywood* (1933), a musical starring Marion Davies and Bing Crosby, he departed for

Paramount in 1934 with a ten-picture contract. Still in the hands of receivers, Paramount needed new talent to put the studio back on its feet.

To bolster MGM's lineup during Thalberg's absence, Mayer lured son-in-law David O. Selznick from RKO in 1933 by giving him a two-year contract to head up his own production unit. Selznick was the youngest son of Lewis J. Selznick, an early motion picture pioneer. He broke into the movies at MGM in 1927 as a script reader and soon became Harry Rapf's assistant, producing the Tim McCoy Westerns. In 1928, Selznick moved to Paramount, where he became an assistant to B. P. Schulberg, the studio chief. In 1930, he married Irene Mayer, Louis B. Mayer's younger daughter. Seeing that the fledgling RKO Radio Pictures was on shaky financial ground, Selznick convinced RCA head David Sarnoff to hire him to replace William LeBaron as vice president in charge of production in 1931. Selznick was 29. Selznick reorganized the studio around individual producer units, like Mayer would later do at MGM. Selznick took charge of the prestige pictures and instituted rigorous coast controls. His record included a string of hits, such as George Cukor's *A Bill of Divorcement* (1932), which introduced Katherine Hepburn; Edward H. Griffith's *The Animal Kingdom* (1932), a Broadway adaptation that starred Ann Harding, RKO's counterpart to MGM's Norma Shearer; and the Merian C. Cooper-Ernest B. Schoedsack production of *King Kong* (1933).

Selznick's tenure at MGM was also brief. His first credits included George Cukor's *Dinner at Eight* (1933), W. S. Van Duke's *Manhattan Melodrama* (1934), and Jack Conway's *Viva Villa!* (1934). Selznick then went on to produce a series of prestige pictures based on literary classics, among them, George Cukor's *David Copperfield* (1935), Jack Conway's *A Tale of Two Cities* (1935), and Clarence Brown's *Anna Karenina* (1935). In 1935, he formed his own independent production company, Selznick International Pictures, and lined up United Artists for distribution.

Hunt Stromberg bolstered MGM's lineup by producing a string of commercial and critical favorites. They included Richard Boleslawski's *The Painted Veil* (1934) starring Greta Garbo; Victor Fleming's *Treasure Island* (1934), an adventure film starring Wallace Beery as Long John Silver and Jackie Cooper as Jim Hawkins; the Thin Man detective series starring William Powell and Myrna Loy; the Jeanette MacDonald–Nelson Eddy operettas; and two big-budget prestige extravaganzas, Robert Z. Leonard's *The Great Ziegfeld* (1936) and W. S. Van Dyke's *Marie Antoinette* (1938). More than Thalberg or Selznick, Stromberg sustained MGM's prestige status through the thirties and more.

While Thalberg was recuperating, Mayer created an executive committee to run the studio. The move was seen as another attempt to dilute Thalberg's authority. It initially comprised Mayer at the helm, Eddie Mannix, vice president and general manager, and producers Harry Rapf, Bernard Hyman, Hunt Stromberg, Walter Wanger, and David O. Selznick. 'People came and went,' but as Eyman (2005: 173) has noted, 'for the rest of Mayer's time at MGM, this board would be the ruling body of the studio.' Later additions to the committee included Benjamin Thau, MGM's casting director and contract officer, J. J. Cohn, MGM's production manager since 1924 now turned producer of low-budget pictures, and Sam Katz. From the start, Howard Strickling, MGM's publicity chief, worked side by side with Mayer in the front office to cover up things when they went wrong.

Sam Katz was hired by Nicholas Schenck in 1934 to function as an executive assistant to Mayer and as a producer. Katz was a cofounder of the Balaban & Katz theater circuit in Chicago, one of the largest in the country. Adolph Zukor bought a controlling interest in the chain in 1926 and placed Katz in charge of Famous Players-Lasky's theater arm, Paramount Publix. Katz remained with the chain until 1932, when John Hertz, the chairman of the finance committee, reorganized operations in a failed attempt to stave off receivership. Katz briefly ventured into independent production before joining MGM, where he remained until 1948.

Thalberg's return

Irving Thalberg returned to work in the summer of 1933 on certain conditions: He would make only big-budget prestige pictures with the pick of MGM's talent pool; he would report directly to Schenck and not to Mayer; and he would continue to participate in the profit-sharing arrangement of the Mayer group. Mayer, Thalberg, and Rubin had signed new five-year personal service contracts with better terms beginning in December 1932. But Thalberg was not satisfied for long. He found himself having to compete with other producers for stars and directors. Mayer, for his part, felt that he had to divide stars and directors equitably among all producers. Schenck interceded again and agreed to set Thalberg up as an independent producer with Loew's financing at the conclusion of his present contract. The terms were generous, but Thalberg did not live long enough to enjoy them. He died on 14 September 1936.

Upon Thalberg's death, the Mayer group profit-sharing arrangement automatically dissolved, and Mayer and Rubin arranged to divide up Thalberg's portion among themselves. However, Norma Shearer threatened to sue the studio if the payments were not continued. A financial settlement was reached in March 1937; Miss Shearer received a new six-picture contract that gave her certain approval rights and a generous $150,000 per picture (Eyman 2005: 251).

Now it was Mayer's turn to complain. He had taken on additional duties after Thalberg died and threatened to quit at the end of his contract in 1937 unless help were forthcoming. Nick Schenck devised a plan to ease Mayer's burden, and in December 1937, Mayer signed on for another five years. To create stability in the executive ranks and to share the burden of production, Schenck included Mayer's executive team in a new profit-sharing arrangement. It was to go into effect on 1 January 1939 and would extend the personal-service contracts of eleven executives from four to seven years and give them the same share of the profits formerly allocated to the Mayer group. The eleven executives comprised Mayer, J. Robert Rubin, Eddie Mannix, Sam Katz, Al Lichtman, Benjamin Thau, Hunt Stromberg, Bernard H. Hyman, Lawrence Weingarten, Harry Rapf, and Mervyn LeRoy. Martin Quigley (1938: 16), the influential publisher of the *Motion Picture Herald*, approved the plan, stating that the profit incentive would ensure 'both continuity and quality of performance' for the benefit of 'theater operators.'

However, such generosity did not sit well with Loew's stockholders. In 1938, nine separate minority stockholder suits were instituted against the company. They claimed that 'the salaries and bonuses were excessive and unreasonable' and sought to set aside the profit-sharing agreements before they could take effect ('Loew's Stockholders' 1938: 2). The consolidated suit, which was filed in the New York State Supreme Court in December 1938, claimed that six Loew's-MGM executives received 31 percent of the net profits, while stockholders received 59 percent. The six included the top four Loew's officers – Nicholas Schenck, president; J. Robert Rubin, vice president; David Bernstein, vice president and treasurer; and Arthur Loew, director – plus MGM vice president Louis B. Mayer and the estate of Irving Thalberg. *Motion Picture Herald* ('Film Salaries' 1939: 44) reported that in 1937 Loew's Inc. paid 'the three highest salaries in the nation.' Mayer ranked number one with a salary of $1,296,503, Rubin ranked number two with $754,254, and Schenck number three with $541,602.

After presenting testimony from industry leaders, counsel for the defendants argued that the executives were 'worth all they received because it was due entirely to their efforts, ability and genius that the profits of the corporation were so enormous' ('6 Top' 1938: 1). The court ruled in favor of Loew's in January 1939 and approved the profit-sharing agreements, stating that 'contracts between the company and its executives for the payment of compensation were proper in principle and not out of reasonable proportion to the value of their services, considering the high salaries paid in the motion picture industry and the intense competition between the major companies for talent' ('Loew's Wins' 1939: 4). Loew's could easily afford to be generous: net profit for fiscal 1937 amounted to $14.3 million, up from $10.6 million in 1936, and $7.5 million in 1935 (Gomery 1986: 52).

The Depression

After the great Wall Street crash of 1929, Hollywood felt the effects of the disabled economy beginning in 1931. The movies were not immune to the Depression. Theater admissions slumped, and more than 4,000 theaters, mostly independent, had gone dark. The price of a theater ticket also fell as well. To make matters worse, Hollywood saw production costs for the new talkies more than double and revenues from foreign markets dwindle. When the newly elected President Franklin Roosevelt declared a four-day national bank holiday in March 1933, the cash flow dried up, which prevented the studios from meeting their payrolls. Production chiefs concluded that the studios could be kept open only if employees took a pay cut. The decision led to the rise of labor militancy in Hollywood.

The box-office slump had a devastating impact on the heavily leveraged majors. No longer able to avoid the ignominy of bankruptcy and receivership, RKO went down first, in January 1933, followed soon after by Paramount and Fox. Warner

Bros. was fighting to stay afloat. The bankruptcies and receiverships occurred in the exhibition subsidiaries of the majors and not in the production–distribution ends and stemmed directly from the ferocious battle for theater control at the end of the twenties. Paramount, Warner Bros., and RKO were particularly aggressive and built or acquired hundreds of theaters, thereby encumbering themselves with millions of dollars of debt. When the boom ended in 1931, the so-called deluxe theaters, built in flush times and at recklessly extravagant costs, became white elephants at least for the duration of the Depression. In short, the major companies could not meet their fixed cost obligations, which simply means they did not have the cash to pay their mortgage commitments, short-term obligations, and the heavy charges on their funded debts.

Of the Big Five, only Loew's had yet to show a deficit; however, its earnings plunged from $14.6 million in 1930 to $4.3 million in 1933 (Gomery 1986: 52). Loew's Inc. posted profits every year of the Depression. Two factors were responsible for Loew's outstanding achievement. The first was the company's fiscal conservatism. Loew's had branched out into production during the twenties by absorbing Metro Pictures, Goldwyn Pictures, and Louis B. Mayer Productions to form MGM, but it stood pat with its chain of 125 high-class theaters, which were located mainly in Greater New York and acquired before the boom years 1927–29. The second was MGM's singular success in gauging public tastes. During the depths of the Depression, MGM consistently contributed to the Loew's bottom line. In fiscal 1931, it generated profits of $6.2 million; in fiscal 1932, $3 million; in fiscal 1933, $1.3 million; and in fiscal 1934, $4.7 million ('Metro-Goldwyn Pictures' 1934: 5). By 1935, box-office receipts and theater admissions had rebounded, one thousand theaters were said to have reopened, and Paramount and Fox had successfully undergone reorganization. The film industry had survived the Depression intact.

Labor militancy

The pay cuts instituted by the majors when President Roosevelt declared a four-day bank holiday in March 1933 set in motion a wave of unionization. The Screen Writers Guild was formed in April 1933, followed two months later by the Screen Actors Guild. Until then, the Academy of Motion Picture Arts and Sciences had been the designated mediator of labor disputes for the majors. Louis B. Mayer had conceived the Academy in 1927, in part to ward off attempts to unionize the movie colony. The founders of the Academy comprised the Association of Motion Picture Producers, the Hollywood arm of the Hays Office. Membership was by invitation (in part to keep out undesirables) and comprised five categories of filmmakers – producers, directors, actors, writers, and technicians. Academy members apparently were given sufficient financial rewards to forestall serious labor organizing among their ranks for five years.

The screenwriters' grievances were many. 'They included practices that Thalberg held dear,' said Vieira (2009: 307). 'Writers were lent from studio to studio without consent; writers were made to write on speculation; writers were suspended or laid off without written notice; writers were arbitrarily denied screen credit, regardless of their contribution; writers were made to work simultaneously on the same material without being informed of this by the producer.' Writers who 'complained about any of these practices,' he said, 'were blacklisted.' The majors countered the formation of the Screen Writers Guild by throwing their support behind the Screen Playwrights, an organization of politically conservative screenwriters that was content with the status quo. MGM lent its support to the organization by providing it with meeting rooms, offices, and secretaries and even by giving the founders working at MGM long-term contracts.

To deal with the actors, the studios wrote in obnoxious provisions in the Code of Fair Competition for the Motion Picture Industry, which was signed into law on 27 November 1933 under the provisions of the National Industrial Recovery Act. The code bared star raiding, curbed the activities of agents, and limited the salaries of artistic personnel. While the code was being drafted, actors and writers had bombarded Washington with telegrams, held mass meetings, and launched publicity campaigns opposing the control of salaries on any basis other than an open market. Even members of the producers' group joined the protest. Joseph Schenck, president of United Artists, said the salary provision would 'result in peonage for the artists.' Sam Goldwyn said, 'You can't make a crime out of earning capacity,' adding that 'he would rather pay an artist $250,000 if he earned it, than $2,000 if he did not' ('Two Producers' 1933). The studio heads signed the code nonetheless. It took a personal appeal to President Roosevelt by Eddie Cantor to get the obnoxious provisions of the code suspended by executive order. Afterward, Cantor commented that 'necessary economies could be brought about by cutting useless relatives and highly paid figureheads from the executive and supervisory staffs of motion picture companies' ('Cantor' 1933).

EPIC (End Poverty in California)

The extent to which the studios went to control the lives and political beliefs of employees can be seen in the 1934 California gubernatorial race. Upton Sinclair, the muckraking author, was a Socialist but ran as a Democrat to win the nomination. He ran on a platform to 'End Poverty in California' (EPIC), which advocated the creation of cooperative farms and factories to put the unemployed to work, among other things. When the polls had showed him winning decisively over the Republican Frank Merriman, the Hearst newspapers and the *Los Angeles Times* launched a successful crusade to defeat him. They were aided and abetted by studio chiefs. Irving Thalberg ordered the production of fake newsreels, one of which accused Sinclair of being a Russian puppet. Louis B. Mayer instructed MGM's publicity departments to 'produce scurrilous newspaper, billboard, and radio ads . . . that demonized Sinclair.' Mayer even went so far as to demand that all studio employees contribute one day's salary to fund anti-Sinclair publicity. As Eyman (2005: 203–04) remarked, the studios' heavy-handed behavior 'left every liberal and many moderates . . . muttering "Never again."'

Guild shops

In 1935, Congress passed the National Labor Relations Act, which recognized the rights of employees to bargain collectively. The Screen Playwrights argued that screen writers were really high-salaried independent contractors rather than employees and performed their services 'free from the control of the companies' ('Orders' 1938). As a result, they should not come under the jurisdiction of the National Labor Relations Board. The NLRB rejected the argument by observing that producers had always exercised the right to demand rewrites from screenwriters, among other things. The board ordered a studio-by-studio election that would allow screenwriters to choose between the Screen Writers Guild and Screen Playwrights as their bargaining representative. Although screenwriters voted in favor of the SWG and won certification from the National Labor Relations Board on 10 August 1938, producers stonewalled during the subsequent bargaining sessions.

A guild shop was finally established in May 1941. Needless to say, none of the goals of the original platform was realized. The studios agreed to ban speculative writing, set a minimum wage, and made the guild the sole arbiter of screen credits, but they would have nothing to do with elevating the creative status of the screenwriter. The means producers used to oppose the SWG 'is one of the less flattering commentaries on the men who control movie production,' commented Rosten (1941: 318–19).

The Screen Actors Guild finally won recognition as a bargaining agent on 15 May 1937 only after threatening to strike. 'The victories have been victories for the rank and file,' said Thompson (1938: 383). 'For themselves the stars have asked and won next to nothing.' The rank and file won minimum pay rates, guarantees of continuous employment, and twelve-hour rest periods between calls. Although successive contracts won benefits for all classes of performers, the relationship of the actor to the production process remained unaltered; in fact, it was never an issue. The concessions had relatively minor economic impact on the studios, which explains why they were implemented.

The Browne–Bioff racketeering scandal

In dealing with talent groups, Hollywood proved to be a belligerent and divisive foe; keeping the labor force in line was another matter. In 1934, International Alliance of Theatrical Stage Employees (IATSE) installed a new president, William B. Browne, the former head of the Motion Picture Machine Operators Union in Chicago. Browne had as his personal representative Willie Bioff, a fellow Chicagoan and professional hoodlum. The majors had previously achieved labor peace with craft workers and rank-and-file laborers by the signing of the Studio Basic Agreement in 1926. The agreement formally recognized five important unions but succeeded in keeping an 'open shop,' meaning that employees did not have to be union members in order to work. IATSE, which controlled virtually every studio craft required to shoot a movie, withdrew from the studio basic agreement in 1933 over a jurisdiction issue, and its membership dwindled from 5,000 to 150 ('Willie Bioff' 1941: 16).

To reinstate his union, Browne used IA's deadliest weapon, a strike. On 30 November 1935, he succeeded in closing down all of Paramount's theaters in Chicago, Minneapolis, and Omaha. Browne's price for settlement was high – a closed shop for all IATSE's former members not only at Paramount but throughout the entire industry. Fearing the disastrous financial losses through labor shutdowns, the studios capitulated, and the rolls of IATSE soon swelled to 125,000 members. Within four months, Browne and Bioff demanded 'peace payments' to prevent further projectionist strikes. They succeed in extorting $1,200,000 from Loew's, 20th Century Fox, Paramount and Warner Bros. over five years 'in the biggest shakedown known,' according to a United States prosecuting attorney ('Bioff, Brown' 1941).

Browne and Bioff's racketeering was exposed in the Southern District Court of New York New in October 1941. Nick Schenck testified that David Bernstein, the company treasurer, personally delivered the first peace payment of $50,000 in $100 bills to Browne at the Waldorf, that Loew's executives then wrote fake expense vouchers to cover the payment, that subsequent installments were made to Bioff by way of Bioff's brother-in-law, a DuPont sales agent, in the form of commissions from the sale of raw film to MGM, and that Loew's had hired an intermediary in Chicago for $100,000 to settle a projectionists' strike in sixty Loew's theaters in New York in 1935 ('Schenck, Bernstein' 1941).

Browne and Bioff were convicted of racketeering and sentenced to ten and eight years, respectively. Joseph Schenck, 20th Century Fox chairman, had also paid bribes to Browne and Bioff. In a separate trial, Schenck had been convicted of income tax fraud. But because he helped the government build its case against the pair, his three-year sentence for tax fraud was suspended, and he was allowed to plead guilty to a perjury account regarding the payoffs, for which he served four months and five days in a minimum-security prison. With Browne and Bioff out of the way, labor peace was secured for the war's duration.

Double features and shorts

To counter a declining box office during the Depression, theaters started offering two pictures for the price of one. The practice got a foothold in New England as early as 1930, and by the middle of 1932, theaters everywhere had adopted the practice. First-run theaters, which were owned mostly by the majors and located in the larger cities, enjoyed a competitive advantage over subsequent-run houses in the distribution chain. They were located in large metropolitan areas and offered an array of inducements to lure in moviegoers such as comfortable appointments, air conditioning, proximity to public transportation, and live entertainment. Subsequent-run houses, which were owned mostly by independents and were located in smaller communities, lowered ticket prices initially to attract customers then devised other tactics such as double features, two-for-one tickets, half-priced student tickets, free ladies' matinees, and prizes to keep the doors open.

Although the majors opposed double features, fearing the practice would open the exhibition market to more independent producers, the NRA legalized the practice in August 1934. In reacting to the new market conditions, studios divided production more or less into two groups – 'A' and 'B' – and formed special production units to handle the lower-grade product. Unlike the upper-grade product, B movies were sold to exhibitors for a flat fee. Although flat fees were low out of necessity, producers could predict with great accuracy the amount of revenue such pictures could generate and scale production costs accordingly. By the end of the decade, double features had become an institution, prevailing in most of the nation's theaters.

MGM never admitted publicly that it produced B movies. MGM took this stand even though Loew's announced in 1935 that all its subsequent-run houses were converting to double features. No one was fooled by MGM's posturing. Mayer considered B movies to be a valuable training ground for aspiring actors and fledgling directors. During the thirties, producers Lucien Hubbard, Harry Rapf, and J. J. Cohn oversaw the lower-budget product, but MGM's Bs looked like no others and sometimes cost as much as a class-A picture at another studio. 'When Metro goes out to make a class B picture,' said *Variety*, 'they give it plenty of production, steady direction and a certain amount of class. It may not have big draw stars and the situation may be overdone, but it certainly will stand up on the second picture shelf in the theatres for which it was designed' (*VFR*, 6 October 1937).

Shorts

Double features left less time on theater playbills for shorts. In 1935, Hal Roach, MGM's principal supplier of shorts, took a hard look at his business and decided to phase out short film production, with one exception, *Our Gang*, which he kept going until 1938, but in a shortened version. MGM now had to pick up the slack by producing more shorts in-house beginning in 1935. Jack Chertok, Harry Rapf's assistant, was placed in charge of production and was soon turning out sixty shorts a year. The Shorts Department 'became a studio within a studio, with its own staff of fifty, including writers, directors, editors, and supervisors,' said Eyman (2005: 272). The directors on the roster included Jacques Tourneur, Roy Rowland, Felix Feist, George Sidney, Joseph Sherman, and Harold Bucquet. The most popular series comprised *Pete Smith Specialties* (1935–54), *Crime Does Not Pay* (1935–37), and *MGM Miniatures* (1935–44).

Pete Smith had moved into short film production in 1931 with *Fisherman's Paradise* and *Sports Champions*. Smith 'took great liberties with the silent sports and fishing footage presented to him, using optical effects such as slow motion and reverse action. He then wrote and recorded rather sarcastic narration, and the Pete Smith formula was set,' said Ward (2003: 225). To make his *Pete Smith Specialties*, which came out once a month, Smith treated anything that 'might be of interest to a large number of customers. He has shown how to prepare a meal in seven minutes, how pictures are transmitted by telegraph, how to play ping-pong and what wrestlers do for amusement,' said Churchill (1937). Two of Smith's shorts, *Penny Wisdom* (1937) and *Quicker'n a Wink* (1940), won Oscars for Best Short Subject and sixteen others received nominations. The Crime Does Not Pay series were dramas of criminals brought to justice. Each short was a dramatic reenactment of a case allegedly taken from FBI files that exposed one particular racket. J. Edgar Hoover himself endorsed the series as helping to curb crime. *MGM Miniatures* were narrated by the humorist Robert Benchley. The first in the series, *How to Sleep* (1935), won an Academy Award for the Best Short Comedy. It was followed by such 'educational and scientific' subjects as *How to Train a Dog, How to Behave, How to Raise a Baby.*

Animation

In 1936, Fred Quimby, who had been handling the sales of MGM's shorts out of New York since 1927, moved to Culver City to better coordinate production and distribution. In 1937, MGM reorganized its entire short subject operation by placing it on a unit basis with Chertok in charge. One such unit was a new in-house animation department. As mentioned earlier, MGM had attempted to go up against Mickey Mouse by releasing the *Flip the Frog* cartoons independently produced by the ex-Disney staffer Ub Iwerks.

Walt Disney had dominated the animation field since he introduced Mickey Mouse in *Steamboat Willie* in 1928. Disney released his first cartoons through Columbia Pictures but switched to United Artists in 1932. In addition to his Mickey Mouse cartoons, Disney produced a popular series of *Silly Symphonies*, for which he had the exclusive use of Technicolor's three-strip process for cartoon production until 1935. *Flip the Frog* cartoons were black and white and did not measure up. MGM dropped Iwerks in 1933 and the following year contracted with independent producers Hugh Harmon and Rudolf Ising to release the Happy Harmonies series in Technicolor's two-strip process. Harmon and Ising had formerly coproduced the popular Looney Tunes and Merrie Melodies series for Leon Schlesinger at Warner Bros. They frequently fought with Schlesinger over budgets, and MGM got them to sign by simply doubling their budgets.

But the *Happy Harmonies* did not measure up as well, and that was when MGM went into animation production and brought in Fred Quimby to take charge. MGM thus became the first and only major studio to operate its own cartoon department. Quimby was an odd choice, since he had been involved exclusively in sales throughout his career and was not known for his sense of humor. After a false start, Quimby was forced to rehire Harmon and Ising in 1938. They returned as contract employees – not independent producers – and set up shop in a rundown bungalow on Lot 2. The two would be gone by 1942. During their stay, Ising created the Barney Bear continuing-character series, which lasted until 1954, and picked up an Oscar for *The Milky Way* (1940); Harmon's one-shot cartoon *Peace on Earth* (1939) was nominated for an Oscar and a Nobel Peace Prize.

In 1940, MGM discovered a new pair of cartoon stars, Tom and Jerry. Quimby needed more cartoons and set up a production unit for two young animators on the lot, William Hanna and Joseph Barbera, in 1939. The Tom and Jerry series was an outgrowth of a stand-alone cartoon, *Puss Gets the Boot* (1940), about a cat and a mouse tormenting each other. After the picture was nominated for an Academy Award, Quimby gave the go-ahead to develop a series. As Eyman (2005: 273) stated, 'Soon, Tom and Jerry were the profit centers for the entire MGM animation department.' *Tom and Jerry* lasted until 1958 and won seven Academy Awards, more than any other series with the same characters.

Quimby was always on the lookout for new talent, and in September 1941, he scored a coup by signing the great Tex Avery, recently of Warner Bros., to a five-year contract. As Morris (1998) stated, Avery 'steered the Warner Bros. house style away from Disneyesque sentimentality and made cartoons that appealed equally to adults, who appreciated Avery's speed, sarcasm, and irony, and to kids, who liked the nonstop action.' Disney's 'cute and cuddly' creatures, under Avery's guidance, were transformed into 'unflappable wits like Bugs Bunny, endearing buffoons like Porky Pig, or dazzling crazies like Daffy Duck.' Avery's first assignment for MGM, *Blitz Wolf* (1942), a *Three Little Pigs* parody satirizing Hitler, was nominated for an Academy Award. Avery went on to direct such classics as *Red Hot Riding Hood* (1943), *What's Buzzin' Buzzard* (1943), and *Who Killed Who?* (1943) and the popular Droopy series. 'Avery's counterpart to Tom and Jerry,' said Eyman (2005: 273), 'was a deadpan bassett hound named Droopy, an imperturbable, waddling understatement in total control of Avery's hyperbolic valley of exaggeration.' The cartoon series lasted for fourteen years and comprised sixty-seven shorts. As Gomery (1986: 73–4) has noted, 'At last MGM had achieved profits in the field of animation to rival its achievements in feature films.'

Production trends

Prestige pictures

Analyzing MGM a second time, *Fortune* ('Loew's Inc.' 1976: 278) reported in 1939 that the studio 'has for at least eight years made far and away the best pictures of any studio in Hollywood. Metro's gross revenue from film rentals has been consistently higher than that of other studios, and as a result Loew's, Inc., has been and still is the most profitable movie company in the world.' A second wave of prestige pictures hit the market early in 1934 'in numbers so thick as to constitute the champion of cycles since sound came in,' said *Variety* ('Biographical Cycle' 1934: 3). The number of prestige pictures rose dramatically afterward, and for the remainder of the decade, they constituted 50 percent of pictures on *Film Daily*'s Top Ten. Motion picture attendance picked up beginning in 1934, and people had more disposable income to spend on entertainment, which reduced the risks of producing big-budget extravaganzas. Thereafter, biopics, costume-adventure pictures, adaptations of literary classics, and even the class-A Westerns became the staples of prestige production. Given its star roster and financial resources, MGM easily retained its preeminent position in the trend.

During Walter Wanger's brief tenure at MGM, he produced one important prestige picture, Greta Garbo's *Queen Christina* (1933), directed by Rouben Mamoulian. *Queen Christina* marked Greta Garbo's return to the screen after eighteen months. Garbo had announced that she would retire from the screen after completing *As You Desire Me* and departing for Sweden. Mayer disabused her of such an idea by signing her to a new contract, which essentially made her a producer of her pictures. The contract set up a company called Canyon Productions and called for Garbo to star in two pictures. She was given the right to choose her own directors, the principal cast, and the start dates, plus other considerations. Her compensation: a magnificent $250,000 for each film (Walker 1980: 132).

Queen Christina was a fictional biopic by Salka Viertel and Margaret Levino about the seventeenth-century Swedish monarch, who abdicates the throne for love of a Spanish envoy who had been sent to the Swedish court with a marriage proposal from the King of Spain. Garbo had originally wanted Lawrence Olivier for the envoy, but she felt uncomfortable with him during rehearsals and insisted that John Gilbert be brought back for the part. *Queen Christina* premiered in New York at the Astor on 26 December 1933. 'The sign above the theatre said to be the largest illuminated theatrical sign on Broadway, carried the single "Garbo" in flashing electric lights over a massive likeness of the Swedish star,' reported the *Motion Picture Herald* ('Garbo's' 1934: 67). Mordaunt Hall said, '*Queen Christina* is a skillful blend of history and fiction in which the Nordic star, looking as alluring as ever, gives a performance which merits nothing but the highest praise. She appears every inch a queen' (*NYTFR*, 27 December 1933). *Queen Christina* ranked number one on MGM 1933–34 roster, turning in a handsome profits of $623,000.

David O. Selznick's two-year stint at MGM rivaled Thalberg as a producer of prestige pictures. Five of his pictures made it to *Film Daily*'s Ten Best Films. His biggest hit was George Cukor's *Dinner at Eight* (1933), a multistar vehicle along the lines of *Grand Hotel* with a cast headed by Marie Dressler, John Barrymore, Wallace Beery, and Jean Harlow. It was based on the George S. Kaufman–Edna Ferber comedy of manners containing interlocking stories about the behind-the-scenes events leading up to a posh Manhattan dinner party. Selznick chose Frances Marion and Herman Mankiewicz to write the screenplay. The picture cost $435,000 to make, received excellent reviews, and earned a profit of $998,000. It premiered in New York at the Astor on a roadshow basis in September 1933.

Selznick then went on to adapt a series of literary masterpieces to the screen. His first, George Cukor's *David Copperfield* (1935), was based on the Dickens classic and starred Freddie Bartholomew, Selznick's newest discovery, in the title role. In a bit of offbeat casting, Selznick cast W. C. Fields as Micawber and Roland Young as Uriah Heep. Although Selznick and Cukor had scouted England for suitable locations, the film was ultimately shot on the MGM lot at a cost of more than $1 million. The *New York Times* hailed it as a 'gorgeous photoplay which encompasses the rich and kindly humanity of the original so brilliantly that it becomes a screen masterpiece in its own right. The immortal people of *David Copperfield* . . . troop

FIGURE 4.1 Jean Harlow and Wallace Beery in George Cukor's *Dinner at Eight* (1933)

across the . . . screen like animated duplicates of the famous Phiz drawings, an irresistible and enormously heartwarming procession' (*NYTFR*, 19 January 1935).

Selznick's second, Clarence Brown's *Anna Karenina* (1935), was based on the Tolstoy classic and starred Greta Garbo. In 1927, Garbo made a silent version of the novel, *Love*, opposite John Gilbert. (*Anna Karenina* followed Garbo's *The Painted Veil* [1934], directed by Richard Boleslawski. It was produced by Hunt Stromberg and constituted the second entry under the terms of the Canyon Productions deal. The production company was liquidated afterward for federal income tax purposes. MGM then gave her a new contract with a boost in salary to make *Anna Karenina*.) For the remake, Selznick cast Fredric March as Vronsky, the dashing young officer to whom Anna turns for love; Basil Rathbone as Karenin, her unloving and hypercritical husband, and Freddie Bartholomew as her son Sergei, whom she gives up to go to her lover. The picture premiered in New York at the Capitol on 30 August 1935 to rave reviews and was held over for four weeks. The *Hollywood Reporter* called it 'Garbo's best picture' ('Anna' 1935: 3). Selznick's version, which was written by Clemence Dane, Salka Viertal, and S. N. Behrman, linked 'the plight of the lovers to the decadent and hypo-critical society which doomed them.' 'The photoplay is literate, intelligent and moving drama, visually handsome and brilliantly performed by Miss Garbo,' said Andre Sennwald. 'From the splendidly staged meeting between Anna and Vronsky in the railroad station to her death under the grinding locomotive wheels, the drama moves along with sureness and dignity' (*NYTFR*, 8 September 1935). 'Garbo's pedestal is not only restored but is made to look unbreakable in this picture . . . Showmen should and must get behind this attraction, build it for one of their greatest openings. The rest will take care of itself.' *Karenina* played well in larger cities but withered in small towns. It turned in a modest $320,000 profit. After making *Anna Karenina*, Garbo signed a two-picture contract on 30 May 1935. The films were *Conquest* and *Camille*.

For his final MGM entry, Selznick turned to another Dickens classic, *A Tale of Two Cities* (1935) directed by Jack Conway. It starred Ronald Colman as Sydney Carton and Elizabeth Allan as Lucie Manette. Andre Sennwald greeted it as fol-lows: 'Having given us David Copperfield, Metro-Goldwyn-Mayer now heaps up more Dickensian magic with a prodigally stirring production of A Tale of Two Cities, which opened at the Capitol Theatre yesterday.' 'For more than two hours,' he said, 'it crowds the screen with beauty and excitement, sparing nothing in its recital of the Englishmen who were caught up in the blood and terror of the French Revolution and of Sydney Carton, who gave his life for his friends'(*NYTFR*, 26 December 1935). W. P. Lipscomb and S. N. Behrman wrote the screenplay and dramatized memorable episodes of the French Revolution, among them, 'the starving populace rioting for the meat that is being fed to Evremonde's dogs, Darnay's mock trial before the bloody tribunal and the impassioned plea of Dr. Manette for the life of his son-in-law, and, finally, the magnificent re-enactment of the fall of the Bastille,' said Sennwald. Because of its high production cost, the picture earned only a modest profit.

FIGURE 4.2 Fredric March and Norma Shearer in Sidney Franklin's *The Barretts of Wimpole Street* (1934)

Thalberg threw himself into a vehicle for Norma Shearer upon his return, *The Barretts of Wimpole Street* (1934), directed by Sidney Franklin. It was based on Rudolf Besier's 1931 Broadway hit starring Katharine Cornell as the invalid poetess Elizabeth Barrett. Thalberg teamed her with two other Oscar winners, Fredric March as the celebrated poet Robert Browning and Charles Laughton as Elizabeth's domineering father. It premiered on 28 August 1934 at the Capitol. Andre Sennwald said, 'Miss Shearer's Elizabeth is a brave and touching piece of acting, and she is successful in creating the illusion of a highly sensitive and delicate woman who beats her luminous wings in vain against the chains which bind her' (*NYTFR*, 29 September 1934). The picture gave Shearer her most widely acclaimed great-lady-of-the-theater role and ranked number one on *Film Daily's* Top Ten.

Ernst Lubitsch's *The Merry Widow* (1934), a remake of MGM's 1925 silent version of the Franz Lehar operetta directed by Erich Von Stroheim, followed. It starred Jeanette MacDonald and Maurice Chevalier, who had previously worked together in two 'continental' musicals at Paramount, Ernst Lubitsch's *The Love Parade* (1929) and Rouben Mamoulian's *Love Me Tonight* (1932). *The Merry Widow* premiered in New York at the Astor on 11 October 1934. 'Under the guidance of the mighty Ernst Lubitsch,' said Watts (1934), '*The Merry Widow*, that sturdy veteran among the operettas, emerges as a debonair and witty photoplay that reveals the master of cinema high comedy in his brightest mood.' The picture demonstrated once more Lubitsch's 'vast skill at genuine cinema wit,' he added. 'You will find little that is touchingly sentimental about the Balkan romance of the handsome widow and the dashing officer. Instead you will encounter, amid a thousand of those superb pictorial epigrams that are known as "Lubitsch touches," an amused, ironical and curiously detached treatment of the old time light operatic plot.' *The Merry Widow* performed best in urban spots, but because of its high production cost, it posted a small loss. Cedric Gibbons and Fredric Hope won an Oscar for their sumptuous set design, which helped explain the high cost. The returns did not sour MGM's interest in operettas. MGM gave Jeanette MacDonald a new five-year contract afterward, which resulted in the Jeanette MacDonald–Nelson Eddy operetta series.

Thalberg's next entry, Frank Lloyd's *Mutiny on the Bounty* (1935), was his top box-office draw. Based on novels by Charles Nordhoff and James Norman Hall, this adventure classic starred Charles Laughton as the sadistic Captain Bligh of the *H.M.S. Bounty* and Clark Gable and Franchot Tone as the mutineers, Fletcher Christian and Roger Byam. *Mutiny on the Bounty* cost more than $2 million to make and was shot largely on location in the South Pacific using life-size reproductions of the ships *Bounty* and *Pandora*. It premiered in New York at the Capitol on 8 November 1935. Sennwald called it 'just about the perfect adventure picture' (*NYTFR*, 9 November 1935). *Variety* said that Bligh, 'due to the faithful portrait drawn by Laughton, is as despicable a character as has ever heavied across a screen.

FIGURE 4.3 Clark Gable and Charles Laughton in Frank Lloyd's *Mutiny on the Bounty* (1935)

Hateful from scratch, Bligh gets worse as he goes along, and when the mutiny arrives, the audience most everywhere will applaud, as did the more or less sophisticated clientele at the Capitol' (*VFR*, 12 November 1935). The picture grossed nearly $4.5 million in rentals and more than $900,000 in profit, making it one of the top moneymakers of the decade. *Film Daily* ranked it number one on its top ten poll. In the Academy Award sweepstakes, all three leads – Laughton, Gable, and Tone – were nominated as Best Actor, a first in the history of the awards. They lost to Victor McLaglen in *The Informer*, but *Mutiny on the Bounty* captured the Oscar for Best Picture.

Afterward, Thalberg embarked on his most ambitious venture, *Romeo and Juliet* (1936), directed by George Cukor, another vehicle for Norma Shearer. Leslie Howard costarred. The picture followed in the wake of the Warner Bros. production of *Midsummer Night's Dream* (1935), directed by Max Reinhardt, which started a brief Shakespeare production cycle. *Romeo and Juliet* was lavish in scope. To assist Cedric Gibbons and Adrian in the design of the sets and costumes, the studio dispatched Oliver Messel, a British art expert, to Verona, Italy, where his staff took thousands of pictures so that the Renaissance could be captured on the screen as never before. Talbot Jennings created a cinematic adaptation of the play by trimming about a fourth of the verse and by opening up the action beyond the confines of the stage. Choreographer Agnes de Mille staged the period dances at the Capulet ball. 'Never before, in all its centuries, has the play received so handsome a production,' said an ecstatic Frank Nugent. 'The picture reflects great credit upon its producers and upon the screen as a whole. It's a dignified, sensitive and entirely admirable Shakespearean – not Hollywoodean – production' (*NYTFR*, 21 August 1936). MGM gave it an equally lavish sendoff at the Astor on 20 August 1936, but the picture languished at the box office and posted a $900,000 loss. Most moviegoers were not particularly interested in Shakespeare.

Thalberg died shortly after the New York premiere, on 14 September 1936. The cause was pneumonia. 'The Metro lot was in turmoil. Company's executives and everybody stopped work to see what service they could be to the bereaved family. In fact, all of Hollywood practically came to a standstill when it realized Thalberg was gone,' reported *Variety* ('Regard' 1936: 2), adding, 'Condolence messages poured into the home. Newspapers received thousands of notices from important people throughout the world as to the great loss the community had suffered in Thalberg's death.' In 1937, the Academy established the Irving Thalberg Memorial Award; the first award went to Darryl F. Zanuck, production head of 20th Century Fox.

Thalberg had an elaborate production program lined up to be released. *The Good Earth* and *Camille* were nearly finished and were given over to Al Lewin and David Lewis to complete. *Marie Antoinette*, *Maytime*, and *A Day at the Races* were in development and were given over to others. *Goodbye, Mr. Chips* and *Pride and Prejudice* were shelved, and *The Prisoner of Zenda* rights were sold to David O. Selznick.

Thalberg had been supervising the cutting of *The Good Earth* (1937) when he fell ill and 'had expressed the hope that this film would be his crowning

FIGURE 4.4 Luise Rainer and Paul Muni in Sidney Franklin's *The Good Earth* (1937)

achievement,' said *Variety* ('Regard' 1936: 2). Thalberg was inspired to produce *The Good Earth* in 1932 after attending a Theatre Guild dramatization of Pearl S. Buck's Pulitzer Prize–winning novel about the rise to riches of a simple Chinese farmer. Thalberg spent four years and $2.8 million on the picture, MGM's most expensive outlay since *Ben-Hur*. To make this epic about Chinese life as authentic as possible, Thalberg dispatched a second unit to China, where it shot two million feet of footage to be used for process shots and for atmosphere. Cedric Gibbons and unit art director Harry Oliver worked two years designing and constructing a replica of a Chinese province complete with peasant huts, palace, and rice paddies on 500 acres in the San Fernando Valley. Meanwhile, the script by Talbot Jennings, Tess Schlesinger, and Claudine West underwent constant revision. Paul Muni was borrowed from Warner to play the farmer Wang, Luise Rainer was chosen to play his wife O-lan, and Sidney Franklin was selected to direct.

The Good Earth had its world premiere at the Carthay Circle Theater in Los Angeles on 29 January 1937 as a roadshow. MGM released the picture with the dedication 'To the memory of Irving Grant Thalberg,' which marked the first time a Thalberg picture carried his name. MGM gave it lavish a sendoff, and as Edwin Schallert (1937) stated, 'the minds of some must have turned to the man who carried it almost to completion.' He called it 'a courageous production, on which earnestness and care have been literally lavished, and which shines as a photographic triumph and an emotionally moving event of the screen. Indeed, it is a contribution that should live on and on.' The New York opening at the Astor on 2 February received equal praise. A. Arnold Gillespie's special effects depicting a plague of locusts attacking the crops and Karl Freund's camerawork created a picture of immense visual appeal. The New York Film Critics crowned Rainer Best Actress of 1936 for her performance of O-Lan, the 'beaten and incoherent slave girl who is suddenly dignified by marriage to an ambitious peasant' (Watts 1937). At the 1937 Academy Awards, Rainer won the Oscar for Best Actress, making her the only actress to win the award two years in a row. She received her first Oscar in MGM's *The Great Ziegfeld* (1936). Because of its high production cost, *The Good Earth* lost nearly $500,000.

The 1937 Academy Awards honored another MGM star that night, Spencer Tracy. He received his first Oscar for Best Actor in *Captains Courageous* (1937) directed by Victor Fleming. It was based on Rudyard Kipling's 1897 coming-of-age classic about 'an imperious and detestable young scamp who toppled from a liner's rail off the Grand Banks, was picked up by a Portuguese doryman . . . and became a regular fellow during an enforced three-month's fishing cruise' (*NYTFR*, 12 May 1937). Freddie Bartholomew and Spencer Tracy headed a star cast comprising Lionel Barrymore and Melvyn Douglas. Thalberg purchased the property in 1934 and assigned the project to Louis D. Lighton, a former Paramount associate producer, who was hired by MGM in 1935. *Captains Courageous* was his first assignment, which MGM promoted 'As Great as *Mutiny on the Bounty*.' It premiered in New York at the Astor on 11 May 1937. Frank Nugent called the picture 'another of those grand jobs of moviemaking we have come to expect of Hollywood's most prodigal studio. With its rich production, magnificent marine photography, admirable direction and performances, the film brings vividly to life every page of Kipling's novel and even adds an exciting chapter or two of its own' (*NYTFR*, 12 May 1937). Howard Barnes (1937) described Spencer Tracy's performance of Manuel, the Portuguese fisherman who rescued little Harvey from the sea, as 'perfect. His Manuel is by turns grave, gay, volatile, serene and dauntless. Certainly there could have been no better choice for the role.' Freddie Bartholomew's performance, he said, made Harvey's transition 'from a mean brat to a gallant little fisherman's apprentice utterly persuasive.' *Captains Courageous* 'belongs with the screen's few masterpieces,' he concluded.

Thalberg considered *Camille* (1937) based on the Alexandre Dumas, fils' novel *The Lady of the Camellias* an ideal choice for Greta Garbo. After making *Anna Karenina*, Garbo signed a two-picture contract on 30 May 1935 at $250,000 each with the same approval rights as before and then left for Sweden for a rest. She returned to the United States in May 1936 to begin the film. *The Lady of the Camellias*, the tragic love story of Marguerite Gautier, a consumptive courtesan in Paris, and the rich young Armand Duval had been a theatrical and motion picture warhorse since it was first published in 1848, but this would be the first talking version. Thalberg, with Garbo's approval, chose 25-year-old Robert Taylor to play Armand. He tapped George Cukor to direct and Zoe Akins, Frances Marion, and James Hilton to adapt the script. The picture premiered in New York at the Capitol on 22 January 1937. Frank Nugent said, 'Having passed its fiftieth anniversary, *Camille* is less a play than an institution. Just as Hamlet is the measure of the great actor, so has the Dumas fils' classic become the ultimate test of the dramatic actress.' 'Greta Garbo's performance,' he said, 'is in the finest tradition: eloquent, tragic, yet restrained . . . Miss Garbo has interpreted Marguerite Gautier with the subtlety that has earned for her the title, "first lady of the screen"' (*NYTFR*, 23 January 1937). The New York Film Critics named Garbo Best Actress of 1938.

   Marie Antoinette (1938), the last prestige picture Thalberg had in his queue, was given over to Hunt Stromberg to see it through. *Marie Antoinette*, directed by W. S. Van Dyke, marked Norma Shearer's triumphant return to the screen after two years. It was based on Stefan Zweig's 1933 biography of the last Queen of France, who dies at the guillotine during the French Revolution, and was adapted by Claudine West, Donald Ogden Stewart and Ernest Vajda. Miss Shearer 'was immediately taken with it, and envisioned the "part of a lifetime,"' said Vieira (2009: 383). Shearer chose Tyrone Power, a rising contract player at 20th Century Fox, to play her lover, Axel de Fersen. The eminent supporting cast included Robert Morley, John Barrymore, and Joseph Shildkraut.

FIGURE 4.5 Norma Shearer in W. S. Van Dyke's *Marie Antoinette* (1938)

Produced at a cost of nearly $3 million, *Marie Antoinette* was MGM's most lavish extravaganza of the decade. Bosley Crowther (1957: 244) described why: 'Mayer and Stromberg instructed Cedric Gibbons, the studio's head designer, to prepare the most exquisite and impressive settings that could be conceived. Versailles itself was slightly tarnished alongside the palace Gibbons whipped up. He did some exquisite reproductions of the buildings of eighteenth century France.' 'Ed Willis, the head of the prop department,' he added, 'was sent to Europe to buy furniture and rugs. He stocked his department for all time with the antiques he bought for *Marie Antoinette*. The costumes [by Adrian] were nigh museum items. There were 152 roles to be garbed. The studio's great technical departments were triumphantly tested on this film.'

The 160-minute film premiered at the Carthay Circle Theatre in Los Angeles on 8 July 1938 and began its initial release as an extended roadshow. It premiered in New York at the Astor on 16 August. Edwin Schallert (1938) reported that in Los Angeles, Miss Shearer 'received a dazzling tribute not only from those who actually viewed the story of the fall of the French monarchical rule, but also from the public that thronged outside the playhouse to watch the great procession of stars – an unrivaled procession, almost, in the cinema chronicles.' Thalberg's last prestige picture opened strong in urban situations, but attendance soon dropped off. Although the picture grossed a handsome $3 million in rentals, it was not enough to recoup the negative cost and turned in a loss of $767,000. Shearer received her sixth Academy Award nomination but lost to Bette Davis in *Jezebel*.

Musicals

Musicals had been flooding the market during the conversion to sound and had become box-office poison by 1930. Beginning in 1933, the musical had made a comeback beginning with the release of the Busby Berkeley backstage musicals at Warner Bros. and the Fred Astaire–Ginger Rogers dance musicals at RKO. In the second half of the thirties, MGM dominated the production trend. The studio launched not only a popular series of operettas designed around Jeanette MacDonald and Nelson Eddy but also a series of dance pictures around Eleanor Powell. And for good measure, MGM produced a few blockbuster prestige musicals as well.

Louis B. Mayer got the idea to team MacDonald with a relatively unknown Nelson Eddy after the modest success of *The Merry Widow* and persuaded Hunt Stromberg to cast him opposite Miss MacDonald in Victor Herbert's *Naughty Marietta* (1935). Eddy, a 'deep-throated baritone' who made his Metropolitan Opera debut in 1924 at the age of 23, had been on the lot since 1933. He was discovered by Ida Koverman, Mayer's private secretary, who had attended a recital of his at the Shrine Auditorium in Los Angeles. 'He had fourteen encores and innumerable curtain calls,' reported the *New York Times* ('Nelson' 1967), which was enough to persuade Mayer to give him a long-term contract. His first MGM assignments amounted to nothing.

Stromberg started afresh on the property and assigned the husband-and-wife team of Albert Hackett and Frances Goodrich to adapt Victor Herbert's beloved libretto. The picture premiered in New York at the Capitol on 22 March 1935 and was greeted with raves. Watts (1935) said, 'Now, amid a handsomely, beautifully managed screen production by W. S. Van Dyke, [Victor Herbert's] music at last has the chance to be appreciated properly, and my illiterate suspicion is that the result is virtually a perfection of cinema light opera.' With all due respect for Miss MacDonald's 'shrewd gift for productions of this type,' he added, 'The triumph of the Van Dyke version is registered by Nelson Eddy . . . Mr. Eddy has a brilliant baritone voice, he seems thoroughly masculine, he is engaging and good looking and he gives the appearance of being unaffected.' Herbert Stothart adapted Victor Herbert's music, which was preserved intact and featured such favorites as 'I'm Falling in Love With Someone' and 'Ah, Sweet Mystery of Life.' *Naughty Marietta* was nominated for an Academy Award as Best Picture and won *Photoplay*'s coveted Movie of the Year award.

Jeanette MacDonald and Nelson Eddy made eight operettas together. The other favorites included W. S. Van Dyke's *Rose Marie* (1936), Robert Z. Leonard's *Maytime*

FIGURE 4.6 Jeanette MacDonald and Nelson Eddy in W. S. Van Dyke's *Rose Marie* (1936)

(1937), and W. S. Van Dyke's *Sweethearts* (1938). *Rose Marie* was an adaptation of the Oscar Hammerstein II and Otto Harbach operetta with a score by Rudolf Friml and Herbert Stothart that enjoyed a long run on Broadway beginning in 1924. It premiered in New York at the Capitol on 31 January 1936. *Variety* said, 'Scriptists Frances Goodrich, Albert Hackett and Alice Duer rate the bouquets for the skillful writing job as they shift the action from the backstage tantrums of a spoiled and petulant diva into the woodlands' (*VFR*, 5 February 1936). Much of the picture was shot on location at Lake Tahoe. Frank Nugent said, 'To paraphrase Fletcher, let Jeanette MacDonald and Nelson Eddy sing an operetta's love songs and we care not who may write its book.' The film retained the well-known 'Indian Love Call,' 'Rose Marie, I Love You,' and 'Song of the Mounties' from the original score and provided opportunities for Miss MacDonald 'to test her lyric soprano with grand opera and with popular – not to say "hotcha" – music as well,' he said (*NYTFR*, 1 February 1936). *Rose Marie* was the second-highest grosser and the second most profitable picture of the 1935–36 season. It was surpassed in both categories by *San Francisco*, the blockbuster disaster picture starring Clark Gable and Jeanette MacDonald.

Robert Z. Leonard's *Maytime* (1937) was an adaptation of a Sigmund Romberg operetta and premiered in New York at the Capitol on 18 May 1937. Noel Langley wrote the script, which was based on Rida Johnson's play, and Herbert Stothart did the musical adaptation. Frank Nugent called it 'the most entrancing operetta the screen has given us. It establishes Jeanette MacDonald as the possessor of the cinema's loveliest voice . . . and it affirms Nelson Eddy's pre-eminence among the baritones of filmdom' (*NYTFR*, 19 May 1937). Critics admired the skillful blending of the music and acting. *Variety* described *Maytime* as Herbert Stothart's 'best filmusical achievement.' 'The vocal piece-de-resistance, of course, is the Romberg waltz ballad, "Will You Remember?" perhaps better known as "Sweetheart, Sweetheart." This has been artfully backgrounded throughout the extended running time by Herbert Stothart . . . His is a painstaking contribution on the musical collaboration, original composition and expert interpretive score' (*VFR*, 24 March 1937).

And thanks to Douglas Shearer's efforts, the movie 'sounded clearer and more musical than any other film musical,' reported Schaffer (1937: 15). *Maytime* was the most expensive picture in the series and grossed nearly as much as *Rose Marie* but generated a profit of only $594,000 compared to *Rose Marie*'s $1,488,000.

Sweethearts was the first MGM musical to be released in Technicolor and the first in the series set in the present. Company founder Herbert Kalmus had perfected Technicolor's three-color process by 1936, which started a color boom. By the end of the decade, it had become the industry standard until the fifties, when it was supplanted by Eastman Kodak's single-strip color process. Shooting a picture in Technicolor was expensive, however. A studio was required to use Technicolor's cumbersome Tri-Pak cameras, film stock, cameramen, a special color consultant, and film processing. Hollywood, as a result, adopted the process only for its top productions. Dorothy Parker and Alan Campbell structured the picture as a 'show within a show.' Jeanette MacDonald and Nelson Eddy are 'real-life sweethearts' and stars of a long-running Victor Herbert operetta who are celebrating 'both their and the musical's sixth anniversaries' (*VFR*, 21 December 1938). Jeanette MacDonald and Nelson Eddy were at the top of their form. The *New York Times* said that they 'have never been more flattering recorded or photographed' and they 'have never sung or acted with more fire or abandon' (*NYTFR*, 23 December 1938). *Sweethearts* received Oscar nominations for Sound Recording and Scoring. Oliver Marsh and Allen Davey received a special Oscar for Best Color Cinematography. *Sweethearts* performed well at the box office but barely broke even.

By now, Miss MacDonald 'was at the pinnacle of her powers as a singer and an actress,' said Turk (1998: 230), yet 'the creative bite of her partnership with Nelson Eddy had reached its limits.' 'Jeanette craved straight dramatic films with only incidental songs,' he said, 'Nelson Eddy was also reviewing priorities. The upshot was that Louis B. Mayer attempted to get extra mileage from the team by pairing them with other singers to no avail.' The box-office returns on these pictures declined steadily, and by 1942, both had secured release from their contracts. They were replaced on the studio's roster by a pair of teenagers, Mickey Rooney and Judy Garland.

MGM, meanwhile, countered the Busby Berkeley's *Gold Diggers* pictures at Warner Bros. by producing a backstage musical series built around the virtuoso tap-dancing talents of Eleanor Powell. The pictures comprised *Broadway Melody of 1936* (1935), *Born to Dance* (1936), and *Broadway Melody of 1938* (1937). The series took its name from MGM's 1929 hit *Broadway Melody*. Nacio Herb Brown and Arthur Freed wrote the songs for the *Broadway Melody* pictures and Cole Porter the songs for *Born to Dance*. All three pictures were directed by Roy Del Ruth and shared many of the same production staff that included screenwriters Jack McGowan and Sid Silvers, choreographer Dave Gould, art director Cedric Gibbons, costume designer Adrian, orchestrator Roger Edens, and editor Blanche Sewell.

Structurally, the Powell pictures are a cross between the backstage musicals of Busby Berkeley and the dance films of Fred Astaire. Like the former, the films contain thin plots that furnish the pretext for the musical numbers; and like the latter, the films spotlight the virtuoso dancing of the star. To broaden the appeal of these pictures, MGM provided Miss Powell with plenty of backup. In *Broadway Melody of 1936*, her supporting cast included comedians Buddy Ebsen, Sid Silvers, and Jack Benny; in *Broadway Melody of 1938*, the cast included singers Frances Langford, Sophie Tucker, and the 16-year-old Judy Garland who sang 'a plaint to Clark Gable's photograph' entitled 'Dear Mr. Gable.'

Exploiting the musical even further, MGM had other tricks up its sleeve. In 1936, it produced the first disaster musical, W. S. Van Dyke's *San Francisco*, and the first big musical biopic, Robert Z. Leonard's *The Great Ziegfeld*. Irving Thalberg had greenlighted the *San Francisco* project shortly before his death at the urging of Anita Loos, who wrote the screenplay. Bernard Hyman saw the production through. Set in the Barbary Coast of San Francisco in 1906, the picture starred Clark Gable as Blackie Norton, the owner of a music hall saloon, and Jeanette

FIGURE 4.7 Clark Gable in W. S. Van Dyke's *San Francisco* (1936)

MacDonald as Mary Blake, an aspiring prima donna torn between the cabaret and the opera house. Spencer Tracy in a supporting role played Father Mullin, 'the two-fisted chaplain of a Barbary Coast mission.' MacDonald's numbers alternated between rousing popular songs ('San Francisco'), religious numbers ('Hosannah'), and operatic arias.

A ten-minute earthquake sequence, the creation of special effects artist A. Arnold Gillespie and editor John Hoffman, marked the climax, which Nugent described as 'a shattering spectacle, one of the truly great cinematic illusions; a monstrous, hideous, thrilling debacle with great fissures opening in the earth, buildings crumbling, men and women apparently being buried beneath showers of stone and plaster, gargoyles lurching from rooftops, water mains bursting, live wires flaring, flame, panic and terror' (*NYTFR*, 27 June 1936). Produced at a cost of $1.3 million, the picture turned in a profit of more than $2.3 million, making it MGM's most profitable film of the thirties. In addition, the picture made it to *Film Daily*'s honor rolls and was nominated for six Academy Awards, including Best Picture. The chemistry between Clark Gable and Tracy so impressed audiences that the studio paired them in two more blockbusters, *Test Pilot* (1938) and *Boom Town* (1940).

The Great Ziegfeld was a highly romanticized story of the life of the master showman Florenz Ziegfeld. With a running time of three hours, it was the most lavish Hollywood production up to that time. The picture 'cost Metro about

$500,000 an hour,' said Nugent. 'It is there . . . in the glittering sets, the exuberantly extravagant song and dance numbers, the brilliant costumes, the whole sweeping panoply of a Ziegfeld show produced with a princely disregard for the cost accountant.' The backstage musical was written by William Anthony McGuire and starred William Powell in the title role and Luise Rainer and Myrna Loy as his two wives, Anna Held and Billie Burke. A thin plot provided the excuse to introduce 'a medley of guest stars impersonated or in the flesh' and 'specialty numbers of no relevance to plot or characters' (*NYTFR*, 9 April 1936).

Roadshowed for five months in twenty-three theaters, *The Great Ziegfeld* was MGM's highest-grossing film of the 1936–37 season and went on to become one of MGM's most successful pictures of the decade. At Academy Award time, it picked up Oscars for Best Picture and Best Actress (Luise Rainer). As might be expected, *The Great Ziegfeld* inspired imitations, which included MGM's own *The Great Waltz* (1939), a musical biopic about Johann Strauss, Paramount's *The Great Victor Herbert* (1939), RKO's *The Story of Vernon and Irene Castle* (1939), and Fox's *Rose of Washington Square* (1939), an homage to Fannie Brice.

Describing the appeal of MGM's Technicolor spectacle, *The Wizard of Oz* (1939), *Variety* said, 'There's an audience for "Oz" wherever there's a projection machine and a screen' (*VFR*, 16 August 1939). Inspired by the success of Walt Disney's musical fantasy, *Snow White and the Seven Dwarfs* (1937), MGM turned to L. Frank Baum's popular children's saga, *The Wonderful World of Oz*, which was published in 1900 and formed the basis for a hit Broadway musical and two silent films. Writers Noel Langley, Florence Ryerson, and Edgar Allan Woolf thoroughly Americanized the story by introducing a screwball aunt, a busybody spinster witch, a Brooklyn clown lion, and a Midwestern horsetrader wizard. Produced by Mervyn LeRoy and directed by Victor Fleming at a cost of $2.8 million, *The Wizard of Oz* made a star out of 17-year-old Judy Garland and contained a flawless cast that included Frank Morgan, Billie Burke, Margaret Hamilton, Ray Bolger, Jack Haley, and Bert Lahr.

The picture's charms include the now-familiar songs by E. Y. Harburg and Harold Arlen, particularly the Academy Award winning 'Over the Rainbow,' which Judy Garland sings in the opening sequence; the fanciful settings by Cedric Gibbons and William A. Horning that used color in countless imaginative ways; and the special effects of Arnold Gillespie that included 'a cyclone made out of a woman's stocking and an army of flying monkeys suspended by thousands of piano wires,' said Green (1981:306). *The Wizard of Oz* grossed more than $3 million in rentals, but because of the record production costs, the picture did not break even the first time out.

Woman's films

The sheer box-office draw of MGM's top stars enabled the studio to remain the most important producer of woman's films. Garbo and Shearer made fewer and fewer pictures each year, but each one was an event that riveted media attention.

By the end of the decade, however, the public had wearied of Mayer's veteran female stars. As Bob Thomas (1978: 135) pointed out, 'Garbo, Shearer, and Crawford had been on the screen since silent films, Jeanette MacDonald for a dozen years. Moviegoers sought newer faces and fresh talent, and Mayer supplied them with Judy Garland, Lana Turner, Hedy Lamarr, Kathryn Grayson, Ann Sothern, and an actress Mayer had discovered in a London play, Greer Garson.' 'All that remained,' he said, 'was for the older stars – now in their mid- or late thirties – to be removed gracefully from the studio payroll. That could be accomplished by giving them bad pictures.'

After *Camille*, Garbo's career went into decline. Her next picture, *Conquest* (1937), was based on a fictional story about a Polish patriot, Countess Marie Walewska, who becomes Napoleon's camp follower in an attempt to free Poland from Czarist rule. The script was written by Samuel Hoffenstein, Salka Viertel, and S. N. Behrman. Charles Boyer, on loanout from Walter Wanger at United Artists, costarred as Napoleon. The picture was produced by Bernard H. Hyman and directed by Clarence Brown. MGM pulled out all the stops to make it: palaces and ballrooms were built to scale, and more than 2,000 extras were used to shoot the ballroom sequences, military reviews, and the retreat from Moscow. Nugent said that *Conquest*, 'with all the munificence of its production, with all the starring strength of a Greta Garbo and a Charles Boyer, is merely a surface show. It goes no deeper than the images its screen reflects.' 'Mr. Boyer's Napoleon does not fire the imagination or encourage respect,' he said, and 'Miss Garbo's Marie Walewska is a creature built upon illogic. We view the destinies of both with interest but not with compassion; and compassion is all-important in a romantic tragedy' (*NYTFR*, 5 November 1937). Nugent's review was in the minority, but after the accounting, *Conquest* showed a loss of $1.4 million, the highest of the 1937–38 season. After the failure of *Conquest*, a group of independent theater owners in New York listed her and others as 'Box Office Poison' in 1938. Again her career was in peril, and again she threatened to retire.

MGM revived her career by offcasting her in *Ninotchka* (1939), a screwball comedy produced and directed by Ernst Lubitsch. Writers Charles Brackett, Billy Wilder, and Walter Reisch were given the task of devising a fresh formula that would increase Garbo's drawing power in the domestic market. The team fashioned *Ninotchka*, a gem about a gloomy Communist envoy from Moscow who falls in love with a Parisian playboy (Melvyn Douglas). MGM marketed the picture as 'Garbo laughs!' which formed a nice bookend to 'Garbo talks!' her first talkie. *Ninotchka* premiered in New York at the Radio City Music Hall, where it enjoyed a three-week run to capacity houses. Nugent said, 'Garbo's '*Ninotchka* is one of the sprightliest comedies of the year, a gay and impertinent and malicious show which never pulls its punch lines . . . and finds the screen's austere first lady of drama playing a dead-pan comedy role with the assurance of a Buster Keaton.' 'Nothing quite so astonishing has come to the Music Hall since the Rockefellers landed on Fiftieth Street,' he added, 'and not even the Rockefellers could have imagined M-G-M getting a laugh out of Garbo at the U.S.S.R.'s expense' (*NYTFR*, 10 November 1939).

Variety assessed the picture as 'high caliber entertainment for adult audiences, a top attraction for the key deluxers, and rates better grosses from the subsequent houses than has been the case in Garbo's last three pictures' (*VFR*, 11 October 1939). *Ninotchka* turned in only a small profit of $138,000, but it signaled a revival of her career.

To keep up the momentum, MGM cast her in *Two-Faced Woman* (1941), another screwball comedy costarring Melvyn Douglas. It was a remake of a 1925 MGM silent, *Her Sister from Paris*, about a wife who tries 'to lure her husband back to bed by masquerading as her own madcap twin sister.' *Two-Faced Woman* was produced by Gottfried Reinhardt, Ernst Lubitsch's former assistant, and directed by George Cukor. Marketed as 'Garbo dances!' it appeared to be a sure win. To keep costs in line with a diminished foreign market, Garbo came forward to request a 50 percent cut in salary before agreeing to do the picture. But the picture ran into trouble when it received a C or 'condemned' rating from the Legion of Decency with this notation: 'Immoral and un-Christian attitude toward marriage and its obligations' ('Yields' 1941). The picture was subsequently denounced from the pulpit by Cardinal Francis J. Spellman of New York and banned in several cities. MGM withdrew the picture as a result and revised it to the satisfaction of the Legion to get a more satisfactory B or 'objectionable in part' rating. Reviewing the cleaned-up version, the *New York Times* said, '*Two-Faced Woman*' is one of the more costly disappointments of the year.' 'The film decisively condemns itself by shoddy workmanship,' it said. 'Miss Garbo's current attempt to trip the light fantastic is one of the awkward exhibitions of the season, George Cukor's direction is static and labored, and the script is a stale joke, repeated at length' (*NYTFR*, 1 January 1942). *Two-Faced Woman* completed Garbo's contractual obligations to the studio. Afterward she retired from the screen.

Norma Shearer's first choice after *Marie Antoinette* was *Idiot's Delight* (1939) based on Robert E. Sherwood's Pulitzer Prize-winning antiwar play that was presented by the Theatre Guild on Broadway in 1936. Hunt Stromberg produced it and Clarence Brown directed. The play was set in a cocktail lounge of a hotel in the Italian Alps at the outbreak of war in Europe. Conditions were so incendiary that the Italian government detained the guests pending further developments. Lynn Fontanne played a vaudeville acrobat who passes herself off as a Russian countess and becomes the mistress of an armaments tycoon and Alfred Lunt, a song-and-dance man. Norma Shearer took Lynn Fontanne's part and Clark Gable Alfred Lunt's.

To get the film past the Breen Office and not offend the totalitarian governments Sherwood's play lampooned, Sherwood had to emasculate his work by adding a prologue, rewriting the ending, and avoiding all references to the current political scene, among other things. The *New York Times*, nonetheless, praised the picture: 'For all the accustomed and too, too predictable fury of its soft-pedaling, *Idiot's Delight*, by the very nature of its theme, exposes the essential idiocy and pointlessness of militarism, and that is the important thing' (*NYTFR*, 3 February 1939). Despite the favorable reviews in the *New York Times*, *Variety*, and other publications, the picture wound up with a $374,000 loss.

Shearer's next choice was *The Women* (1939) based on Clare Booth's 1936 smash Broadway hit. Hunt Stromberg produced it and George Cukor directed. The adaptation by Jane Murfin and Anita Loos contained not a single male role; the cast of 130 was headed by a galaxy of stars consisting of Norma Shearer, Joan Crawford, Rosalind Russell, and Paulette Goddard. Frank Nugent described the picture as 'a sociological investigation of the scalpel-tongued Park Avenue set, entirely female, who amputate their best friends' reputations at luncheon, dissect their private lives at the beauty salon and perform the postmortems over the bridge table, while the victims industriously carve away at their surgeons. It is a ghoulish and disillusioning business' (*NYTFR*, 22 September, 1939). Audiences loved it nonetheless, especially the Technicolor segment, which featured a fashion show staged by Adrian. At year's end, the picture was named to *Film Daily*'s Top Ten and the *New York Times*'s Ten Best.

Shearer followed *The Women* with *Escape* (1940) based on Ethel Vance's anti-Nazi thriller. Lawrence Weingarten produced it and Mervyn LeRoy directed. Shearer played Countess Von Treck, a widow living in Germany and the mistress of a Nazi general, who assists a young American (Robert Taylor) in rescuing his actress mother (Alla Nazimova) from a concentration camp. 'The outlook for Norma's career was . . . beginning to look unsettled,' said Lambert (1990: 291). Shearer 'hadn't really wanted to make *Escape* but felt obligated to; the picture's very modest success with the public, and her own relatively small part in it, was anticlimactic after *Marie Antoinette*, *Idiot's Delight*, and *The Women*. . . . Her next choices, Robert Z. Leonard's *We Were Dancing* (1942) and George Cukor's *Her Cardboard Lover* (1942),' he said, 'were out of sync with the times. Both were café society romances.' Crowther called the former 'another of those frivolous marital comedies' and the latter 'just a lot of witless talk' (*NYTFR*, 1 May 1942; *NYTFR*, 17 June 1942). Shearer had lost touch with the movie audience and knew it. After turning down Mayer's offer of a new contract, she left the studio 'with no royal farewell, and to the gateman, The Queen of the Lot was simply going home,' said Lambert (1990: 300).

Joan Crawford was one of the top ten money-making stars from 1932 to 1936 and one of the highest-paid actresses in the industry. She continued playing working-class girls in Clarence Brown's *Sadie McKee* (1934) and *Chained* (1934), but that type of role became outmoded as economic conditions improved in the second half of the decade. Like Garbo, she tried her hand at screwball comedy by making W. S. Van Dyke's *Forsaking All Others* (1934) and *Love on the Run* (1936). *Forsaking All Others* costarred Clark Gable and Robert Montgomery. Joseph L. Mankiewicz's screenplay contained the usual screwball elements, said *Variety* – 'scintillating, gay and sophisticated dialog,' 'such hoke as a bicycle ride with Joan Crawford on Robert Montgomery's handlebars,' and Crawford, a bride-to-be, 'left waiting at the church.' 'On the performance end,' said *Variety*, 'it is one of Crawford's best. She is believable throughout' (*VFR*, 31 December 1933). *Forsaking All Others* earned the highest profit of the 1933–34 season. *Love on the Run* costarred Clark Gable and Franchot Tone and was a spinoff of Frank Capra's *It Happened*

One Night (1934). 'Crowded with ludicrous situations, considerable action and popular gagging, the film is lightweight and synthetic,' said *Variety*. 'In the hands of less capable studio people, many of the more absurd proceedings might have been pretty hard to stomach' (*VFR*, 31 December 1935). But Crawford's fans loved it, and the picture turned out to be another big box-office hit.

Crawford followed this up with her one and only period piece, Clarence Brown's *The Gorgeous Hussy* (1936), a romanticized biography of an innkeeper's daughter, Peggy O'Neill Eaton, who becomes a trusted advisor to President Andrew Jackson. Most critics found the picture dull and stodgy. Even her fans rejected it. As Walker (1983: 115) noted, 'Crawford's career at this stage exemplifies the uncertainty that MGM was feeling about her. She was still a top star, but she was approaching an awkward age, her mid-thirties, and what roles she could play had to be considered in relation to what films the public wanted to see.' 'MGM was none too sure of either,' he said, 'Crawford was too mature to be convincing working girl; too modern for a historical heroine; too easily confused in comedy with other stars who had an earlier patent on the role of screwball comedienne.'

Producer Joseph L. Mankiewicz, who had been nurturing Crawford's career since 1934, failed to come up with winning properties. There followed three uninspired films, Richard Boleslawski's *The Last of Mrs. Cheyney* (1937) with William Powell and Robert Montgomery, Dorothy Arzner's *The Bride Wore Red* (1937) with Franchot Tone and Robert Young, and Frank Borzage's *Mannequin* (1937) with Spencer Tracy. Through a series of bad choices, bad judgment, and bad luck, Crawford had begun a five-year slide, and by 1938, exhibitors had dubbed her 'Box Office Poison.'

However, MGM still had confidence in her and signed her to a five-year contract in 1938 to make fifteen films. *The Women* was thought to signal a comeback. Hunt Stromberg checked her decline only temporarily by casting her as Crystal, a hard-boiled perfume clerk who steals the heroine's husband, a part that resembled her Flaemchen role in *Grand Hotel*. Frustrated by formula films, which she termed 'undiluted hokum,' Miss Crawford asked Metro to drop her contract in 1942, and she left the studio after eighteen years (Flint 1977).

Comedies

After the sentimental comedy cycle of Marie Dressler and Wallace Beery had run its course, Irving Thalberg enlivened MGM's roster with the Marx Brothers. Thalberg had always admired the team and saw an opportunity to revive their careers after Paramount dropped them in 1933. At Paramount they had made a remarkable series of anarchistic comedies that included Norman McLeod's *Monkey Business* (1931) and *Horse Feathers* (1932) and Leo McCarey's *Duck Soup* (1933). The Marx Brothers style was a blend of vaudeville, the musical stage, and slapstick comedy, and the butts of their satire were institutions, social fads, and the movies themselves.

But anarchistic comedy had lost much of its appeal by 1933, and the brothers found themselves without a studio until 1935, when Thalberg signed them to a contract with the proviso that he would have artistic control. Thalberg hedged his bet by offering the trio (Zeppo had dropped out of the act to become a talent agent) only a fraction of the salary they had received at Paramount. 'The Marx Brothers agreed and signed,' said Vieira (2009: 277). 'Hollywood was littered with has-beens too proud to accept a reasonable comeback offer.'

Irving Thalberg revamped the Marx Brothers' anarchistic comedy to conform to Hollywood entertainment norms. For their first MGM venture, Sam Wood's *A Night at the Opera* (1935), Thalberg instructed writers George S. Kaufman and Morrie Ryskind to cut the number of gags and arranged for the team to pretest new material before live audiences in West Coast theaters. Thalberg also wanted to balance their routines with romantic subplots and musical numbers. The love interest was provided by Allan Jones and Kitty Carlisle. Their song, 'Alone,' written by Nacio Herb Brown and Arthur Freed, became a big hit. The perennial Margaret Dumont still served as the butt of Groucho's insults, and *A Night at the Opera* still contained plenty of buffoonery; 'The Marxist assault on grand opera makes a shambles of that comparatively sacred institution,' said Sennwald (*NYTFR*, 7 December 1935). Thalberg's renovation worked and led to four more pictures – Sam Wood's *A Day at the Races* (1937), Edward Buzzell's *At the Circus* (1939) and *Go West* (1940), and Charles Riesner's *The Big Store* (1941). But none was as inspired as the Marx Brothers' romp in *A Night at the Opera*, and they all lost money.

MGM's first foray into the screwball comedy occurred in 1934 with the release of W. S. Van Dyke's *The Thin Man*. It followed on the heels of two surprise madcap hits from Columbia, Frank Capra's *It Happened One Night* (1934) and Howard Hawks's *Twentieth Century* (1934). Van Dyke, a murder mystery buff, came up with the idea to make the film when he learned that the studio had recently acquired the rights to the Dashiell Hammett novel; and he also had a good idea who should play Nick and Nora Charles: William Powell and Myrna Loy, whom he had just finished directing in *Manhattan Melodrama* (1934). It was an inspired bit of casting. Hunt Stromberg, the producer, then set screenwriters Frances Goodrich and Albert Hackett to work on the screenplay. Because the novel contained 'sadism, masochism and kindred unfilmable stuff,' said *Variety* ('Inside Stuff' 1934: 52), they had to clean it up, while retaining 'some of the flavor of the book that brought the advance plugs.'

MGM apparently conceived the picture as a programmer by scheduling an eighteen-day shoot and by budgeting a modest $200,000 on the production. Like *It Happened One Night*, *The Thin Man* was a comic variation of a dramatic genre. Goodrich and Hackett closely followed Hammett's murder mystery line but inserted into it a secondary plot involving Nick and Nora Charles. Describing the comic/romantic interplay between Powell and Loy, *Variety* said, 'What appears to have been the most successful part of the Hackett-Goodrich team's adaptation is that they captured the spirit of the jovial, companionable relationship of the characters, Nick, retired detective, and Nora, his wife.' 'Their very pleasant manner of loving each other and showing it, was used as a light comedy structure upon which the screen doctors' performed their operation on the Hammett

FIGURE 4.8 William Powell and Myrna Loy in W. S. Van Dyke's *After the Thin Man* (1934)

novel,' it said. 'For its leads, the studio couldn't have done better than to pick Powell and Miss Loy, both of whom shade their semi-comic roles beautifully,' it added. (*VFR*, 3 July 1934).

The Thin Man was a big hit. Nick and Nora soon became a national craze and elevated Powell and Loy to stardom. However, MGM discovered that William Powell and Myrna Loy were not bankable as a team outside the *Thin Man* context. MGM, therefore, initiated a series. It was produced by Hunt Stromberg and reunited director Van Dyke and the Goodrich–Hackett screenwriting team. The pictures were released at a leisurely pace so as not to satiate demand. *After the Thin Man* (1936), the second picture in the series, grossed twice as much as the original to become MGM's most profitable film of 1936–37. *Another Thin Man* (1939), the third, failed 'to measure up to the high entertainment standard set by its predecessors,' said *Variety* (*VFR*, 15 November 1939). MGM had domesticated the couple by giving them an infant son. Still, the picture made it to MGM's top ten and earned a respectable profit. *Shadow of the Thin Man* (1941) sustained the momentum, but the series was suspended in 1942 shortly after the attack on Pearl Harbor when Myrna Loy went on suspension to join the war effort.

Social problem films

Warner Bros. produced more social consciousness films than any other studio during the thirties. MGM produced the fewest, but three are worth discussing: Gregory La Cava's *Gabriel Over the White House* (1933), Fritz Lang's *Fury* (1936), and Norman Taurog's *Boys Town* (1938). *Gabriel Over the White House* was Walter Wanger's first picture for the studio. As the Depression deepened, Hollywood offered various solutions to solve the country's economic dilemma, and this was MGM's entry. *Gabriel Over the White House* was a political allegory about the president of the United States (Walter Huston), who is indifferent to his duties until he is visited by the Archangel Gabriel while recuperating from a serious automobile accident and becomes a changed man. He 'proclaims himself a "dictator" and addresses the problems of unemployment, crime and the foreign debts facing the country,' said Mordaunt Hall (*NYTFR*, 1 April 1933). The picture was produced for MGM by William Randolph Hearst's Cosmopolitan Productions and was to be released shortly before the president's inauguration. When Louis B. Mayer, a staunch Republican, viewed the picture at a preview, he 'considered it a calculated slap at recent Republican presidents,' said Crowther (1960: 180) and demanded cuts and revisions, which Wanger was forced to accede to before it could be released. The experience did little to endear Wanger to Mayer and led to Wanger's swift departure from the studio. *Variety* called the picture 'A cleverly executed commercial release, it waves the flag frantically, preaches political claptrap with ponderous solemnity, but won't inspire a single intelligent reaction in a carload of admission tickets' (*VFR*, 29 March 1933).

Fury was produced by Joseph L. Mankiewicz. MGM made it only to secure the talents of the noted German director Fritz Lang, who had recently fled Nazi

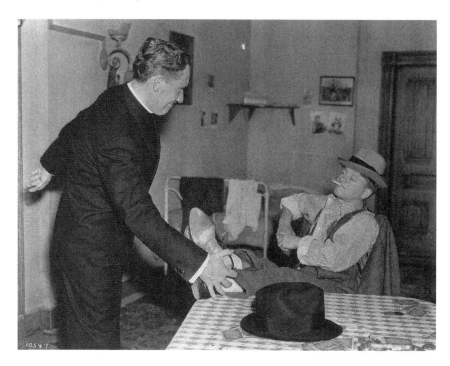

FIGURE 4.9 Spencer Tracy and Mickey Rooney in Norman Taurog's *Boys Town* (1938)

Germany. Lang waited around for more than a year on payroll before the studio found a project fitting for his American debut. Norman Krasna's original screenplay, which was 'elemental in its simplicity,' satisfied him. *Fury* did not involve a Black victim nor is the action set in the South; the central character is a white auto mechanic played by Spencer Tracy, who is stopped by the police on his way to visit his fiancé, Sylvia Sidney, in rural Illinois and is booked on suspicion of kidnapping a little girl. Lang was basically interested in mob psychology and presented the 'great American institution' of lynching 'as the victim sees it, as the mob sees it, as the public sees it. We see a lynching, its prelude and its aftermath, in all its cold horror, its hypocrisy and its cruel stupidity,' said Nugent (*NYTFR*, 6 June 1936). However, the plot contrivances and the happy ending placed *Fury* squarely in the tradition of Hollywood entertainment and undermined the social criticism. The picture was praised by the critics and established Lang's career in Hollywood, but it withered at the box office.

Boys Town, produced by John W. Considine Jr., followed in the wake of Sam Goldwyn's production of William Wyler's *Dead End* (1937), a prestige picture based on Sidney Kingley's 1935 stage play that showed how slums formed a breeding ground for criminals. *Boys Town* implied that if big-city slums breed wayward children, then take the kids into the country. It starred Spencer Tracy as Father Flanagan and Mickey Rooney as Whitey Marsh, a super-tough delinquent. *Boys Town* depicted Father Flanagan's orphanage in Nebraska in its beginning, experimental stage; it is an idealized community in which 'boys of all nationalities and faiths work side by side in harmony, under the benevolent care of a purpose-ful leader.' Into this scene comes Mickey Rooney, 'the Dead End gang rolled into one . . . with a pack of butts in his left-hand pocket, a deck of cards in his right, a Tenth Avenue Homburg cocked over one ear and his mind made up to blow the joint,' said Nugent (*NYTFR*, 9 September 1938). Although Mickey eventually succumbs to Father Flanagan's and the home's refining influences, *Variety*, which called the picture 'a tear-jerker of the first water,' pointed out that 'the delinquents are reformed without any change in the slums or in the economic structure that produced them' (*VFR*, 7 September 1938). Spencer Tracy won an Oscar for Best Actor, his second in a row after *Captains Courageous*, and screenwriters Dore Schary and Eleanore Griffin won an Oscar for Best Original Screenplay. *Boys Town* was the highest-grossing picture of the 1938–39 season and the most profitable.

Gone With the Wind

On 15 December 1939, MGM released the greatest box-office hit of the sound era, *Gone With the Wind*, which had its world premiere that day in Atlanta and became a cultural phenomenon of great significance. It was produced by Louis B. Mayer's son-in-law, David O. Selznick, an independent producer who nurtured the project for nearly four years. Selznick acquired the motion picture rights to Margaret Mitchell's 1,037-page novel for $50,000 in June 1936, just as it hit the market. Rave reviews, the Pulitzer Prize, and word-of-mouth publicity made *Gone With the Wind*, the first novel of a 35-year-old Atlanta housewife, the most popular American novel ever written up to that time, and Selznick's bid was the highest price paid for a novel up to that time.

The project could have easily gone to Irving Thalberg. Vieira (2009: 320) reports that Albert Lewin had handed Thalberg a fifty-page synopsis of *Gone With the Wind* in 1936 before Selznick acquired the rights and urged him to take it on. Thalberg declined, stating that recent Civil War films had flopped. He did read the synopsis and agreed it would make a good picture for Clark Gable but again declined to bid on the property. After making *Romeo and Juliet* and *The Good Earth*, he said, 'I've just been to Verona and China. Now you want me to burn Atlanta. No, Al. It's out of the question. No more epics for me now. Just give me a little drawing-room piece. I'm tired. I'm just too tired' (Vieira 2009: 320). With MGM out of the bidding, Selznick made his move.

Selznick had been distributing his pictures through United Artists since 1935. His production company – Selznick International Pictures – had an eight-picture contract. In March 1937, Selznick announced that *Gone With the Wind* would be among the pictures released through UA. He had the assurance that United Artists 'would meet any outside bids for the distribution,' reported *Variety* ('UA's' 1937: 7). *Variety* added, 'Clark Gable looked set for the Rhett Butler characterization, but with the UA distrib decision, Selznick may have to find a new male lead. He is still confident that Norma Shearer may play Scarlett O'Hara.'

That September, Selznick entered into negotiations with MGM to distribute his next batch of pictures after he completed his commitment to UA. *Gone With the Wind* was to be included in the deal. Selznick had never been happy with UA. But the deal soon fell through when MGM declined 'to handle Selznick product on an individual basis, standing firm on the policy that it should be sold with run-of-the-mill pictures from the main studio.' As a result, the *New York Times* ('News' 1937) reported, 'it is probable that Selznick will renew his contract with United Artists and that *Gone With the Wind* – when, as and if made – will be distributed by that concern.'

Selznick did not have a free hand in the casting. Clark Gable, named in a national poll as the 'King of Hollywood,' was the public's unanimous choice for the part of Rhett Butler. However, he was securely tied to MGM. To borrow Gable from the studio as well as money to complete the financing of the picture, Selznick approached his father-in-law. Driving a hard bargain, Mayer offered Gable's services and $1.25 million in financing but demanded in return the distribution rights to the picture and 50 percent of the profits for five years (Eyman 2005: 259). Selznick had no choice but to sign on the dotted line on 24 August 1938. The deal had to be Mayer's shrewdest.

To play his Scarlett O'Hara, Selznick had mounted a massive talent hunt. The stars he auditioned included Norma Shearer, Paulette Goddard, Susan Hayward,

FIGURE 4.10 Vivien Leigh and Hattie McDaniel in David O. Selznick's production of *Gone With the Wind* (1939), directed by Victor Fleming

and Joan Fontaine. On 23 June 1938, Selznick made his choice – Norma Shearer. The picture was scheduled to begin after Shearer and Gable completed *Idiot's Delight*. But Shearer withdrew from the role within a month. She attributed 'her decision to fan mail, in which a substantial number of correspondents voiced their opinion that she was unsuited for the part' ('Shearer' 1938). Selznick announced on 13 January 1939 that the Scarlett O'Hara sweepstakes had been won by Vivien Leigh, a young British actress who was comparatively unknown in the US.

Gone With the Wind cost more than $4 million to make – more than any picture had ever cost in the entire history of the American film industry. Running more than three hours and forty-two minutes, the picture was nearly twice the length of a conventional feature. Following its Atlanta premiere, it opened in New York on 19 December at both the Capitol and the Astor on a reserved-seat basis. On 27 December, it opened in Los Angeles at the venerable Carthay Circle Theater. January 1940 marked the beginning of the national roadshow playoff.

At Academy Award time, *Gone With the Wind* won an unprecedented ten Oscars. Hattie McDaniel received an Academy Award for supporting actress, which marked the first time a Black person had ever been nominated let alone honored. In recognition of Menzies's contribution to *Gone With the Wind*, Selznick created the special credit 'Production Designed by William Cameron Menzies.' Menzies was responsible for the overall look of the picture. Since there was no precedent for what Menzies had done, the Academy awarded him a special plaque at the Oscar ceremonies to recognize his 'outstanding achievement in the use of color for the enhancement of dramatic mood.' Clark Gable did not win the Oscar for Best Actor; the honors went to Robert Donat for his title role in *Goodbye, Mr. Chips*. Nor did Max Steiner win an Oscar for his score, oddly enough, because the Academy rules for the music category did not distinguish between dramas and musicals. The Oscar that year went to the musical classic *The Wizard of Oz*. However, Selznick won the Irving G. Thalberg Memorial Award for his efforts as producer.

The box-office returns matched the picture's epic scope. By the end of May 1940, the picture had grossed an astonishing $20 million (Balio 1993: 211). No picture had ever come close to this. This gross was from the first roadshow playoff. Yet to come were the general release and the return engagements, of which there would be many. When the results were in, *Gone With the Wind* had established a box-office record that stood for more than twenty years.

Although MGM had acquired the distribution rights to the picture for five years, by 1942, the company owned it outright. Selznick liquidated Selznick International in 1942 for tax purposes and sold his half share of *Gone With the Wind* to Jock Whitney, his partner, for $500,000. Because wartime taxes were prohibitive, Whitney 'turned around and sold, not only the former Selznick holdings, but his own as well, to MGM for $2.8 million,' reported Shearer (1947: 56). MGM thus became the owner of the picture since 1942, and it was a cash cow that saved the studio more than once.

5

MGM AT THE HOME FRONT (1940–46)

The domestic market

By 1940, all the majors were again making hefty profits. Widespread unemployment continued throughout the thirties. It took the U.S. entry into World War II to break the back of the Depression, when conditions on the home front created the best market Hollywood had ever seen. During the war, dollars were plentiful but basic goods such automobiles, refrigerators, and other commodities were not. Movies were the most readily available entertainment. Although gasoline restrictions hurt attendance in some rural areas, the integrated companies, whose theaters were more favorably situated, flourished. Domestic film rentals for the eight majors escalated as well. 'Every night was Saturday night' at the movies. B pictures, low-grade pictures, pictures featuring unknown players – all commanded an audience. Weekly attendance by the end of the war reached ninety million, it was estimated, the highest ever.

As business improved, pictures ran longer and longer to capacity houses, with a significant result; the eight majors cut back on production. B movies were the most affected. Although the decision was motivated in part by wartime rationing of film stock, it became apparent early on that more and more dollars could be earned from fewer and fewer top-grade films. At MGM, the number of releases dropped steadily from forty-eight in 1941–42 to twenty-seven in 1945–46. While the 'average production cost climbed from $650,000 in 1941–1942 to $1,680,000 in 1945–1946,' said Glancy (1992: 137), the number of box-office failures 'dropped sharply, and it was not uncommon for the top 10 grossing films of each season to earn profits over $1,000,000 each.' Looking at the Loew's bottom line, the company posted profits of $9.5 million in 1939. They dipped somewhat in 1940 to $8.7 million and then rose steadily to $17.9 million in 1946 (Gomery 1986: 52).

Antitrust

Agitation over block booking and monopolistic trade practices had reached its peak by 1938, prompting the Justice Department to bring suit against the Big Eight, charging them with combining and conspiring to restrain trade unreasonably and to monopolize the production, distribution, and exhibition of motion pictures. The specific charges were nearly identical to those leveled at the majors during the days of President Roosevelt's National Recovery Act.

So were the remedies; the government petitioned for the divorcement of production from exhibition, the elimination of block booking, unfair clearances, the forcing of shorts and other producer-distributor trade practices. Nick Schenck believed 'that the government will either drop its suit . . . or lose it' ('Loew's Inc.' 1976: 279). He was wrong on both counts.

The case was originally scheduled for trial in June 1940, but after a period of negotiation, the government entered the amended complaint providing for the entry of a consent decree that was to run for three years. During this period, the government agreed not to press for divorcement of the affiliated theaters from their distribution companies. Certain trade practices specified in the complaint were either modified or eliminated. They had the effect of removing an important prop from the studio system. The consent decree reduced the number of pictures that could be included in blocks to five and did away with the forcing of shorts. No longer could the majors force B movies and program filler on exhibitors. Such films had enabled studios to stabilize production. They filled out double bills and were rented to exhibitors at flat fees. So long as a producer kept costs in line, B movies supplied a steady stream of profits. Because class-A product was playing longer runs, the full impact of the decree could not be felt until war's end.

The foreign market

To guarantee worldwide distribution of MGM's pictures, Loew's was prepared to build or buy theaters wherever necessary. As of 1936, Loew's operated twenty-six theaters in South America, India, South Africa, Australia, and elsewhere with twelve more under construction. As Glancy (1999: 69) has noted, 'Between 1930 and 1945 MGM films, on average, made 66 percent of their total earnings from the domestic market and the remaining 34 percent from the foreign markets, and only the final 19 percent of earnings were realized as profit.' 'The greatest earnings,' he said, 'then came from the domestic market, but it was the foreign markets that supplied the studio's profits.' He added that prestige pictures did best overseas and that MGM's 'were produced with an unusual attention toward the tastes of the foreign market. The studio was clearly adept at this strategy. It combined stars who had a strong foreign following with genres that had a particular appeal in the foreign markets.'

MGM-British

As hostilities spread in Europe and in Asia, revenues from foreign markets declined. Before the Nazis came to power, the German film industry was second to the United States in prestige and sales in the major European markets. With the exception of the United States, no other country had an international film market to speak of. When the U.S. entered the war, Hollywood severed all relations with Germany and the Axis. The largest overseas market for Hollywood films was Great Britain, which accounted for nearly half of the overall foreign gross, and it was here that American companies fought hardest to maintain a stronghold (Balio 1993: 32). In 1938, Parliament renewed its efforts to protect Britain's film industry by passing the Cinematograph Films Act of 1938. It replaced the old Quota Act of 1927, which required distributors, American companies included, to release a certain percentage of British pictures each year. Because the act did not specify quality, it led to the production and distribution of 'quota quickies,' which further damaged the reputation of British pictures. Now, to meet Britain's quota require-ments, a picture had to cost a certain minimum and be produced in Britain by an all-British cast and crew, with the exception of the director and one star. The law assumed that the presence of these talents in a picture would be enough to make it palatable for an American audience. To encourage the distribution of British films in the United States, American companies were permitted to satisfy the British quota by acquiring the distribution rights to completed British films instead of making them there ('Film Quotas' 1938).

To make pictures that would be satisfactory in both the U.S. and Great Britain, MGM in 1936 leased the Denham Studios outside London belonging to Alexander Korda. Spread out on 165 acres were seven stages, two theaters, dressing rooms, machine shops, and other facilities. In January 1937, MGM hired Michael Balcon, the former head of production for British Gaumont, as production chief. The subsidiary was called MGM-British. Establishing a production base in England allowed the company to recruit British actors, directors, producers, and writers. The actors included Robert Donat, an international star, and new talent such as Vivien Leigh, Greer Garson, and Deborah Kerr. Korda lost control of Denham at the end of 1938 when his London Films went under. MGM ceased its production in England in 1940, although it continued to lease the Denham studio until 1943, when it purchased a new headquarters for its British subsidiary – Elstree Studios in Borehamwood.

Before the war, MGM made successful prestige pictures that satisfied Britain's quota requirements – Jack Conway's *A Yank at Oxford* (1938), King Vidor's *The Citadel* (1938), and Sam Wood's *Goodbye, Mr. Chips* (1939). The pictures were indistinguishable from anything MGM turned out in Culver City; only the locales and supporting cast were British. All three made it to MGM's top ten each season. *A Yank at Oxford* (1938) was produced by Michael Balcon and starred Robert Taylor as a 'brash American student' who wins an athletic scholarship to Oxford, clashes with the cultured British students, and eventually wins their respect. He was supported by Maureen O'Sullivan, who supplied the love interest. 'Robert

Taylor brings back from Oxford an entertaining rah-rah film which is full of breathless quarter-mile dashes, heartbreaking boat race finishes and surefire sentiment,' said *Variety*. 'What Conway has caught is the humor of student life at the university. This is the background for Taylor's adventures, the wall against which a cocky Yank bounces his somewhat enlarged head, eventually regaining his poise a better and tamed human being' (*VFR*, 2 February 1938). *A Yank at Oxford* went on to inspire an entire sub-genre of films based on 'Yanks in Britain.' In each, 'The "Yank" repeatedly comes into conflict with British manners and customs, but each time his discomfort is overcome by the traditions and ambience of the "Oxford environment,"' said Glancy (1999: 84).

The Citadel and *Goodbye, Mr. Chips* were produced by Victor Saville, and both starred Robert Donat, who gave *tour de force* performances. *The Citadel* was based on A. J. Cronin's best-seller about an idealistic Scottish doctor, Andrew Manson, M.D., who loses his way but rights himself and becomes a crusader for medical reforms. Rosalind Russell played Manson's wife. Ian Dalrymple Williams adapted the screenplay. 'Mr. Donat was a felicitous choice for the role of Dr. Manson,' said Barnes (1938). 'He has communicated to a remarkable degree the subjective responses of the doctor to various situations.' 'Not only has he succeeded in being credible as the loutish apprentice physician, blowing up a sewer which is spreading typhoid or crawling through a mine shaft to perform an amputation, but as the sleek specialist catering to rich hypochondriacs,' he said. It grossed nearly $2,600,000 and returned a profit of $983,000.

Goodbye, Mr. Chips was based on James Hilton's sentimental novella about a gentle schoolmaster of an English public school. 'The Mr. Chips of the Hilton biography,' said Nugent, 'was the somewhat dull young pedant who came to Brookfield's ivy-grown walls in his twenties, took quiet root there, languished miserably for a decade or two and then, under the tender cultivation of a woman's hand became such a human, quizzical and understanding person that all Brookfield eventually began to regard him as an institution' (*NYTFR*, 16 May 1939). R. C. Sherriff, Claudine West, and Eric Maschwitz adapted the screenplay. Donat's performance, in which he aged from 'young schoolmaster' to 'octogenarian institution,' was so subtle and convincing that he beat out Clark Gable in the Academy Award balloting for Best Actor during the *Gone With the Wind* sweepstakes. Greer Garson, who made her screen debut as Chips's wife, was also nominated for an Oscar. Louis B. Mayer had seen her on stage in 1938 and was so riveted by her performance that he signed her to a movie contract.

Before the war, MGM also released a British-made prestige picture, *Pygmalion* (1938), directed by Anthony Asquith, which starred Leslie Howard and Wendy Hiller. It was produced independently by Gabriel Pascal, who succeeded in acquiring the first movie rights to a George Bernard Shaw play. MGM picked up domestic distribution after the picture was favorably reviewed in London. *Pygmalion* premiered in New York on 7 December 1938 at the Astor as a roadshow. 'Mr. Shaw's first film has been most happily served,' said Nugent. 'His story of a modern Pygmalion, a phonetics expert named Henry Higgins, who molds the common clay of Eliza Doolittle, cockney flower girl, into a personage fit to meet an

FIGURE 5.1 Greer Garson and Robert Donat in Sam Wood's *Goodbye, Mr. Chips* (1939)

Archduchess at an embassy ball, has been deftly, joyously told upon the screen.' 'Miss Hiller [as Eliza] is a Discovery (She deserves the capital),' he said. 'We cannot believe that even Mr. Shaw could find a flaw in her performance of Pygmalion's guttersnipe Galatea' (*NYTFR*, 8 December 1938).

Louis B. Mayer at the helm

During the war, Louis B. Mayer's executive committee comprised Eddie Mannix, Al Lichtman, Sam Katz, Ben Goetz, Harry Rapf, J. J. Cohn, Dore Schary, Larry Weingarten, James K. McGuinness, Pandro S. Berman, and Joe Pasternak. Schary was a newcomer to the group. After sharing an Oscar for Best Writing for *Boys Town* (1938), Schary went on to earn credits on *Young Tom Edison* (1940) starring Mickey Rooney and its sequel *Edison, the Man* (1940) starring Spencer Tracy. But Schary aspired to be a director. In 1941, he went to producer John Considine for permission to write and direct a Paul Gallico story about an ammunitions factory worker who is abducted by Nazi spies. After Considine consulted Mayer on the matter, Mayer convinced Schary to become a producer instead and run MGM's B-movie unit with Harry Rapf. Schary was to function as executive producer and

Rapf as administrative head. The goal of the unit was to produce quality B movies that could get top billing in smaller communities. Schary, a pro-Roosevelt New Dealer, preferred making films with strong social themes, such as *Joe Smith, American* (1942) and *Pilot No. 5* (1943). But his unit is best remembered for *Journey for Margaret* (1942) and *Lassie Come Home* (1943). The former launched the career of the 5-year-old child star Margaret O'Brien and the latter the career of 10-year-old Elizabeth Taylor. Schary resigned in 1943, when Mayer rejected a project he had in mind written by Nobel Prize winner Sinclair Lewis, and joined David O. Selznick's new independent production venture, Vanguard Films, at United Artists.

The star roster

Going into the forties, MGM's leading men comprised Mickey Rooney, Clark Gable, Spencer Tracy, James Stewart, Wallace Beery, William Powell, and Robert Taylor. After Pearl Harbor, Clark Gable, James Stewart, Robert Montgomery, Gene Kelly, and Robert Taylor enlisted, temporarily leaving Mickey Rooney and Spencer Tracy as the only big male stars left on the lot. Myrna Loy took a leave of absence to work for the Red Cross. After Greta Garbo, Norma Shearer, Joan Crawford, and Jeanette MacDonald departed the studio, MGM nurtured a new crop of female stars – Katharine Hepburn, Greer Garson, Kathryn Grayson, and Hedy Lamarr. The studio also nurtured a new generation of younger talent, such as Judy Garland, Van Johnson, Robert Walker, Lana Turner, and two precocious child actors, Margaret O'Brien and Elizabeth Taylor.

Gone with the Wind had cemented Clark Gable's reputation as the 'King of Hollywood.' He remained near the top of exhibitors' polls, and his films continued to turn a profit. His first big hit after *Gone With the Wind* was Jack Conway's *Boom Town* (1940), an adventure film costarring Spencer Tracy. Gable and Tracy were teamed up for the third time. They had previously appeared together in two big blockbusters, *San Francisco* (1936), the disaster movie, and *Test Pilot* (1938), an aviation drama. *Boom Town* also brought Gable and Claudette Colbert together for the first time since *It Happened one Night* (1934). *Boom Town*, 'the tale of wildcat oil drilling, with fortunes won and lost just as quickly as a roller coaster dips and rises,' said *Variety*, was a 'dashing, rough-and-tumble yarn of modern adventure. Interspersed is romance and love interest of more than minor importance' (*VFR*, 29 December 1939). It was produced by Sam Zimbalist and earned more than $5 million in profits.

Gable made four more pictures for MGM before he enlisted – King Vidor's *Comrade X* (1940) opposite Hedy Lamarr, Clarence Brown's *They Met in Bombay* (1941) opposite Rosalind Russell, and two big hits opposite Lana Turner, MGM's newest sex symbol – Jack Conway's *Honky Tonk* (1941) and Wesley Ruggles's *Somewhere I'll Find You* (1942). The Gable–Turner pairings were produced by Pandro S. Berman. Crowther described *Honky Tonk* as 'distinctly in the tradition of Gable pictures – you know, the sort in which he slugs it out, toe to toe, with equally impetuous women. In the present instance Lana Turner acts as his sparring partner, which helps matters no end because Miss Turner is not only beautifully but ruggedly constructed.' He added, 'One can only whisper that this story of a gambling hall sharpster and his snarled romance with a virtuous young lady is enveloped in a faint aroma of mothballs. The dead hand of *Cimarron* and a dozen subsequent frontier extravaganzas lies heavy upon it' (*NYTFR*, 3 October 1941). *Somewhere I'll Find You* 'provides even more of the same,' said the *New York Times*, for it 'is the sort of synthetic fiction that has no other purpose than to exploit the respective charms of its twin stars. Mr. Gable is "bad news, poison" and the women love him for it' (*NYTFR*, August 28 1942).

Spencer Tracy, like Gable, remained an exhibitor favorite during the prewar years. After winning Oscars back to back for *Captains Courageous* (1937) and *Boys Town* (1938), he went on to make Clarence Brown's *Edison, the Man* (1940), a biopic; King Vidor's *Northwest Passage* (1940), an outdoor epic in Technicolor; and Victor Fleming's *Dr. Jekyll and Mr. Hyde* (1941), a horror tale. His success in these pictures was eclipsed in 1942, when he teamed up with Katharine Hepburn to make *Woman of the Year*.

Hepburn staged her own triumphant return to Hollywood after being declared 'Box Office Poison' by exhibitors in 1938. She bought out her contract at RKO and returned to Broadway to star as the socialite Tracy Lord in Philip Barry's play *The Philadelphia Story*, which was written especially for her. The play was produced by the Theatre Guild and ran for a year. Studios vied to buy the screen rights only to discover that Hepburn had already owned them. She selected MGM to make the movie and sold the rights to the studio on the condition that she play the lead. She also chose George Cukor to direct. She wanted Spencer Tracy and Clark Gable as her costars, but they had other commitments. MGM instead cast Cary Grant as her former husband and Jimmy Stewart as the reporter and assigned Joseph L. Mankiewicz to produce.

The Philadelphia Story (1940) opened at the Radio City Music Hall on 26 December 1940 and ran for a record six weeks to capacity houses. As *Variety* predicted, 'The smarties are going to relish *Philadelphia Story* a lot more than the two-bit trade' (*VFR*, 26 November 1940). Crowther opined that the picture had 'just about everything that a blue-chip comedy should have – a witty, romantic script derived by Donald Ogden Stewart out of Philip Barry's successful play; the flavor of high-society elegance, in which the patrons invariably luxuriate, and a splendid cast of performers headed by Katharine Hepburn, James Stewart and Cary Grant.' 'If it doesn't play out this year and well along into next,' he added, 'they should turn the Music Hall into a shooting gallery' (*NYTFR*, 27 December 1940). The picture ranked number two on the 1940–41 roster behind *Strike up the Band* and earned a profit of $1.3 million.

Hepburn's next picture was *Woman of the Year* (1942). Here is how it came about: After the success of *Philadelphia Story*, she dictated, 'what is considered to be one of the most astonishing contracts to be signed by Metro-Goldwyn-Mayer,' said Churchill (1941). 'In addition to naming her own salary (estimated

FIGURE 5.2 John Howard, Cary Grant, Katharine Hepburn, and Jimmy Stewart in George Cukor's *The Philadelphia Story* (1940)

at $150,000), obtaining Spencer Tracy as her costar, and persuading the studio to go outside of its own staff and engage George Stevens to direct,' he said, 'Miss Hepburn garnered $111,000 for the rights to *The Woman of the Year*, reputedly the highest price paid for an original screenplay.' The screenplay was written by 'two comparatively unknown screenwriters, Ring Lardner Jr. and Michael Kanin.'

MGM acquiesced to her demands and again assigned Joseph L. Mankiewicz to produce. Like *Philadelphia Story*, *Woman of the Year* opened at the Radio City Music Hall on 5 February 1942. 'Miss Hepburn is as courageous in playing this role as she was shrewd in in choosing it,' said Richard Griffith (1941). 'She herself has often been lampooned and mimicked for certain rather "blue-stocking" traits of the characters she plays and, by underlining these traits, she uses the familiar caricature of herself to make the role all the more convincing.' 'The result is a tour de force of acting for which reviewers cannot find enough praise.' He added that reviewers 'are equally admiring of Spencer Tracy in a part as cleverly tailored in his measure as Miss Hepburn's is to her.' *Woman of the Year* marked the beginning of one of the great screen partnerships which lasted until 1967. It earned a profit of $753,000. Hepburn was nominated for an Oscar but lost out to Greer Garson for *Mrs. Miniver*. Ring Lardner Jr. and Michael Kanin won an Oscar for Best Original Screenplay.

MGM's series pictures

By 1939, 19-year-old Mickey Rooney had become MGM's most valuable property. That year, theater owners voted him the number-one box-office draw, and the Academy awarded him and Deanna Durbin Special Academy Awards 'for bringing to the screen the spirit and personification of youth.' Rooney remained the top box-office draw in 1940, over Spencer Tracy, and in 1941, over Clark Gable. MGM signed up Mickey Rooney in 1936. He had become an instant sensation as Puck in Max Reinhardt's Hollywood Bowl production of *A Midsummer Night's Dream* in 1934 and in Reinhardt's movie version for Warner Bros. in 1935 starring James Cagney, Dick Powell, and Olivia de Havilland. Under contract at MGM, he brought vitality even to bit parts like a Brooklyn shoeshine boy in *Little Lord Fauntleroy* (1936), the kid brother in the film version of Eugene O'Neill's *Ah, Wilderness!* (1935), and a young deckhand on a fishing boat in *Captains Courageous* (1937), said Harmetz (2014). His breakthrough came in 1937 with George Seitz's *A Family Affair*, a routine domestic drama about a small-town judge and his family who live in Carvel, Idaho. It was based on Aurania Rouverol's play, *Skidding*, which ran for a year on Broadway in 1928. Lionel Barrymore played Judge Hardy and Mickey Rooney his teenage son, Andy. Lucien Hubbard and Samuel Marx produced it, and Kay Van Riper and Hugo Butler adapted the screenplay.

Fan mail for *A Family Affair* prompted a sequel, *You're Only Young Once* (1938), that focused more attention on the judge's son, Andy. In this picture, the Hardys go on a vacation to Catalina Island, where Andy discovers the excitement of kissing girls. Three changes were made in the cast – Lewis Stone replaced Lionel Barrymore as the judge, Fay Holden replaced Spring Byington as the mother, and Ann Rutherford was added to the cast as Polly Benedict, Andy's girlfriend. Four months later came *Judge Hardy's Children* (1938), which developed the father–son relationship further. And the forth in the series, *Love Finds Andy Hardy* (1938), introduced Judy Garland as the young girl visiting next door.

'The word had got out that [the Andy Hardy pictures] were grossing three or four times their cost. And well they might, for they were genuinely charming, warm and likeable little films. Mickey Rooney was the new sensation and Andy Hardy was the all-American boy,' said Crowther (1957: 256). *Love Finds Andy Hardy* earned the distinction of making it to both the *Film Daily* and *Variety* top ten lists. Produced at a little more than $200,000, it grossed $2.2 million in rentals and generated a profit of $1.3 million.

The Andy Hardy series became the most profitable film series during the heyday of Hollywood. MGM produced sixteen Andy Hardy pictures, thirteen of which were directed by George B. Seitz, one of MGM's busiest B movie directors. The series served as a training ground for MGM's budding young actresses, among them Judy Garland, Lana Turner, Donna Reed, Kathryn Grayson, and Esther Williams. Judy Garland appeared in three, *Love Finds Andy Hardy* (1938), *Andy Hardy Meets Debutante* (1940), and *Life Begins for Andy Hardy* (1941), and

FIGURE 5.3 Mickey Rooney in Busby Berkeley's *Babes in Arms* (1939)

introduced a musical element to the series. As Crowther (1943) observed, 'The only essential difference between one film and the next has been the girl for whom Andy conceived a burning but brief fancy.' Crowther predicted that the series would possibly come to an end with the thirteenth film, *Andy Hardy's Double Life* (1942). Andy was now a young adult and college bound. Andy had grown up, said Crowther, and 'the world that moves outside of Carvel, the family's home town, has seen some change.' Moreover, 'Andy can't go on being a girl-crazy college boy, and he certainly can't run home to papa every time a little problem comes up.' But MGM milked the series for three more pictures before it fizzled out in 1946.

MGM took advantage of Mickey Rooney's multiple talents by casting him in a musical in 1939, *Babes in Arms*. It was the first musical produced by the Freed unit. After writing songs and music for MGM's top musicals with collaborator Nacio Herb Brown for more than a decade, Freed aspired to be a producer. Mayer was receptive to his proposal and told Freed to find a property to develop. It was *The Wizard of Oz*, a vehicle for Judy Garland. Because it was a fantasy and an expensive one to produce, Mayer hired Mervyn LeRoy, an experienced producer, to see it through and appointed Freed as his associate. Afterward, Mayer elevated Freed to producer. *Babes in Arms* was based on the 1937 Rodgers and Hart musical and designed as a vehicle for Mickey Rooney and Judy Garland. Kay Van Riper and Jack McGowan adapted the screenplay. It told the story of a group of talented youngsters who decide to put on a show to raise money for their out-of-work vaudevillian parents. Busby Berkeley was selected to direct it. Roger Edens adapted, arranged, and supervised the musical score. '*Babes in Arms* – to express it in two words – is Mickey Rooney,' said Nugent (*NYTFR*, 20 October 1939). Produced for a relatively modest $748,000, the picture generated the highest gross of the 1939–40 season and earned a profit of $1.5 million. Mickey Rooney was nominated for an Oscar, and Arthur Freed was catapulted 'from a $300-a-week novice producer to the position of the Number One man for musicals on the Metro lot,' said Fordin (1975: 31).

MGM teamed up Mickey Rooney and Judy Garland in three more musicals produced by Arthur Freed. 'That the plots were more or less the same did not matter,' remarked Harmetz (2014). In *Strike Up the Band* (1940), they raise money for a high school band contest; in *Babes on Broadway* (1941), they stage 'a settlement house show to raise funds to send some underprivileged children to the country'; and in *Girl Crazy* (1943), they stage a Wild West rodeo to save their college. 'What really mattered were Mickey's brash charm, Judy's sincerity and the songs by the Gershwin brothers, Rodgers and Hart, and others,' Harmetz said.

The perfect pairing of Mickey Rooney and Judy Garland was best summed up in the *New York Times* review of *Girl Crazy*. Describing the 'I've Got Rhythm' production finale staged by Busby Berkeley, the *New York Times* reviewer said, 'Mickey does everything but play Hamlet. He sings, bears the brunt of an Apache dance, impersonates the sundry characters at a prizefight, mugs his way through several hilarious scenes, bangs a piano with considerable finesse, and finally does a hep-cat hoedown with Miss Garland in the finale that must have caused a minor earthquake.' 'Amid these frantic shenanigans,' he said, 'Miss Garland's songs, such as "Biding My Time," should sooth even the most savage breast; of all the child prodigies of Hollywood, Miss Garland has outgrown her adolescence most gracefully and she still sings a song with an appealing sincerity which is downright irresistible' (*NYTFR*, 3 December 1943). Needless to say, the Rooney–Garland musicals all made money and plenty of it.

In 1938, MGM hit pay dirt a second time with another B movie, *Young Dr. Kildare* starring Lionel Barrymore and Lew Ayres. Lionel Barrymore, who suffered from severe arthritis, was now confined to a wheelchair. Lew Ayres had risen to stardom as a disillusioned German soldier in *All Quiet on the Western Front* in 1930 but had been making mostly B movies for Universal, Fox, and Poverty Row studios before MGM signed him up for the movie. In Harold S. Bucquet's *Young Dr. Kildare*, he played a young doctor who declines to follow his father's footsteps as a general practitioner and becomes an intern in a large city hospital, where he comes under the tutelage of the grouchy Dr. Gillespie. *Young Dr. Kildare* opened at the Radio City Music Hall on 27 October 1938. Nugent (1938) called it 'a likable film, quiet in tone and performance; suspenseful . . . and pleasantly above most of the melodramatic explosions of the men-in-white opera.' He added, 'Mr. Ayres's successful comeback can be taken as a fait accompli.' *Variety* agreed, saying, 'it is rather frank and almost entirely devoid of the hokum with which the healers usually feed the public in book, or other entertainment form. Unfolding of the yarn, in fact, denotes the careful research by the writers and director, and the result is a believable interesting picture that should add prestige to Metro's B schedule' (*VFR*, 19 October 1938).

Young Dr. Kildare cost only $199,000 to make but turned in a profit of $367,000. Thereafter, MGM turned out two to three of these low-budget pictures a year until 1942. The series was based on stories written by Frederick Schiller Faust (as Max Brand). MGM acquired the film rights to the stories in 1938 after noting the success of *Internes Can't Take Money* (1937), a Paramount picture based on the Kildare character starring Joel McCrea. As part of the deal, Brand agreed to work with MGM to help develop stories for the series. The production team was headed by Lou Ostrow, a former producer at Universal and Monogram, who joined MGM's B movie department in 1937; Harold S. Bucquet, a former MGM assistant director, helmed the pictures; and Willis Goldbeck, an MGM veteran, wrote the screenplays.

Each picture in the series depicted the young doctor's latest problem. Laraine Day as Nurse Mary Lumont joined the cast in the second picture, *Calling Dr. Kildare* (1939), to provide a love interest. By 1941, MGM thought that Day was too good for B movies and wrote her out of the series. In *Dr. Kildare's Wedding Day* (1941), she was killed by a truck as she was out shopping for furniture. Dr. Kildare fans were not happy with the decision and how it was done. *Photoplay* ('Dr Kildare's' 1941: 97), for example, said, 'It comes as a shock that jars the emotions – the sudden, tragic death of Laraine Day as Nurse Lamont, the beloved of Lew Ayres . . . Although we'd been forewarned, it still seemed a rather brutal demise for a character so beloved.'

Dr. Kildare carried on bravely after the death of his sweetheart in the final film of the series, *Dr. Kildare's Victory* (1942). It opened in New York on 4 February 1942. Ayres was drafted soon after. He filed as a conscientious objector and was sent to a CO camp in Oregon for two months. Exhibitors, meanwhile, pulled his pictures from release and cancelled future bookings. MGM, to its credit, kept the pictures in distribution 'because the public has shown more tolerance in the matter than theater men,' said an MGM spokesman ('Metro to Continue' 1942). After his dismissal from the labor camp, Ayres served as a noncombatant in the Medical Corps for more than three years and won three battle stars. He resumed his career after the war and made scores of movies but never reached the peak of his early Hollywood stardom.

MGM continued the series under a new name, *Dr. Gillespie*. Willis Goldbeck took over as the principal director, but the behind-the-camera personnel remained pretty much the same. Lionel Barrymore became the central focus of the series, and now a succession of young interns vied for a position as his assistant. Van Johnson, who was just starting out at the studio, appeared in four of the pictures as Dr. Gillespie's assistant, Dr. Randall 'Red' Ames. The series lasted for six more pictures, expiring in 1947.

In 1939, MGM hit pay dirt a third time with another B movie, *Maisie* (1939) starring Ann Sothern. The series originated with producer J. Walter Ruben, who was impressed with Sothern's bit role as a wisecracking blonde in Walter Wanger's *Trade Winds* (1938) at United Artists and cast her for the part. Sothern had plenty of experience working in B movies for Columbia and RKO. *Maisie* was based on the novel *Dark Dame* by Wilson Collison and directed by Edwin L. Martin. Sothern played 'a small-time showgirl stranded in a Wyoming cow-town.' *Variety* described her as 'sexy, smart, and resourceful – and decidedly likeable.' The picture was a 'top programmer,' it said, and demonstrated 'advantages of perfect blending of crackerjack script, crisp dialogue, zestful direction, and consistently fine performances, for favorable results' (*VFR*, 7 June 1939).

Maisie was an instant hit, and MGM signed Miss Sothern to a long-term contract. Instead of breaking into A films at MGM, as she had hoped, she became the queen of the Bs. She went on to make nine more pictures in the series, 'traveling to every part of the globe as conceived by set decorators' (Harmetz 2001). Sothern typically played 'the hapless little Miss Fixit all too often hurt by the people she helps, the good fairy from the honky tonks who behaves as if the world were filled with nothing but the nicest people. Her taste is not precisely refined. It runs to furbelows, bric-a-brac and ugly little dogs. Her conversation is not always as elegant as it aspires to be. But Maisie has a very strict credo even if it never got beyond the grammar-school stage. Above all she has a heart' (*NYTFR*, 10 September 1943). The pictures had no continuing characters; her costars were drawn mainly from MGM's contract-player ranks. Sothern eventually begged Louis B. Mayer to allow her to quit the series, but he would always answer, 'No. Your movies pay for our mistakes' (Harmetz 2001). *Swing Shift Maisie*, a wartime movie that had Maisie working an aircraft factory, for example, cost $535,000 to make, grossed three times as much ($1.4 million), and made a profit of $447,000. By 1946, all of MGM's long-running series had run their course. *Undercover Maisie* (1947), the last picture in the series, was the first to lose money.

Production trends

When war broke out in Europe in 1939, Hollywood shied away from specific war-related themes. The European markets remained opened, and a strong isolationist movement existed at home. Moreover, overt criticism of foreign 'institutions, prominent people and citizenry' was forbidden by the Production Code under the heading 'National Feelings.' Recall that Robert E. Sherwood had to emasculate his antiwar film *Idiot's Delight* to get it past the Breen Office. Once the United States entered the war in 1941, the constraints were mostly removed. Immediately after Pearl Harbor, President Roosevelt enlisted Hollywood's support of the war effort unfettered by censorship. And on 13 June 1942, he created the Office of War Information (OWI) headed by Elmer Davis 'to enhance public understanding of the war at home and abroad.' Dealing with Hollywood, the OWI created the Bureau of Motion Pictures, which reviewed scripts before production began and advised studios how they could help the cause. By then, Crowther (1942) had lamented the 'disquieting flabbiness' of many wartime pictures being released by Hollywood. 'No one expects or desires that every film now made give a realistic picture of war . . . But one can expect – and demand – that those films which do touch this vital theme do so with truth, discretion and a full respect for its gravity. It is obvious they have not.'

Action pictures

Before the war, MGM made its share of routine action pictures. Frank Borzage's *Flight Command* (1940), for example, was made when the U.S. was beginning to think about national preparedness. It starred Robert Taylor and glorified the Navy Hellcats. The best thing about it, said Crowther were the 'actual air shots . . . the scenes of planes flying in tight formations above the majestic clouds, dropping away in screaming power dives, taking off and landing on a carrier's deck. Then you feel it really has wings' (*NYTFR*, 17 January 1941).

MGM also produced two anti-Nazi pictures of note, *The Mortal Storm* (1940) and *Escape* (1940). *The Mortal Storm*, produced and directed by Frank Borzage, was based on Phyllis Bottome's 1937 best seller about a 'non-Aryan' university biology professor (Frank Morgan), who refuses to accept Nazi racial theories and is sent to a concentration camp. It starred Margaret Sullavan, James Stewart, Robert Young, and Frank Morgan. *Variety* stated, 'With the devastating directness of a Stuka diver, *The Mortal Storm* is a film bomb which is about to explode in American theatres with such force as to dispel public equanimity if, in fact, any exists towards the vicious operation of Nazism and its fanatical proponents' (*VFR*, 12 June 1940).

Escape, produced and directed by Mervyn LeRoy, was based on Ethel Vance's 1940 best seller about the 'rescue of a famous German actress from a concentration camp' and starred Norma Shearer, as previously mentioned. Crowther said, 'This is far and away the most dramatic and hair-raising picture yet made on the sinister subject of persecution in a totalitarian land, and the suspense which it manages to compress in its moments of greatest intensity would almost seem enough to blow sizable holes in the screen' (*NYTFR*, 1 November 1940). The two films so angered the Germans that they banned MGM films from the country and from Nazi-occupied territories and forced the closing of MGM's Berlin office.

As of August 1940, Paramount was the only American company still doing business in Germany.

Home-front dramas – American

Once the United States entered the war, MGM went full throttle to build morale at home and to support the war effort. War-related themes permeated all of MGM's production trends, the most important of which were the home-front dramas, combat pictures, and musicals. At MGM, home-front came in two types, American and British. The American comprised Richard Thorpe's *Joe Smith, American* (1942) and Clarence Brown's *The Human Comedy* (1943). *Joe Smith, American* was the first release of Dore Schary's new B movie unit. It starred Robert Young and was based on a Paul Gallico story about a factory worker, a regular American guy, who is kidnapped by Nazi agents and tortured in an unsuccessful attempt to get him to reveal the workings of a new secret bombsight. As the *New York Times* reviewer said, 'It was the little things, the small remembrances of what his life had been, that pulled him through' (*NYTFR*, 2 April 1942).

The Human Comedy was based on a story by William Saroyan, the Pulitzer Prize–winning playwright who wrote *The Time of Your Life*. The picture starred Mickey Rooney; he played Homer Macauley, a telegram messenger who delivers messages from the War Department informing families in a small California town that their sons have died. MGM hired Saroyan to write the original screenplay, which he turned out in eighteen days, it was reported. Although MGM loved it, ardor cooled when it was determined that the running time of the film would be four hours. Thinking that the project had died, Saroyan converted his screenplay into a novel, which became a Book-of-the-Month Club selection and a best seller. Meanwhile, Clarence Brown convinced the front office to go ahead with the project under his supervision and with Mickey Rooney in the lead. Saroyan's novel appeared shortly before the picture premiered in New York at the Astor on 2 March 1943. Crowther praised Mickey Rooney's performance. 'There is a tenderness and restraint in his characterization, along with a genuine youthfulness, such as he has not shown for a long time.' But he added, 'The tone of Mr. Saroyan's writing and the mood in which Mr. Brown has directed the film make the characters seem more sanctified than human. They are so full of beatitudes that they slip out of normal perspective. *The Human Comedy* is sentimental showmanship' (*NYTFR*, 3 March 1943). The picture was a big hit, earning a profit of $1.5 million and ranking number four in the 1942–43 season. Mickey Rooney received his second Academy Award nomination for his performance, and William Saroyan won an Oscar for Best Original Story.

Home-front dramas – British

MGM's British home-front films were produced by Sidney Franklin, the studio's veteran director who turned to producing in 1939 after helming such prestige favorites as *Private Lives* (1931), *The Barretts of Wimpole Street* (1934), and *The Good*

Earth (1937). Following the closure of MGM-British, MGM resumed production of the British home-front pictures in Culver City. The most important were *Mrs. Miniver* (1942), *Random Harvest* (1942), and *The White Cliffs of Dover* (1944). 'While Britain was threatened with invasion and bombings, MGM created the most idealized portrayals of Britain and the British,' said Glancy (1999: 89–91). 'Each of the Franklin melodramas centres on the pain and anxiety caused by wartime separation or loss, and each offers a strong, maternal and caring woman as a source of safety and serenity amid the heartaches of war.' 'Class distinctions are overwhelmingly apparent in these idyllic rural settings,' he added, 'but they are a source of order and harmony rather than conflict. Everyone knows their place and is happy with it.' And the leading roles went to British actors such as Vivien Leigh, Greer Garson, and Ronald Colman.

William Wyler's *Mrs. Miniver* (1942) starred Greer Garson and Walter Pidgeon. It was based on Jan Struther's *Mrs. Miniver* stories that had first appeared in the *London Times* and 'centered on the heroine's leisurely observations about life amid the upper-middle class' (Glancy 1999: 93). Arthur Wimperis, George Froeschel, James Hilton, and Claudine West collaborated on the screenplay. *Mrs. Miniver* 'depicted a thoroughly decent English couple suffering through the London blitz. . . . The maternal heroine of *Mrs. Miniver* comforts her younger children during the Blitz, sees her husband and elder son off to Dunkirk, and creates goodwill

FIGURE 5.4 Greer Garson, Walter Pidgeon, and Richard Ney in William Wyler's *Mrs. Miniver* (1942)

throughout her war-torn village,' said Glancy (1999: 93, 90). *Mrs. Miniver* premiered in New York on 4 June 1942 at the Radio City Music Hall. It ran for a record-breaking ten weeks, was seen by 1,500,000 people, and took in a reported $1,000,000 at the box office (Schatz 1997: 152). Produced at a cost of $1.3 million, it grossed $8.9 million worldwide, the best results since *Ben-Hur*, and turned in a profit of $4.8 million, making it the most profitable MGM picture of the decade. Crowther called it 'the finest film yet made about the present war, and a most exalting tribute to the British, who have taken it gallantly.' 'This is a film about the people in a small, unpretentious English town on whom the war creeps up slowly, disturbing their tranquil ways of life, then suddenly bursts in devastating fury as the bombs rain down and the Battle of Britain is on. Crowther praised the four writers who imbued the script with a 'natural, literate quality' and William Wyler, who directed it with 'a sensitivity that rarely shows in films.' 'Greer Garson's performance as Mrs. Miniver,' he said, 'glows with compassion and womanly strength.' And 'Walter Pidgeon is a real inspiration to masculine stamina and resource as Clem,' her husband (*NYTFR*, 5 June 1942). The reviews were unanimous. At the Academy Awards, the picture won seven Oscars, including Best Picture, Best Director, and Best Actress. Louis B. Mayer rewarded Garson with a $30,000 bonus and a new seven-year, no-option contract at $4,000 a week (Eyman 2005: 367). Greer Garson had now inherited Norma Shearer's mantle as 'Queen of the Lot,' but she would remain typecast for the remainder of her career, which ended in 1954.

MGM quickly followed up on the success of *Mrs. Miniver* by producing *Random Harvest* (1942) directed by Mervyn LeRoy. It teamed Greer Garson and Ronald Colman and was based on James Hilton's novel about a wife who abandons her career as a music-hall entertainer to care for her husband, a shell-shocked veteran of World War I suffering from amnesia. It too premiered at the Radio City Music Hall – this time it was presented as the Music Hall's annual Christmas show – and again set an attendance record at the theater. In the earnings department, it turned in a profit of $4.4 million, nearly as much as *Mrs. Miniver*.

Garson went on to make three additional hits during the war, *Madame Curie* (1944), *Mrs. Parkington* (1944), and *The Valley of Decision* (1945). They were period pieces, unlike the home-front films. But the roles were pretty much in the same mold. As Flint (1996) stated, 'In her high-toned M-G-M pictures she was invariably serene, polite, elegant in a slightly unreal way, too good to be true, always prepared to meet any emergency and staunchly middle-class.' Like always, they premiered in New York at the Radio City Music Hall. In *Madame Curie* and *Mrs. Parkington*, Garson continued to play the devoted wife of Walter Pidgeon. Crowther said of the pairing, 'Greer Garson and Walter Pidgeon have been ingrained in the popular mind as the ideal connubial couple to be seen upon the screen' (*NYTFR*, 13 October 1944). In *The Valley of Decision* (1945), the most successful of the group, Garson was teamed with a new leading man, Gregory Peck. It was based on the Marcia Davenport best seller about Mary Rafferty, an in-between-maid back in 1873 who entered the family of a pioneering Pittsburgh steel baron and rises to the post of family confidante. The picture, produced by Edwin H. Knopf and directed by Tay Garnett, ranked number one on MGM's 1944–45 roster. Garson was nominated for Best Actress for the fifth consecutive time.

Wartime tributes

The White Cliffs of Dover was MGM's contribution to the OWI's 'Brothers in Arms' campaign, which encouraged Hollywood to produce films that paid tribute to wartime allies – not only to the British but also to Soviet Russia and China. Clarence Brown's *The White Cliffs of Dover* starred Irene Dunne and Alan Marshall and was based on Alice Duer Miller's popular verse novel, *The White Cliffs*, published in 1940, that chronicled the trials and tribulations of a courageous American woman who loses her British husband and son in the two world wars. Crowther said, *The White Cliffs of Dover* 'has virtually gotten down on its knees and kissed the ground – the ground, that is, of England and all that it represents.' 'But it is not of the modern England that this film most affectionately tells – and certainly not of the England of shopkeepers and simple folks,' he said. 'Rather it is an England of grand baronial estates, of gracious and elegant patricians and of militant old-school ties. It is an England of frumpy old codgers with hearts made of Bank-of-England gold and of weatherworn class traditions which stretch back for centuries' (*NYTFR*, 12 May 1944). The picture was a hit on both sides of the Atlantic, grossing $6.3 million in rentals and earning a profit of $1.8 million.

MGM's tribute to Russia, Gregory Ratoff's *Song of Russia* (1944), was produced by Joseph Pasternak and Pandro S. Berman. 'If one studio would try to turn the grimness of war into a musical it would be Metro,' remarked Koppes and Black (1987: 215). 'It offered *Song of Russia*, built around the romance of a fictional composer (played by Robert Taylor) and a young pianist (Susan Peters).' The Office of War Information applauded, they said, 'as the performers' touring offered a panorama of a modern Soviet Union, peopled by industrious folk who liked to relax after hours to Jerome Kern's tunes in glittering nightclubs.' This was Robert Taylor's last picture before he joined the Navy. The movie suffered no political backlash in the U.S. during its initial release and was even popular, turning in a profit of $782,000.

MGM's tribute to China, Jack Conway's *Dragon Seed* (1944), was produced by Pandro S. Berman and starred Katharine Hepburn. It was based on Pearl S. Buck's novel, which told how the peaceful villagers in China resisted their Japanese invaders and intended as a follow up to *The Good Earth* starring Luise Rainer. As described by the *New York Times*, 'The familiar pattern for such things is followed: curiosity about the enemy; bewilderment at enemy atrocities; the inevitable quisling; a sporadic reign of terror, and, finally, grim and determined guerrilla warfare. Throughout all of it there is the painful stress and strain on the relationships of the closely knit family (*NYTFR*, 21 July 1944). MGM spent two years and $3 million to make a two-and-a-half–hour epic that was pilloried by the critics. As Koppes and Black (1987: 242) reported, 'James Agee thought it was an "unimaginably bad movie." He could not recall having seen another film "so full of wrong slants." The Japanese were played by Chinese while the Chinese were played by Caucasians "with their eyes painfully plastered in an Oriental oblique." Agee continued: 'I shan't even try to say how awful and silly they looked – Miss Hepburn especially, in her shrewdly tailored Peck-&-Peck pajamas.' But audiences liked it. The picture ran eight weeks at the Radio City Music Hall and was Hepburn's best wartime gross. 'Her films with Spencer Tracy paled by comparison,' said Glancy (1992: 139). But because of the picture's high production cost, it incurred a relatively small loss.

Combat films

The combat film was another popular wartime trend, as would be expected. The practice of dramatizing actual military battles began with Paramount's *Wake Island* (1942). MGM contributed three important pictures to the cycle, Tay Garnett's *Bataan* (1943), Mervyn LeRoy's *Thirty Seconds Over Tokyo* (1944), and John Ford's *They Were Expendable* (1945). All three were big box-office hits. *Bataan* was produced by Dore Schary's B movie unit. It starred Robert Taylor and told the story of thirteen soldiers from different races, classes, and religious beliefs who volunteer to fight a rear-guard action on the Bataan peninsula to stall the Japanese advance while the American and Filipino armies fell back on Corregidor. They are killed by the Japanese one by one to the last man. Crowther said, 'This time, at least, a studio hasn't purposely "prettified" facts. This time it has made a picture about war in true and ugly detail. There is nothing bright or exultant about this new film at the Capitol – nothing except the admiration inspired by the image of brave men hanging on' (*NYTFR*, 4 June 1943).

Thirty Seconds Over Tokyo (1944) was produced by Sam Zimbalist. Dalton Trumbo's screenplay was inspired by Lieutenant Ted W. Lawson's 1943 memoir about Lieutenant Colonel Jimmy Doolittle's raid on Japan just months after the attack on Pearl Harbor. It starred Van Johnson in his first major role. Crowther called the war epic 'the best yet made in Hollywood' (*NYTFR*, 6 November 1944). The film won an Academy Award for Best Special Effects.

They Were Expendable (1945) was released three months after the Japanese sur-rendered on 2 September 1945 and came near the end of the combat film cycle. It was produced and directed by John Ford and starred Robert Montgomery and John Wayne. Frank Wead adapted W. L. White's 1942 best seller about 'the gal-lantry and daring of that handful of Navy men who threw their fast PT-boat squadron against the Japanese in the first days of the war' (*NYTFR*, 21 December 1945). John Ford, an officer in the U.S. Naval Reserves, was furloughed to make the movie. 'John Ford has lost none of his cunning or artistry during the years he has been in Navy uniform,' said Barnes (1945). 'There has been a notion around that war pictures were dated. Messrs. Ford and Montgomery give it the lie . . . *They Were Expendable* is an enthralling tribute to nice youngsters who fought gallantly in defeat. It is more than merely entertaining. It is an abiding testament to the valor that made victory possible.'

Musicals

The musical was MGM's most prolific and most profitable production trend of the decade. During the war, they boosted the morale 'of fighting men and women, and the families awaiting their return,' said Hay (1991: 192). Musicals with war-related themes included Arthur Freed's production of *For Me and My Gal* (1942) and *Meet Me in St. Louis* (1944) and Joe Pasternak's *Thousands Cheer* (1943), *Two Girls and a Sailor* (1944), and *Anchors Aweigh* (1945). Busby Berkeley's *For Me and My Gal* marked the first time Judy Garland's name appeared above the title. She had turned twenty and was given her first dramatic role as an adult. The picture also marked Gene Kelly's film debut. He had arrived in Hollywood in 1941 after starring in the 1940 Rodgers and Hart Broadway hit, *Pal Joey*. *For Me and My Gal* was based on an original story by Howard Emmett Rogers about two hoofers from the sticks in the days before the first world war who aspire to play the Palace in New York, the Mecca of vaudeville. Kelly becomes a draft dodger when the war breaks out by deliberately breaking his hand but redeems himself by entertaining the troops at the front. 'Miss Garland is a knockout as the warm-hearted young song-and-dance girl, selling a number of songs persuasively, getting by neatly in the hoofing routines with Kelly, and giving a tender, affecting dramatic performance,' said *Variety*, 'while Gene Kelly gives a vividly drawn portrayal of the song-and-dance man and imperfect hero, practically another "Pal Joey" character that he played so well on Broadway (*VFR*, 9 September 1942).

Meet Me in St. Louis (1944), Vincente Minnelli's nostalgic piece of Americana, ranked among the top musicals of the period. Minnelli joined the Freed unit in 1940 after a successful career on Broadway directing musicals. His first directing job was *Cabin in the Sky* (1943), an all-black musical headed by Ethel Waters, Eddie 'Rochester' Anderson, and Lena Horne. *Meet Me in St. Louis* starred Judy Garland and featured Margaret O'Brien, Mary Astor, Leon Ames, and Lucille Bremer. Garland had to be persuaded to accept the lead role as Esther, and for good reason; playing another teenager, she thought, would set back her career.

Meet Me in St. Louis was based on Sally Benson's *New Yorker* short stories about growing up in St. Louis around the turn of the century. Irving Brecher and Fred Finklehoffe adapted the screenplay. The story was divided into four segments, each corresponding to a season of the year, and led up to the opening of the St. Louis World's Fair of 1904. The focus was the daily routines of the Smith clan. As described by Crowther, the Smiths comprised the 'long-suffering papa and mama, four daughters, a saucy elder son, grandpa (who is something of a crack-pot) and a tautly tyrannical maid. And the tempests which occur in this large hen-roost derive from such grand necessities as meeting the right boy at the right time and not moving to New York' (*NYTFR*, 29 November 1944).

FIGURE 5.5 Lucille Bremer, Margaret O'Brien, Judy Garland, and Tom Drake in Vincente Minnelli's *Meet Me in St. Louis* (1944)

Judy Garland sang three original songs by Hugh Martin and Ralph Blane – 'The Trolley Song,' 'The Boy Next Door,' and 'Have Yourself a Merry Little Christmas.' *Meet Me in St. Louis* was released in glorious Technicolor and premiered in New York at the Astor as a roadshow at the start of the Christmas season. The picture was an enormous success and embellished MGM's reputation as the producer of Hollywood's greatest musicals. The picture was nominated for numerous Academy Awards. Margaret O'Brien, who played the 7-year-old Tootie in the movie, won a special Academy Award as the Most Outstanding Child Actress of 1944.

Judy Garland finally established her bona fides as a dramatic actress in Arthur Freed's production of *The Clock* (1945) directed by Vincente Minnelli before moving on to other hit musicals. In *The Clock*, she played her first nonsinging dramatic role opposite Robert Walker in what Crowther called 'A tender and refreshingly simple romantic drama' about 'a soldier on a forty-eight-hour furlough in Manhattan and his chance meeting with a lonely girl.' He added, '*The Clock* is the kind of picture that leaves one with a warm feeling toward his fellow-man, especially toward the young folks who today are trying to crowd a lifetime of happiness into a few fleeting hours' (*NYTFR*, 4 May 1945).

Joe Pasternak's musicals were cut from a different cloth. Unlike Freed's integrated musicals, which used music to advance the narrative, Pasternak's musicals were musical extravaganzas which contained a pastiche of classical music, big-band sounds, and comic skits, plus assorted cameos and appealing young newcomers in the leading roles – all tied together with the thinnest of plots. Pasternak, a Hungarian immigrant, had saved Universal from bankruptcy by producing a series of musicals around Deanna Durbin, a teenage soprano. She was 15 when Pasternak cast her in *Three Smart Girls* (1936). The picture was a huge box-office hit and launched her acting and singing career. Pasternak moved to MGM in 1942. Louis B. Mayer wanted him to work his magic on the studio's young singing talent like Judy Garland, Kathryn Grayson, June Allyson, Gene Kelly, and Frank Sinatra.

George Sidney's *Thousands Cheer* (1943) starred Kathryn Grayson and Gene Kelly. 'It told the story of an Army officer's daughter who puts on camp show for the troops with MGM's "big box-office artillery."' 'It's been a long time since Metro spread itself so lavishly as in *Thousands Cheer*, and it's been longer than that since the screen provided such a veritable grab-bag of delights,' said Pryor. 'Musically, there is something for all tastes, from José Iturbi to boogie woogie, from Kathryn Grayson and "Semper Libre" to Judy Garland and "The Joint Is Really Jumpin'!" and for extra measure, there is a circus sequence with an aerialist act that is as thrilling as anything ever seen under the big top' (*NYTFR*, 14 September 1943).

Richard Thorpe's *Two Girls and a Sailor* (1944) starred Van Johnson, June Allyson, and Gloria De Haven. Allyson and De Haven are two singing sisters who are helped by a sailor to set up a canteen to entertain lonesome soldiers. Van Johnson, the sailor, turns out to be a millionaire and ends up falling in love with the plain sister, June Allyson. The canteen format allowed Pasternak to stuff the picture with a 'salmagundi of band numbers by Harry James and Xavier Cugat, with their soloists, plus Jimmy Durante, of whom there isn't enough and various other specialties ranging from Lena Horne to Jose Iturbi,' said *Variety* (*VFR*, 26 April 1944). June Allyson playing the girl-next-door roles and Van Johnson playing the boy next door would be romantically paired four more times.

George Sidney's *Anchors Aweigh* starred Frank Sinatra, Kathryn Grayson, and Gene Kelly. Two decorated sailors on a four-day leave in Hollywood help an aspiring young singer get an audition with Jose Iturbi. MGM gave Kelly a chance to do his own choreography. One such dance number combined Kelly's live action with a Tom and Jerry cartoon sequence. Crowther called Kelly 'the Apollonian marvel of the piece, dancing, singing and performing in a delightfully gay and graceful style' (*NYTFR*, 20 July 1945). *Anchors Aweigh* 'earned the best gross ($7,475,000) of all the wartime musicals, but it was closely followed by the lavish aquacades of Esther Williams,' said Glancy (1992: 138).

MGM signed up Esther Williams in 1941. She was 18 and a three-time national swimming champion. Williams earned a place on the 1940 U.S. Olympic Team, but her hopes for an Olympic medal were dashed when the games were cancelled after Hitler invaded Poland. She was lead swimmer in Billy Rose's Aquacade at the San Francisco World's Fair when MGM spotted her. Louis B. Mayer hired her with the intent of making her a rival to Fox's figure skating star and Olympic medalist, Sonja Henie. Williams made her MGM debut in *Andy Hardy's Double Life* (1942) as one of Mickey Rooney's girlfriends. It contained a swimming pool sequence in which she plants a kiss on Mickey Rooney under water.

George Sidney's *Bathing Beauty* (1944) made her a star. It was produced by Jack Cummings, Louis B. Mayer's nephew, who worked his way up from office boy to staff producer in MGM's B movie unit by 1934. Two years later, he was assigned his first major project, the Cole Porter musical *Born to Dance* (1936) starring Eleanor Powell. Cummings continued producing Powell musicals until she departed the studio in 1943. By then Cummings had joined Arthur Freed and Joe Pasternak as one of MGM's top musical producers. *Bathing Beauty* teamed Esther Williams with Red Skelton. The picture was originally called *Mr. Co-ed*, a comedy designed for Red Skelton, but during production MGM retitled it and built up Esther Williams's part. A thin plot about a swimming instructor in an all-girls school who is being pursued by her estranged fiancé allowed Skelton to perform his specialty numbers and Williams her water ballets. 'Metro has put on another of its spectacular musical shows combining all the Technicolors of the rainbow and much of the talent on its lot,' said Crowther. 'Miss Williams' talents as a swimmer – not to mention her other attributes,' he said, 'make any title the studio wants to put on it okay by us. When she eels through the crystal blue water in a rosy-red bathing suit or splashes in limpid magnificence in the gaudy water carnival which John Murray Anderson has brought to pass, she's a bathing beauty for our money' (*NYTFR*, 28 June 1944). *Bathing Beauty* was the top-grossing picture of the 1943–44 season and earned a profit of more than $2 million. Williams remained a top box-office draw for the next decade. Joe Pasternak, Jack Cummings, and Arthur Freed all had a hand in nurturing her career.

Family classics

A remarkable series of family films starring a new lode of child stars helped boost morale. To maintain its hold on the family trade, MGM again turned to making 'British' pictures. They comprised Fred M. Wilcox's *Lassie Come Home* (1943), Clarence Brown's *National Velvet* (1944), and Victor Saville's *The Green Years* (1946). *Lassie Come Home* was produced by Samuel Marx for Dore Schary's B movie unit. Marx had previously worked for Thalberg as story editor from 1930 to 1936, before turning to producing. The picture was set in Yorkshire and Scotland during the dark days before the war and shot in Technicolor. Hugo Butler adapted Eric Knight's *Lassie*, a best-selling young person's novel published in 1940 about a collie who is sold by his caring and struggling family, the Carracloughs, to a Scottish duke. The faithful Lassie finally manages to escape with the help of the duke's daughter and treks hundreds of miles to return home to the boy he loves in time for Christmas. Roddy McDowell played the young Joe Carraclough and Pal, a trained collie owned by Rudd Weatherwax, his dog Lassie. The 10-year-old Elizabeth Taylor played the duke's daughter. McDowell, a British adolescent actor, had just completed *My Friend Flicka* (1943) at Fox about a little boy's love for an outcast colt before being loaned out to MGM to make the Lassie picture. The supporting cast was also British and included seasoned professionals such as Donald Crisp, Elsa Lanchester, Dame May Whitty, Ben Webster, and Edmund Gwenn, as well as Miss Taylor.

Lassie Come Home premiered at the Radio City Music Hall on 7 October 1943. Bosley Crowther's verdict: 'The Radio City Music Hall should be filled with young folks these next few weeks,' said Crowther, 'young folks and their wistful elders who still pulse to the joys and sorrows of youth. For the picture which opened there yesterday tells the story of a boy and a dog, tells it with such poignancy and simple beauty that only the hardest heart can fail to be moved.' The most remarkable performer in the film, was Lassie: 'The beauty of this dog and her responsiveness go far to make the picture a thorough delight' (*NYTFR*, 8 October 1943). *Lassie Come Home* became MGM's most profitable picture of the 1943–44 season, earning a profit of $2.3 million, and spawned six sequels and even a radio show which ran for three years on NBC. To secure Pal's services, MGM signed Rudd Weatherwax to a long-term contract. Lassie had become the most famous dog in the world. Robert Sisk produced four of the sequels. They were all set in the rugged outdoors and told poignant stories about the great love of a dog for its owner. The supporting casts remained mostly the same and featured up-and-coming stars such as Peter Lawford, June Allyson, Janet Leigh, and Elizabeth Taylor. Miss Taylor received top billing in the third picture, *Courage of Lassie* (1946). MGM sold off the rights to the series in 1951, mistakenly thinking that it had run its course with *The Painted Hills*, but Lassie lived on in television.

Elizabeth Taylor's performance in *Lassie Come Home* so impressed MGM that she was given a starring role in *National Velvet* opposite Mickey Rooney and Donald Crisp. Produced in Technicolor by Pandro S. Berman, *National Velvet* was based on Enid Bagnold's novel about Velvet Brown, a 12-year-old girl living on the Sussex Coast who is obsessed with horses and rides 'a magnificent sorrel gelding' to victory in the Grand National Steeplechase. It premiered at the Radio City Music Hall on 14 December 1944 in time for Christmas. As Lusk (1944) reported, 'It is a perfect, a glorious attraction, the first picture keyed to the season to reach Broadway, where it will remain long after the holly and mistletoe are taken down.' The picture made Elizabeth Taylor a star. Crowther said, little Elizabeth Taylor's 'face is alive with youthful spirit, her voice has the softness of sweet song and her whole manner in this picture is one of refreshing grace' (*NYTFR*, 5 December 1944). *National Velvet* became a children's classic.

The Green Years, produced by Leon Gordon, was based on A. J. Cronin's story about the coming of age of a young Irish-Catholic orphan who is raised by his stingy and dour grandparents in Scotland. It starred Charles Coburn, Tom Drake, Beverly Tyler, Hume Cronyn, and Dean Stockwell. *Variety* said, 'Metro, with the skill it has so often demonstrated in transforming a best-selling novel to a best-selling picture, turns the trick again with this filmization of A. J. Cronin's *The Green*

FIGURE 5.6 Mickey Rooney and Elizabeth Taylor in Clarence Brown's *National Velvet* (1944)

Years.' 'Ten-year-old Stockwell,' it said, 'is the particularly bright spot in the well-turned cast, as well as a top addition to the list of Hollywood juve players . . . In the present film he gets real opportunity to demonstrate a sensitivity and true dramatic poignancy that definitely set him off from the usual studio moppets' (*VFR*, 13 March 1946). Charles Coburn played Stockwell's great grandfather, who develops a tender relationship with the young man and guides his destiny. Crowther said, 'Charles Coburn plays the swag-bellied old rascal with a beautifully fustian air but laces into his comicality a great deal of moving sentiment. His bearded and brummagemed performance in this role will be remembered for a long time' (*NYTFR*, 5 April 1946). *The Green Years* premiered at the Radio City Music Hall on 4 April 1946 in time for Easter and went on to earn the highest profit on MGM's 1945–46 roster.

MGM's family dramas with a distinctly American bent included Roy Rowland's *Our Vines Have Tender Grapes* (1945) and Clarence Brown's *The Yearling* (1946). *Our Vines Have Tender Grapes* premiered in New York at the Radio City Music Hall on 6 September 1945 and starred Edward G. Robinson and Margaret O'Brien, the recent winner of a Special Academy Award for her performance as Tootie in *Meet Me in St. Louis. Our Vines Have Tender Grapes* was another piece of Americana. Dalton Trumbo's screenplay was based on George Victor Martin's novel about a small Norwegian farming settlement in Wisconsin. Robert Sisk produced it. Edward G. Robinson played a 'benevolent farmer' and Margaret O' Brien, his 7-year-old daughter who leads the community out of a series of calamities. Pryor said, 'It would indeed be a cold and distant heart that failed to respond to the homey philosophy and the tenderly sentimental vignettes of family life which are sketched with loving care and understanding by a knowing group of players in this beautifully made Metro-Goldwyn-Mayer production' (*NYTFR*, 7 September 1945).

The Yearling (1946) was released at the end of 1946 and is included here, in part because it was five years in the making. Producer Sidney Franklin started work on the picture in 1940, but the production was interrupted several times and then shelved until 1944. MGM had invested heavily in the picture when it was first abandoned, but Franklin persisted in bringing the story to the screen. It was based on Marjorie Kinnan Rawlings's 1938 Pulitzer Prize winner and told 'the heart-warming story of good earth, family ties, and the love of the 11-year-old Jody Baxter for the fawn which he is compelled to put out of life as it becomes a yearling,' said *Variety* (*VFR*, 27 November 1946). It starred Gregory Peck, Jane Wyman, and Claude Jarman Jr. Clarence Brown selected Jarman for the part of Jody after personally conducting a six-month talent search in the South and shot much of the picture on locations in the Florida scrub country described in Rawlings's book. The picture premiered in Los Angeles on 25 December 1946 to qualify for that year's Oscar balloting. It opened in New York on 23 January 1947 at the Radio City Music Hall and went on to become a huge critical and commercial success. Crowther pretty much summed up the critical response, saying '*The Yearling* is a cheerful and inspiring film about the coming to

FIGURE 5.7 Claude Jarman Jr. in Clarence Brown's *The Yearling* (1946)

manhood of a youngster.' He singled out Claude Jarman Jr.'s 'incredibly fine performance.' 'As Jody, the tow-headed farm boy, this youngster who had never acted before achieves a child characterization as haunting and appealing as any we've ever seen,' he said. 'Spindly, delicate of features and possessed of a melting Southern voice, he makes not a single sound or movement which does not seem completely genuine. And his confident handling of the animals reveals him plainly as their natural, primal friend' (*NYTFR*, 24 January 1947).

The Yearling posted the highest gross on MGM's 1946–47 roster – more than $7.5 million – but earned only a modest profit of $451,000 because of its high production cost. At the Academy Awards, it received a total of six Oscar nominations. Peck and Wyman were nominated for Best Actor and Best Actress, and Jarman was given a Special Academy Award. The picture also won Oscars for Art Direction (Color) and Cinematography (Color).

Wartime prosperity

Wartime prosperity for the American film industry spilled over to 1946. By then, attendance had reached a peak of around 90 million per week, and studio profits had ballooned. Loew's Inc. recorded a profit of $17.9 million, an all-time high for the company (Gomery 1986: 52). Studios with larger theater chains were more profitable. But what the figures don't show is the relative potency of the studios' pictures. At year's end 1946, *Variety* ('60 Top' 1947: 8) published a list of the sixty top-grossing films – pictures that earned more than $2,250,000 in domestic rentals for the year. MGM had the highest number on the list with thirteen and one-third of the films in the over-$4,000,000 category. Some of the pictures on the top-sixty list not previously discussed include Victor Fleming's *Adventure* (1946), which teamed Greer Garson with Clark Gable in his first postwar film; Vincente Minnelli's *Undercurrent* (1946), which teamed Katharine Hepburn and Robert Taylor in his first postwar film; Tay Garnett's *The Postman Always Rings Twice* (1946), which starred Lana Turner and John Garfield; and three musicals produced by Arthur Freed, Joe Pasternak, and Jack Cummings, respectively – George Sidney's *The Harvey Girls* (1946) starring Judy Garland, Henry Koster's *Two Sisters from Boston* (1946) starring Kathryn Grayson and June Allison, and Edward Buzzell's *Easy to Wed* (1946) starring Van Johnson and Esther Williams.

6

DORE SCHARY

'A new Thalberg' (1947–58)

Postwar recession

After the war, an era had come to an end. Beginning in 1947, the movie industry entered a ten-year recession during which motion picture attendance declined by half and 4,000 theaters closed their doors. Veterans swarmed into colleges and universities to take advantage of the GI Bill. They married, had children, and moved to the suburbs. Young families far removed from the downtown movie palaces found a substitute for the movies in radio, which enjoyed unprecedented growth in the late forties. And acquiring new houses, cars, appliances, and other consumer goods cut into disposable income. Abroad, governments erected trade barriers to limit the number of films allowed in and froze the earnings of American companies. At home, the landmark *Paramount* antitrust case reached the U.S. Supreme Court in 1948. The court abolished block booking and a range of unfair trade practices that had kept independent theaters in a subservient position and forced the Big Five to divorce their theater chains.

The studio system went by the boards during the postwar recession as companies produced fewer films and pared producers, directors, and stars from the payrolls. The *Paramount* decrees, changing demographics, and the rise of television made the venerable studio system an outmoded form of production. Before television, when movie going was a national pastime, Hollywood's fine honed-method of producing motion pictures was ideal to meet audience demand. But no more. The most efficient means of operating under these circumstances was to tailor make big-budget pictures on an individual basis; in this way, the personnel best suited for a project could be hired to contribute their talents and afterward let go. A studio, as a result, would not be burdened with high fixed salary costs, the largest component of which was studio overhead. United Artists and Columbia, members of the Little Three, were not encumbered with theaters and were the first studios to open their doors to independent producers by offering them profit-participation deals. During the fifties, every studio, with the notable exception of MGM, had followed suit. By then, the independent producer ranks contained a mix of creative producers, packagers, directors and stars, and combinations thereof.

The *Paramount* decrees restructured the industry, but by no means did they reduce the strength of the majors. By allowing the Big Five to retain their distribution arms, the court, wittingly or not, gave them the means to retain control of the market. The reason, simply stated, is that decreasing demand for motion picture entertainment during the fifties foreclosed the distribution market to newcomers. Distribution presents high barriers to entry. To operate efficiently, a distributor requires a worldwide sales force and capital to finance twenty to thirty pictures a year. Since the market absorbed less and less product during this period, it could support only a limited number of distributors – about the same as existed at the time of the *Paramount* case. Without new competition, the majors continued to collect the lion's share of film rentals.

Overseas, the majors fared just as well, despite trade restrictions and stiffer competition from foreign producers. After the war, Hollywood, with its tremendous backlog of pictures yet to be released abroad, flooded foreign markets. Protective barriers established during the twenties and thirties had disappeared, and national film industries, with the exception of Great Britain's, had been disrupted by the war. To strengthen Hollywood's interests overseas, the Motion Picture Association of America formed the Motion Picture Export Association (MPEA) in April 1946 to function as the sole distributor of Hollywood pictures in thirteen countries closed to American films during the war. The MPEA had even more clout than other legal cartels, because Hollywood's economic interests coincided with Washington's foreign policy. The State Department saw the movies as a means to inculcate American ideology in the reopened countries. And The Marshall Plan of 1948, which aimed at restoring the economies of war-ravaged Europe, also pressed for the elimination of trade barriers.

Great Britain remained the most lucrative market for Hollywood, and it was here that Hollywood fought the hardest to retain its presence. After the war, the British Labour government devised various ways to prop up Britain's film industry. The Films Act of 1948 perpetuated a government policy instituted twenty years earlier stipulating a quota for exhibitors and distributors; the former were required to devote a certain amount of their playing time to British pictures, while the latter were required to release a certain percentage of British pictures. Then in 1950, Parliament created the Eady Pool to stimulate production. Under this plan, a levy was placed on the price of admission and the proceeds rebated to producers of quota pictures. The amount divvied out depended on the distribution gross of the picture and the size of the pool in the given year. Anyone who made a film in Great Britain could qualify for this rebate, including a foreign subsidiary of an American company. Similar protectionist measures were established in France and Italy, in particular, leading to the postwar phenomenon of runaway production.

MGM originally turned to Alexander Korda to meet its quota commitments after the war and had hired him as a producing partner in 1943 to take charge of MGM-British. The plan was for him to produce a dozen or so pictures a year for ten years using MGM talent at Denham Film Studios. But the partnership came to naught. MGM, therefore, acquired its own studio to make quota pictures and placed Benjamin Thau in charge. In 1944, Loew's purchased the Amalgamated Studios in Borehamwood outside London from Prudential Assurance and renamed it MGM British Studios. The studio had eight large stages which, at the time, were being used for war production. MGM refurbished the studio and released its first postwar British production in 1949, George Cukor's *Edward, My Son* starring Spencer Tracy and Deborah Kerr. Thereafter, the studio produced selected pictures in England to meet quota requirements and to take advantage of British locations. During the fifties, all the Hollywood majors, through their British subsidiaries, had followed suit, with devastating effect on Hollywood's labor force.

Assessing MGM's responses to the cataclysmic changes in the postwar film industry, Hughes (1957: 100) observed, 'MGM has always been a deliberate beast, almost always last in the industry to take every great forward step.' The management of Nicholas Schenck, he said, 'behaved with a sullen contempt for the forces that, in the decade from 1946 to 1956 drove down corporate income.' 'Action – or inaction on three fronts,' he said, 'contributed to this dismal decline. While the other members of the Big Five capitulated to the Supreme Court's decision by divorcing their theaters and moving on, Loew's stalled and did not complete the split until 1959.' 'During the commercial expansion of network television,' he added, 'Loew's stood on the sidelines thinking that television would need Hollywood and MGM in particular.' And 'when other studios welcomed independent producers by offering them profit-sharing deals to strengthen their distribution rosters, MGM retained its central producer status until the sixties.' 'It had this effect,' he said, 'Stars deserted the MGM lot as fast as their contracts expired. Literary agents sold their best material (*The Caine Mutiny*, *Stalag 17*, etc.) to studios willing to make percentage deals. And the greatest studio extended its near-hitless streak: in fifteen years MGM has produced but one Academy Award–winning film.'

After posting consolidated profits of $17.9 million in 1946, an all-time high for the company, Loew's consolidated earnings dropped precipitously – to $10.5 million in 1947 to $4.2 million in 1948 (Gomery 1986: 52). MGM, for its part, had its best year in 1944–45, the last year of the war; afterward the studio's earnings also dropped precipitously, hitting rock bottom in 1947–48 and posting a deficit of $6.5 million (Glancy 1992: 140). That season, 'MGM lost money for the first time in its history,' reported Eyman (2005: 380). Sixteen of the studio's twenty-five releases lost money, among them Arthur Hornblow Jr.'s production of *Desire Me* (1947) starring Greer Garson and Robert Mitchum; Pandro Berman's *Living in a Big Way* (1947) starring Gene Kelly; Joe Pasternak's *The Unfinished Dance* (1947) starring Margaret O'Brien and Cyd Charisse; and Arthur Freed's *Summer Holiday* (1948) starring Mickey Rooney and *The Pirate* (1948) staring Judy Garland and Gene Kelly.

Production costs rose substantially after the war due to inflation and higher labor costs, audiences had become more selective in their moviegoing tastes, and MGM's top stars such as Greer Garson, Margaret O'Brien, Judy Garland, and Mickey Rooney were beginning to lose their luster. Greer Garson never recovered from the *Desire Me* debacle, which lost more than $2 million. She was being typecast, and audiences had grown tired of her roles. Margaret O'Brien failed to transition into adult roles and retired from the screen in 1949. Judy Garland, who suffered from alcohol and drug abuse and exhibited erratic behavior on the set, was finally released from her contract in 1950. After *Summer Holiday*, Mickey Rooney's career slumped. He was too old to play a teenager, and he was too short to play an acceptable adult male character.

Studio reorganization

Louis B. Mayer's first response to postwar conditions was to realign the executive committee that had guided the studio through the war. In December 1947, he concentrated production authority in a triumvirate comprising Eddie Mannix and Benjamin Thau with himself as chair. The former executive duties of Mannix as general manager and Thau as casting director were assigned to Louis K. Sidney and J. J. Cohn. The other producers on the committee – Larry Weingarten, Pandro S. Berman, Joe Pasternak, Al Lichtman, Sam Katz, and James K. McGuinness – returned to full-time producing and now reported to the triumvirate. Announcing the reorganization, Mayer ('Metro Abandons' 1947) said that 'the boom days' of the film industry are over and 'indicated that the executive shuffle is aimed to ensure concentration of effort on individual pictures in an attempt to economize and improve quality.'

Mayer's reorganization got rid of some excess baggage at the executive level, but Nick Schenck insisted the studio needed 'a new Thalberg' to turn the studio around. Mayer considered David O. Selznick, Walter Wanger, and Joeseph Mankiewicz for the job and then decided on Dore Schary. Dore Schary was at liberty, having resigned as vice president in charge of production at RKO on 30 June 1948, eight weeks after Howard Hughes took control of the studio. Schary joined RKO in January 1947 after leaving the David O. Selznick's Vanguard independent outfit at United Artists. He was 42. Schary's in-house productions for RKO comprised a string of *film noirs*, such as *Crossfire* (1947), *Out of the Past* (1947), and *They Live by Night* (1948), and commercial fare, such as *The Bachelor and the Bobby-Soxer* (1947) and *I Remember Mama* (1948). On 14 July 1948, he signed a seven-year contract with MGM as vice president in charge of production at a salary of $5,000 a week (Eyman 2005: 410). Much was made of the division of responsibilities: 'Mayer, as head of the studio, establishes long-range policy and determines such matters as budgetary ceilings, while Schary confines himself to direct production problems,' reported Brady (1949).

Schary, a liberal Democrat, was an odd fit for MGM. 'Of all the Hollywood studios, MGM was the most Republican, hence the most anti-Communist,' said

FIGURE 6.1 Dore Schary

Eyman (2005: 382). MGM had most of the members of the Motion Picture Alliance for the Preservation of American Ideals on its rolls. The Alliance was a militant right-wing organization formed in 1944 that welcomed the House Committee on Un-American Activities to Hollywood. Schary was the rare Hollywood studio executive to stand up to HUAC when it held hearings in Hollywood in 1947 to investigate the alleged Communist infiltration into the motion picture industry. He told the committee ('Movies' 1947) 'that he would not discharge an employee because he was a Communist.' However, he sided with the industry leaders who convened a two-day closed session at the Waldorf-Astoria Hotel in November and voted unanimously 'to refuse employment to Communists and to "discharge or suspend without compensation" the ten Hollywood figures who have been cited for contempt of Congress.' Two RKO employees – Adrian Scott and Edward Dmytryk, the producer and director of *Crossfire* – were members of the Hollywood Ten and lost their jobs. Schary explained to the press, 'What I told the Un-American Activities Committee was my own personal view. However, I also stated that the ultimate policy would have to be made by the president of RKO. That policy has now been established. As an employee of the company, I will abide by the decision.'

Mayer didn't seem to care what writers did in their spare time; he was only concerned about results. At the 1947 HUAC hearings, Mayer denied that Communist propaganda could be injected into any MGM picture and enumerated the anti-Communist pictures the studio had made, such as *Ninotchka* and *Comrade X*. Regarding *The Song of Russia*, Mayer pointed out that the picture was made with the approval of the OWI and was simply a musical salute to America's wartime ally. However, he went on to say that he would not knowingly employ any card-carrying Communist. Two MGM employees – screenwriters Dalton Trumbo and Lester Cole – were also members of the Hollywood Ten. They too lost their jobs and were sent to federal penitentiary along with the others.

Production trends

Schary's first three seasons

Taking charge, Schary trimmed production budgets, wrote off dubious properties, and devised ways to better utilize contract players. Like Thalberg, he intended to personally produce one or two pictures a year, but unlike Thalberg, he intended to take screen credit for them. At the end of Schary's first year as production chief, 1948–49, MGM rebounded from a $6.5 million deficit the year before and posted a modest profit of $300,000. In fiscal 1949–50, the studio posted profits of $3.9 million, and in fiscal 1950–51, profits of $8.1 million (Eyman 2005: 418, 441). For a while, MGM was outperforming the other majors.

Top hits of the 1948–49 season included Pandro S. Berman's production of *The Three Musketeers* (1948) and Jack Cummings's *Neptune's Daughter* (1949) and *The Stratton Story* (1949). George Sidney's *The Three Musketeers*, was a swaggering, tongue-in-cheek swashbuckler starring Gene Kelly, Lana Turner, and June Allyson. It ranked number one on the season's roster. Eddie Buzzell's *Neptune's Daughter* (1949) was an Esther Williams vehicle which Crowther described as 'a great big beautiful musical, full of slickness and Technicolored plush, models and Xavier Cugat rhythm and Esther Williams in a water ballet' (*NYTFR*, 30 June 1949). Frank Loesser's 'Baby, It's Cold Outside,' a duet sung by Ricardo Montalban and Williams, won an Oscar for Best Song. Sam Wood's *The Stratton Story* (1949) was a biopic of the Chicago White Sox pitcher Monty Stratton starring James Stewart and June Allyson.

Top hits of the 1949–50 season included two Spencer Tracy pictures – Lawrence Weingarten's production of *Adam's Rib* (1949) and Pandro S. Berman's *Father of the Bride* (1950) – and Dore Schary's *Battleground* (1949). After starring in MGM's ill-considered *Edward, My Son* (1949), the studio's first postwar British production, Tracy staged a comeback in *Adam's Rib*, a screwball comedy directed by George

FIGURE 6.2 Elizabeth Taylor and Spencer Tracy in Vincente Minnelli's *Father of the Bride* (1950)

Cukor. It was the sixth Tracy–Hepburn pairing, with a supporting role featuring Judy Holliday, the star of Garson Kanin's Broadway farce, *Born Yesterday*. Ruth Gordon and Garson Kanin wrote the screenplay. As described by Crowther, 'Miss Gordon and Mr. Kanin, who also are husband and wife, mix up their charming people by a far-fetched but clever device,' he said. 'They make the husband the prosecutor of a woman who has shot her spouse and they make the wife defense counsel for this miserably unhappy dame. And then they introduce a question of female equality between the two and let them fight it out roundly in the courtroom and in their home' (*NYTFR*, 26 December 1949). Regarding Judy Holliday's performance, *Variety* said, 'A better realization on type than Holliday's portrayal of a dumb Brooklyn femme doesn't seem possible' (*VFR*, 2 November 1949). Her performance led to a starring role in Columbia's *Born Yesterday* (1950) directed by George Cukor, which earned her an Academy Award for Best Actress.

Father of the Bride, directed by Vincente Minnelli, was based on Edward Streeter's 1949 novel about a middle-class tribal matrimonial rite. Frances Goodrich and Albert Hackett wrote the screenplay. As Maslin (1991) described it, '*Father of the Bride*' is an affectionate reminder of the days when parties required stiff protocol, suburban life was martini-filled and gracious, a majority of one's college classmates were likely to be married and a father was truly a patriarch, valiantly meeting the fiscal and emotional needs of everyone in his household.' Crowther described

FIGURE 6.3 John Hodiak, Van Johnson, and Thomas E. Breen in William Wellman's *Battleground* (1949)

Tracy's performance by saying, 'As a father, torn by jealousy, devotion, pride and righteous wrath, Mr. Tracy is tops' (*NYTFR*, 19 May 1950). Eighteen-year-old Elizabeth Taylor played the bride and Joan Bennett the mother. The picture was nominated for three Oscars, for Best Picture, Best Actor, and Best Screenplay.

Dore Schary had intended to make *Battleground* at RKO. He had commissioned Robert Pirosh, a former soldier and veteran of the Battle of the Bulge, to write the screenplay, but Howard Hughes ordered Schary to cancel the project. After joining MGM, Schary bought the screenplay from Hughes and hired Pirosh to see it through. Mayer thought that audiences had grown weary of war pictures, but Schary persisted and got Nick Schenck to approve it. Schary's movie directed by William Wellman eschewed war movie heroics and focused on the loneliness and struggles of a group of men from the 101st Airborne during the Battle of the Bulge in 1944. The principal cast included Van Johnson, John Hodiak, James Whitmore, George Murphy, and Ricardo Montalban. The picture premiered in New York on Armistice Day, 11 November 1949, at the Astor as a roadshow. Crowther described *Battleground* as *The Big Parade* of World War II and 'the best of the World War II pictures that have yet been made in Hollywood. 'For here, without bluff or bluster or the usual distracting clichés that have somehow crept into the war films . . . is a smashing pictorial re-creation of the way that this last one was for the dirty and frightened foot-soldier who got caught in a filthy deal.' 'Here,' he said, 'is the unadorned image of the misery, the agony, the grief and the still irrepressible humor and dauntless mockery of the American GI' (*NYTFR*, 12 November 1949). *Battleground* was a huge hit and became the studio's most profitable picture of the year. The picture was nominated for four Oscars, including Best Picture and Best Director, and won awards for Best Writing (Robert Pirosh) and Best Black-and-White Cinematography (Paul Vogel). 'The film's commercial success became a personal vindication for Schary, who had successfully stood his ground against Mayer,' said Hay (1991: 262).

Top hits of the 1950–51 season included two exotic adventure films – *King Solomon's Mines* (1950) and *Kim* (1950) – and a biblical epic, *Quo Vadis* (1951). *King Solomon's Mines*, produced by Sam Zimbalist and directed by Compton Bennett, starred Deborah Kerr and Stewart Granger. It was based on the Victorian novel by Sir H. Rider Haggard, which told the story of an African hunter who takes an English lady and her brother in search of her missing husband. As *Variety* noted, the picture had 'all the ingredients to capture public fancy.' It was shot 'against an authentic African background' and contained 'several socko, ticket-selling values,' among them 'an elephant hunt, a lion pack, hippos, rhinos, monkeys, crocodiles, and an animal stampede, minutes long, that roars across the screen to the terrifying noise of panic-driven hoofbeats' (*VFR*, 27 September 1950). The

FIGURE 6.4 Peter Ustinov, Patricia Laffan, and Robert Taylor in Mervyn LeRoy's *Quo Vadis* (1951)

picture earned a profit of more than $4 million, making it MGM's top money earner of 1950. *Kim*, produced by Leon Gordon and directed by Victor Saville, starred Errol Flynn and Dean Stockwell. It was based on Rudyard Kipling's novel about the strange adventures of an orphan boy during the British Raj. Like *King Solomon's Mines*, *Kim* was shot on authentic locations and contained elements that 'fill and bedazzle the eye,' said Crowther – 'elephants, caravans, bazaars and brilliant British regiments on parade' (*NYTFR*, 8 December 1950).

In 'size, scope, splash and dash,' *Quo Vadis* 'gave for the first time in a long while credence to the now "super-colossal term,"' said *Variety*. 'It's right up there with *Birth of a Nation* and *Gone With the Wind* for boxoffice performance' (*VFR*, 14 November 1951). The three-hour Technicolor spectacle set in Nero's Rome, was based on Henryk Sienkiewicz's novel first published in 1895, which enjoyed continued popularity due 'to the fact that it is a dramatic synthesis of purported religious history and highly colored fictional romance spiced with an arrestingly frank presentation of moral depravity among the ruling Romans,' said Spiro (1950). The picture was produced by Sam Zimbalist and directed by Mervyn LeRoy. It starred Robert Taylor as Marcus Vinicius, the Roman military commander, Deborah Kerr as Lygia, the converted Christian slave girl, Leo Genn as Petronius, and Peter Ustinov as Nero.

MGM set up production in Rome's Cinecittà Studios to release blocked funds and to take advantage of cheap Italian labor. MGM's production crew comprised more than fifty people. MGM needed thousands of extras for the picture and hundreds of workmen to build Nero's palace, the Circus Maximus, Roman shops and streets, and other costly sets. *Quo Vadis* had its world premiere in New York on 8 November 1951 at two theaters – the Astor on a reserved-seat basis and the Capitol. Scenes such as 'the triumphal greeting of victorious legions returned from far-off wars, the slaughter of Christian martyrs in the vast arena, the horrendous burning of Rome . . . huge orgies of drinking and love-making' provided the mass appeal,' said Crowther (1951). 'But within and around these visual triumphs and rich imagistic displays is tediously twined a hackneyed romance that threatens to set your teeth on edge,' he said. 'And the notion that Nero was a monster and a numbskull is pounded at such length, in scenes of unending conversations, that patience is sorely tried.' 'We have a suspicion,' he concluded, 'that this picture was not made for the overly sensitive or discriminate. It was made, we suspect, for those who like grandeur and noise – and no punctuation. It will probably be a vast success' (*NYTFR*, 9 November 1951). *Quo Vadis* was MGM's biggest-grossing picture since *Gone With the Wind*, earning a profit of $5.4 million.

Schary's message pictures

After *Battleground*, Schary wanted MGM to remain relevant in the postwar period, and during his watch, the studio soon released a number of so-called message pictures, among them, *Intruder in the Dust* (1949), *Go for Broke!* (1951), and *The Red Badge of Courage* (1951). *Intruder in the Dust*, produced and directed by Clarence Brown, was based on the William Faulkner novel about a white boy and older woman who save an innocent black man falsely accused of murdering a white man. *Go for Broke!*, produced by Schary and directed by Robert Pirosh, was based on a true story of Japanese Americans who volunteered to serve in the 442nd Regimental Combat Team to prove their allegiance to the United States.

The Red Badge of Courage, produced by Wolfgang Reinhardt and directed by John Huston, was based on Stephen Crane's Civil War novel published in 1895. This was John Huston's second picture on his two-picture contract for MGM. His first, *The Asphalt Jungle* (1950), based on the W. R. Burnett novel, was a classic caper movie and the latest in a string of MGM *film noirs* that included *The Postman Always Rings Twice* and *Lady in the Lake* (1947), and *Caught* (1949). *The Red Badge of Courage* was John Huston's idea, but Mayer hated it and wanted to cancel the project. Schary, however, liked it very much and again appealed to Nick Schenck for a final decision. Schenck decided to side with Schary.

According to Lillian Ross (1993: 15), 'Huston, like Stephen Crane, wanted to show something of the emotions of men in war, and the ironically thin line between cowardice and heroism.' To play Henry Fleming, the young Union soldier who is sent into battle for the first time, Huston cast Audie Murphy, the most decorated hero of World War II. The preview was a disappointment, which led Schary to take drastic action. He had the picture recut and shortened and added a voice-over narration, among other things. MGM's sales force, nonetheless, lost faith in the picture and failed to support its release. The picture received positive reviews in the *New York Times* and *Los Angeles Times*, but *Variety*, with its finger on the moviegoing pulse, said, 'Boxoffice appeal in the general market is rather limited . . . There is some merit for either presentation in the sureseater art house or the small showcase theatre where a run can be stretched to the maximum but, in any case, big returns do not appear likely' (*VFR*, 15 August 1951). *The Red Badge of Courage* ended up losing $1 million and validated Louis B. Mayer's earlier assessment of its commercial potential.

Although Mayer's prediction had proven correct, Schenck's decision to greenlight the movie brought Mayer's grievances to a head. Mayer had detested Schary's message pictures all along; he felt Schary was not properly deferential towards him, and he felt that he was no longer top man at the studio. These and other grievances, real and imagined, led Mayer to resign from the studio on 23 June 1951. Actually, he might have been fired. Reports later stated that Mayer gave Schenck an ultimatum – 'It's either him or me!' – and Schenck chose Schary. Mayer announced his intention to remain in motion picture production. 'It will be at a studio and under conditions where I shall have the right to make pictures – decent, wholesome pictures for Americans and for people throughout the world who want and need this type of entertainment,' he said. As part of the settlement, Mayer retained 'a 10 percent interest in the future earnings of all the pictures produced or initiated during his long incumbency' (Brady 1951).

Dore Schary at the helm

With Mayer gone, Nicholas Schenck gave Dore Schary full charge of the studio. Unlike other Hollywood studios that were opening their doors to independent producers by putting up production financing and making profit-participation deals, MGM remained under the control of a central producer. Like Louis B. Mayer before him, Schary worked with an executive committee, which now comprised Eddie Mannix, Benjamin Thau, and Louis K. Sidney. But he had to make do with less. In July 1952, Nick Schenck instituted a sweeping economy move, the first since the Depression, that slashed the salaries of executives in the home office and reduced the number of people working at the studio. At its peak, the studio employed 6,000. In 1952, MGM had 4,000 employees on its payroll ('MGM Slashes Pay' 1952). By 1953, the number had been reduced to 2,700.

Production trends

The big picture

In an attempt to rekindle interest in the movies during the rise of television, Hollywood adopted the adage 'We'll give them something television can't.' The motion picture industry, as a result, decided to make moviegoing a special event by differentiating its product from television fare. It would exploit the 'Big Picture,' big budget items based on presold properties that were often shot in authentic locales around the world in color utilizing widescreen processes, such as Cinema-Scope and VistaVision. At the exhibition level, such pictures were often initially released as roadshows on a reserved-seat basis, two a day at advanced prices.

The widescreen revolution was launched by two short-lived novelties in 1952, Cinerama and 3-D. CinemaScope, the one process to make a real impact on the entire industry, was the innovation of 20th Century Fox. CinemaScope made its debut in *The Robe*, which opened at the Roxy in New York on 16 September 1953. After a week of sensational business, the picture opened in a hundred other cities with the same results. Partly because of the widescreen process and partly because of the narrative, *The Robe* set an industry record, grossing more than $30 million (Lev 2003: 118). Here was the signal the industry wanted to jump on the widescreen bandwagon. On the eve of *The Robe*'s release, Schary announced, 'We at MGM – all of us – believe that the future of the motion picture industry will depend, number one, on the quality of the stories that are told and the use of a variety of presentations best suited to the individual story.' He said this in rebuttal to Darryl F. Zanuck, Fox's production chief, who stated that 'Hollywood will rise or fall on the success of *The Robe*' (Pryor 1953).

Once again, MGM relied on swashbucklers to do the job. British star Stewart Granger had been given a seven-year contract after his success in *King Solomon's Mines*. He went on to make two more Technicolor swashbucklers, George Sidney's

Scaramouche (1952) and Richard Thorpe's *The Prisoner of Zenda* (1952). He was perfect for such roles, said Crowther: 'He has the build of an athlete, a chest that can proudly be exposed and the face of a dauntless Adonis who gallantly leaps to muscular deeds' (*NYTFR*, 5 November 1952). *The Prisoner of Zenda* fared the best. It was the third remake of Anthony Hope's 1897 Ruritanian adventure novel and costarred Deborah Kerr. 'Fanciers of costumed swashbucklers will find this remake of the venerable *Prisoner of Zenda* a likeable version,' said *Variety* (*VFR*, 5 May 1952).

Pandro Berman and Richard Thorpe, the producer–director team responsible for *The Prisoner of Zenda*, went on to make two more swashbuckler hits starring Robert Taylor, *Ivanhoe* (1952) and *Knights of the Round Table* (1953). They were set in medieval England when knighthood was in flower and based at MGM-British Studios outside London to enable MGM to recover frozen funds and to take advantage of authentic locations. *Ivanhoe* was based on Sir Walter Scott's classic novel about a young knight's quest to restore Richard the Lion Heart, the imprisoned Saxon King, to the throne. It costarred Elizabeth Taylor, Joan Fontaine, George Sanders, and Emlyn Williams. After Robert Taylor's brilliant performance as Marcus Vinicius in *Quo Vadis*, he was a natural for the role of Ivanhoe. MGM-British spent two years reproducing Scott's Torquilstone Castle, which was nearly as large as the sets for *Quo Vadis*. 'Ivanhoe is no ordinary swashbuckler, but a big

FIGURE 6.5 Robert Taylor in Richard Thorpe's *Ivanhoe* (1952)

screen creation of knights and their ladies and the spirit of battle and romance as they might be imagined moviewise for the Middle Ages,' said Schallert (1952). There was a lot to keep action fans happy: 'the jousting of the title character with five successive opponents in the tournament, the siege and conquest of the Norman castle by the Robin Hood-like band of archers collaborating with the Saxons, and the final ghastly, horrible duel between Ivanhoe and De Bois Guillbert, armed with the deadly axe and the almost as lethal mace and chain.'

Crowther admired the handling of the 'original sub-theme of anti-Semitism in medieval England.' Aeneas MacKenzie and Noel Langley, the writers, 'have kept the story of Rebecca, the beautiful Jewess, and Isaac, her father, well to the fore. And they have emphasized such episodes in the novel as the beating of Isaac and the trial of Rebecca as a witch to highlight the sobering implications of the universal injustice of social bigotry' (*NYTFR*, 1 August 1952). *Ivanhoe* was nominated for three Academy Awards, for Best Picture, Best Score, and Best Cinematography. It was MGM's first British picture to be successful at the box office and was MGM's top-grossing picture of the year.

Knights of the Round Table was inspired by Thomas Malory's classic *Morte d'Arthur*, the Camelot tale of King Arthur, Sir Lancelot, and Queen Guinevere. It starred Taylor, Ava Gardner, and Mel Ferrer. Talbot Jennings, Jan Lustig, and Noel Langley adapted the screenplay. *Knights of the Round Table* was MGM's first picture in CinemaScope and was released just four months after *The Robe*. Because most theaters had yet to convert to the widescreen process, MGM shot a flat version of the film as well. Berman wanted his picture to surpass *The Robe* in spectacle. Like *Ivanhoe*, it was filled with jousts, tournaments, and knightly battles. A battle sequence shot in Ireland along the Liffey River used 1,000 members of the Irish Free State Army and was designed 'to top any battle scene ever filmed, including the surging, long-remembered one in Olivier's *Henry V*,' said Hudgins (1953). Crowther described the battle as 'awesome to see.' But the picture itself, he said, was 'straight Hollywood.' 'This highly scenic conglomeration of panoply and horse opera is standard, unsubtle entertainment on a panoramic scale' (*NYTFR*, 22 November 1953). *Variety* admitted the picture was 'storybook stuff – and must be accepted as such – but the astute staging results in a walloping package of entertainment for all except, perhaps, the blasé' (*VFR*, 23 December 1953).

Musicals

The musical remained MGM's signature production trend during Schary's reign. As Schatz (1997: 375) has pointed out, MGM 'actually increased its musical output' after the war. . . . In the decade following World War II,' he noted, 'musicals comprised more than 25 percent of MGM total output (81 of 316 total releases), while MGM musicals comprised more than half the total made in Hollywood.' Most were shot in Technicolor. The appeal of Technicolor in *Meet Me in St. Louis* convinced the company of the market value of the medium. MGM's musical units headed by Arthur Freed, Joe Pasternak, and Jack Cummings continued to work semi-autonomously under Schary. But musicals were no longer the most profitable items on MGM's roster. None could compare to such hits as *Father of the Bride* or *Quo Vadis*. Musicals were expensive to produce; during the fifties, motion picture attendance was declining rapidly, and there were fewer theater admissions to support MGM's bigger-budget items. Moreover, teenagers, who comprised the largest segment of the audience during the rise of television, were developing a subculture of their own that was more in tune with rock 'n roll than with the Tin Pan Alley melodies proffered by MGM. And lastly, MGM's producers were too often content with tried-and-true formulas rather than innovating.

Arthur Freed hit his stride after the war, producing three hit stage adaptations: *On the Town* (1949), based on the 1944 Broadway musical by Leonard Bernstein, Betty Comden, and Adolph Green about 'three sailors who hit New York on a twenty-four-hour leave with two intentions: to see the sights and meet three girls'; *Annie Get Your Gun* (1950), based on the Richard Rodgers and Oscar Hammerstein II production starring Ethel Merman as Annie Oakley, a backwoods marksman who joins Buffalo Bill's Wild West Show; and *Show Boat* (1951), the third film adaptation of the Jerome Kern and Oscar Hammerstein II Broadway musical based on the novel by Edna Ferber. *On the Town* was the most inventive. It was directed and choreographed by Gene Kelly and Stanley Donen and starred Gene Kelly and Frank Sinatra. Kelly and Donen 'invested it with so much that was new and exciting,' said Hirschhorn (1981: 308). 'They changed the entire concept of the film musical, opening it out (some of it was actually filmed on location in New York and its environs) and relying on the dance for its chief mode of musical expression. The underlying feeling of the film was essentially balletic.' The film was an instant box-office success and won the Academy Award for Best Music, Scoring of a Musical Picture.

Show Boat was the most profitable. Freed's latest version of the American musical classic was directed by George Sidney and adapted for the screen by John Lee Mahin. It starred Kathryn Grayson as Magnolia Hawks, Howard Keel as Gaylord Ravenel, and Ava Gardner as Julia Laverne. Crowther said, *Show Boat* 'has never reached the screen . . . in anything like the visual splendor and richness of musical score as are tastefully brought together in this brilliant re-creation of the show.' 'As often as one may have listened to "Make Believe" and "You Are Love",' he said, 'they still sound original and exciting as sung by Kathryn Grayson and Howard Keel. "Ol' Man River" has been blunted by thousands of bass baritones, yet it thrusts to the heart when William Warfield sings it on the banks of the muddy river in the misty dawn.' 'And even though "Bill" is as banal as "La Vie en Rose" in the night club realms,' he added, 'it is haunting and moving as it ripples from Ava Gardner's throat' (*NYTFR*, 20 July 1951).

Freed achieved his greatest critical success with *An American in Paris* (1951), *Singin' in the Rain* (1952), and *The Band Wagon* (1953), prime examples of Freed's 'integrated musicals' with their 'seamless combination of music, dance, narrative, art direction, and camera movement' (Lev 2003: 34). Freed's unit now comprised an impressive array of artists: they included producer Roger Edens; director Vincente Minnelli; choreographer-directors Gene Kelly, Stanley Donen, Charles Walters,

FIGURE 6.6 Howard Keel and Kathryn Grayson in George Sidney's *Show Boat* (1951)

and Robert Alton; arrangers Conrad Salinger, Johnny Green, Saul Chaplin, Adolph Deutsch, and André Previn; writers Alan Jay Lerner and the team of Betty Comden and Adolph Green; and musical stars Gene Kelly, Fred Astaire, Cyd Charisse, Leslie Caron, Frank Sinatra, Debbie Reynolds, and Donald O'Connor.

Vincente Minnelli's *An American in Paris* starred Gene Kelly and Leslie Caron. Alan Jay Lerner wrote the script, and the songs were by George and Ira Gershwin. *Variety* stated that the film was 'one of the most imaginative musical confections turned out by Hollywood in years.' It was most impressed with Kelly's choreography: 'There's a lengthy ballet to the film's title song for the finale, which is a masterpiece of design, lighting, costumes and color photography. It's a unique blending of classical and modern dance with vaude-style tapping, which will undoubtedly trailblaze new terp techniques for Hollywood musicals' (*VFR*, 29 August 1951). Crowther was equally impressed with Caron, who made her screen debut: 'Miss Caron is not a beauteous thing, in the sense of classic features, but she has a sweet face and a most delightful smile. Furthermore, she has winsomeness, expression and youthful dignity – and she can dance like a gossamer wood-sprite on the edge of a petal at dawn' (*NYTFR*, 5 October 1951). Among the standout Gershwin songs were 'I Got Rhythm,' which Kelly sang and danced to a group of 'French moppets,' and 'Embraceable You,' which 'served to introduce Miss Caron's terp talents in highly imaginative style,' said *Variety* (*VFR*, 29 August 1951). *An American in Paris* won six Academy Awards for Best Picture, Writing (Story & Screenplay), Cinematography, Art Direction (Color), Best Score of a Musical Picture, and Costume Design (Color).

Singin' in the Rain, directed by Gene Kelly and Stanley Donen, starred Kelly, Donald O'Connor on loan from Universal, and a 19-year-old Debbie Reynolds in her first major role. This 'breezy, good-natured spoof at the film industry' during the early sound period was written by Adolph Green and Betty Comden and built around the song catalogue of Arthur Freed and Herb Nacio Brown. The songs dated back to the earliest days of the talkies and populated many an MGM musical. Among the many delights of the picture were the ballet sequence 'Broadway Ballet,' choreographed by Kelly and danced by Cyd Charisse; Gene Kelly's rain-soaked dance solo, 'Singin' in the Rain'; the song and dance duet by Kelly and Debbie Reynolds, 'You Were Meant For Me'; and the slapstick song-and-dance number 'Make Them Laugh' by Donald O'Connor. Although *Singin' in the Rain* went on to become an American classic, it earned only a modest amount of $666,000, compared to profits of $1.5 million for *An American in Paris* and $2.3 million for *Show Boat*. And it received only two Academy Award nominations, for Best Musical Score and for Best Supporting Actress. The latter went to Jean Hagen, who played Lina Lamont, the glamorous, screechy-voice movie queen.

Vincente Minnelli's *The Band Wagon* (1953) starred Fred Astaire, Cyd Charisse, Jack Buchanan, Oscar Levant, and Nanette Fabray. It was a putting-on-a-show musical written by Betty Comden and Adolph Green about a has-been Hollywood hoofer trying to make a Broadway comeback. Howard Dietz and Arthur Schwartz, who wrote the songs, were best known for writing some of Broadway's greatest shows of the thirties, including the 1931 *The Band Wagon*, produced by Flo Ziegfeld, which starred Fred Astaire and his sister Adele. The musical highlights in the film include the Astaire–Charisse 'Dancing in the Dark,' the Fabray and Chorus 'Louisiana Hayride,' the Astaire–Buchanan 'I Guess I'll Have to Change my Plan,' and the rousing finale with the cast singing 'That's Entertainment,' which Dietz and Schwartz wrote especially for the movie. The ballet sequence in this movie,

FIGURE 6.7 Donald O'Connor, Debbie Reynolds, and Gene Kelly in Gene Kelly and Stanley Donen's *Singin' in the Rain* (1952)

performed by Astaire and Cyd Charisse and staged by Michael Kidd, was titled 'The Girl Hunt' and was a parody of Mickey Spillane crime thrillers. The *Band Wagon* received rave reviews. Crowther called it 'one of the best musicals ever made' (*NYTFR*, 19 July 1953). *Variety* said that Arthur Freed and director Vincente Minnelli 'have come up with another show biz musical that looks a sure b.o. winner' (*VFR*, 8 July 1953). But sadly, *The Band Wagon* failed at the box office and posted a loss of more than $1 million.

After Louis B. Mayer departed the studio, 'both the quantity and quality of Freed's work dropped sharply,' said Eyman (2005: 462). 'He averaged one picture a year from 1953 to 1958.' Freed relied mostly on pretested material – long-running Broadway shows, such as Alan Jay Lerner and Frederick Loewe's *Brigadoon* (1954), Robert Wright and George Forrest's *Kismet* (1955), and Cole Porter's *Silk Stockings* (1957). To no avail; they were all box-office failures.

Joe Pasternak, MGM's most prolific producer of musicals, continued to nurture MGM's top female singing talent, in particular Esther Williams, Lana Turner, and Jane Powell. And in 1947, he took charge of MGM's newest musical discovery, Mario Lanza, a young tenor from Philadelphia with a spectacular voice. After *Bathing Beauty* in 1944, Esther Williams went on to make a dozen more musicals until 1955. They adhered to the same predictable formulas, which typically featured elaborate aquatic sequences choreographed by Busby Berkeley, music by

FIGURE 6.8 Cyd Charisse and Fred Astaire in Vincente Minnelli's *The Band Wagon* (1953)

Xavier Cugat and his orchestra, dance numbers performed by Ann Miller or Cyd Charisse, and gags performed by Red Skelton, Lucille Ball, or Keenan Wynn.

Pasternak found the perfect vehicle for Esther Williams after the war, Charles Walters's *Easy to Love* (1953). She was again teamed with Van Johnson, this time in a Cypress Gardens, Florida, setting. 'The Pasternak touch is amply evident in the film,' said *Variety*. 'Every possible advantage is taken of the Cypress Gardens location as the camera moves to the water skiing climax which has sock visual appeal as some 20 or 30 motorboats peal across the waters, leaving a foamy wake and forming an exciting pattern with the water skiers themselves.' 'Too bad that the story had to be so lightweight,' it said. 'Esther Williams, shapely and vivacious as the much sought-after aquatic star whose only aim in life is to "hook" Van Johnson, delivers her usual cheerful performance' (*VFR*, 11 November 1953).

Esther Williams was at the top of her career when she made *Easy to Love*. She went on to star in Pasternak's *On an Island with You* (1948), Jack Cummings's *Neptune's Daughter* (1948), Arthur Hornblow Jr.'s *Million Dollar Mermaid* (1952), and George Sidney's *Jupiter's Darling* (1955). *Jupiter's Darling* marked her fall. It was based on Robert E. Sherwood's 1927 satirical antiwar comedy *Road to Rome* dealing with Hannibal's invasion of Rome. Howard Keel costarred. 'Esther Williams must be getting bored with water. She goes swimming only three times in MGM's *Jupiter's Darling*,' said Crowther, 'and two of these times are forced upon her. She dunks only once for fun. And that, we might note, is the most attractive and buoyant thing in the film' (*NYTFR*, 18 February 1955). The picture lost more than $2 million. Williams had grown weary of appearing in inferior films and walked out on her MGM contract, forfeiting $3 million in deferred salary that had been set aside for her for income tax purposes ('Jupiter's Darling' 1955).

Casting Lana Turner in Pasternak's *The Merry Widow* (1952), the Franz Lehar war horse, was Dore Schary's idea to revive a faltering career. Turner was not a trained singer, and any singing her part required would have to be dubbed. MGM signed Lana Turner to a contract in 1938, when she was 17. After appearing in Mickey Rooney's *Love Finds Andy Hardy* (1938) and other inexpensive pictures, MGM gave her a new contract and teamed her with the studio's top male star, Clark Gable, in Pandro S. Berman's *Honky Tonk* (1941) and *Somewhere I'll Find You* (1942), Gable's last picture before joining the Army. They were big hits. Around this time, Howard Strickling, MGM's publicity chief, came up with a sobriquet 'The Sweater Girl' for Miss Turner, which stayed with her to the end of her career. During World War II, she was one of the armed forces' favorite pinups. Her next big opportunity came in 1946, when she was cast as a femme fatale opposite John Garfield in Tay Garnett's *The Postman Always Rings Twice* (1946), a *film noir* based on the James M. Cain's crime novel about a doomed love affair. The picture made more than $1 million in profit. MGM then cast her in a series of successful costume pictures, among them *The Three Musketeers* (1948) with Gene Kelly. Afterward, her career faltered.

Curtis Bernhardt's *The Merry Widow* was Turner's comeback film. It costarred Fernando Lamas. Crowther described the picture as 'the most colorful and exquisite' version of the operetta. 'The brilliance in Technicolor of the palaces, grand hotels and a replica of Maxim's in Paris that craftsmen at Metro have contrived is something to take your breath away, and the richness of the costumes and the staging of the dance and choral groups will deal the knockout blow' (*NYTFR*, 25 September 1952). Scheuer (1952a) said, Miss Turner 'has never given a performance of comparable warmth . . . [S]he is portraying an American girl, and she brings to the role all the peculiarity attractive qualities of one – including a certain air of little-girl defiance, of impulsiveness bordering on brashness – in which many a shop clerk and deb will recognize themselves.' Turner received a new seven-year contract afterward. She acquitted herself well in John Houseman's *The Bad and the Beautiful*, costarring with Kirk Douglas, but then slipped in popularity after appearing with Fernando Lamas in *Latin Lovers* (1952), a witless tongue-in-cheek romance directed by Mervyn LeRoy, and other ill-chosen pictures. She finally bought out her MGM contract in 1956.

Pasternak had been grooming Jane Powell since 1946, when she appeared in her first MGM musical, George Sidney's *Holiday in Mexico* (1946). MGM signed her to a contract in 1944 after she had won a spot on the Los Angeles radio talent show, *Stars Over Hollywood*. Her first two pictures were made at United Artists on loanout to producer Charles R. Rogers. Crowther said they were 'best forgotten in light of the way she shines' in *Holiday in Mexico*, which he described as 'lovely to look at and delightful to hear.' Miss Powell 'doesn't have as yet the easy charm Deanna Durbin exhibited,' he said, 'but given a little more time under the expert tutelage of Mr. Pasternak there is no reason why she, too, shouldn't become the moviegoer's singing sweetheart' (*NYTFR*, 16 August 1946). Powell played the precocious teen-age daughter of the American ambassador to Mexico (Walter Pidgeon) who develops a crush on an older singer (Jose Iturbi). The trite story provided her the opportunity to sing Schubert's 'Ave Maria,' Victor Herbert's 'Italian Street Song,' Delibes's '*Les Filles de Cadiz*' and 'I Think of You,' based on Sergei Rachmaninoff's Second Piano Concerto, among other songs. She had plenty of musical backup from Illona Massey, Jose Iturbi, and Xavier Cugat. The picture was a hit, and MGM gave her a new three-year contract.

Powell made a dozen musicals for MGM, nine of which were produced by Pasternak. Her two biggest hits were Richard Thorpe's *A Date With Judy* (1948) and Stanley Donen's *Royal Wedding* (1951). *A Date With Judy*, based on characters in the weekly radio program created by Aleen Leslie, was a 'romantic fable about young love and complications,' in *Variety*'s words, which provided the excuse for songs by Powell and musical backup support by Carmen Miranda and Xavier Cugat (*VFR*, 23 June 1948). The picture turned in the highest profit of the 1947–48 season for the studio: $1.5 million. *Royal Wedding* was produced by Arthur Freed. Miss Powell and Fred Astaire played a brother–sister musical team who take their act to London while preparations are made for the royal wedding of Elizabeth II and Prince Phillip. In between the musical numbers, 'Astaire falls in love with Sarah Churchill, a show hoofer, and Miss Powell catches the love bug from Peter Lawford, an English lord-romeo.' The story and screenplay by

Alan Jay Lerner, with music by Burton Lane, was inspired by Fred Astaire's dance partnership with his sister Adele, which broke up when she married into nobility in England. As *Variety* noted, 'two of the numbers are sock enough to almost carry the picture by themselves. They are Astaire's solo dance on a ceiling upside-down, and the teaming with Miss Powell in a sort of Frankie-and-Johnny-apache-hepcat presentation that will click with audiences' (*VFR*, 7 February 1951).

Powell's subsequent pictures save one, *Seven Brides for Seven Brothers* (1954), followed a predictable formula. 'On the assumption that a snugly familiar tale, with a clock-work sprinkling of song and dance and a fine supporting cast will turn the trick,' as a *New York Times* critic said of *Small Town Girl*, 'that seasoned impresario, Joe Pasternak, the producer, has mechanized a dandy array of talent along wholesome but standard lines. Minus, we might add, the two most important ingredients of any musical, originality and pace' (*NYTFR*, 7 May 1953). Powell tired of playing the perennial adolescent. Her last picture for MGM was *Hit the Deck* (1955). MGM could no longer find suitable roles for her, and she was let go at age 29.

Mario Lanza had been brought to Louis B. Mayer's attention by Ida Koverman, his private secretary, after attending Lanza's Hollywood Bowl debut in August 1947. Mayer signed him to a multiple-picture and turned him over to Pasternak to groom him as the singing Clark Gable. It took Pasternak a year to get him ready for his first MGM picture, *That Midnight Kiss* (1949) directed by Norman Taurog, a romanticized story that was loosely based on Lanza's life about a singing truck driver who makes his operatic debut. Pasternak loaded the picture with 'music and talent galore,' which was supplied by José Iturbi, Kathryn Grayson, Ethel Barrymore, Thomas Gomez, and J. Carrol Naish. The slim plot allowed Lanza to perform operatic arias, a duet with Miss Grayson, and a song by Jerome Kern. Crowther's verdict: 'As for the budding Mr. Lanza, the opinion rendered of him by the sanguine Mr. Iturbi is good enough for us. "His voice," says Mr. Iturbi, "has quality and warmth and he has a very nice personality." Check. We'll wait to see how he can act' (*NYTFR*, 23 September 1949).

Lanza would never be known for his acting. In his next picture, Norman Taurog's *The Toast of New Orleans* (1950), Lanza played a singing fisherman and again was surrounded by 'music and talent galore.' In addition to the usual opera arias, Lanza and Kathryn Grayson sang the Oscar-nominated ballad, 'Be My Love,' music by the Nicholas Brodszky and lyrics by Sammy Cahn. Although the picture barely broke even, MGM figured that it might have another Jeanette MacDonald–Nelson Eddy singing team. Lanza's third picture, Richard Thorpe's *The Great Caruso* (1951), was his biggest hit. Crowther described the fictionalized biopic of the great Italian tenor Enrico Caruso written by Sonya Levien and William Ludwig as 'perhaps the most elaborate "pops" concert ever played upon the screen.' But, he added, 'All of the silliest, sappiest clichés of musical biography . . . have been written into the script . . . And Richard Thorpe has directed in a comparably mawkish, bathetic style' (*NYTFR*, 11 May 1951). The picture strung together twenty-seven numbers sung by Lanza and Metropolitan Opera

FIGURE 6.9 Mario Lanza in Richard Thorpe's *The Great Caruso* (1951)

stars Dorothy Kirsten, Blanche Thebom, and others. In addition, Ann Blyth, who played Caruso's wife, sang 'The Loveliest Night of the Year,' which became a huge popular hit. The picture ran for ten weeks at the Radio City Music Hall and made a profit of nearly $4 million, making it MGM's biggest hit of the year. Clive Hirschhorn (1981: 320) called it 'the high-water mark of producer Joe Pasternak's career, and the most successful long-haired entertainment ever to emerge from Hollywood.' As for Mario Lanza, he had become the most famous tenor in America.

Lanza's next picture, Alexander Hall's *Because You're Mine* (1952), was a change of pace. Lanza played an opera star who is drafted into the Army. At training camp, he falls in love with his sergeant's sister, an aspiring young singer played by Doretta Morrow. Lanza apparently hated the script and proved difficult to work with. Pasternak showered the picture with the usual ingredients, enough to earn a respectable profit; Lanza's title song, 'Because You're Mine,' written by Nicholas Brodszky with lyrics by Sammy Cahn, was nominated for an Academy Award and became Lanza's third and final million-selling single.

Lanza's career at MGM went downhill afterward. Lanza could not control his weight, he drank too much, and he was abusive on the set. Lanza's last MGM picture was *The Student Prince* based on the 1924 Sigmund Romberg operetta.

Production started in 1952, and Lanza had recorded the soundtrack. But on the first day of shooting, Lanza failed to appear and was suspended. Threats and confrontations followed, which led to his dismissal. In 1954, MGM remounted the picture using Lanza's recordings and cast Edmund Purdom in his place. Although audiences were initially disconcerted with the lip-syncing, the songs carried the day.

Cummings reunited Kathryn Grayson and Howard Keel, the stars of *Show Boat*, in two more remakes, *Lovely to Look At* (1952) and *Kiss Me, Kate* (1953). Mervyn LeRoy's *Lovely to Look At* was a remake of RKO's *Roberta* (1935), the Jerome Kern–Otto Harbach musical starring Fred Astaire and Ginger Rogers. Cummings's version was written by George Wells and Harry Ruby. *Variety* described it as 'A pleasant round of light musical comedy entertainment. Kathryn Grayson and Howard Keel for songs; Red Skelton for comedy; Marge and Gower Champion and Ann Miller for terps . . . All deliver expertly' (*VFR*, 28 May 1952). George Sidney's *Kiss Me, Kate* was a remake of Sam and Bella Spewack's adaptation of Shakespeare's *The Taming of the Shrew* with music and lyrics by Cole Porter, which played on Broadway in 1948. This was Grayson's last picture for the studio. She had secured a release from her contract following *Lovely to Look At* but then agreed to return to play the title role in *Kiss Me, Kate*. MGM shot two versions of the picture, in 3-D and 2-D. Exhibitors could choose either one. *Variety* asked, 'Why 3-D? "Kate" has all the dimension it needs in 2-D. The pictorial effects achieved with the 3-D lensing mean little in entertainment value. The necessity of wearing viewing glasses, to us, proved a pain in the eyebrows.' 'But the play's the thing,' it added, 'and "Kate" has it.' 'Under George Sidney's skilled direction, "Kate" unfolds smoothly all the way as it goes back and forth from backstage story to the play within the play and works in the numerous and brilliant Cole Porter tunes' (*VFR*, 28 October 1953).

Lovely to Look At and *Kiss Me, Kate* both lost money due in part to their high production costs. MGM produced eleven musicals in 1951–52 and thirteen in 1952–53; it just might have been that audiences were becoming satiated with MGM musicals.

Cumming's greatest commercial and critical success was Stanley Donen's *Seven Brides for Seven Brothers* (1954). Howard Keel and Jane Powell headed a cast that included Jeff Richards, Russ Tamblyn, and Tommy Rall. Frances Goodrich, Albert Hackett, and Dorothy Kingsley wrote an original script inspired by Stephen Vincent Benét's folk tale *The Sobbin' Women* and Plutarch's *Legend of the Sabine Women*. Gene de Paul and Johnny Mercer supplied the music and lyrics and Michael Kidd did the choreography. *Variety* described the picture as 'a happy, hand-clapping, foot-stomping, country type of musical with all the slickness of a Broadway show.' 'The Broadway show touch comes from having Michael Kidd to stage the dance and musical numbers,' it said. 'A real standout is the acrobatic hoe-down staged around a barn-raising shindig, during which six of the title's seven brothers vie in love rivalry with the town boys for favor of the mountain belles. From a square dance, to acrobatics, to a spirited free-for-all brawl, it's a rousing sequence, packed

FIGURE 6.10 Howard Keel and Jane Powell in Stanley Donen's *Seven Brides for Seven Brothers* (1954)

with rhythmic fun and mayhem' (*VFR*, 2 June 1954). *Seven Brides* turned in a profit of $3.2 million.

Biopics of famous singers

Audiences might have been growing tired of musicals by mid-1950s, but MGM managed to wring extra mileage from the trend by producing a series of biopics of famous female singers. Jack Cummings's *Interrupted Melody* (1955), directed by Curtis Bernhardt, starred Eleanor Parker as Marjorie Lawrence, the Australian-born Metropolitan Opera star who overcame polio and reached new heights in her career. Joe Pasternak's *Love Me or Leave Me* (1955), directed by Charles Vidor, starred Doris Day as the torch singer Ruth Etting who struggled to escape the clutches of a gangster, the man who made her a star. Lawrence Weingarten's *I'll Cry Tomorrow* (1955), directed by Daniel Mann, starred Susan Hayward and was based on Lillian Roth's autobiography describing her harrowing descent into alcoholism and her remarkable return to stardom. Audiences had first heard of her sixteen-year struggle with alcohol in 1953 when she appeared on Ralph Edward's TV show, *This Is Your Life*. Her autobiography, published in 1954, sold more than a million and a quarter copies in its first printing. Crowther described Susan Hayward's performance 'as thoroughly authentic and convincing, shattering and sad. And when her excesses finally take her down, down the hill to Skid Row and to the brink of suicide out a window, she is almost too tragic to behold' (*NYTFR*, 13 January 1956). Hayward was nominated for an Academy Award for Best Actress and won the Golden Globe Award for Best Actress at the 1956 Cannes Film Festival. The overwhelming positive audience response to the New York and Los Angeles premieres convinced MGM to release the picture initially as a roadshow. Not until 1957 did it go into general release, and at the end of the day, it turned in a profit of nearly $3 million.

Prestige pictures

MGM produced more than song-and-dance pictures during this period. To add some class to MGM's roster, Schary signed John Houseman to a contract in 1951. Houseman had worked for Schary at RKO, where he produced *They Live by Night* (1948), a classic *film noir* directed by Nicholas Ray. Romanian-born Houseman was best known for his joint ventures with Orson Welles, most famously their 1938 *Mercury Theater on the Air* broadcast of the legendary radio drama *The War of the Worlds*, an adaptation of an H. G. Wells story about an invasion from Mars, which accidentally created mass panic along the East Coast. Houseman moved to RKO with Welles in 1939. When work began on *Citizen Kane*, Houseman helped Herman Mankiewicz write the screenplay and acted as the preproduction advisor to the film. After the release of *Citizen Kane* in 1941, the partnership broke up, and Houseman went to work for the Voice of America during the war. Afterward, he moved to Paramount, where he produced George Marshall's *The Blue Dahlia* (1946) and Max Ophüls's *Letter from an Unknown Woman* (1948), among others, before joining RKO.

Houseman produced a series of intelligent pictures for Schary; Vincente Minnelli's *The Bad and the Beautiful* (1952), Joseph Mankiewicz's *Julius Caesar* (1953), Robert Wise's *Executive Suite* (1954), and Vincente Minnelli's *Lust for Life* (1956). *The Bad and the Beautiful* starred Kirk Douglas and Lana Turner and was part of a show-business cycle that began in 1950 with Joseph L. Mankiewicz's *All About Eve* and Billy Wilder's *Sunset Boulevard*. Houseman's picture was based on a short story, *Memorial to a Bad Man* by George Bradshaw, about a ruthless Hollywood producer. Like *Citizen Kane*, the picture unfolds in flashbacks as three people – a writer, a director, and an actress – who were 'raised to the pinnacle of wealth and fame' by the producer reveal how he wrecked their personal lives. Scheuer (1952b) said, '*The Bad and the Beautiful* makes "success" an empty and mocking word in Hollywood – and in the process makes a success of itself to the extent of being one of the three best movies about Hollywood, if not the best.' The picture earned a respectable profit – $484,000 – but won an astonishing five Oscars for Best Screenplay, Best Cinematography, Best Art Direction/Set Decoration, Best Costume Design, and Best Supporting Actress (Gloria Grahame). Kirk Douglas was nominated for Best Actor but lost to Gary Cooper in *High Noon* (1952).

Executive Suite was based on Cameron Hawley's best seller about the maneuverings of six corporate vice presidents who compete to take over a large furniture company after the founder dies unexpectedly without leaving a named successor. The picture contained a galaxy of stars reminiscent of MGM's *Dinner at Eight* that comprised William Holden, June Allyson, Barbara Stanwyck, Fredric March, Walter Pidgeon, Shelley Winters, Paul Douglas, and Louis Calhern. Ernest Lehman adapted Hawley's book into 'a dramatically interesting motion picture humanizing big business and its upper echelon personalities,' said *Variety*. The characters represented different executive types. 'Fredric March's characterization of the controller, a man with a bookkeeper's mind and cold drive will be remembered among the really sock [*sic*] delineations,' said *Variety*. 'So will William Holden's portrayal of the idealistic, but practical, young executive.' *Executive Suite* was 'a class drama for class bookings' (*VFR*, 24 February 1954).

There were precedents for producing a Shakespeare movie after the war. England had sent over two commercially successful and critically acclaimed Shakespeare adaptations produced by Lawrence Olivier, *Henry V* (1944) and *Hamlet* (1948). Houseman explained his choice of *Julius Caesar* as follows: 'Of all Shakespearean plays, this one is probably the most modern,' he said. 'It's a melodrama about the lust for power which breeds dictatorship and political violence, about the twin tyrannies of totalitarian government and mob rule and about the human conflict of people who are caught between such forces.' 'Those are realities of which people in the world today are well, and all too sadly, aware,' he added (Pryor 1952). This was Houseman's second attempt at producing *Julius Caesar*; his first was a modern-dress version, which launched his Mercury Theater in 1937. It starred Orson Welles as Caesar and alluded to the rise of fascism in Europe.

Houseman's cast for the film contained a mix of American and British actors headed by Marlon Brando as Mark Anthony, James Mason as Brutus, John Gielgud as the lean and hungry Cassius, and Louis Calhern as Caesar. In design, it was presented in traditional classic form. The picture used stylized settings and was shot in black and white in a conventional Academy format. *Julius Caesar* premiered in New York at the Booth, a legitimate house, on 4 June 1953 as a roadshow. *Variety* called it 'a triumphant achievement in filmmaking.' 'Every performance is a tour de force,' it said. 'Any fears about Marlon Brando appearing in Shakespeare are dispelled by his compelling portrayal as the revengeful Mark Antony. The entire famous funeral speech takes on a new light' (*VFR*, 3 June 1953).

Crowther concurred: 'The delight and surprise of the film is Mr. Brando's Mark Antony, which is something memorable to see. Athletic and bullet-headed, he looks the realest Roman of them all and possesses the fire of hot convictions and the firm elasticity of steel . . . In him a major talent has emerged' (*NYTFR*, 5 June 1953). Houseman kept costs to a minimum, which enabled the picture to eke out a profit of a little more than $100,000.

Lust for Life was a biopic of Vincent van Gogh, the tortured Dutch Impressionist painter, starring Kirk Douglas. John Huston's *Moulin Rouge* (1953), a biopic of Toulouse-Lautrec starring José Ferrer, had demonstrated that biopics about French painters could win awards and make money. *Lust for Life* was based on Irving Stone's sensational biographical novel first published in 1934 and was adapted for the screen by Norman Corwin. Anthony Quinn costarred as van Gogh's contentious friend, Paul Gaugin, and James Donald as his brother, Theo van Gogh.

Vincent van Gogh was America's favorite modern painter. His canvases were exhibited at New York's Metropolitan Museum and had toured the country, where they were seen by hundreds of thousands. MGM secured permission to photograph original van Gogh paintings in numerous museums in the U.S. and Europe, which were interspersed throughout the film. The picture was shot in CinemaScope and Ansco Color on locations in the Netherlands, Belgium, and France where van Gogh actually worked. *Lust for Life* premiered in New York at the Plaza Theatre, a prominent art house, on 17 September 1956. The picture broke a house record at the Plaza and received unanimous praise from the critics.

After an initial art-house run, *Lust for Life* went into general release, where it met a different fate. *Variety*, which was better attuned to mainstream moviegoing, stated, 'This is a slow-moving picture whose only action is in the dialog itself. Basically a faithful portrait of Van Gogh, *Lust for Life* is nonetheless unexciting. It misses out in conveying the color and entertainment of the original Irving Stone novel.' 'Kirk Douglas plays the title role with undeniable understanding of the artist,' it said. 'He's a competent performer all the way, conveying the frustrations which beset Van Gogh in his quest for knowledge of life and the approach to putting this on canvas. But somehow the measure of sympathy that should be engendered for the genius who was to turn insane is not realized' (*VFR*, 5 September 1956). Produced at a cost of more than $3 million, *Lust for Life* racked up a deficit of $2 million. Kirk Douglas was again nominated for Best Actor but lost to Yul Brynner in *The King and I* (1956). However, an Oscar did go to Anthony Quinn as Best Supporting Actor. After *Lust for Life*, Houseman accepted the job as artistic director of the American Shakespeare Festival in Stratford, Connecticut, beginning in the summer of 1956. Soon after, he also joined CBS as executive producer of The Seven Lively Arts weekly TV series.

Message pictures redux

Dore Schary personally produced ten pictures at the helm. They were a mixed bag of styles, and most lost money. *Bad Day at Bad Rock* (1954), a message picture directed by John Sturges, was Schary's best effort. *Variety* described Schary's message pictures as having 'a flair for offbeat story values' that had 'word-of-mouth and editorial-getting' ingredients. The pictures 'say a lot of fairly grim and unpretty things about human nature and yet leave the spectator feeling the good guys beat the bad guys' (*VFR*, 3 August 1955). *Bad Day*, a thriller shot in CinemaScope and in color, starred Spencer Tracy and Robert Ryan. Tracy played a war veteran with a crippling injury to one hand who is deposited by a streamliner at a whistle stop in the desert in search of a Japanese farmer. He wants to present him the Medal of Honor for heroism his son won in an action that left him dead and Tracy crippled. 'Tracy is greeted with an odd hostility and his own life is endangered when he puts together the reason for the cold, menacing treatment. At the height of the anti-Jap feeling after Pearl Harbor, the farmer had been killed by Robert Ryan, rancher, in a mob scene in which the other townsmen had

FIGURE 6.11 Spencer Tracy and Robert Ryan in John Sturges's *Bad Day at Bad Rock* (1954)

participated.' As *Variety* noted, 'Besides telling a yarn of tense suspense, the picture is concerned with a social message on civic complacency, whether in a whistlestop or city. Fortunately for entertainment purposes, the makers have wisely underplayed this social angle so it seldom gets out of hand' (*VFR*, 15 December 1954). The picture opened in New York at the Rivoli on 1 February 1955 and earned a profit of $947,000. Spencer Tracy received an Academy Award nomination for Best Actor and won the Golden Globe Award for acting. *Bad Day* was Tracy's last picture for the studio.

The message pictures produced under Schary's supervision include Pandro S. Berman's production of *Blackboard Jungle* (1955) and Charles Schnee's *Trial* (1955). *Blackboard Jungle* was directed and written by Richard Brooks and starred Glenn Ford on loanout from Columbia. It was based on Evan Hunter's controversial bestseller about a novice teacher, played by Ford, whose first assignment is a tough inner-city school at which he confronts a classroom filled with delinquents. Brooks cast relative unknowns for the student roles, among them Vic Morrow, Rafael Campos, Paul Mazursky, and Sidney Poitier, and shot the picture in black and white to give it a documentary feel. Juvenile delinquency had been in the news ever since a Senate committee had begun investigating the problem early in the fifties. Crowther described the picture as 'a full-throated, all-out testimonial to

FIGURE 6.12 Vic Morrow and Glenn Ford in Richard Brooks's *The Blackboard Jungle* (1955)

the lurid headlines that appear from time to time, reporting acts of terrorism and violence by uncontrolled urban youths' (*NYTFR*, 21 March 1955). MGM attempted to justify its portrayal of juvenile delinquency in a disclaimer at the beginning, which stated in part, 'We believe that public awareness is a first step toward a remedy for any problem.' The picture offered no clear-cut solution to the problem, but it did end on a high note: 'The use of a black student (played by Sidney Poitier) as the leader of those who aid the teacher suggests that cooperation between races, classes, and generations is possible in 1950s America,' said Lev (2003: 245). The picture generated an enormous amount of controversy, to the benefit of the box office. For example, Clare Booth Luce, the United States ambassador to Italy, forced the removal of the picture for consideration at the 1955 Venice International Film Festival because an unflattering portrayal of American youth would feed anti-American propaganda, she believed. It returned a profit of $4.4 million and outperformed *Mogambo* (1953) and *Seven Brides for Seven Brothers*. MGM's decision to use the song 'Rock Around the Clock' by Bill Haley and His Comets as the picture's theme song contributed in no small measure to the film's success. Decca had first released the song as a B side of a single in 1954. After the film's release, the song became a best-selling single, rising to the number-one spot on the *Billboard* chart for twenty-nine weeks.

After *Blackboard Jungle*, MGM signed Ford to a new seven-year contract and rushed him into another message film, Mark Robson's *Trial* (1955), a courtroom drama adapted by Don Mankiewicz from his *Harper's* prize-winning novel about a Mexican boy, Angelo Chavez, who is accused of murdering a young white woman. Glenn Ford played another idealistic character, a young law professor in need of courtroom experience who defends the boy and saves him from the gallows. Unknown to Ford, the lawyer who hires him to defend the boy was actually a Communist who wanted to pump up the case 'into a national cause célèbre for the raising of funds and the making of a class-war martyr.' 'This picture gives the public fresh information on timeless social problems, justice and tolerance, and those who falsely pose as morality's champions,' said *Variety*. 'Perhaps the most offbeat angle in *Trial*, on a par with the Communist Party stuff, is having the presiding judge a Negro. In the careful, temperate, judicious rulings which he is constantly making, Hernandez proves himself one of the great rhetoricians among current players.' '*Trial* gives the Negro race its greatest break in terms of a fully-felt, many-sided, warm human being,' the review concluded (*VFR*, 3 August 1955).

Prestige pictures redux

Tea and Sympathy (1956), produced by Pandro S. Berman, was adapted by Robert Anderson from his 1953 landmark play that ran for more than 700 performances on Broadway. It was directed by Elia Kazan and starred Deborah Kerr, John Kerr, and Leif Erickson, who reprised their roles for MGM with Vincente Minnelli directing. *Variety* said, 'Let Metro be congratulated for not being discouraged and for going ahead with a boxoffice property that presented unique problems right from the start. This is the story of a youngster regarded by fellow students as "not regular" (i.e., not manly). The spotlight is on clearly implied homosexuality – and that was explicit to the stage play's plot' (*VFR*, 26 September 1956). MGM and Anderson overcame the Production Code's objections to the play by dropping the word 'queer' from the script, by deleting Laura's recognition of her husband's latent homosexuality, and by adding a '"voice for morality" (a favorite PCA device) when an older Tom returns to school and finds Laura's letter saying their brief sexual encounter was wrong,' said Lev (2003: 92). Crowther described John Kerr's performance as 'incredibly sure, as sensitive as a fine mechanism and yet reflective of the callowness of youth. And Miss Kerr, who is no relative, reveals as the housemaster's wife one of the most genuine and tender female characters we have seen on the screen in a long, long time. He added that the letter at the end was 'so prudish and unnecessary, we strongly suggest that you leave after Miss Kerr has reached her hand gently toward the boy and spoken the unforgettably poignant line, "Years from now, when you talk about this – and you will – be kind"' (*NYTFR*, 28 September 1956).

Teahouse of the August Moon (Scope 1956), produced by Jack Cummings, was adapted by John Patrick from his 1953 Pulitzer Prize–winning play that ran for more than 1,000 performances on Broadway. MGM acquired the screen rights to the play and the underlying novel by Vern J. Sneider even before the play had gone into production. *Teahouse* was directed by Daniel Mann and starred Marlon Brando, Glenn Ford, Machiko Kyo, and Eddie Albert. Machiko Kyo, the Japanese actress who played Lotus Blossom the geisha girl, was well known to American art-house audiences for her starring roles in films by Akira Kurosawa and Kenji Mizoguchi. Patrick's play was a clash-of-cultures comedy about a young army officer, Captain Fisby (Glenn Ford) during the occupation of Okinawa, who attempts to impose democracy and free enterprise on the little village of Tobiki. Marlon Brando played Sakini, 'the amiable Okinawan who engineers the confusion and subversion of the American Army's aims.' Crowther stated that the play, 'though far from a solemn social drama . . . was a studious report in comparison with this rendering of it on the screen.' 'Now, Daniel Mann, the director,' he said, 'has dished up the same material, prepared for the screen by Mr. Patrick, in a style bordering close on burlesque. And he has got Mr. Ford and Mr. Brando playing their leading roles as though they were out to make Dean Martin and Jerry Lewis look slightly repressed' (*NYTFR*, 30 November 1956). *Variety*'s opinion was more temperate, stating that *Teahouse* 'retains the basic appeal that made it a unique war novel and a legit hit' and predicted fine box office prospects' (*VFR*, 17 October 1956). It was correct; the picture turned in a profit of $1.5 million.

Segue into independent production

Not until 1955 did MGM release an independent production. The picture was *Guys and Dolls* (1955) and the producer Sam Goldwyn. Nick Schenck announced that the Goldwyn distribution agreement represented 'a significant step for us in our new policy of joining with the leading independent producers in the market-ing of outstanding pictures' (Pryor 1955). *Guys and Dolls* was based on Frank Loesser's hit musical, which ran on Broadway for three years beginning in November 1950. Goldwyn acquired the movie rights for a record $1 million against 10 percent of the picture's gross and spent more than $5 million of his own money to pro-duce it (Pryor 1955). Joseph L. Mankiewicz wrote and directed it. The cast was headed by Marlon Brando, Jean Simmons, Frank Sinatra, and Vivian Blaine. The picture grossed more than $9 million worldwide to become a top money earner of 1955.

A year before, MGM had entered into a partnership deal with Desi Arnaz and Lucille Ball's Desilu Productions, the producer of the *I Love Lucy* show. It was a two-picture, profit-participation deal that anticipated that the couple would be moving into feature film production. The first picture, *The Long, Long Trailer* (1954), produced by Pandro S. Berman and directed by Vincente Minnelli, marked Lucille Ball and Desi Arnaz's first screen appearance together since 1940. Albert Hackett and Frances Goodrich adapted Clinton Twiss's novel about two newly-weds who go off on their honeymoon intending to live in a trailer. 'The Long, Long Trailer is especially designed for those who simply want to watch their TV favorites on a large screen, in color,' said Guernsey (1954). 'Most of the time there is nothing else on the screen except Desi and Lucille, kissing and making up after each happy scheme misfires.' He added, '*The Long, Long Trailer* is as unmanageable as the ponderous rig behind the Desi Arnaz-Lucille Ball convertible, and not nearly as shiny.' The picture was a hit, however, earning a profit of more than $1.5 million.

To produce their first independent picture, *Forever Darling* (1956), Arnaz and Ball formed Zanra (Arnaz spelled backward) Productions. The property was suggested by Schary and went against type. It was a fantasy comedy, which Weiler described as 'a thin, overdrawn, weak caper about a chemist and his wife, whose once-rosy marriage has deteriorated into bickering and boredom and then is saved through the intervention of the lady's "guardian angel"' (*NYTFR*, 10 February 1956) 'Lucy and Desi are engaging people, but *Forever Darling* is every bit as terrible as it sounds,' said Zinsser (1956). 'The script [by Helen Deutsch] is heavy and the jokes are bad. This is quite a switch on the entertainment pattern of the day – the two stars devote their best energies to television and toss a quickie for the movies. Movie fans deserve a better break – there are still quite a few of us around.' The picture failed at the box office, and plans for Desilu to go into independent production were dropped by mutual consent.

In 1955, MGM finally moved into the new era by signing Sol C. Siegel, former 20th Century Fox producer, to a multiple-picture contract. The deal called for him to produce ten pictures over the next five years. Siegel was born in New York in 1903 and graduated from the Columbia University School of Journalism. He started out as a reporter for the *New York Herald Tribune* and later worked as a sales executive for Columbia-Brunswick Records. In 1934, he joined his brother, Moe Siegel, who was assisting Herbert J. Yates, the founder and president of Consolidated Film Industries, with the merger of six Poverty Row studios to form Republic Pictures in 1935. At Republic, Siegel became a producer and was placed in charge of up-and-coming Western stars Gene Autry, Roy Rogers, and John Wayne. In 1940, Siegel moved to Paramount Pictures to head the studio's B movie unit, and in 1947 he moved to 20th Century Fox as an A-list producer responsible for such hits as *Three Coins in the Fountain* (1954), *There's No Business Like Show Business* (1954), *Gentlemen Prefer Blondes* (1953), and *Call Me Madam* (1953).

Siegel's first MGM picture was Charles Walters's *High Society* (1956), a musical remake with a Cole Porter score of MGM's screwball comedy, *Philadelphia Story* (1940), which starred Katharine Hepburn, Jimmy Stewart, and Cary Grant. Siegel's version was shot in VistaVision and starred Grace Kelly as Tracy Lord and Bing Crosby and Frank Sinatra in the Cary Grant and Jimmy Stewart roles. John Patrick wrote the screenplay. Siegel figured he needed a big name to carry the picture and willingly gave Crosby 5 percent of the worldwide gross against a minimum guarantee of $200,000 to sign him. Crowther (1956) called it an implausible choice, since Crosby was 52, old enough to be Grace Kelly's father. He also found fault with the choice of Grace Kelly: 'As we well recall the Main Line matron that Miss Hepburn brilliantly played, she was a beautifully netted creature whose every dart contained a lively sting. Miss Kelly, whose manners are elegant, is more like a petulant girl who is almost apologetic for her occasional audacities.' But the chemistry worked for audiences; *High Society* made more than $1 million. *High Society* was Grace Kelly's last Hollywood picture before becoming Princess Grace of Monaco.

The divorcement

On 30 August 1954, Loew's Inc. signed a consent decree divorcing its theater chain from MGM. It was the last company to fall into line in the *Paramount* antitrust case. RKO, Paramount, 20th Century Fox, and Warner Bros. had signed consent decrees by 1951. Loew's presented its plan for the split-up to the Department of Justice in January 1952, which was approved by the court on 6 February 1952. Loew's agreed to divest twenty-four theaters, sixteen of which were located in New York City, within two years. This would leave the chain with fifty-one houses in New York and sixty-three elsewhere in the United States after the divorce ('M'Grath Approves' 1952). As stipulated by the 1954 consent decree, Loew's created a new subsidiary, Loew's Theatres, Inc., which took over the theater chain. Joseph Vogel, the general manager of the chain, was elected president. Vogel, a New Yorker, started out as a part-time usher and at age 18 was appointed manager of the Loew's Fulton Theatre in Brooklyn. He rose steadily through the ranks until he was named top man of the chain in 1945. Loew's Inc. had until 6 February 1957 to work out the details of the divorcement, but the proceedings were delayed until 1959, when the company finally came up with a satisfactory plan to divide up the $32 million funded debt among each separated company – Loew's Theatres and Loew's Inc. (Conant 1976: 347).

Dissident stockholders

During the divorce proceedings, Loew's had come under withering criticism from Wall Street and dissident stockholders alike. Loew's had 'the greatest prestige in the industry,' a 'matchless studio in Culver City,' and a potent sales force, said Hughes (1957: 99–100), 'Yet critics noted that a company earning no more than 2 percent on its investment was scarcely worth keeping alive.' Nicholas Schenck, who had reached retirement age at 73, took stock of the situation and stepped aside as president, a position he had held since 1927. On 14 December 1955, he became president emeritus and moved up to board chairman. He was succeeded by Arthur M. Loew, the former head of Loew's International, a position he held since 1920. Taking the top job made him the only son of a film pioneer to reach the same position held by his father.

Arthur Loew had been reluctant to take on the job as president. He acquiesced only to soothe Loew's dissident stockholders. But the dissidents were not assuaged. At the February 1956 annual meeting, for example, disgruntled stockholders ('Loew's Stockholders Highly' 1956) asked why 'should the former giant of the motion picture industry now be close to the bottom in earning power unless the management of "old men, out of imagination" were to blame?' 'Why,' they insisted, 'did MGM not sell its old films to television? Had the company missed the market?' And, why, they wanted to know, wasn't anyone willing to provide an accurate evaluation of the company's assets?

Arthur Loew got the message. He wisely decided not to sell off MGM's film library to television; rather, he announced in June 1956 that MGM would enter the television field, first by leasing its pre-1950 pictures for showing on TV and second by going into television production. Loew also made several independent deals, instituted another economy drive and strove to bring closure to the divorcement proceedings. But Loew sensed that a battle for the control of Loew's was in the offing and quit in October 1956 with four months remaining on his contract.

Joseph Vogel management

He was replaced by Joseph Vogel, president of the still-to-be-divorced Loew's Theatres, on 18 October 1956. Vogel, in turn, was replaced by Leopold Friedman, financial vice president and a director of the theater chain. Arthur Loew resumed his old position as head of Loew's International but retired in 1957 due to health concerns. He was succeeded by Morton A. Spring, a vice president of the department. Vogel faced a barrage of complaints from the start. Chief among them was that Nick Schenck exercised too much influence over Loew's affairs as board chairman. Under pressure from the stockholders, Schenck resigned from the board effective 1 January 1957.

Vogel's first big move after assuming the presidency was to seek the ouster of Dore Schary, and on 28 November 1956, the board called for his resignation. Schary remained at the studio until the end of the year to complete his last personal production, *Designing Woman* (1957), a romantic comedy starring Lauren Bacall and Gregory Peck. Schary's $200,000-a-year contract remained in force until in January 1958. As part of the settlement, Schary was retained by the studio as a consultant until 1968 at $100,000 a year, reported Esterow (1956). Vogel replaced Schary with Benjamin Thau as vice president and head of studio operations. Thau vowed to restore the company to its former eminence by essentially reverting to the status quo. He chose to run the studio with another executive committee, this time comprising Louis B. Mayer's old guard – Eddie Mannix, J. J. Cohn, Lawrence Weingarten, Marvin Schenck, Kenneth MacKenna and Saul Rittenberg, the head of MGM's legal department.

Vogel claimed that MGM under Schary had been 'mismanaged' for years ('Sale' 1958). MGM's 1957 releases, all begun by Schary's team, constituted 'the worst collection of pictures in its history,' said Vogel (Lev 2003: 198). Nineteen MGM pictures lost money, and Loew's ended up posting a loss of $455,000 for the year, a first in the company's thirty-four-year history (ibid.). Hughes (1957: 101) substantiated Vogel's assessment in a 1957 *Fortune* article: 'Over the ten year period, 1947–56, the net result of all MGM film production was a *loss* of more than

$6 million,' he said. 'In 1956 alone, losses on film production hit $4,600,000. Losses were offset (and hidden) only by profits from the reissue of *old* films. These netted more than $16,800,000; the reissue of *Gone With the Wind* netted over $11,500,000. All the while, MGM facilities were maintained at a level capable of producing forty to fifty films a year, and these facilities cost the studio as much as $10 million in overhead in 1956. Actual production in 1956, however, was a mere twenty pictures.'

But as Glancy (1992: 141) has pointed out, Schary's 'MGM's record in the fifties is very similar to that of the late forties, with only a few huge successes making up for a plethora of losses each season.' 'The safety mechanisms of the studio system had been removed, and MGM was unable to prosper without them,' he said. MGM's stars faded fast after the war, 'and with most of the industry's top stars going independent, there was little chance of restoring the star roster at MGM.' More importantly, B movie production, which provided a steady revenue stream to offset the risks of producing expensive films, had ceased. 'Thus, the 1948 reshuffle that brought Dore Schary to MGM as "the new Thalberg," and eventually resulting in the ousting of Louis B. Mayer, actually had little effect,' Glancy concluded (1992: 141).

Proxy fights

Joseph Tomlinson, a board member who was the largest single shareholder of Loew's stock, believed that Vogel was failing to turn the company around and launched a battle in December 1956 to take control. Tomlinson, a Canadian, had interests in hotels, construction, and trucking. He was joined in his attack by fellow board member Stanley Meyer, a minor television producer and a former theater executive. Working behind the scenes was Louis B. Mayer, who was staging a comeback as MGM production chief. Tomlinson demanded the resignation of five board directors who were officers in the company. They included Howard Dietz, vice president of advertising and publicity; Charles C. Moskowitz, vice president and treasurer; Ben Melnicker, vice president and general counsel (who succeeded J. Robert Rubin); Charles M. Reagan, vice president; and George A. Brown, an attorney. Tomlinson ('Big' 1956) stated that 'he had met with Louis B. Mayer . . . who has offered to return in a production capacity, but not under the present management.'

Vogel managed to head off a proxy fight at the 1957 annual meeting by agreeing to remove all management personnel from the board and accepting a perilous compromise: six seats on the board for insurgents, six for Vogel, and an 'independent' thirteenth man. Both factions chose businessmen, lawyers, and bankers. 'Strong-minded men, successful in their own fields,' said Pryor (1957), 'but babes in the movie woods' when it came to producing movies. The independent was Ogden R. Reid, president and editor of the *New York Herald Tribune*.

But Tomlinson was still not happy. He called a meeting of the insurgent directors on 30 July 1957 and unilaterally 'elected' Louis B. Mayer and Samuel J.

Briskin, a former Hollywood producer, to the board. Vogel called the meeting illegal. A quorum of seven was required by the by-laws, and only five had attended the meeting. The matter was ultimately settled in the Delaware Chancellory Court, which declared that the July rump committee had acted improperly and that Mayer and Briskin were to be removed at once from the board. Vogel finally won control of the board at a special meeting of stockholders on 15 October 1957. He had the backing of a majority of the outstanding stock with proxies for 2,746,000 shares or 51 percent (Reckert 1957). Just two weeks later, Louis B. Mayer died of leukemia on 29 October 1957.

Vogel lost little time instituting economy measures. He set up strict cost accounting and rigid budget controls, placed buying on a competitive basis (to overcome the nepotism charges), scrapped twelve dubious picture projects, pared unproductive directors, writers, and stars from the payroll, and downsized the home office. Howard Dietz, the exploitation wizard behind MGM's lion's head trademark, resigned amicably on 10 January 1958. At the same time, fourteen employees in MGM's advertising and publicity department and fifty people in the Loew's distribution department were dismissed. On the production side, he set up a large-scale television department and signed veteran producers Sol Siegel, Pandro S. Berman, and Lawrence Weingarten to long-term contracts with profit-participation terms.

Vogel made two significant hires. After accepting the retirement of Charles C. Moskowitz, vice president and treasurer, in August 1957, Vogel replaced him with Robert H. O'Brien. O'Brien was a real catch. An attorney and former commissioner of the Securities and Exchange Commission (1942–44), O'Brien joined Paramount Pictures in 1944 as special assistant to Paramount President Barney Balaban and later became treasurer. He handled the divorcement of Paramount's theaters after the consent decree in 1950 and became a director and financial vice president of United Paramount Pictures, the successor theater chain. After UPT took over the struggling American Broadcasting Company in early 1953, O'Brien became executive vice president of the network and financial vice president of American Broadcasting-Paramount Theatres, where he remained until Vogel hired him.

On 23 April 1958, Vogel replaced Ben Thau with Sol Siegel as studio chief. Thau's appointment had been a stopgap measure until someone with significant filmmaking experience could be found. Vogel had approached Siegel to take the job in 1957, but negotiations stalled over financial terms. Siegel initially wore two hats – as an independent producer and studio chief – until he fulfilled the terms of his original contract with the studio.

Vogel's plan to bring closure to the divorcement proceedings had been stymied for a year by a group of dissident stockholders who insisted that MGM be split off from the company instead of the other way around. The dissidents contended that motion picture production was 'a losing business.' A greater return would accrue to Loew's stockholders 'by concentrating on the theatre, TV, records and publishing end of the business than from any further major efforts on production' ('Divestment' 1958). But Loew's finances were in better shape by 1958. After going deep in the red in 1957, the company posted a profit of $774,000 in fiscal 1958 (Loew's in Black' 1959). The turnaround at MGM convinced Loew's stockholders to accept management's divorcement plan to divide up the funded debt, and on 29 October 1958, the Loew's board formally approved it. The plan was approved by the federal district court on 6 March 1959. At the 1960 annual meeting on 25 February 1960, stockholders approved the name change for Loew's Inc. to Metro-Goldwyn-Mayer, Inc.

7

ADJUSTING TO THE SIXTIES (1959–69)

Sol Siegel at the helm

When Siegel took over as production chief, the following three pictures had been placed in the pipeline: *Gigi* (1958), *North by Northwest* (1959), and *Ben-Hur* (1959). He was a lucky man. *Gigi*, Arthur Freed's first independent venture, was his biggest commercial hit and MGM's last great musical. It was directed by Vincente Minnelli and starred Leslie Caron, Maurice Chevalier, and Louis Jourdan. Alan Jay Lerner adapted the Collette novella set in fin-de siècle Paris about a carefree young girl who is being brought up by her grandmother and great aunt to be a courtesan. American theatergoers had seen Anita Loos's version of the work on Broadway in 1951 starring Audrey Hepburn. The lyrics and music for the film were by Lerner and Frederick Loewe, the team responsible for *My Fair Lady*, which was in its third year on Broadway. Cecil Beaton, another *My Fair Lady* veteran, designed the costumes and scenery.

Minnelli shot the film in CinemaScope and in Metrocolor against authentic backgrounds in Paris such as Maxim's, the Bois de Boulogne, the Palais de Glace, and the Tuileries. Metrocolor was the name MGM gave to Eastman Kodak's single-strip color negative stock. The Eastman Kodak stock supplanted Technicolor's three-strip color process beginning in the fifties mainly because it simplified shooting in color and at a significantly lower cost. Branding the Eastman Kodak stock to reflect the studio doing the film processing was a common practice. *Gigi* premiered in New York as a roadshow at the Royale Theatre, a legitimate house on Broadway, on 15 May 1958. '*Gigi* is destined for a global boxoffice mopup,' said *Variety*. 'It has all the ingredients. It's a naughty but nice romp of the hyper-romantic naughty 90s of Paris-in-the-spring, in the Bois, in Maxim's, and in the boudoir. How can it miss? Despite the sex and, to the credit of all concerned including the censorial authorities who abstained, it is replete with taste from its sartorial investiture to the ultimate histrionic performances' (*VFR*, 20 May 1958).

FIGURE 7.1 Cary Grant in Alfred Hitchcock's *North By Northwest* (1959)

Gigi won nine Academy Awards, the most any film had won before then, and was the last MGM musical to win the Best Picture award. At the Oscar ceremony, Maurice Chevalier, who had not made a picture in Hollywood for twenty-two years, was presented with an Honorary Academy Award, which revitalized his movie career. *Gigi* grossed nearly $10 million worldwide and earned a profit of nearly $2 million.

Alfred Hitchcock made only one film for MGM, *North By Northwest* (1959), but it was one of his best. Hitchcock was at the top of his popularity when he struck a deal with MGM in 1957. His fifties films included *Dial M for Murder* (1954) for Warner Bros. and *Rear Window* (1954), *To Catch a Thief* (1955), and *Vertigo* (1958) for Paramount. And his hit TV show, *Alfred Hitchcock Presents*, had been airing on CBS since 1955. *North By Northwest* was based on an original script by Ernest Lehman and starred Cary Grant, his fourth pairing with Hitchcock, Eva Marie Saint, and James Mason. Hitchcock shot his picture in Paramount's VistaVision widescreen process, and it featured a score by Bernard Herrmann. *North By Northwest* premiered at the Radio City Music Hall on 6 August 1959, where it enjoyed a long run. Weiler described it as 'a suspenseful and delightful Cook's Tour of some of the more photogenic spots in these United States.' Cary Grant 'was never more at home than in this role of the advertising-man-on-the-lam,' he said. 'He handles the grimaces, the surprised look, the quick smile, the afore-mentioned spooning and all the derring-do with professional aplomb and grace.' 'In casting Eva Marie Saint as his romantic vis-à-vis,' he added, 'Mr. Hitchcock has plumbed some talents not shown by the actress heretofore. Although she is

FIGURE 7.2 Charlton Heston in William Wyler's *Ben-Hur* (1959)

seemingly a hard, designing type, she also emerges both the sweet heroine and a glamorous charmer' (*NYTFR*, 7 August 1959). The picture earned a profit of $837,000.

MGM had started work on the *Ben-Hur* remake in 1953, but the picture was postponed during the turmoil leading up to Nick Schenck's and Dore Schary's departures. By 1957, Vogel was ready to move ahead, convinced that another biblical epic like MGM's own *Quo Vadis*, Fox's *The Robe* (1953), and Paramount's *The Ten Commandments* (1956) could save his company. William Wyler was set to direct, and after considering Burt Lancaster, Tony Curtis, and Kirk Douglas for the title role, MGM signed Charlton Heston, who played Moses in *The Ten Commandments*.

Ben-Hur was shot in Rome's Cinecittà Studios from May 1958 to January 1959, during which the budget ballooned to more than $15 million, a new record. The chariot race itself cost a fortune to produce. Everything about the production, which was photographed in MGM Camera 65 in Technicolor, was colossal. The production had taken over nearly all the facilities of the studio, the largest in Europe. After six months in postproduction, *Ben-Hur* opened in New York at Loew's State on a reserved-seat basis on 18 November 1959. *Variety* said, Metro's $15,000,000 bet 'should result in the biggest payoff in the history of film business.

Ben-Hur is a majestic achievement, representing a superb blending of the motion picture arts by master craftsmen.' 'The big difference between *Ben-Hur* and other spectacles, biblical or otherwise,' it added 'is the sincere concern for human beings. They're not just pawns reciting flowery dialog to fill gaps between the action and spectacle scenes. They arouse genuine emotional feeling in the audience. This has been accomplished without sacrificing the impact of the action, panoramic, and spectacle elements' (*VFR*, 18 November 1959). Crowther said, William Wyler's 'big scenes are brilliant and dramatic – that is unquestionable.' 'There has seldom been anything in movies to compare with this picture's chariot race,' he said. 'It is a stunning complex of mighty setting, thrilling action by horses and men, panoramic observation and overwhelming dramatic use of sound. But the scenes that truly reach you and convey the profound ideas are those that establish the sincerity and credibility of characters' (*NYTFR*, 19 November 1959).

Ben-Hur ran for seventy-four weeks as a roadshow at Loew's State. Elsewhere, it played as a roadshow for more than a year, by which time it had reached breakeven. At the Academy Awards, the picture won eleven Oscars, including Best Picture, Best Director, Best Actor, and Best Supporting Actor, a record that held until James Cameron's *Titanic* (1997). At the end of the run, *Ben-Hur* grossed more than $66 million in rentals to rank number two behind *Gone with the Wind* and turned in a profit of $20.4 million. It saved the day for MGM.

Profit-participation deals

MGM's move into independent production was cautious. It initially offered profit-participation deals to in-house producers – Sol Siegel, Pandro S. Berman, Joe Pasternak, and Arthur Freed – and not to new talent. Siegel followed up *High Society* with George Cukor's *Les Girls* (1957), a Cole Porter musical starring Gene Kelly, Mitzi Gaynor, Kay Kendall, and Taina Elg. This was Gene Kelly's last musical for the studio. *Variety* described it as 'an exceptionally tasty musical morsel that should help satiate the somewhat emaciated Metro lion and, at the same time, provide the necessary fodder to satisfy hungry theater turnstiles' (*VFR*, 2 October 1957). But audiences stayed away, and the picture was a bust. Siegel made three more pictures for MGM, Ranald MacDougall's *Man On Fire* (1957) starring Bing Crosby in a straight dramatic role; Michael Kidd's *Merry Andrew* (1958), a musical starry Danny Kaye and Pier Angeli; and Vincente Minnelli's *Home from the Hill* (1960), a melodrama starring Robert Mitchum and Eleanor Parker. None compared commercially to Siegel's first entry for the company.

Blackboard Jungle (1955) had demonstrated the market potential for movies targeted at modern youth. Pandro S. Berman's first entry as an independent, which he made under the Avon Productions banner, was *Jailhouse Rock* (1957) starring Elvis Presley. This was Presley's third picture, which he made on loanout from Paramount. Presley's contract with Hal Wallis at Paramount allowed him to make one picture a year at another studio. After 'Heartbreak Hotel' and other rock 'n' roll songs reached the top of the pop music charts in 1956, Presley had become a national pop star who had appeared several times on national TV. *Jailhouse Rock* was directed by Richard Thorpe and released in CinemaScope in black and white. Unlike his previous films, *Jailhouse Rock*, with a script by Nedrick Young and Guy Trosper, was built entirely around Elvis's rags-to-riches story. He played a hot-headed ex-con who learns how to play the guitar and becomes a rock star. His six songs grew naturally from the story. The title song, 'Jailhouse Rock' by Jerry Leiber and Mike Stoller, sold two million copies within weeks of the film's release. Mainstream critics deplored Elvis's acting and his screen persona, but *Variety* was right on the mark: 'Film is packed with the type of sure-fire ingredients producers know Presley followers go for,' it observed, 'and it's likely a considerable portion of the populace, particularly the cats, will find this Metro release in their alley' (*VFR*, 16 October 1957). The picture earned a profit of more than $1 million.

MGM turned out a spate of teenpics afterward. Probably the best was Albert Zugsmith's *High School Confidential* (1958) starring Russ Tamblyn, Jan Sterling, John Drew Barrymore, and Mamie Van Doren. Zugsmith was an outside producer, who signed with MGM in 1957. At Universal, he had previously produced such highly regarded pictures as Douglas Sirk's *Written on the Wind* (1957) and *The Tarnished Angels* (1958) and Orson Welles's last American film, *Touch of Evil* (1958). *High School Confidential*, which *Variety* described as a 'sensational account of pills, marijuana and narcotics among the high school set,' made a nice profit (*VFR*, 28 May 1958), but Zugsmith's next efforts, *The Big Operator* (1959) and *The Beat Generation* (1959), were critical and box-office failures.

After *Jailhouse Rock*, Berman went on to produce two big hits starring Elizabeth Taylor, Richard Brooks's *Cat on a Hot Tin Roof* (1958) and Daniel Mann's *Butterfield 8* (1960). Taylor was nearly at her peak when she made these pictures, having established herself as a dramatic actress in *Giant* (1956) for Warner Bros. and *Raintree County* (1957) for MGM. *Cat on a Hot Tin Roof* was based on Tennessee Williams's Pulitzer Prize–winning play, which played for more than 700 performances on Broadway. The picture was produced for Berman by Lawrence Weingarten and adapted for the screen by Brooks and James Poe. It costarred Paul Newman as Brick and Burl Ives, who reprised his Broadway role as Big Daddy. To get a Production Code seal, MGM had to remove any hint of homosexuality from Paul Newman's character. Elizabeth Taylor as Maggie the Cat 'surpasses all her previous portrayals as the loveless, childless wife,' said Scheuer (1958). *Variety* concurred: 'The frustrations and desires, both as a person and a woman, the warmth and understanding she molds, the loveliness that is more than a well-turned nose – all these are part of a full-accented, perceptive interpretation.' Paul Newman as Big Daddy's son Brick, 'who has left his material bed for the solace of the bottle, again proves to be one of the finest actors in films.' And Burl Ives, it said, 'is a vibrant and convincing plantation king' (*VFR*, 13 August 1958). Taylor was nominated for an Academy Award for her performance. The picture was the top money earner of the year for MGM, earning a profit of $2.4 million.

FIGURE 7.3 Paul Newman and Elizabeth Taylor in Richard Brooks's *Cat on a Hot Tin Roof* (1958)

Butterfield 8 was Elizabeth Taylor's last picture for the studio. It was based on John O'Hara's 1935 novel and costarred Laurence Harvey. Crowther described it as a 'hackneyed story of the tinseled but tarnished prostitute who thinks she has finally discovered the silver lining for her life in Mr. Right.' 'By the odds, it should be a bomb,' he said, 'But a bomb it is not . . . At least, it is not the sort of thing to set you to yawning and squirming, unless Elizabeth Taylor leaves you cold. In the first place, it has Miss Taylor, playing the florid role of the lady of easy virtue, and that's about a million dollars right there.' 'You can take it from us,' he added, 'at no point does she look like one of those things. She looks like a million dollars, in mink or in negligée' (*NYTFR*, 17 November 1960). Taylor won her first Academy Award for her performance, and the picture turned in a profit of $1.9 million.

Joseph Pasternak in partnership with Sam Katz helped fill MGM's roster until 1966, making sixteen pictures under their Euterpe Productions banner. They included Charles Walters's *Ask Any Girl* (1959) and *Please Don't Eat the Daisies* (1960), Henry Levin's *Where the Boys Are* (1960), Vincente Minnelli's *The Courtship of Eddie's Father* (1963), and a batch of musicals starring Jimmy Durante, Doris Day, Connie Francis, and Elvis Presley. *Ask Any Girl* (1959), Euterpe's first hit, was a romantic comedy starring Shirley MacLaine, David Niven, and Gig Young.

Shirley MacLaine, fresh from her Academy Award nomination in Vincente Minnelli's *Some Came Running* (1958), played a small-town girl 'who comes to New York not to seek fame and fortune, but in search of a husband.' *Variety* described Miss MacLaine as a 'pert and effervescent actress, who gains increased stature as a performer and a personality with each new outing.' In *Ask Any Girl*, she 'again comes through with a performance that is a sheer delight,' it said (*VFR*, 13 May 1959). *Where the Boys Are* (1960), a teen pic about college kids on spring break in Fort Lauderdale, starred Dolores Hart, George Hamilton, Yvette Mimieux, and Jim Hutton. The picture allowed MGM to give 'Hollywood's fresh, young up-and-coming players . . . a chance to cut loose and show their thespic wares,' said *Variety* (*VFR*, 10 November 1960). Paula Prentiss and recording star Connie Francis made their screen debuts. Francis sang the title song by Howard Greenfield and Neil Sedaka, which became her signature piece. *Please Don't Eat the Daisies* (1960) starring Doris Day and David Niven and *The Courtship of Eddie's Father* (1963) starring Glenn Ford and Shirley Jones were popular domestic comedies aimed at the family trade.

International operations

Great Britain

The decline of the domestic theatrical market after World War II forced all of Hollywood to rely on overseas markets more and more. At one time, American films could at least break even at home, but no more. Foreign sales, which by 1960 accounted for a hefty share of Hollywood's total income, spelled the difference between profit and loss. The majors operated through wholly owned subsidiaries in the largest overseas markets – Great Britain, Italy, Germany, France, and Japan – and licensed local distributors in smaller markets. To retrieve blocked funds and to conform to European quota restrictions, American companies moved much of their production to Europe after the war – a practice known as runaway production. Operating through their foreign subsidiaries, they produced films on their own, by American independent producers working abroad, and by local producers.

During the sixties, England remained Hollywood's most important overseas market. American film producers had become enamored of British popular culture and had entered into coproduction deals with British producers, creating the phenomenon known as 'Hollywood on the Thames.' MGM linked up with its first important British producer, Sir Michael Balcon, in 1956. Balcon's former company, Ealing Studios, was best known for a series of quixotic comedies about English life starring Alec Guinness and Stanley Halloway, among them *Passport to Pimlico* (1949), *Kind Hearts and Coronets* (1950), and *The Lavender Hill Mob* (1951). In the U.S., they helped nurture a burgeoning art film market after the war. Balcon sold his studio to the BBC in 1956. To get back into production, he sought Arthur Loew's help, which resulted in a six-picture contract. Balcon set up operations at MGM British Studios and produced a series of pictures that mainly lost money, with one exception, Leslie Norman's *Dunkirk* (1958), an 'epic war adventure' about the evacuation of British forces from the beaches of Dunkirk using a fleet of little boats at the outset of World War II. *Variety* stated that Dunkirk 'is a splendid near-documentary which just fails to reach magnificence. The pic should prove a deserved, resounding success' (*VFR*, 26 March 1958).

To ramp up its output of British pictures, Siegel hired Lawrence P. Bachmann as executive producer of MGM-British in 1959. Bachmann had held a similar position at Paramount British the previous three years. Before that, he worked for MGM as a screenwriter in J. J. Cohn's B movie unit, where he wrote scripts for the Dr. Kildare and Dr. Gillespie series, among other pictures. Under Bachmann, MGM-British turned out mostly low-budget items, whodunits, thrillers, melodramas, comedies, and even a sci-fi horror picture. Some played the art-house circuit in the U.S. while others played in neighborhood theaters, where they were relegated to the lower half of double bills. As a group, they were undistinguished, and nearly all lost money. The best of the lot were a series of four Miss Marple films based on Agatha Christie's murder mysteries that starred Margaret Rutherford; *Village of the Damned* (1960), a sci-fi horror picture; and *The V.I.P.s* (1963), a commercial vehicle with an all-star cast headed by Elizabeth Taylor and Richard Burton.

During the fifties, the British seemed 'to have relied almost solely on bright sophisticated comedy, supplemented by an occasionally brittle whodunit or two, to tap the U.S. market,' said Canby (1961: 1). The Miss Marple pictures were directed by George Pollock and were adapted by David Pursall and Jack Seddon. In New York, they premiered at some of the better art houses on the Upper East Side. The first, *Murder, She Said* (1961), was based on Agatha Christie's *4.50 from Paddington*. 'This modest whodunit comes off as a thoroughly satisfying and suspenseful diversion,' said Weiler. 'This "Murder" would be a thin and transparent affair if it were not for its redoubtable author, Agatha Christie, who has been tossing red herrings at detective fiction readers for as long as they have been suspecting the butler.' 'As the indomitable spinster with a beagle's nose for crime,' he added, 'Margaret Rutherford leads the chase and the cast with a flair for this school of genteel and restrained detection that would do credit to the great Holmes himself.' (*NYTFR*, 8 January 1962) The other pictures in the series were *Murder at the Gallop* (1963), *Murder Ahoy* (1964), and *Murder Most Foul* (1964). By 1964, the series had worn thin, and Bachmann dropped it.

Village of the Damned (1960), produced by Ronald Kinnoch and directed by Rolf Rilla, was based on John Wyndham's sci-fi novel *The Midwich Cuckoos*. As *Variety* described it, 'A little British village comes under a spell of some strange, supernatural force which first puts everybody out for the count. Then the villagers come to and find that every woman capable of being pregnant is. Snag is that all the children are little monsters.' In *Variety*'s opinion, it was a 'rather tired and sick film with little marquee value; interesting idea gone awry, result being just a mediocre filler' (*VFR*, 29 June 1960). Thompson was closer to the mark: 'As a quietly civilized exercise in the fear and power of the unknown this picture is one of the trimmest, most original and serenely unnerving little chillers in a long time' (*NYTFR*, 6 December 1960). The picture was a sleeper and went on to become a cult classic. Produced on a budget of $320,000, it grossed more than $2 million and turned in a profit of $860,000.

The V.I.P.s was produced by Anatole de Grunwald, the Russian-born producer who teamed up with director Anthony Asquith and screenwriter Terence Rattigan to craft a portmanteau film that told four interwoven stories about very important people headed for New York who were fogged in at London Heathrow Airport. The principal story revolved around Richard Burton, Elizabeth Taylor, and Louis Jourdan and was perhaps inspired by Burton's scandalous affair with Taylor during the filming of *Cleopatra*. Crowther compared the structure to the 'always service-able pattern of the old multi-character *Grand Hotel*' and described the picture as 'a gratifyingly, a lively, engrossing romantic film' (*NYTFR*, 20 September 1963). The picture opened in New York at the Music Hall on 19 September 1963, three months after *Cleopatra*, and went on to break box-office records. Anatole de Grunwald produced a second portmanteau film for MGM-British, *The Yellow Rolls-Royce* (1965), which had an international cast headed by Rex Harrison, Jeanne Moreau, George C. Scott, and Shirley MacLaine, but the film did not measure up to *The V.I.P.s*.

MGM's British production record paled in comparison to that of other companies. During the sixties, Hollywood became enamored of British popular culture and absorbed nearly all the directors with proven track records working in Britain. A case in point, United Artists backed Tony Richardson's *Tom Jones* (1963) starring Albert Finney; Richard Lester's *A Hard Day's Night* (1964) starring the Beatles; and the James Bond films. 'The great explosion of new British producers and directors which has occurred so spectacularly during the past five years . . . might never have happened so far as MGM is concerned,' Byron (1969: 30) remarked. 'While UA, Columbia, Embassy, Paramount, and later 20th Century Fox and Universal were busy trying to mine this phenomenon for potential gold, MGM, despite the fact that it was the only U.S. major to actually have a studio in Britain, looked aside.'

Europe

American runaway production to Italy started in the fifties with the goal of unlocking blocked-lira accounts and continued in earnest in the sixties to take advantage of Italian film subsidies. Rome had many things going for it. The city was within easy reach of the most disparate and colorful backdrops and had a mild climate that allowed a long season of location shooting, just like Hollywood. Rome also had an abundance of trained extras and horses for all those biblical epics that came into vogue. The showplaces of Italian cinema were Rome's Cinecittà, Italy's state-owned studio built by Mussolini in 1939, and Dinocittà, a huge $11 million facility containing four immense sound stages Dino De Laurentiis built outside Rome on a 750-acre site. By the sixties, Rome was being referred to as 'Hollywood on the Tiber.'

MGM International, headquartered in New York, was run by Maurice Silverstein. As the Italian market opened up, Hollywood signed coproduction pacts with top-ranked producers starting with Goffredo Lombardo, Carlo Ponti, and Dino De Laurentiis. The producers typically teamed up with French counterparts to take advantage of French subsidies as well. Goffredo Lombardo's Titanus Films was the biggest film producer in Italy. MGM's 1961 pact with the company yielded but two art films – Valerio Zurlini's *Family Diary* (1962) and Nanni Loy's *The Four Days of Naples* (1963) – but no pot of gold.

MGM's pact with Carlo Ponti was the most productive. Ponti broke into the international film scene in the early fifties in partnership with Dino De Laurentiis. They were best known for producing two early art-house hits, Federico Fellini's *La Strada* (1954) and *The Nights of Cabiria* (1956), both winners of the Academy Award for Best Foreign Film. On his own, Ponti advanced the career of his wife, Sophia Loren. She was best known in the U.S. for her starring roles in three Vittorio DeSica hits, *Two Women* (1961), *Yesterday, Today & Tomorrow* (1964), and *Marriage Italian Style* (1964). They were produced by Ponti and released by Joseph E. Levine's Embassy Pictures. Capitalizing on her performance in *Two Women*, Levine waged a successful publicity campaign, which resulted in Loren winning the 1961 Academy Award for Best Actress, the first for a non–U.S. actor in a foreign film. For MGM, Ponti made nearly a dozen pictures, but his most successful ventures were pictures in which his wife did not appear – David Lean's *Doctor Zhivago* (1965) and Antonioni's *Blow-Up* (1966), discussed later.

MGM's involvement in French production began in 1960 when it signed a coproduction deal with the Cipra Company of Paris headed by Jacques Bar. The venture yielded three pictures starring Jean Gabin – Gilles Grangier's *Money, Money, Money* (1962) and Henri Verneuil's *A Monkey in Winter* (1963) and *Any Number Can Win* (1963) – and Louis Malle's *A Very Private Affair* (1962) starring Brigitte Bardot and Marcello Mastroianni. They were released in the U.S. subtitled, played the art-house circuit, and yielded miniscule returns. *A Very Private Affair*, loosely based on Bardot's life as a movie star, was part of a wave of Bardot imports that swamped the American market after her first big hit, Roger Vadim's *And God Created Woman* (1957).

MGM's brand of independent production

Siegel finally put a stake in the heart of MGM's outmoded central producer system by making deals with outside producers – among them Edmund Grainger, Julian Blaustein, Samuel Bronston, Aaron Rosenberg, Albert Zugsmith, Martin Ransohoff, and Seven Arts, headed by Ray Stark and Eliot Hyman. MGM's brand of independent production was similar to that of the other majors – save one. MGM formed partnerships with independent producers by signing multiple-picture deals that provided them with complete production financing, creative control over their work once a project was greenlighted, and a share of the profits. In greenlighting a picture, the studio retained the right to approve the main ingredients – the director, cast, script, and budget. After completion, the studio acquired the distribution rights to the picture and a share of the profits. MGM remained a producer's studio, however. As late as 1969, MGM 'was practically the last studio you'd bring a director's project to,' reported Byron (1969: 30). Almost always they came through the '"intermediary" agency of a producer with which the studio had a long-term commitment.'

The main difference between MGM's brand of independent production and United Artists,' which had become an industry leader during the fifties, was the overhead charge. MGM expected its independent producers to make their pictures mostly on the lot, but they could make them anywhere to suit the needs of the story and to take advantage of foreign subsidies. In either case, the studio tacked on an overhead charge to the budgets to help relieve the burden of running the studio. As Aaron Rosenberg, the producer of *Mutiny on the Bounty* (1962), put it (Scheuer 1962), 'MGM was still operating under its old system, which meant that for every $1 spent, the picture was charged $1.30.' United Artists did not own a studio and functioned exclusively as a financier-distributor. As a result, it cost less money to make the same film at UA than at MGM.

The legacy of Ben-Hur

Ben-Hur's success had a downside. It convinced Siegel to produce a series of large-scale epics to carry the studio. MGM was not alone in adopting such a policy, but the practice nearly sank the company again and led to another management upheaval. Between 1960 and 1963, MGM released six such pictures: four remakes – *Cimarron* (1960), *King of Kings* (1961), *Four Horsemen of the Apocalypse* (1961), and *Mutiny on the Bounty* (1962) – and two originals, *The Wonderful World of the Brothers Grimm* (1962) and *How the West Was Won* (1963). The remakes were produced by independent producers and the originals in partnership with Cinerama Inc. Four were released as roadshows in wide-screen formats and, with one exception, all suffered massive losses.

Cimarron, shot in CinemaScope, was a remake of RKO's 1931 Oscar-winning Western based on Edna Ferber's novel about the Oklahoma land rush of 1889. It was produced by Edmund Grainger, directed by Anthony Mann, and starred Glenn Ford and Maria Schell. Grainger, a former independent producer at RKO, had signed a five-year contract with MGM in April 1957. He produced five pictures for MGM prior to *Cimarron*, and only one, *The Sheepman* (1958), a tongue-in-cheek Western directed by George Marshall starring Glenn Ford and Shirley MacLaine, earned a profit. *Cimarron* opened at the Radio City Music Hall on 16 February 1961 and went quickly into general release after the reviews. After the noisy and colorful land rush sequence that begins the movie, it 'simmers down to a stereotyped and sentimental cinema saga of the taming of the frontier' (*NYTFR*, 17 February 1961). The picture lost big, $3.6 million.

King of Kings, a remake of Cecil B. DeMille's 1927 biblical epic about the crucifixion of Christ, was produced by Samuel Bronston, directed by Nicholas Ray, and starred Jeffrey Hunter and Siobhan McKenna. Bronston had set up operations in Spain after going independent and set out to make big-budget historical epics. In Spain, he could take advantage of the warm climate, cheap labor, and creative offshore financing to bankroll his pictures on his own. Bronston's first production, *John Paul Jones* (1959), distributed by Warner Bros., was a dismal failure. Bronston financed *King of Kings* by securing Spanish subsidies, by preselling the foreign distribution rights to twelve local distributors, and by securing funds from private investors such as Pierre S. Du Pont III. MGM acquired the domestic rights to the picture as a pickup during production.

King of Kings opened in New York at Loew's State as a roadshow in Technicolor Super Technirama 70 on 11 October 1961. It had a running time of 168 minutes. With a screenplay by Philip Yordan, the picture depicted 'familiar episodes in the Saviour's life,' which were linked together by a voiceover narration spoken by Orson Welles. *Variety* described it as a 'carefully, reverently and beautifully made . . . retelling of the ministry and agony of Jesus Christ.' The box-office prospects looked good, it added, by steering 'a tactful course between Christian and Jew, dogma and drama' and avoiding 'the banalities of religious calendar art.' Jeffrey Hunter's portrayal of the Saviour came 'remarkably close to being ideal,' it said. 'Hunter's blue orbs and auburn bob (wig, of course) are strikingly pictorial' (*VFR*, 11 October 1961). *King of Kings* was produced for $5 million and eventually earned a profit of $1.6 million, which was less than the company hoped. A *Ben-Hur* or a *Quo Vadis* it was not.

Four Horsemen of the Apocalypse (1962), a remake of the 1921 Metro hit starring Rudolph Valentino, was produced by Julian Blaustein, directed by Vincente Minnelli, and starred Glenn Ford and Ingrid Thulin. Blaustein had worked for Columbia Pictures as an independent producer for three years before signing with MGM in June 1958. Blaustein's first two pictures for MGM, Michael Anderson's *Wreck of the Mary Deare* (1959) and Charles Walters's *Two Loves* (1961), lost money, but *Four Horseman* fared the worst. Blaustein's picture was an updated version of the Vicente Blasco Ibáñez's novel and was set in Occupied Paris during World War II. Crowther called the story written by Robert Ardrey and John Gay 'a pompous and idiotic fiction.' Vincente Minnelli's staging, he said 'reeks of the sound stages and the painted sets of a Metro-Goldwyn-Mayer studio' and conveyed 'no more illusion of actuality than did *Snow White and the Seven Dwarfs*.' And Glenn Ford 'as the gay hidalgo from the pampas who hits the boulevards wearing a gray fedora, black gloves and swinging an ebony cane is about as convincingly Argentine and possessed of urbanity as a high-school football coach from Kansas who has never been out of the state.' 'The less attention paid to this picture, the better for the simple dignity of the human race,' he concluded (*NYTFR*, 10 March 1962). The picture lost nearly $6 million.

Mutiny on the Bounty (1962), a remake of MGM's 1935 Oscar winner starring Clark Gable and Charles Laughton, was produced by Aaron Rosenberg and starred Marlon Brando as Fletcher Christian, Trevor Howard as Capt. Bligh, and Richard Harris as Seaman John Mills. Rosenberg moved to MGM as an independent from Universal-International in 1957 and produced four undistinguished pictures for MGM before taking on the *Mutiny* remake project. At Universal, he was best known for producing Anthony Mann's *Winchester '73* (1950) starring Jimmy Stewart. Stewart received 50 percent of the profits from the picture, a deal that was brokered by MCA head Lew Wasserman. The profit-participation deal was a new high and demonstrated just how desperate studios had become to retain and attract new talent.

Mutiny on the Bounty was filmed in Tahiti and other South Sea locations in Ultra Panavision 70 in color and was released with a running time of 179 minutes at a cost of $18.5 million, which eclipsed *Ben-Hur's* by about $3.5 million. *Variety* ('Brando's' 1962: 2) called the picture 'by far the costliest picture ever made.' The production got off to a bad start beginning in November 1960. Carol Reed

FIGURE 7.4 Marlon Brando in Lewis Milestone's *Mutiny on the Bounty* (1962)

started out as the director without a complete script and quit after three months of shooting over story differences with the producer. He was replaced by Lewis Milestone. Brando and the producer demanded endless rewrites, which required new footage to be shot, and the weather sometimes did not cooperate. The delays were reported in the press, which attributed most of the troubles to Brando. Milestone told Murray Schumach (1962c) that 'if Brando did not like something he would just stand in front of the camera and not act.' Milestone also said that Siegel and Vogel contributed to the delays as well by making script suggestions of their own. Brando gave his side of the story to Bob Thomas (1961): 'There have been 30 different versions of the script, but never have I received a finished script. We went to Tahiti with no idea of how the final third of the picture was going to be . . . How could an actor play a character if he doesn't know how he is going to end up?

Joseph Vogel ('Vogel' 1962: 5) came to Brando's defense, stating that published stories blaming Brando for the picture's high production cost were 'gravely unfair.' 'Actually a combination of circumstances [also] contributed to the final cost,' he said, among them 'a delay in completion and delivery of our specially built ship' [the replica of the *H.M.S Bounty*, cost $750,000], 'a break-out of a fire on the ship on its way to Tahiti, tropical storms and otherwise unfavorable weather,' 'illness and death among the cast,' and 'other problems which not infrequently arise on a location far-distant from the facilities of a Hollywood studio.' Vogel may have come to Brando's defense to calm Wall Street jitters. *Variety* ('Marlon' 1962: 3) had reported that 'Never before has a single motion picture influenced the trading value of a film company listed on the New York Stock Exchange as has *Mutiny on the Bounty*.' When reports came out stating that *Bounty*'s original budget of $10 million had nearly doubled, MGM's stock sank to a new low of around $43 a share from a high of $57 (ibid.). Wall Street people rightly feared that the picture could sink the studio. The end result, nonetheless, was a critical success. Crowther described the picture as 'robust and rousing . . . a high mark of filmed adventure on the sea' (*NYTFR*, 9 November 1962). *Variety* described *Mutiny on the Bounty* as 'superlative entertainment' and stated that 'Brando in many ways gives the finest performance of his career' (*VFR*, 14 November 1962).

Mutiny on the Bounty opened as a roadshow attraction. After twin premieres in New York and Los Angeles on 8 November 1962, the picture eventually played in eighty other situations on a reserved-seat basis. But given the enormously inflated budget, MGM could not expect even to break even, and the picture incurred a huge loss the first time out. The following May in time for the summer season, MGM rereleased the picture widely at general admission to some 600 theaters and captured over $1 million the first month ('Mutiny' 1963). *Mutiny on the Bounty* was nominated for seven Oscars, including Best Picture, Best Cinematography, Best Special Effects, Best Film Editing, Best Music Score, and Best Art Director-Set Decoration, and Color. It lost in all categories, with five of the awards going to *Lawrence of Arabia* (1962).

Cinerama pictures

Siegel doubled-down on MGM's big-picture policy by teaming up with Cinerama Inc. in 1960 to produce four narrative features in Cinerama's improved three-strip wide-screen process. The deal was proposed by Nicolas Reisini, Cinerama's new president and chairman, who wanted Cinerama to branch out from the travelogue format that characterized its first releases. He was motivated to do so because the novelty of the format had worn thin and the company was losing money. MGM agreed to be equal partners with Cinerama and to put up half the financing for a share of the profits. The pictures were to be released first to 125 Cinerama-equipped theaters worldwide on a reserved-seat basis and then to conventional theaters in 35mm reduction prints.

MGM and Cinerama placed two projects into production initially, *How the West Was Won* and *The Wonderful World of the Brothers Grimm*. *The Wonderful World of the Brothers Grimm* (1962) produced by George Pal was completed first. Pal had acquired the screen rights to the Grimm property in 1956 and had unsuccessfully pitched the project to Siegel on several occasions. But once the Cinerama deal was set, Siegel gave the go-ahead. *The Wonderful World of the Brothers Grimm* had its world premiere in New York on 7 August 1962 at the newly refurbished Cinerama-equipped Loew's Capitol Theatre, now renamed Loew's Cinerama. The picture starred Lawrence Harvey and Karl Boehm as the brothers Wilhelm and Jacob Grimm. A fanciful story about the struggles of the brothers for recognition served as the framework to dramatize three classic Grimm fairy tales, each with its own cast of stars. Henry Levin directed the main story and Pal the fairy tale segments. Morgenstern (1962) said, 'It seems a pity that the promise of the process is not fully realized, that a really good fairy hasn't come along to make the seams disappear between the panels of the monumental triptych and put an end to the jiggling and the distortion, and make the bad acting as good as the good acting.' The picture itself, he said, was 'an amiable, undistinguished and curiously unaffecting story in which little children 15 feet tall are apt to act as badly as more modestly proportioned moppets in conventional movies.' The framework, he added was 'less believable than the tales themselves.' *Brothers Grimm* was produced for $6.25 million but earned only $4.8 million in domestic rentals – far less than the $15 million earned by *This Is Cinerama* a decade earlier.

How the West Was Won (1963) premiered in New York at the Loew's Cinerama on 31 March 1963. The $15 million epic picture written by James R. Webb told how three generations of pioneers opened the American West. The three segments were directed by Henry Hathaway, George Marshall, and John Ford, respectively. *Variety* called it a 'blockbuster supreme, a magnificent and exciting spectacle which must, inevitably, dwarf the earnings of the travelogues in the three-screen process.' 'Technically, there's a vast improvement in the process,' it noted. 'The print joints are barely noticeable, and the wobble, which beset earlier productions, has been eliminated.' 'It would be hard to imagine a subject which lends itself more strikingly to the wide-screen process than this yarn of the pioneers who opened the American West' (*VFR*, 7 November 1962). The *New York Times* described it as 'a mammoth patchwork of Western fiction clichés' (*NYTFR*, 1 April 1963). *How the West Was Won* became one of the highest grossing pictures of the year. It ran for ninety-two weeks at the Stanley Warner Cinerama Theater in Hollywood and enjoyed record-breaking runs in Minneapolis, Denver, and other cities. But when marketing and distribution costs were factored in, the picture actually lost money, and it severed the MGM–Cinerama partnership. The losses Cinerama endured on the two pictures nearly bankrupted the company.

O'Brien–Weitman management

Siegel had resigned as vice president in charge of production in January 1962 with two more years to go on his contract. He stated that he wanted to return to independent production and would continue his distribution arrangement with MGM. In 1961, MGM generated a profit of $2.6 million, thanks mainly to the continued earnings of *Ben-Hur*, *King of Kings*, and yet another release of *Gone With the Wind* ('MGM Reports' 1963). But looking forward, Siegel might have also anticipated the economic fallout from the big-budget blockbusters in the works.

Vogel immediately replaced Siegel with Robert M. Weitman, MGM's vice president in charge of TV production since 1960. A Cornell University graduate, Weitman started out as a theater man. By 1935, he was managing Paramount's flagship theater on Times Square. To drum up business, he presented big-name bands such as Tommy Dorsey, Benny Goodman, and Harry James and popular singers such as Frank Sinatra, which attracted huge audiences. He rose to become vice president of Paramount's houses in the South. When Paramount divorced its theaters in 1949, Weitman stayed on. When the chain – now called United Paramount Theatres – merged with the ABC television network in 1953, he became vice president of program and talent development. In 1956, he moved to CBS Television as a program developer under James Aubrey. Vogel hired him to help revitalize MGM's television division, which was falling behind in its sales of series to the networks. Taking over from Siegel as head of the studio, Weitman retained his position as vice president in charge of TV production. As Schumach (1962a) noted, 'Mr. Weitman, although he has considerable experience in television, theater management, and the business end of the movie industry, has not produced movies.'

A year later in January 1963, Joseph Vogel resigned as well and was immediately replaced by Robert H. O'Brien, MGM's vice president and treasurer. As *Variety* reported, ('Proxy' 1969: 4), 'Vogel was entirely aware of the disharmony at the top echelon over company's state of affairs and when the board met on 9 January 1963, Vogel, weary of the aggravations of the job, tendered his resignation.' Vogel was 'kicked upstairs' to board chairman, a position he held for four months. At the end of the year, MGM posted a loss of $17.5 million thanks mainly to *Mutiny on the Bounty* ('MGM Reports' 1963).

The top management changes at MGM prompted Schumach (1962b) to remark that 'the businessmen have just about completed their conquest of Hollywood's major movie companies. . . The era of the moviemakers, which brought to Hollywood many of the most colorful men – as well as the greatest affluence – seems to be finished,' he said. He noted that the new production heads of 20th Century Fox (Peter G. Levathes), Warner Bros. (William T. Orr), Columbia Pictures (Sol Schwartz), and Paramount (Hack Karp) had all come from television, advertising, theater management, or distribution. During the breakdown of the studio system, said Crowther (1963), 'it became more important to have a man who could negotiate deals with stars, directors, producers, agencies; who could grasp, and utilize, the fine points of tax laws, the intricacies of international quota systems.' 'What was needed, in short,' he said, 'was a good businessman more than a moviemaker. For the important movies were now being produced, for the most part, by independents.' Taking the reins at MGM, O'Brien resolved 'to tackle the company's problems with scientific managerial techniques, a practice that motion picture companies have shunned.'

MGM-TV

Hollywood had entered a new phase in its relationship to commercial television by the fifties. After broadcast television took off in 1952, the year the FCC lifted its freeze on the granting of new television licenses, the film industry entered into a period of collaboration with its competitor. It was obvious that the new medium – given its goal of programming a full day, every day of the week – could not exist economically without feature films. It was equally obvious during the early days of television why the majors refused to help out. Not only did the majors see television as a competitor, they also saw it as incapable of generating the advertising revenue to pay a fair price for filmed programming.

The studios were free to dispose of their pre-1948 film libraries since they controlled television performance rights and all ancillary rights to their pictures. But the Screen Actors Guild, the Writers Guild of America, and the Screen Directors Guild demanded residual compensation to guild members who appeared in features made after 1 August 1948 that were leased to television. Exhibitors, however, characterized the sale of any feature to television as 'unfair competition' and threatened to boycott the studios that collaborated with the enemy.

The majors kept their vaults locked until 1955. In that year, RKO withdrew from motion picture production and sold its assets to General Teleradio, a subsidiary of General Tire & Rubber Company that operated five independent TV stations. Needing ready cash, Warner Bros. disposed of its backlog of old films in 1956 for $21 million. Paramount, which had been holding on to its films for possible use on subscription television, finally sold its pre-1948 film library to MCA in 1958 for $50 million. Within three years, then, an estimated 3,700 features, mostly of the pre-1948 vintage, had been sold off by the majors for more than $220 million. The average price per feature rose from $10,000 to $75,000 in this period (Balio 1990a: 30–2). The sales represented windfall profits for the studios. However, increasing demand for theatrical films revealed that the majors had undervalued their libraries. Within eighteen months after the RKO film library hit the market, pre-1948 features grossed an estimated $150 million in the syndication market (Balio 1990a: 31–2). When the majors decided to release their post-1948 features to television in the sixties, they would not make the same mistake of undervaluing their product again.

MGM moved into television in July 1956, when it set up a new department, MGM-TV, and hired Charles C. Barry to run it. Barry, an industry veteran and former vice president in charge of radio and television programming for NBC, operated out of the Loew's headquarters in New York. His job was to lease the 770 features and 900 shorts in MGM's pre-1948 library to TV. As previously noted, MGM's dissident stockholders wanted the company to score a quick profit by unloading the film library. MGM had received several offers for it, one for $50 million, but Arthur Loew held firm and rejected them. The wisdom of this decision became apparent immediately. In July 1956, Barry leased *The Wizard of Oz* to CBS-TV for four showings at a total cost of $900,000 ('MGM Leases' 1956). This was MGM's first sale to television. A month later, he sold a package of 725 features to CBS's owned-and-operated stations for $20 million (ibid.). Excluded from the package were *Gone With the Wind* and *The Wizard of Oz*, among other big hits. Thereafter, the pre-1948 film library consistently buttressed MGM's bottom line.

Having released their old films to TV, Hollywood found it easy to collaborate again by producing original television programming. The majors entered telefilm production beginning in 1955. Unlike the early independent telefilm producers who catered to the first-run syndication market, the majors supplied programming to the networks during prime time. As the proportion of live prime-time programming on all three networks declined after 1955, the working relationship between the film industry and the networks became Hollywood (the supplier) and New York (the exhibitor).

MGM's entry into television production was tentative like those of the other majors. The leading telefilm producers during the fifties were MCA/Revue, Columbia's Screen Gems, and Desilu. MGM's first entry was *The MGM Parade*, which aired over ABC in 1955. The weekly half-hour series contained segments from MGM's older films and interviews with stars promoting upcoming MGM releases. It was essentially a television commercial and not a very good one. *The MGM Parade* was cancelled after one season. To supply programming for prime time, MGM conformed to the standard practice dictated by the networks and self-financed pilots that were pitched to the networks during the selling season. Starting out, it produced seven pilots but failed to sell a single TV series. Barry managed to produce only two prime-time series, *The Thin Man* starring Peter Lawford and Phyllis Kirk as Nick and Nora Charles, which aired on NBC for two seasons from 1957 to 1959, and *Northwest Passage* starring Keith Larsen and Buddy Ebsen, which aired on ABC in 1958. Adapting old features for telefilm production would characterize MGM's output to the end. It made a certain amount of sense; the titles of such programs had name recognition, and MGM had to pay nothing for the television rights.

Barry's successor, George T. Shupert, had better luck by producing *National Velvet* (1960), a drama series starring Lori Martin as Velvet Brown; *The Asphalt Jungle* (1961), a police drama starring Jack Warden, Arch Johnson, and Bill Smith; and *Dr. Kildare*, a medical drama starring Richard Chamberlain and Raymond Massey – all inspired by older MGM features. *Dr. Kildare* was the most successful, lasting five seasons on NBC. Shupert resigned after one year, and when Weitman took over, MGM-TV became a major telefilm producer responsible for *Mr. Novak* (1963–65), a dramatic series starring James Franciscus and Dean Jagger; *The Man from U.N.C.L.E.* (1964–68), a sci-fi series starring Robert Vaughn and David McCallum; *Flipper* (1964–67), a family show starring Brian Kelly, Luke Halpin, and Tommy Norden; and *Please Don't Eat the Daisies* (1965–67), a sitcom starring Patricia Crowley and Mark Miller.

The long-running television series did a lot to fill MGM's excess capacity after it cut back on film production during the fifties. 'A studio is like an airplane,' said Smith (1964). 'if you don't fly it, it goes to pot. It must produce in order to exist – to keep its scenic division, its shops, its technicians, its artisans. These various departments are vital to both TV and feature production – film is film – and move effortlessly between the two.

MGM-TV hit the doldrums in 1967 after Robert Weitman resigned, presumably over a falling out with O'Brien, and moved to Columbia Pictures as film production chief. O'Brien replaced him in the TV slot with Herbert F. Solow, a 36-year-old former production chief at Desilu where he launched a string of network hits, such as *Mission: Impossible*, *Star Trek*, and *Mannix*. Solow brought the television division back to life by producing three pilots and selling them to each of the networks for the 1969–70 season: *Medical Center* to CBS, *Then Came Bronson* to NBC, and *The Courtship of Eddie's Father* to ABC. To fill the film production slot, O'Brien appointed Clark Ramsey, Weitman's executive assistant. It was an interim appointment.

Independent production continued

O'Brien returned MGM to profitability. After the 1963 debacle, profits rose steadily from $7.4 million in 1964 to $14 million in 1967 ('Loew's and MGM' 1967). MGM's main producers during the O'Brien-Weitman management were Filmways, Carlo Ponti, Seven Arts Productions, John Frankenheimer, and Stanley Kubrick. Filmways was headed by Martin Ransohoff, who founded the company in 1952 shortly after college in partnership with Ed Casper. With $200 in hand, they started out making commercials then branched out into television by putting together packages of stars, story, and director and obtaining financing from the networks. Their biggest hits – *Mr. Ed*, *The Beverly Hillbillies*, and *Petticoat Junction* – were rural comedies that kept CBS at the top of the ratings in the early sixties. MGM released ten Filmways pictures beginning in 1963, among them Arthur Hiller's *The Americanization of Emily* (1964) starring Julie Andrews and James Garner; Vincente Minnelli's *The Sandpiper* (1965) starring Elizabeth Taylor and

Richard Burton; and Norman Jewison's *The Cincinnati Kid* (1965) starring Steve McQueen and Edward G. Robinson.

The Sandpiper received the worst reviews but made the most money of the group. Ransohoff signed Taylor to a contract in May 1963, a month before the release of *Cleopatra*. *The Sandpiper* premiered in New York at the Radio City Music Hall on 15 July 1965. By then Taylor and Burton had divorced their spouses and married. The movie was based on a story by Ransohoff about a married Episcopal priest who has an illicit affair with a free-thinking hippie with an illegitimate 9-year-old son. Dalton Trumbo and Michael Wilson wrote the screenplay, and the setting was the majestic California Big Sur coast. Crowther (1965) said the movie offered 'some striking presentments of the famous Taylor-Burton affair' and was contemptible for endowing a 'cheap story with spiritual grandeur and recti-tude.' *Variety* called the picture 'trite and often ponderous in its philosophizing' (*VFR*, 30 June 1965). Gottfried (1965) said, 'This new film meets all the standards of Hollywood mediocrity. It is a stock triangle, this time in a hopeless imitation bohemia; slack, superficial and insipid.' MGM launched the picture with a steamy ad campaign – 'She gave men a taste of life that made them hunger for more!' – and opened it widely for the summer breakout. *The Sandpiper* became MGM's top-grossing picture of the year.

Carlo Ponti delivered two big pictures, David Lean's *Doctor Zhivago* (1965) and Michelangelo Antonioni's *Blow-Up* (1966). Ponti had acquired the rights to Boris Pasternak's Nobel Prize–winning novel in 1963. It had been smuggled out of the Soviet Union, where it was banned, and had gone on to become an international best seller. To direct the movie, Ponti tapped David Lean, the two-time Oscar winner for *The Bridge on the River Kwai* (1957) and *Lawrence of Arabia* (1962). The international cast was headed by Omar Sharif in the title role and featured Julie Christie, Geraldine Chaplin, Tom Courtenay, Rod Steiger, Alec Guinness, and Sir Ralph Richardson. Ponti had originally proposed Sophia Loren for the part of Lara, but Lean quashed the idea, preferring instead a younger Julie Christie, who had been nominated and would later win an Oscar for her performance in John Schlesinger's *Darling* (1965). Lean had worked with both Sharif and Guinness in *Lawrence*, and it was from that picture that he selected his crew – screenwriter Robert Bolt, cinematographer Freddie Young, production designer John Box, costume designer Phyllis Dalton, and composer Maurice Jarre. Lean set up pro-duction in Madrid, where he shot his interiors at the C.E.A. Studios and on the Moscow set constructed on a 10-acre site near Madrid's airport. Location scenes were shot in the Spanish mountains and in Finland. It took two years to complete the epic.

Variety's review was right on the mark: 'The sweep and scope of the Russian revolution, as reflected in the personalities of those who either adapted or were crushed, has been captured by David Lean in *Doctor Zhivago*, frequently with dra-matic intensity. Director has accomplished one of the most meticulously designed and executed films.' Carlo Ponti's production, it added, 'is an excellent achievement in filmmaking and seems destined for good hardticket action' (*VFR*, 29 December

FIGURE 7.5 Omar Sharif and Julie Christie in David Lean's *Doctor Zhivago* (1965)

1965). *Doctor Zhivago* won five Academy Awards, for Adapted Screenplay, Cinematography, Art Direction, Costume Design, and Original Score. It grossed $38 million in domestic rental compared to $39 million for *Ben-Hur* ('All-Time Boxoffice' 1970: 25).

Blow-Up was based on a short story by the Argentine writer Julio Cortázar and the fashion photography of David Bailey, who captured the 'Swinging London' pop culture scene. Ponti persuaded Michelangelo Antonioni, who was contemplating making a film in English, to direct it. Antonioni worked with his long-time collaborator, writer Tonino Guerra, to develop the screenplay. Ponti set up at MGM British Studios to qualify for Eady subsidies and to have easy access to London locations. When Antonioni was asked, 'Would the picture be clear or ambiguous?' he answered, 'Definitely ambiguous' (Watts 1966: 3). *Blow-Up* premiered in New York 18 December 1966 at the Coronet, a prominent art house on the Upper East Side. MGM released the picture through a subsidiary, Premier Productions, without a seal rather than cutting it to meet Production Code standards. *Life* ('Antonioni's' 1967: 62–7) magazine helped the cause by publishing full-page photographs of the scenes that 'lost *Blow-Up* the Seal.' Driving home the point, MGM gave Vanessa Redgrave star billing and prominently displayed a photo of her with crossed arms covering her bare chest on all the ads. David

FIGURE 7.6 David Hemmings and Vanessa Redgrave in Michelangelo Antonioni's *Blow-Up* (1966)

Hemmings, who was in practically every shot, received costar billing along with Sarah Miles, who had a small part.

Variety said, 'It is doubtful that the general public (any more than this reviewer) will get the "message" of this film, shrouded as it is in shadings and symbols, in mysterious mummery and way-out treatment. As a commentary on a sordid, confused side of humanity in this modern age, it's a bust' (*VFR*, 21 October 1966). But Crowther gave it a rave review, as did others. 'This is a fascinating picture, which has something real to say about the matter of personal involvement and emotional commitment in a jazzed-up, media-hooked-in world so cluttered with synthetic stimulations that natural feelings are overwhelmed. It is vintage Antonioni fortified with a Hitchcock twist, and it is beautifully photographed in color' (*NYTFR*, 19 December 1966). *Blow-Up* went into national release within weeks of the New York art-house premiere. *Blow-Up* was named Best Film of the year and Antonioni Best Director by the newly organized National Society of Film Critics. It also won the Grand Prix at Cannes in 1967 and many other awards. Produced at a cost of $1.8 million, *Blow-Up* took in $20 million in the U.S. box office alone (Balio 2010: 245).

John Frankenheimer made four pictures for MGM, but only one was a success, *Grand Prix* (1966), an action picture about international Formula One auto racing.

FIGURE 7.7 James Garner in John Frankenheimer's *Grand Prix* (1966)

Frankenheimer started out directing award-winning dramas for CBS's *Playhouse 90* and other live anthology series during the 'golden age' of television. His screen credits included the highly regarded *Birdman of Alcatraz* (1962), *The Manchurian Candidate* (1962), *Seven Days in May* (1964), *The Train* (1964), and *Seconds* (1966). His producing partner was John Lewis. *Grand Prix*, with a cast headed by James Garner, Eva Marie Saint, and Yves Montand, followed the professional and romantic rivalries of four drivers making the grand-prix circuit in the 1966 season. The picture was shot in 70mm Super Panavision and premiered at the Warner Cinerama Theater in New York as a roadshow on 21 December 1966. It had a three-hour running time. The main attraction, of course, was 'roar and whine of engines sending men and machines hurtling over the 10 top road and track courses of Europe, the U.S. and Mexico. . . . The real stars of *Grand Prix*,' said *Variety*, 'are the cameramen – Lionel Lindon and his second unit team . . . who worked out intricate business of running with the racing cars, all within the overall production design by Richard Sylbert.' *Variety* added, '*Grand Prix* is one of those rare pictures that draws its basic strength, excitement and interest-arresting potential through the visual, the pure art of cinema' (*VFR*, 28 December 1966). *Grand Prix* went on to become one of the top ten releases of 1966 and the winner of three Oscars, for Film Editing, Sound, and Sound Effects.

MGM's relationship with Seven Arts Productions began in 1962 with the release of Stanley Kubrick's *Lolita* (1962). Seven Arts, headed by Eliot Hyman, financed independent productions and arranged for their distribution. *Lolita* was produced by James B. Harris, Kubrick's partner, and starred James Mason, Shelley Winters, Peter Sellers, and Sue Lyon. It was shot in England but not at MGM-British Studios. In adapting Vladimir Nabokov's controversial bestseller, Kubrick and Harris had to make crucial concessions to get a Production Code seal and a pass from the Legion of Decency, and it showed. *Variety* said the film version is 'like a bee from which the stinger has been removed . . . The novel has been stripped of its pubescent heroine and most of its lively syntax, graphic honesty and sharp observations on people and places in a land abundant of clichés' (*VFR*, 13 June 1962). Crowther agreed, saying, 'The character of Lolita, the perversely precocious child who had such effect on the libido of the middle-aged hero in the book, is not a child in the movie. She looks to be a good 17 years old, possessed of a striking figure and a devilishly haughty teen-age air.' 'The distinction is fine,' he said, 'but she is definitely not a "nymphet." As played by Sue Lyon, a new-comer, she reminds one of Carroll Baker's *Baby Doll*' (*NYTFR*, 4 June 1962). *Lolita* did well at the box office initially, but faded in subsequent release.

Afterward, MGM partnered with Seven Arts to make Sidney Lumet's *The Hill* (1965) and Robert Aldrich's *The Dirty Dozen* (1967). Both were made at MGM-British Studios and produced by Kenneth Hyman, Eliot Hyman's son. *The Hill*, set in a British military prison during World War II, was Sean Connery's first attempt to establish himself as something other than James Bond. It received a lukewarm reception. 'Mr. Connery is stark and sturdy as the usual underdog hero – quite a departure from the flashiness of his characterization of James Bond,' said Crowther (*NYTFR*, 4 October 1965).

The Dirty Dozen, Aldrich's picture 'about 12 soldiers, all condemned-to-die criminals, who are given a chance to redeem themselves by carrying off a suicidal mission prior to the D-Day invasion,' contained an all-male cast headed by Lee Marvin, Ernest Borgnine, Charles Bronson, and Jim Brown. Aldrich shot the movie in 35mm, but after a favorable rough-cut screening to a preview audience, MGM decided to reprocess the picture and release it in 70mm to suitable equipped theaters backed by an extensive promotional campaign. *Boxoffice* ('The Dirty' 1967) called it 'one of the most convincing and exciting and the most savage war films ever made.' Crowther called it 'an astonishingly wanton war film' and a 'studied indulgence of sadism that is morbid and disgusting beyond words' (*NYTFR*, 16 June 1967). The graphic violence in the movie was something new. Nothing like it was ever seen in a John Wayne war movie. No doubt that was the appeal. *The Dirty Dozen* premiered in New York on 15 June 1967 and became MGM's highest-grossing film of the year.

Stanley Kubrick's *2001: A Space Odyssey* (1968) ranked among MGM's top ten of the decade and was largely responsible for averting a major financial disaster for MGM in 1968. Kubrick's sci-fi epic was based on Arthur C. Clarke's 20-year-old short story, *The Sentinel*. Kubrick had pitched the project to MGM while his popular Cold War comedy *Dr. Strangelove* (1964) was in release. Kubrick set up production in England to qualify for Eady subsidies and to have easy access to the sound stages at Shepperton Studios and MGM-British Studios to create his realistic special effects. His picture was filmed almost entirely within a studio situation and tied up the sound stages at MGM-British for nearly two years. To play the two astronauts, Kubrick chose Keir Dullea and Gary Lockwood.

Kubrick kept the picture under wraps during the filming, and it was eagerly awaited. The picture was released in 70mm Super Panavision, MGM's second such release, and opened as a roadshow in Cinerama theaters with a 160-minute running time first in Washington, DC, at the Uptown Theater on 2 April 1968, then in New York and Los Angeles the next two days. New York critics initially panned the movie, including Renata Adler, who replaced Bosley Crowther as chief film critic of the *New York Times* in 1967. The 29-nine-year-old Bryn Mawr graduate had never before been a regular film critic. Her appointment was viewed as part of the newspaper's new generation rejuvenation. In her opinion: 'The uncompromising slowness of the movie makes it hard to sit through without talking – and people on all sides when I saw it were talking almost throughout the film. . . . With all its attention to detail, a kind of reveling in its own I.Q.,' she explained, 'the movie acknowledged no obligation to validate its conclusion for those, me for example, who are not science-fiction buffs. By the end, three unreconciled plot lines – the slab, Dullea's aging, the period bedroom – are simply left there like a Rorschach, with murky implications of theology' (*NYTFR*, 4 April 1968).

After its third public screening, Kubrick cut nineteen minutes from the picture. Out-of-town reviewers and second-look critics in New York were more receptive to the picture after MGM released the shorter version. *2001* became a cult classic, playing long runs on a reserved-seat basis for months in many theaters around the world. 'Stanley Kubrick and MGM based their $10-million gamble on the belief that the mass audience for films was ready for way-out [science fiction] speculations *visually* presented,' said Lee (1968). 'This belief has a strong foundation: The current motion picture audience is composed mostly of young adults under 25. This is the first group in history to grow up with the massive exposure to visual presentations made possible by television.'

Proxy fights with Philip J. Levin

MGM's track record under O'Brien failed to impress one MGM shareholder, Philip J. Levin, who launched two proxy fights against the company in 1966 and 1967. Levin, a real estate developer in New Jersey and one of the largest builders of supermarkets and shopping malls in the northeast, had been elected to the MGM board and executive committee in 1965. He launched his first proxy fight in May 1966 with the goal of unseating O'Brien. Levin narrowly lost the fight and in November launched a second proxy battle to place a slate of like-minded members on the board and take control of the company. Levin asserted that much of MGM's 182 acres in Culver City 'could be used for building apartment houses, office buildings and shopping centers.' The land was being carried on the company's books for less than $2 million, but it had been estimated that the property could be sold for $150,000 an acre, for a total of $27 million, reported Penn (1967). Levin also complained 'that much of MGM's earnings were derived from leasing films to television rather than to theaters' ('MGM Struggle' 1967). He claimed that MGM would have lost $5.7 million rather than made $15.3 million in 1966 before interest and taxes from production and distribution of features had the impact of television rentals not been included. Levin wanted MGM to produce more and better pictures that could make it exclusively in the theatrical market. 'Income from TV should be a bonus, not a refuge,' he stated.

At the annual meeting of MGM stockholders on 23 February 1967, a management-backed slate of directors defeated the move. O'Brien defended MGM's earnings record under his management and told stockholders that the profits resulted 'from planning, from progress, from thinking ahead and moving forward' ('MGM Struggle' 1967). O'Brien stated that management was fully aware of the land's potential and was considering a proposal to lease land in Thousand Oaks to a new studio but that no decision had been made. Earlier, O'Brien had accused Levin of having 'a shallow understanding, if any at all, of the development of feature pictures as the banner programming on TV networks prime time' ('MGM Executive' 1967).

What was going on? Television had changed the way the American film industry conducted its business. By the sixties, network television had become an important ancillary market for post-1948 feature films. Anticipating a boost in demand for newer pictures when the networks converted to color television, Hollywood reached a settlement with the actors and writers in 1960 regarding residual payments. Afterward, the networks beginning with NBC launched weekly series of recent vintage Hollywood features until by the end of the decade, every night was Saturday night at the movies. The average price for a run-of-the-mill feature leased to the networks jumped from $150,000 to $400,000 by 1965. The following year, a new high was reached when ABC paid Columbia $2 million for *The Bridge on the River Kwai* and opened a new era of motion picture blockbusters on TV (Balio 1990a: 38). Afterward, competitive bidding by the networks became hectic. In 1964, MGM was licensing pictures for as much as $800,000 for first-run network showings. MGM had been offered $10 million for just a single network showing of *Gone With the Wind*, which O'Brien turned down because the film remained a top grosser in the theatrical market as a reissue (Penn 1967). 'Film makers will be benefitting from an ideal supply–demand situation for some years to come if TV keeps on gobbling up pictures,' said Penn (1967). 'Last year, about 225 American-made films were released to movie houses – but in New York City alone, the six VHF commercial stations telecast over 140 feature films in a single week.' Conventional theatrical exhibition had been considered the primary source of revenue, with anything from TV just 'gravy.' But as relations between the two industries stabilized, television income became expected and planned for. So long as the 'ideal supply–demand situation' continued, this proved to be a safe way to budget new releases. As the following chapter reveals, the situation changed, with disastrous consequences for the majors. Levin's proscription was correct.

Mergers and acquisitions

The networks' voracious appetite for feature films help stabilize the motion picture business, but it also made Hollywood studios attractive takeover targets. Champlin (1966) said in November 1966, 'It has been a remarkable, a watershed year for Hollywood. Never in modern times has the actual financial control of the studios been in contention on such a scale. The thrones of the overseers of production have been tottered and they continue to totter.' The takeovers began in 1966 when Paramount merged with Gulf + Western Industries Inc. Headed by Charles G. Bluhdorn, an Austrian émigré, Gulf + Western started out as a small auto-parts company and then swiftly acquired sixty companies in such diverse fields as food products, natural resources, financial services, chemicals, and real estate. Paramount had been a setup for outside raiders. The company was nearly moribund. Paramount had a backlog of newer films that had yet to be licensed to network television and was anything but aggressive in its dealing with the networks. The studio had experienced continued production losses and had shied away from television production. Moreover, Barney Balaban, its president, was in his seventies, and the average age of the board of directors was not far behind. Paramount Pictures marked Gulf + Western's entry into the growing leisure-time field. In 1967, Bluhdorn added Desilu Productions and the Famous Players Canadian theater chain to its new division.

In 1967, United Artists was acquired by the San Francisco-based Transamerica Corporation, a full-line financial service company involved in insurance, consumer loans, and more than twenty-five other related firms. Unlike Paramount, United Artists was in excellent financial shape at the time of the takeover. The management team headed by Arthur Krim and Robert Benjamin that had taken over a moribund United Artists from company founders Mary Pickford and Charlie Chaplin in 1951 had transformed the company into an industry leader by devising a successful plan to finance and distribute independent producers. The strategy turned the company around. UA went public in 1957 and, ten years later, had become the largest producer-distributor in the world. As the ranks of independent producers swelled during the sixties, UA's roster contained a mix of creative producers, packagers, talent, and combinations thereof, such as Harry Saltzman and Albert 'Cubby' Broccoli, producers of the James Bond series, actors Burt Lancaster and Frank Sinatra, producer-directors Stanley Kramer and Otto Preminger, and the Mirisch company, a successful packager that produced sixty-seven pictures for UA over fifteen years, three of which won Oscars for Best Picture: Billy Wilder's *The Apartment* (1960), Robert Wise and Jerome Robbins's *West Side Story* (1961), and Norman Jewison's *In the Heat of the Night* (1967). The management team owned a large block of stock in the company and was searching for a buyer as a way to realize capital gains. Transamerica, for its part, was searching for an entree into the leisure-time field. As John Beckett, Transamerica president, explained (Penn 1967), 'With the declining work week and the growing affluence of Americans, people have more free time and the money to enjoy it.'

Also in 1967, Kinney National Services, a conglomerate headed by Steve Ross that operated funeral homes, a car rental agency, parking lots and garages, and a building maintenance service, purchased the Ashley Famous talent agency. Venturing further into entertainment, Ross acquired Warner Bros.-Seven Arts in 1969. Seven Arts had acquired the ailing Warner Bros. studio from founder Jack Warner in 1967, along with its post-1948 films and record labels. Ross added toys, cosmetics, video games, and other businesses to his company, which he renamed Warner Communications in 1972 after selling off the old Kinney business. This was just the start. Mergers and acquisitions would continue apace as Hollywood adjusted to the arrival of new technologies and changes in the global economy.

Edgar M. Bronfman management

In August 1967, Levin decided to cash out and sold his stake in MGM to Edgar M. Bronfman, the 38-year-old president of Joseph E. Seagram & Sons, and to Time Inc., the magazine publisher. Levin received $33 million for his shares, which was about $20 million more than he had paid for them. Bronfman purchased 420,000 shares and Time 300,000 (Canby 1967). Both said they were buying MGM stock for investment and were acting independently. The buyout brought relief to O'Brien. Bronfman had earlier bought a big block of MGM shares but chose not to become embroiled in the proxy fight. The shares were privately purchased by Bronfman and his family and not by Seagram or its parent company, Distiller Corporation-Seagrams, Ltd. of Montreal.

In 1966, the Bronfman family bought into Paramount Pictures with the intent of taking it over, but Bluhdorn moved in more aggressively, and the Bronfmans sold their holdings. Bronfman ('Time' 1967: 3) said 'he saw no need for management or operational changes in MGM, terming the film company "the best-managed company in a very exciting industry."' Bronfman was given two seats on the MGM board after the purchase, one for himself and one for Leo Kolber, director of the Bronfman family's private investment company. Time was given one seat on the board, which was filled by Edgar Baker, a Time vice president. Baker explained that Time has 'a generic interest in the moving image. We wanted to be an outside insider so we could contemplate our compatibility with it' (Welles 1969). Bronfman augmented his holdings in MGM from other sources and eventually emerged as the largest single stockholder.

In April 1968, Bronfman sought a bigger voice in MGM's affairs. He wanted O'Brien to 'relinquish the presidency to a younger man' and increased representation on the board, among other things. The conglomerate takeovers had gone hand in hand with the accent on youth. A new generation of younger talent took over the production reins of Hollywood   Ken Hyman, age 38, at Warner Bros. Seven Arts, Robert Evans, age 37, at Paramount, Richard Zanuck, age 34, at Fox and David Picker, age 36, at United Artists. These young executives were supposed to be more in tune with the sixties audience. At MGM, O'Brien was approaching age 64, with no provision for an orderly transition once his contract expired in August 1969. O'Brien tried to be a 'one-man band,' explained an MGM executive (quoted in Welles 1969): 'There was practically no staffing at the top. There were no top financial people, no system of financial controls, no marketing organization, no research staff. No effort was made to leverage all those assets.' Bronfman was dissatisfied with two seats on the board given the amount of stock that he owned. In May, the MGM board expanded its number and elected two different members representing Bronfman and one representing Time. At the October board meeting, O'Brien yielded to demands from Edgar M. Bronfman that he step down as chief executive officer. The plan was to move O'Brien up to chairman once the new president was found. The board formed a committee of six directors chaired by Bronfman to find O'Brien's replacement. 'Mr. Bronfman seems to have succeeded in the long-sought after role of king-maker,' said the *Wall Street Journal* ('O'Brien' 1968).

On 14 January 1969, after a much-publicized talent hunt, the board chose O'Brien's successor, Louis F. Polk Jr., the 38-year-old former financial vice president of General Mills, Inc. He was the first chief executive of a major studio to be brought in from outside the industry. Polk received a BS degree in electrical and industrial engineering from Yale and an MBA from the Harvard Business School. At General Mills, Polk had hired numerous business school grads and, with the full support of the young managers, closed nine of the company's seventeen flour mills and used the cash to diversify into toys, crafts, and games via acquisitions of Play-Doh, Parker Bros., and other companies. As Byron noted (1968: 24). 'Many have long felt that letting a young bizschool-trained "whiz kid" loose on a major film company could result in revolutionizing the field. Many standard assumptions in the industry could, it was argued, fall by the wayside as sentiment was brushed aside in favor of the slide rule.'

To take charge of production in Culver City, Polk elevated Herbert F. Solow to the dual posts of vice president in charge of theatrical and television production in April 1969, replacing Clark Ramsey. Solow reorganized the production department and began to build his slate. It would be targeted mainly at young audiences. 'These are the kind of pictures MGM has never made, yet they are what most moviegoers want to see,' he said (Warga 1969). As part of Polk's 'accent on youth' policy, he instituted a sweep of MGM's top management and replaced veteran executives with 'young blood.' With a cadre of MBAs, he analyzed all facets of the company's operations, established 'profit centers,' shelved existing film and record projects, and announced plans to dispose of MGM's 2,000-acre ranch in Conejo Valley and a big chunk of Lot I in Culver City to reduce overhead and to raise working capital. As *Variety* ('Bronfman' 1969: 3) pointed out, MGM was 'determined to write off and write down everything possible so as to present a "clean slate" for Polk in 1970.'

MGM was a wounded company when Polk took control. MGM's performance lagged beginning in 1968. Earnings were off by 33 percent, due in part to a slump in its MGM Records division, the cancellation of three of the four network series produced by the company, and a string of money-losing pictures, such as John Schlesinger's *Far From the Madding Crowd* (1967) starring Julie Christie and Peter Glenville's *The Comedians* (1967) starring Elizabeth Taylor and Richard Burton. They were produced by Joseph Janni and Glenville, respectively. At a board of directors meeting in Los Angeles on 26 May 1969, the company announced that its loss for the year could be as much as $19 million. At that meeting, Robert O'Brien resigned as chairman and was replaced by Edgar Bronfman (Sloane 1969a).

8

KIRK KERKORIAN AND THE BUYING AND SELLING OF MGM, PART 1 (1969–85)

Kirk Kerkorian takes control

On 22 July 1969, Kirk Kerkorian, the 51-year-old Las Vegas casino operator, made a tender offer to buy one million shares or 17 percent of MGM stock at $35 a share with the announced goal of acquiring working control of the company (Sloane 1969b). Through his Tracy Investment Company, Kerkorian was the principal owner of the refurbished 767-room Flamingo Hotel and Casino in Las Vegas, which Bugsy Siegel had opened on the strip twenty years earlier. He owned a large stake in Western Air Lines, which had just received some lush rights to serve Hawaii. And he was chairman and principal shareholder of International Leisure Corporation, the developer of the 3,000-room International Hotel in Las Vegas, which was under construction.

MGM dug in and moved to block the tender offer by taking Kerkorian to court. Since Kerkorian intended to borrow the needed money from Transamerica, the suit argued that Transamerica's backing of Kerkorian would be in violation of antitrust laws. The court ruled in MGM's favor. Undaunted, Kerkorian immediately turned to Europe and secured loans at high interest from German and British banks. The tender offer gave Kerkorian 24 percent of MGM's outstanding stock. Kerkorian had wanted to acquire Bronfman's shares from the offer, but Bronfman held tight. Kerkorian therefore made a second tender offer at $42 a share in September, which increased his holdings to 47 percent of shares outstanding and gave him working control of the company. Total cost: $72 million in debt (Sloane 1969b). Rather than fight the takeover, Edgar Bronfman resigned from the board on 21 October 1969. He had no stomach to start a new proxy fight. 'The passing of control of the destiny of Metro-Goldwyn-Mayer, Inc. . . . from Edgar M. Bronfman, the liquor heir, to Kirk Kerkorian, the self-made millionaire, after just 10 months marked the end of one of the shortest reigns in filmdom,' said Sloane (1969b). Bronfman held on to his stock and took a paper loss, since MGM shares were selling at around $40, considerably less than he had paid for his holdings.

Kerkorian's story 'makes Horatio Alger seem like an underachiever,' said Egan (2004: 5). Kerkorian was born in Fresno, California, on 6 June 1917, one of four children of Armenian immigrants. His father, a fruit merchant, lost his money in the 1921 recession and moved his family to Los Angeles, where he 'repeatedly went in and out of business,' Kerkorian recalled (Bedingfield 1969). To help support his family, Kerkorian quit school at 16 and took jobs wherever he could find them. As a student at the Los Angeles Metropolitan Trade School, he was 'average or maybe a little bit below average,' he said (ibid.). At the onset of the Depression, he did a stint with the Civilian Conservation Corps then took up amateur boxing but quit in 1939 and learned to fly. When World War II broke out, he joined the British Royal Air Force and ferried Canadian-built Mosquito bombers from Labrador to Scotland. Only one in four made it over the treacherous North Atlantic. After the war, he bought and sold military surplus planes and earned enough to purchase a small Los Angeles charter service in 1947. He eventually grew this into Trans International Airlines, which became the source of his wealth. In 1967, he sold the airline to Transamerica Corp. for $90 million in TA stock (ibid.). Transamerica was the parent company of United Artists. Kerkorian had the chance to closely observe the workings of a successful motion picture company as a result of the sale, which may have influenced his decision to acquire MGM.

James Aubrey Jr. management

Kerkorian intended to replace Louis F. Polk Jr. with someone with film industry experience, but he gave no indication where he planned on taking the company. Kerkorian's first choice for the top job was Herb Jaffe, vice president in charge of West Coast production for United Artists, but Jaffe stayed put. Kerkorian then held discussions with Mike Frankovich and Ray Stark, prominent independent producers, and then settled on another outsider who knew little about producing movies, James Aubrey Jr. Aubrey received the same salary as Polk's – $208,000 a year, said Sloane (1969b) – but Aubrey did not want a contract because, as he reportedly said, 'a contract is no good if you don't do a good job.' Aubrey, 'the boy wizard,' was president of CBS-TV from 1959 to 1964. During his tenure, CBS's earnings more than doubled with smash 'hick-coms' like *The Beverly Hillbillies*, *Green Acres*, *Gomer Pyle*, and *Petticoat Junction*. Aubrey was educated at Philips Exeter and Princeton and served in the Air Force as a pilot during World War II. He started out in television in 1948 as a salesman for a CBS television station in Los Angeles. In 1956, he was hired by ABC-TV as vice president of programs and talent. ABC was the weakest of the three major networks, but Aubrey boosted ABC's ratings with such hit shows as *Maverick*, *The Rifleman*, *77 Sunset Strip*, and two family comedies, *The Donna Reed Show* and *Leave It to Beaver*. Aubrey's tenure at CBS-TV came to a sudden end in February 1965, when CBS chairman William S. Paley fired him 'in a blaze of publicity and unproved allegations' regarding his conflicts of interest, his arbitrariness, and his private life, reported Kasindorf (1972). At CBS, Aubrey was remembered for 'his almost inaudible voice and coldly unsentimental decisiveness,' which gained him a memorable nickname – 'the Smiling Cobra,' Kasindorf added. Aubrey worked unsuccessfully as an independent film producer before joining MGM.

The 1969 recession

The year 1969 was not a good year to buy a film company. The industry was in the throes of a recession, which in the opinion of A. H. Howe (1969: 15), a Bank of America executive, matched 'in seriousness, dislocation and change by only two events in film history, the sound revolution of 1930 and the television upheaval of the 1950s.' This state of affairs had its roots in the blockbuster philosophy of the majors, when companies came to rely on one or two big hits a year to stay in the black and generate profits. MGM adopted the philosophy following the success of *Ben-Hur* (1959) if not earlier. 20th Century Fox under Darryl Zanuck was its most enthusiastic booster. Fox reversed the company's fortunes after the *Cleopatra* (1963) fiasco by producing *The Sound of Music* (1965). Although the picture cost a hefty $10 million, it went on to become the highest-grossing picture of the decade. All the studios accepted the larger risks of big-ticket pictures by 1968; some of the top hits of the decade included MGM's *Doctor Zhivago* (1965), Disney's *Mary Poppins* (1964), Warner Bros.' *My Fair Lady* (1964), and United Artists' *Thunderball* (1965).

The risks of producing blockbusters were worth taking because network television seemingly had an insatiable demand for feature films. Every night was movie night on the networks, and rental prices skyrocketed. Hollywood became complacent. The thinking became that if a picture didn't make it in the theatrical market, it would break even or earn a profit from the network television sale. In 1969, the bottom fell out of the market. The types of pictures that had been so successful just a year before were now bombing. They included a raft of musicals such as Fox's *Hello, Dolly!* (1969), Paramount's *Paint Your Wagon* (1969), and MGM's *Goodbye, Mr. Chips* (1969), as well as spectacles like Columbia's *Casino Royale* (1967), MGM's *The Shoes of a Fisherman* (1968), and United Artists' *The Battle of Britain* (1969).

The safety net of a network sale had been removed. Confronted with seven movie nights a week during the 1968–69 season, TV audiences became selective, and ratings dropped. And since the networks had acquired enough product to last until 1972, they stopped bidding on theatrical films. And at the exhibition level, the mass audience was staying home. As Champlin (1970) put it, 'The movies entered the 60s as a mass family entertainment medium in trouble and they leave them as a mass but minority art-form, important and newly influential, wildly divergent and addressed to many divergent audiences.' 'Moviegoing as a national habit is over except among the young and unmarried (or the young and married but childless) segment of the population,' he said. 'And even this young audience is, like everyone else who goes to movies at all, enormously selective and discretionary.' All those blockbusters with bloated budgets worked their way through the distribution system at staggering losses. United Artists, 20th Century Fox, Columbia, and MGM were all awash in red ink. Hollywood nearly collapsed. Under pressure from the banks, the majors were forced into another period of retrenchment that lasted four years.

Trimming the fat

Polk had predicted that MGM would report a loss of $25 million in fiscal 1969. Aubrey reassessed the loss at $35 million by writing down the asset value of pictures in release, such as the musical version of *Goodbye, Mr. Chips*, and canceling fourteen projects in various stages of development, including three big-budget projects initiated by Solow – the Carlo Ponti–Fred Zinnemann production of Andre Malraux's *Man's Fate*; Martin Ransohoff's *Tai-Pan* starring Patrick McGoohan; and Blake Edwards's *She Loves Me* starring Julie Andrews. To reduce overhead, Aubrey relocated the company's corporate headquarters and 500 key employees from the MGM Building in New York to Culver City (Sloane 1969c). (MGM under O'Brien moved the original corporate headquarters from the Loew's Times Square building in 1966 to a new building located at the southeast corner of Sixth Avenue and Fifty-Fifth Street, where it leased eleven floors.) In Culver City, he slashed the workforce, sold off two back lots totaling one hundred acres to real estate developers, a warehouse full of costumes and props to an auctioneer, and MGM's cameras to Panavision. The cameras would later be leased from Panavision as needed. Since Aubrey planned on making fewer films in the future, he downsized MGM's distribution arm by closing most of MGM's domestic film exchanges. In England, Aubrey closed the Borehamwood Studio outside London. To take the place of MGM-British, which was operating unprofitably, Aubrey entered into a partnership with Great Britain's Electrical and Musical Industries (EMI) to use EMI's Elstree production facilities and to coproduce and distribute MGM's films in foreign markets. One last thing: 'The new management quietly removed the name Irving Thalberg from MGM's administration building, as if it were an embarrassment to a later generation who had neither the interest in movies nor anything like his innovating flair,' reported Champlin (1973).

   Aubrey even contemplated a merger with 20th Century Fox, which was also being reorganized after the ouster of Richard D. Zanuck, the 36-year-old president and son of the chairman. Fox and Columbia Pictures were the only remaining majors that had not been absorbed by another company. Like MGM, Fox had suffered operating losses during the 1969 recession, and its survival was in jeopardy. Aubrey began discussions with a group of Fox's minority shareholders in early 1971, but they went nowhere. The Fox board refused to consider the matter.

Aubrey nonetheless had done his job. He turned a $35 million loss in 1969 to a profit of $16.4 million in 1971 and reduced MGM's bank debt from $80 million to $15 million (Kasindorf 1972). To help run the company, Aubrey promoted Douglas Netter to vice president in charge of world sales, the second-highest operating post in the company. Netter was Aubrey's first appointment after taking charge and came in as vice president in charge of sales. Before that, he was best known for directing the worldwide roadshow engagements for Sam Goldwyn's *Porgy and Bess* and Columbia's *Lawrence of Arabia*.

Aubrey temporarily saved MGM from disaster mainly by selling off unproductive assets. To survive, MGM decided to diversify. In October 1971, Aubrey announced MGM's intention to branch out into the leisure field first by building the world's largest resort hotel in Las Vegas and second by building a fleet of luxury cruise liners. 'There are peaks and valleys in the motion picture business,' he said (quoted in Dallos and Delugach 1971). 'By expanding into travel and resort fields with a good measure of predictability,' MGM hoped to build a 'steady flow of income.' The impetus for the move came from Kerkorian. Kerkorian had gotten out of the hotel business in 1970, when he sold the International and the Flamingo hotels to Hilton Hotels. He needed the money to repay those high-interest European bank loans he had secured to acquire control of MGM and Western Airlines. But he took a beating on the sale. The value of his International Leisure stock had plunged during the 1969–70 recession. 'His International Leisure stock was worth $180 million at the beginning of 1970, but a year later he was forced to sell half his holdings in the company for $16.5 million.' Kerkorian's response was, 'Sometimes you lose, but that's the nature of the game. There's always another game and another chance to win,' reported Kendall (2015). To build the new hotel, MGM paid Kerkorian about $5 million for a site he owned on the strip. MGM paid an additional amount to the owners of an adjoining plot. The project, overwhelmingly approved by the MGM board in December 1971, was christened MGM Grand Hotel after the 1932 MGM hit starring Greta Garbo and John Barrymore. A subsidiary corporation was formed in Nevada to operate the hotel. It was headed by MGM board chairman Fred Benninger, a Kerkorian insider and former president of International Leisure. To finance the $90 million project, MGM intended to raise the first $50 million from a public offering and the remainder from bank loans and studio funds (Kasindorf 1972). The longer-range cruise ship plan was placed on hold.

No Irving Thalberg

It was an article of faith in Hollywood that pictures targeted at the youth counterculture would revive the business. There was ample evidence for this belief. In 1967, three studio-backed pictures attracted young people in record numbers: Norman Jewison's *In the Heat of the Night* (United Artists) starring Sidney Poitier and Rod Steiger; Mike Nichols's *The Graduate* (Avco Embassy) starring Anne Bancroft and Dustin Hoffman; and Arthur Penn's *Bonnie and Clyde* (Warner Bros.) starring Warren Beatty and Faye Dunaway. By 1969, the first year of the recession, a slew of counterculture pictures had hit the market, led by Dennis Hopper's *Easy Rider* (Columbia) starring Hopper and Peter Fonda; John Schlesinger's *Midnight Cowboy* (United Artists) starring Dustin Hoffman and Jon Voight; and Franco Zeffirelli's *Romeo and Juliet* (Paramount) starring Leonard Whiting and Olivia Hussey. These pictures won Oscars for Best Picture (*In the Heat of the Night* and *Midnight Cowboy*), Best Director (Mike Nichols and John Schlesinger), and other Oscars and topped the box-office charts. Filmmakers could now treat 'once-shocking themes, with a maturity and candor unthinkable even five years ago,' as *Time* put it ('The Shock' 1967: 66). As of 1968, the MPAA under Jack Valenti had replaced the outmoded Production Code with a full-scale rating system administered by the Code and Rating Administration that classified films according to their suitability for different age groups.

By 1970, all the studios were making low-budget pictures with unknowns, directed at (and often by) young people. Aubrey, in tune with the times, wanted to create a new image for the company and resurrected a project initiated by O'Brien and then shelved by Polk – Michelangelo Antonioni's *Zabriskie Point*. Antonioni had been given a two-picture contract after the success of *Blow-Up*. Hoping that Antonioni could make an Americanized *Blow-Up*, O'Brien had invited Antonioni to make his next film in the United States. Antonioni got the idea for *Zabriskie Point* touring counterculture America in 1967. Antonioni saw for himself 'folk-song concerts, discotheques and pot parties. He investigated off-Broadway theater. He spoke with young artists and film makers in their lofts and he met political groups including the Black Panthers and the Yippies,' said Bosworth (1969: 116). Antonioni shot much of his picture in Death Valley. To play the leads, Antonioni chose two young people who had never acted before, Mark Frechette and Daria Halprin. When Polk saw the final results, he balked. The love-in orgy and the student riot scene that showed a police officer being fatally shot so intimidated Polk that he ordered Antonioni to reedit the picture and then shelved it indefinitely.

Aubrey personally flew to Rome and persuaded Antonioni to restore the offending scenes. MGM had high hopes for the picture, in which it had invested $7 million (Balio 2010: 289). It premiered in New York at the Coronet Theater on 9 February 1970 and bombed. Canby said, '*Zabriskie Point* will remain a movie of stunning superficiality' (*NYTFR*, 10 February 1970). Pauline Kael (1970: 95) called *Zabriskie Point* 'a rather pathetic mess.' Antonioni, she said, 'doesn't offer an outsider's view that illuminates what we had never seen for ourselves or what we had taken for granted – he plans and arranges every loaded bit of banality about our sins and vices.' 'Working outside the studio and on a huge scale,' she said, Antonioni 'winds up with an America as false and unconvincing as if it had been manufactured in a studio by foreign craftsmen. Though he uses actual locations, *Zabriskie Point* is as far off of America as the Italian Westerns shot in Spain.' The youth audience had ignored the picture. *Zabriskie Point* grossed a mere $900,000 during an embarrassingly brief theatrical run and was a huge disappointment for all concerned (Balio 2010: 289).

MGM had another campus rebellion picture in the works when Aubrey took over, the Irwin Winkler–Robert Chartoff production of *The Strawberry Statement* (1970). Herbert Solow had greenlighted it under the previous management. *The Strawberry Statement* directed by Stuart Hagmann was based on 'The Strawberry Statement: Notes of a College Revolutionary,' the diary kept by James Simon Kunen, a Columbia University student who witnessed the 1968 campus insurrection. *The Strawberry Statement* fared little better even though it was entered as an official American entry at the 1970 Cannes Film Festival and received a Jury Prize. Released just weeks after the Kent State massacre of four college students on 4 May 1970, the picture was being accused of exploiting the incident and died at the box office. The 'youthpix' phenomenon was dead by 1971.

Herbert Solow departed MGM in April 1971 to venture into independent production. Rather than replacing him, Aubrey took over the production reins of the company as well. Solow left behind two important projects, David Lean's *Ryan's Daughter* (1970) and *Shaft* (1971). *Ryan's Daughter* had gone over budget. Lean may have thought he had carte blanche to make the picture after *Dr. Zhivago*. He shot his epic mostly on the Dingle Peninsula in Ireland, where he constructed an entire village from scratch. Aubrey could do little more than complain since the picture was too far along to jettison. *Ryan's Daughter* was produced by Anthony Havelock-Allan and starred Robert Mitchum, Trevor Howard, Christopher Jones, John Mills, and Sarah Miles. Robert Bolt, Lean's collaborator on *Doctor Zhivago*, wrote the original screenplay about a married Irish woman who falls in love with the new commander of the British occupation force during World War I. MGM released it as a roadshow at the Ziegfeld Theater in New York with a running time of 192 minutes. The picture received a restrictive R rating from the MPAA's Code and Rating Administration (CARA). At issue were a nude love scene between Miles and Christopher Jones and the infidelity theme. The label restricted young people under 17 from attending the movie unless accompanied by an adult guardian. MGM ignored the rating and marketed it without any mention of it. MGM thus became the first MPAA member to defy CARA. Aubrey successfully appealed the decision to CARA's board and secured a more favorable GP rating, admitting all ages 'with parental guidance suggested.' He argued that the R rating would have spelled financial disaster for the company. Regardless, the picture was a disappointment, grossing $14.6 million in the U.S. compared to *Dr. Zhivago*'s $44.4 million take ('Updated' 1975). The critics were not kind to it. *Ryan's Daughter*, said Canby, 'marks a new apogee in [David Lean's] increasingly picturesque – and vacuous – 19th century romanticism' (*NYTFR*, 10 November 1970).

Shaft (1971) was based on Ernest Tidyman's 1970 hard-boiled thriller about a black private eye modeled after Dashiell Hammett's Sam Spade. The picture was brought to Solow's attention by screenwriters Sterling Silliphant and Roger Lewis, who had read the novel in manuscript. Solow's decision to back it was no doubt influenced by the success of such black films as Ossie Davis's *Cotton Comes to Harlem* (1970) and Melvin Van Peebles's *Sweet Sweetback's Baadassss Song* (1971). Silliphant and Lewis formed a partnership with Tidyman and formed Shaft

FIGURE 8.1 Richard Roundtree in Gordon Parks's *Shaft* (1971)

Productions, Ltd., to coproduce the picture with the studio. As part of the deal, MGM included a provision for possible sequels.

Shaft was directed by Gordon Parks and starred Richard Roundtree. Tidyman wrote the screenplay with John D. F. Black. Parks, a respected *Life* photographer, composer, and writer, shot the picture entirely on locations in Harlem, Greenwich Village, and Times Square. It opened with an R rating on 2 July 1971. Greenspan said that *Shaft* 'has surely the best title of any of the one-name movies to have opened in recent years. [*Marlow*, *Harper*, and *Madigan*] And though it doesn't have too much else of the best, it has a kind of self-generated good will that makes you want to like it even when for scenes on end you know it is doing everything wrong.' Describing the Shaft character, he said, 'Shaft is wish-fulfillment: the pad, the girls (whom he treats none too well), the fancy leather clothes, the ability to put down everybody and be paid back in admiration, the instinct for danger, the physical prowess, the fantastic ability that has him up and around after taking three machine guns in the chest' (*NYTFR*, 3 July 1971).

African-American film critics were harsh in their judgments: 'Clayton Riley, the critic for *The Amsterdam News* in Harlem, called it "a disaster," lacking both style and substance and offering whites "a comfortable image of blacks as non-competitors,"' reported Gent (1972). MGM's promotion heavily targeted African-Americans, which helped launch the Blaxploitation film cycle. Isaac Hayes won an Academy Award for Best Original Song for 'Theme from *Shaft*,' making him the first African-American composer to win an Oscar. And Ernest Tidyman, the white novelist who created the Shaft character, received a 1971 Image Award from the NAACP. *Shaft* spun off two sequels starring Richard Roundtree – *Shaft's Big Score!* (1972) and *Shaft in Africa* (1973) – which rapidly declined in popularity.

MGM no longer had writers, directors, composers, or producers under long-term contract. To build his annual slate, Aubrey contracted with independent producers, while eschewing blockbusters and concentrating on 'average' pictures with budgets less than $2 million and containing no big-name stars or directors. They were meant to turn a modest but almost sure profit. Aubrey became known as a hands-on producer, and not everyone liked it. Complaints against Aubrey were first aired in *Variety* and other trade publications in December 1971 (Warga 1971). They carried ads signed by Michael Laughlin, the producer of *Chandler*, and Paul Magwood, the director, that read, 'To those who may be interested: Regarding what was our film *Chandler*, let's give credit where credit is due. We sadly acknowledge that all editing, post-production as well as additional scenes were executed by James T. Aubrey Jr. We are sorry.' Robert Altman, who directed the MGM hit *Brewster McCloud* (1970), responded to the ad by sending the following telegram to Laughlin: 'I understand you're having your problems with the cowardly lion, MGM. I wish I had more sympathy for you, but you should have paid a little attention to some of your predecessors. As I recall, I was not mute about my experiences with Messrs. Aubrey and Netter.' 'When you deal with men of no honor,' he said, 'you can only expect to be treated in that manner' (ibid.). Altman had complained that his picture 'called for special promotion, publicity and advertising and they made a mess of it.' Similar complaints were leveled against Aubrey by Blake Edwards, the director of *The Carey Treatment* (1972); Jack Smight, the producer-director of *The Traveling Executioner* (1970); Carter DeHaven, the producer of *The Last Run* (1971) starring George C. Scott and Michael Clinger; and Michael Caine, the producer and star of *Get Carter* (1971).

'The claims and accusations are various,' reported Warga (ibid.), 'but in talking to the insurgents, one theme constantly emerges; that Aubrey does not understand filmmakers and that once a film is completed, MGM is not at all likely to contribute proper advertising, publicity and distribution. Serious charges against one of the more troubled companies in a troubled industry.'

Aubrey kept a low profile and chose not to be interviewed to get his side of the controversy. However, he had earlier told the *Los Angeles Times* that when his regime took over, 70 percent of MGM's films were failures. Now 'better than 50% make money,' he said (quoted in Dallos and Delugach 1971).

MGM under Aubrey had been releasing around eighteen pictures a year, but only two could be considered hits, *Shaft* and *Westworld* (1973). *Westworld*, a sci-fi satire 'about Doomsday in Disneyland' was written and directed by Michael Crichton, the author of *The Andromeda Strain* and other thrillers. This was Crichton's first attempt at directing. The picture was produced by Paul Lazarus III and starred Yul Brynner, Richard Benjamin, and James Brolin. The setting was a Disney-like theme park where tourists pay $1,000 a day to indulge their fantasies, sexual and otherwise, with life-sized cyborgs, until things begin to go wrong. MGM had high hopes for the picture and opened it wide in 250 first-run theaters backed by a massive TV campaign. It paid off. The picture was a success and later spun off a sequel and TV series.

Exiting the record business

In May 1972, MGM got out of the record business. Aubrey sold off MGM Records and its Los Angeles record-pressing plant, MGM Record Studios, to Polygram Corp., an affiliate of the Dutch-based Philips cartel, for an undisclosed sum of money. For several years, the records division had underperformed. MGM Records was formed in 1947 specifically to market soundtrack albums of MGM musicals. MGM Records was considered one of the major labels in the business, on a par with Columbia, RCA, Decca, Capitol, and Mercury, because it had its own manufacturing facilities. Under Frank B. Walker, who ran the division for ten years, MGM Records transitioned into country and Western and pop and released top singles by Art Lund ('Mamselle,' the first hit single), Hank Williams ('Your Cheatin' Heart'), Connie Francis ('Where the Boys Are'), Sheb Wooley ('Purple People Eater'), and Tommy Edwards ('It's All in the Game'), to name just a few. Walker resigned in 1957 and was replaced by Arnold Maxin, a former artists and repertoire director of Columbia's Epic and Okeh labels. Under Maxin, MGM Records grew into a ten-label operation, among them MGM, Kama Sutra, Deutsche Grammophon, Heliodor, and Verve. MGM acquired Verve Records from its founder Norman Granz in 1960. Verve's vast jazz and pop catalog contained such recording greats as Ella Fitzgerald, Duke Ellington, Stan Getz, Bill Evans, Oscar Peterson, Erroll Garner, and many more. In addition to releasing best-selling MGM soundtrack albums, the company branched out to Off-Broadway and released hit original-cast albums of *The Three Penny Opera* (1954) and *The Fantasticks* (1963).

In 1965, Maxin was placed in charge of MGM's music publishing division, Robbins, Feist & Miller (known as 'the Big Three'), and the record division was taken over by Mort L. Nasatir, a former Decca Records executive. Nasatir turned the division into one of the hottest pop labels by signing such groups as Herman's Hermits, the Animals, the Righteous Bros. and the Lovin Spoonful. However, by the end of the sixties, MGM Records had become a drag on MGM's music business, and under pressure from Edgar Bronfman, Nasatir resigned in September 1968. Maxin was made acting head of the record division but left the company after his contract expired in April 1969.

During the fiscal years 1968 and 1969, MGM Records lost close to $18 million ('Music Records' 1972). To turn MGM Records around, Aubrey hired Mike Curb as the new president in November 1969. He was 25 – the youngest executive in MGM history to hold such a top position and the youngest such executive in the music industry. Curb, a college dropout, had formed his own record label, Sidewalk Productions, at age 18. Starting in 1963, it released mostly soundtrack albums of films released by American International Pictures.

Aubrey signed Curb to a profit-participation pact. Transcontinental Investing Group (TIC) took over manufacturing and distribution, and MGM Records became strictly a producer. Curb reorganized the division by canceling recording contracts, closing the company's pressing plant in Bloomfield, New Jersey, and moving the music headquarters to Los Angeles from New York. Curb had turned the company around by steering it to the middle of the road, relying on standard sets from Eydie Gorme and Steve Lawrence, the Osmond Brothers, Robert Goulet, Lou Rawls, and the Congregation, a group Curb had formed that recorded contemporary rock music in an 'uplifting, sing-along format.' Curb had done his job, and the division was put up for sale. Curb remained president of MGM Records after the takeover. For the time being, MGM continued in the music publishing business by retaining control of its long-established ASCAP music publisher, Robbins, Feist & Miller, which it fully owned after acquiring 20th Century Fox's one-third interest in the company.

Exiting distribution

Aubrey's next move was a shocker. In September 1973, he announced that MGM was withdrawing from film distribution. 'The bottom fell out of the motion picture business,' said Aubrey ('MGM to Cut' 1973). The decision, nonetheless, mystified many industry observers, since distribution and not production was the most profitable arm of the film business. But MGM wanted to be freed from the necessity of producing a full roster of pictures every year and the burden of maintaining a worldwide distribution network. MGM thereupon sold off its seven remaining domestic branches and thirty-seven foreign branches and dismissed nearly 2,000 employees ('MGM to Cut' 1973). Without a distribution arm with the ability to market a picture worldwide, MGM reduced itself to second-tier status in the industry.

To distribute its future lineup, MGM signed a ten-year pact with United Artists in October 1973 covering the U.S. and Canada. Since Kerkorian needed additional cash to support his Las Vegas hotel venture, MGM sold its remaining music property – the Robbins, Feist & Miller music publishing company and Quality Records – to United Artists. In a separate deal, MGM sold its overseas theater holdings to Cinema International Corporation (CIC), the Paramount–Universal joint venture, and also signed a ten-year pact with CIC to distribute its pictures worldwide. Henceforth, MGM announced that it would make 'a limited number of "highly selective films" a year and give greater emphasis to TV production and the gambling operations at the MGM Grand in Las Vegas which was about to open' ('MGM Scrams' 1973).

Immediately after the signing, Aubrey called a special board meeting on 31 October 1973 and resigned as president and chief executive. The decision was not unexpected. Aubrey had accomplished what he set out to do: rescue a debt-laden studio and turning it into a moneymaker three years running. As Canby (1973) remarked, MGM had been kept afloat by reissues of *Gone with the Wind*, *Doctor Zhivago*, and *2001*, by television revenues, and by the systematic liquidation of studio assets. 'The Kerkorian–Aubrey management of MGM during the last four years was the realization of everyone's worst fears of what would happen to Hollywood when the moneymen take over,' he said. Aubrey had once said that the movie industry is a business 'that can work if it's run like a business and not an art form,' which led Canby to remark, 'he proceeded to authorize the production of medium-budget films of hardly any interest to anyone.' Canby went on to note that Paramount (*The Godfather*), Warner Bros. (*A Clockwork Orange*), and 20th Century Fox (*The French Connection*) 'have shown it's possible to survive in this radically changed, much more specialized theatrical market if they are given a certain amount of luck and if the film projects are chosen with even a minimal amount of care.'

Aubrey had been the architect of much of the downsizing, but according to Haber, he opposed abandoning motion picture distribution. Kerkorian needed a cash infusion to finance the MGM Grand Hotel, which had gone substantially over budget, and had his way. As Haber (1973) reported, 'Insiders say it was Aubrey who managed to scuttle negotiations with CIC at least once; they were resumed and concluded exactly two weeks ago by Kerkorian and Paramount lawyer Sidney Korshak.' Aubrey's diminished status as CEO afterward left him little choice but to resign. Douglas Netter, Aubrey's number-two man in charge of worldwide distribution, resigned soon after as well since his primary function no longer existed.

The MGM Grand Hotel

The MGM Grand Hotel opened on 5 December 1973 'with all the hoopla that attended the premieres of [MGM's] movies in the 1930s' (Wright 1973). Dean Martin was the headliner, and the Hollywood celebrities who showed up included Cary Grant, Fred MacMurray, June Haver, Jane Powell, and Shirley MacLaine to name a few. Situated on 43 acres, the MGM Grand Hotel was the largest resort hotel in the world with 2,076 rooms on twenty-six floors. 'The ground floor is dominated by the world's largest gambling casino, a 140-yard-long array of roulette, black-jack and dice tables and 1,000 slot machines,' said Wright (1973). 'There are four restaurants and a delicatessen and coffee shop operating 24 hours a day. Two big show rooms seat 1,200 and 800; entertainment is also provided in the Lion's Den off the casino floor.' Life-size blowups of MGM stars lined the lobbies, and on each room door was affixed a brass 'star' just like a star's dressing room. To greet the guests, 'A massive fountain at the main entrance has a bronze copy of Lorenzo Giambologna's 16th-century statue of Neptune and the Sirens.' Originally budgeted at $90 million, it cost $107 million to complete ('MGM to Cut' 1973).

Frank E. Rosenfelt management

With Aubrey gone, Kerkorian stepped in as chief executive. Kerkorian wanted to prove to skeptics that MGM would remain a force in film and television. Kerkorian would focus principally on policy. To run the day-to-day operations of the company, Kerkorian appointed Frank E. Rosenfelt president. A Cornell Law School graduate, Rosenfelt had been working in MGM's legal department since 1955. He was elected corporate secretary in 1966 and vice president and general counsel in 1969. Kerkorian took the post on an interim basis and relinquished it to Rosenfelt in December 1974. The announcement came just after MGM posted record earnings of $28.6 million for fiscal 1974, nearly three times its 1973 profit. Hotel and gaming accounted for $22 million of the company's net. 'The performance . . . was considered by industry observers to be a vindication of the new course set three years ago by MGM's controlling shareholder, Kirk Kerkorian,' reported Delugach (1974).

Restoring MGM's luster

To produce a limited number of 'highly selective films' as previously announced, Rosenfelt elevated Daniel Melnick, MGM's production chief under Aubrey since 1972, to senior vice president and an officer in the company. Melnick had a long and distinguished career in television. As vice president of programming at ABC-TV, he was responsible for developing such programs as *The Fugitive*, *The Untouchables*, *The Flintstones*, and *77 Sunset Strip*. Later, in partnership with David Susskind and Leonard Stern, Melnick formed Talent Associates, a television production company that turned out a string of hits during the sixties that included *N.Y.P.D.*, *East Side West Side*, and the Emmy-winning spy-spoof series Get Smart starring Don Adams. Melnick personally won two Emmys, for producing *Ages of Man* with John Gielgud doing a Shakespearean turn in 1966 and for a presentation of Arthur Miller's *Death of a Salesman* starring Lee J. Cobb in 1967.

Melnick restored some of the luster to MGM by producing such hits as *That's Entertainment!* (1974), Herbert Ross's *The Sunshine Boys* (1975), Michael Anderson's *Logan's Run* (1976), and Sidney Lumet's *Network* (1976). *That's Entertainment!*, a compilation of segments from MGM's greatest musicals, was produced and directed by Alex Haley Jr. to celebrate MGM's fiftieth anniversary. It was a box-office sensation and spun off at least two sequels. *The Sunshine Boys* (1975), produced by Ray Stark, was adapted by Neil Simon from his long-running Broadway comedy and starred Walter Matthau and George Burns as two feuding vaudevillians who come out of retirement to recreate their act for a TV special. This was Burns's first movie in thirty-six years. *The Sunshine Boys* opened at the Radio City Music Hall as its Christmas attraction and set house records. George Burns won an Academy Award for Best Supporting Actor, and Walter Matthau was nominated for the Best Actor award.

Logan's Run (1976) was a sci-fi thriller based on William F. Nolan and George Clayton Johnson's 1967 dystopian novel about the survivors of an overpopulated and polluted world who retreat to a huge doomed city outside Washington, DC, where everything is regulated by a computer. The survivors live entirely for pleasure, but everyone must commit ritual suicide at age 30 as a form of population control. It starred Michael York, Richard Jordan, and Jenny Agutter. The picture used holography to create special effects. The day after *Logan's Run* premiered in New York at the Astor Plaza on 22 June 1976, United Artists released it widely

FIGURE 8.2 Peter Finch in Sidney Lumet's *Network* (1976)

to five hundred theaters nationwide backed by a massive television campaign. To cross-promote the picture, which became a cult favorite, Bantam Books brought out a paperback version of the novel, which became a best seller.

Network (1976) made the biggest splash. Paddy Chayefsky's dark satire of television and the viewing public was nominated for six Academy Awards and won four, for Best Original Screenplay (Chayefsky), Best Actor (Peter Finch), Best Actress (Faye Dunaway), and Best Supporting Actress (Beatrice Straight). Chayefsky had shown a draft of his screenplay to Arthur Krim at United Artists, the distributor of Chayefsky's Oscar-winning screenplays for *Marty* (1955) and *The Hospital* (1971), but he rejected it as being too controversial. Chayefsky and Howard Gottfried, his producer, then took it to Melnick. By then, United Artists had had second thoughts about the project and agreed to coproduce it with MGM. Chayefsky won a large measure of control over the production and was given the 'By Paddy Chayefsky' credit instead of the typical 'Screenplay by.' To direct his picture, he chose Sidney Lumet, whose credits included *12 Angry Men* (1957), *Fail-Safe* (1964), *Serpico* (1973), and *Dog Day Afternoon* (1975). To top off the cast, he chose William Holden and Robert Duvall. *Variety* said, '*Network* will shake you up. Paddy Chayefsky's absurdly plausible and outrageously provocative original script concerns media running amok.' 'This is a bawdy, stops-out, no-holds-barred story of a TV network that will, quite literally, do anything to get an audience,' it said. 'The strangest thing about the film is that, while often preachy, hysterical, shrill and bizarre, it also makes a compelling statement from amidst its sound and fury' (*VFR*, 13 October 1976).

Melnick had compiled a successful record but called it quits in 1976 and resigned to go into independent production. He cited as a reason 'the tremendous pressure that the administration of an entire production program requires . . . I just got tired. This job was a combination of business management, psychotherapy and creative input and it was the latter I enjoyed the most' (Grant 1976). He was replaced by Richard Shepherd as senior vice president and worldwide head of production. Shepherd started out as an independent producer in partnership with Martin Jurow. They were best known for Blake Edwards's *Breakfast at Tiffany's* (1961) starring Audrey Hepburn. In 1962, he joined Creative Management Associates, where he headed the agency's motion picture and television division for nine years. In 1970, he was named head of production at Warner Bros., where he oversaw such hits as William Friedkin's *The Exorcist* (1973) and John Guillermin's *The Towering Inferno* (1974). Returning to independent production in 1974, he produced *Robin and Marian* (1976) starring Audrey Hepburn and Sean Connery for Columbia and *Alex and the Gypsy* (1976) starring Jack Lemmon and Geneviève Bujold for Fox.

MGM released around four pictures a year under Shepherd. He had the best luck with *The Goodbye Girl* (1977), a Ray Stark–Neil Simon–Herbert Ross romantic comedy starring Richard Dreyfus and Marsha Mason; *Coma* (1978), a suspense film directed by Michael Crichton starring Geneviève Bujold and Michael Douglas; *The Champ* (1979), Franco Zeffirelli's remake of MGM's 1931 Academy Award winner starring Jon Voight and Faye Dunaway; and *Fame* (1980), a teen musical produced by David DeSilva and directed by Alan Parker.

Enter David Begelman

By 1979, MGM could no longer afford to remain a second-tier film studio and decided to ramp up production. The decision was spurred in part by the arrival of two new distribution technologies – pay TV and home video – which created two new lucrative ancillary markets for feature films. MGM hired David Begelman, the deposed president of Columbia Pictures, to do the job. Begelman had been convicted of forging checks and padding his expense account. Begelman and Freddie Fields had cofounded the prominent talent agency Creative Management Associates in 1960. As president of Columbia Pictures from 1973 to 1978, Begelman was credited with saving the studio from financial ruin by overseeing a series of hits that included Hal Ashby's *Shampoo* (1975), Ken Russell's *Tommy* (1975), Herbert Ross's *Funny Lady* (1975), and Steven Spielberg's *Close Encounters of the Third Kind* (1977). Begelman blamed stress and other psychological problems for his self-destructive behavior and pleaded no contest to the embezzlement charge. He was initially sentenced to three years' probation and given a small fine. Begelman bounced back nicely from the scandal; Rosenfelt signed him to a four-year contract in December 1979 that paid him $1,900,000 over that period plus a profit participation, which made him the highest paid-executive at MGM (Sansweet 1982). As the new president of MGM's motion picture division, Begelman's assignment was 'to return MGM to the glory days of Mayer and Thalberg,' Rosenfelt announced (quoted in Cole 1979). Having been passed over for the top post, Richard Shepherd resigned soon after Begelman's arrival.

MGM Grand Hotels

Begelman's appointment was made in anticipation of a major restructuring. MGM had increasingly been perceived as a hotel company. As Rosenfelt explained ('Two Lions' 1979: 5), 'The film side has been living in the shadow of the towering success of the hotels and casinos. More revenue comes from the hotel and casino side than from the film/TV side and we have come to be regarded as a hotel/casino company that makes a few movies a year.' 'As a result,' he continued, 'we are not getting the properties that we should.'

Kerkorian's hotel empire now included the MGM Grand-Reno, which opened in May 1978. In May 1980, MGM divided the company into two separate, publicly held entities, Metro-Goldwyn-Mayer Film Co. and MGM Grand Hotels, Inc. Fred Benninger was named board chairman and chief executive of the hotel company and Alvin Benedict president and chief executive. The company headquarters was moved to Las Vegas.

Acquiring United Artists

Next, MGM had to give serious thought to distribution. Its contract with United Artists expired in 1983. After making unsuccessful attempts to take control of Columbia Pictures Industries and 20th Century Fox, Kerkorian turned his sights on United Artists. Thinking that MGM would soon have a string of big hits in the pipeline, Kerkorian determined how much MGM might have to pay UA in distribution fees and used that amount to make a preemptive bid to buy the company from Transamerica for $380 million in May 1981 (Balio 1987: 341). The sale was completed in July, and United Artists became a subsidiary of Metro-Goldwyn-Mayer Film Co. MGM reacquired the distribution right to its massive film library in addition to United Artists' post-1951 film library and the pre-1950 Warner Bros. and RKO film libraries that UA had earlier acquired. UA's library included more than 1,000 pictures, including the James Bond series, the Pink Panther series, and a string of hits produced by Stanley Kramer, Otto Preminger, Woody Allen, Hecht-Lancaster, and the Mirisch Corporation, among others.

The James Bond franchise

The most important asset in the United Artists buyout was the James Bond franchise. The franchise had been going strong since 1962 and was a gold mine. United Artists had struck a deal with British producers Harry Saltzman and Albert

R. Broccoli to finance the first James Bond picture on 2 April 1962. Saltzman and Broccoli had secured the exclusive motion picture rights from Ian Fleming for all the published James Bond novels in 1959 and incorporated their company in Switzerland for tax purposes under the name Danjaq to hold the Ian Fleming rights. To produce the James Bond pictures, they formed a production subsidiary called Eon Productions. Beginning with *Dr. No* (1962) starring Sean Connery in 1962, United Artists financed and Eon produced twelve James Bond pictures. All had generated profits of various degrees and had sustained their popularity even after three successive star changes. In 1975, Saltzman was under water from his other production ventures, and United Artists acquired his 50 percent interest in Danjaq in December 1975 (Balio 1987: 273). UA paid $36 million for Saltzman's share and became a coproducer of the James Bond series, with Eon retaining creative control. Now that UA and Danjaq were partners, UA effectively had perpetual distribution rights to the franchise.

UA's demise

The sale of United Artists to MGM was the result of the resignation of UA's top management in 1978 in protest over Transamerica's administrative policies. United Artists recovered from the 1969 recession by 1974 and set an industry record by winning the Best Picture Oscar three years in a row, with the Saul Zaentz–Michael Douglas production of *One Flew Over the Cuckoo's Nest* (1975) directed by Miloš Forman; the Robert Chartoff–Irwin Winkler production of *Rocky* (1976) directed by John G. Avildsen, and the Woody Allen production of *Annie Hall* (1977). *Cuckoo's Nest*, moreover, achieved what no other picture in forty years had done – an Academy Awards sweep of the top five Academy Awards. Arthur Krim, UA's chairman, stemmed the losses and put the company solidly in the black by the mid-1970s, but Transamerica's stock was not sensitive to a single subsidiary's performance. In fact, Transamerica's stock had declined during this period, and Krim and his partners watched as their gains from the exchange of stock at the time of the merger were wiped out. In January 1978, Krim and four other top UA executives resigned from the company and formed Orion Pictures, with aspirations of becoming another major studio. After the walkout, UA's new management had the misfortune of producing Michael Cimino's *Heaven's Gate* (1980). Proposed at $7.5 million, budgeted at $11.5 million, and written off finally at $44 million, the fiasco led to at least temporary unemployment for almost everyone associated with the picture and ultimately to the demise of UA itself (Balio 1987: 339). After suffering the humiliation of being associated with one of the most public motion picture failures of all time, Transamerica decided to get out of the motion picture business and was relieved to sell it to Kerkorian.

MGM increased its bank debt to get United Artists up and running with a full slate of pictures. As a result, MGM's creditors placed severe limits on the amounts of money that could be spent on film production. MGM suffered a further setback when it failed to spot certain contractual clauses in the CIC distribution agreement. When MGM withdrew from distribution in 1973, it contracted with CIC to handle its product abroad. In negotiating the purchase of United Artists, no one at MGM thought to shield the UA product from the agreement. This was a costly mistake that deprived MGM of an enormous amount of distribution fees. Since CIC would not let MGM off the hook, UA's entire foreign distribution arm was made redundant, and its employees lost their jobs.

At the time of the takeover, Kerkorian assured the Department of Justice that United Artists 'would keep its own identity, retain its own management and continue to produce its own films' (Sansweet 1981). But two months later, Rosenfelt, in a surprise move, replaced UA's top management with an MGM team headed by David Begelman, who became chairman and CEO of United Artists. Rosenfelt (quoted in 'Begelman' 1981) explained: 'The primary reason for shifting Begelman is that he will do at UA a job comparable to the one he accomplished at MGM. We have a momentum going that we would like to see going at UA.' However, industry skeptics saw the move as a way to run MGM and UA as one studio. Begelman's position at MGM Film was left vacant temporarily.

Frank Rothman management

The restructuring continued. On 15 February 1982, the name Metro-Goldwyn-Mayer Film Co. was changed to MGM/UA Entertainment Co. To run it, Kerkorian turned to Frank Rothman, his long-time friend and a respected Los Angeles trial lawyer. Rothman was the lawyer who had defended Begelman in the check-forgery case and saved him from prison. Under the new structure, Rosenfelt and Begelman became coequals, and both reported to Rothman. To run MGM Film, Rothman appointed Donald Sipes, president and CEO, and Freddie Fields, president of production. Sipes, a lawyer, had been president of Universal Television since 1975. Before that, he worked in business affairs, first at CMA and then at NBC and CBS. Freddie Fields, Begelman's former CMA partner, had five credits as a producer, among them Richard Brooks's *Looking for Mr. Goodbar* (1977) and Paul Schrader's *American Gigolo* (1980) for Paramount.

Exit David Begelman

No sooner had the restructuring been completed than Begelman was forced out on 14 July 1982. Begelman's expensive slate of pictures, which had triggered the United Artists takeover, began its rollout in December 1981. All but one of the eleven flopped. The losers included Billy Wilder's *Buddy, Buddy* (1981) starring Jack Lemmon and Walter Matthau; Robert Aldrich's *All the Marbles* (1981) starring Peter Falk and Vicki Frederick; John Badham's *Whose Life Is It Anyway?* (1981) starring Richard Dreyfus and John Cassavetes; Herbert Ross's *Pennies from Heaven* (1981) starring Steve Martin; and David Ward's *Cannery Row* (1982) starring Nick Nolte and Debra Winger. 'It is likely that the aggregate losses to MGM equaled or surpassed those sustained by UA with *Heaven's Gate*,' said Bach (1985: 418). The impending publication of David McClintick's *Indecent Exposure: A True Story of Hollywood and Wall Street* (1982), which reopened the Columbia scandal, might have been a factor in Begelman's departure, although the company denied it. But clearly, Begelman had become an embarrassment to the company. He still had three years to go on his contract, which the company refused to honor. The matter was later settled by arbitration. Begelman was replaced by Frank Rosenfelt on an interim basis.

Two summer blockbusters

On the plus side, MGM/UA had two summer blockbusters in release. The first, *Rocky III* (1982), was the latest edition of the Robert Chartoff–Irwin Winkler franchise from United Artists, which had been preplanned. Sylvester Stallone directed, wrote, and starred in the picture. 'With *Rocky III*,' said *Variety*, 'Sylvester Stallone has come up with a successful variation on a now-familiar theme which requires merely mathematical progression to predict its probable success. The first generated domestic rentals of more than $55,000,000, the second 77 percent of that and if the third only takes half the second, it's still plenty of money' (*VFR*, 19 May 1982). However, *Rocky III* did 'what no sequel has accomplished – surpass an immensely successful predecessor.' The pictures grossed $63.4 million, reported Harmetz (1982). *Poltergeist* (1982), the second, was Begelman's one and only hit. *Poltergeist* was produced by Steven Spielberg and Frank Marshall and directed by Tobe Hooper of *The Texas Chainsaw Massacre* (1974) fame, with a cast headed by Heather O'Rourke, Craig T. Nelson, and JoBeth Williams. As Canby described it, Spielberg 'has come up with a marvelously spooky ghost story that may possibly scare the wits out of very small children and offend those parents who believe that kids should be protected from their own, sometimes savage imaginations. I suspect, however, that there's a vast audience of teen-agers and others who'll love this film' (*NYTFR*, 4 June 1982). The proceeds from the two pictures enabled the company to post a $27.5 million profit for fiscal 1982, an 18-plus percent jump from $23.2 million in 1981 (Hayes 1982).

Unloading assets

MGM/UA, nonetheless, was still deep in debt, and Rothman started to unload more assets. In December 1982, MGM/UA spun off 15 percent of its new home video division, Home Entertainment Group (HEG), in a public offering, which netted $54 million. The following month, it sold United Artists Music, containing the Big 3 catalog, to CBS for $68 million, 'the largest outlay in dollars ever for a music publishing operation,' said Lichtman (1983: 3).

Enter Frank Yablans

As always, the company needed hits. In February 1983, Rothman hired Frank Yablans as vice chairman of MGM/UA. Yablans was president of Paramount Pictures from 1971 to 1975, during which it released Francis Ford Coppola's first two *Godfather* films, Sidney Lumet's *Serpico* (1973) and *Murder on the Orient Express* (1974), Roman Polanski's *Chinatown* (1974), and Robert Aldrich's *The Longest Yard* (1974). He resigned from the studio after a dispute with Charles G. Bluhdorn, chairman of Gulf + Western, Paramount's parent company, and became a successful independent producer connected with 20th Century Fox, where his credits included Arthur Hiller's *Silver Streak* (1976), Charles Jarrott's *The Other Side of Midnight* (1977), and Frank Perry's *Mommie Dearest* (1981).

Yablans quickly took control. He promoted Freddie Fields to CEO of MGM Films, a position previously held by Donald Sipes, who was appointed the new CEO of United Artists to replace Frank Rosenfelt. He then closed United Artists' New York offices and moved the headquarters to Hollywood. United Artists had been located at 729 Seventh Ave. since the company's founding in 1919. The closing led to the resignations of UA Classics toppers Michael Barker and Tom Bernard, who went over to Orion Pictures and formed Orion Classics.

MGM/UA had another pair of summer blockbusters in 1983, John Badham's *WarGames* (1983) and *Octopussy* (1983), the first James Bond picture under the MGM/UA banner. *WarGames*, an adventure story about a brilliant teenager who accidentally breaks into the Pentagon's top-secret computer system, was written by Lawrence Lasker and Walter F. Parkes and starred Matthew Broderick and Ally Sheedy. It was produced by Leonard Goldberg, a former television producer who was best known for producing ABC's first made-for-television movie, *Brian's Song* (1971), and the hit TV series *Charlie's Angels* (1976–81) in partnership with Aaron Spelling. *WarGames* was his first independent film venture. *Variety* described it as a 'terrifically exciting story charged by an irresistible idea for today's young audi-ence: an extra-smart kid can get the world into a whole lot of trouble and that it also takes the same extra-smart kid to rescue it' (*VFR*, 11 May 1983). The picture was released by United Artists.

Octopussy, the thirteenth James Bond and the sixth starring Roger Moore, was produced by Albert R. Broccoli's Eon Productions. 'The James Bond movies have become such a fact of life that we don't give much thought to their longevity,' said Summers (1983: 52). 'If we did we'd probably appreciate how absolutely amazing it is that they've continued being so entertaining after so many years. . . . Sure, Roger Moore is getting a little thick around the middle,' he said, 'and there are die-hards who say the series hasn't been the same since Sean Connery, but for the most part the James Bond movies are among the most stylish, witty, audience-pleasing movies around.'

Sipes did not last long in his new position at UA. He resigned in August, 1983, feeling that he had become redundant after Yablans's restructuring. He was not replaced, and MGM/UA functioned as a single motion picture company under Yablans. To keep the distribution pipeline full, Yablans linked up with two aspiring mini-majors, the Cannon Group and the Dino De Laurentiis Entertainment Group. Cannon was a minor independent film producer when Menahem Golan and Yoram Globus, two little-known Israeli filmmakers, took over the company in 1979. They started out producing low-budget films known as 'Cannon fodder'

FIGURE 8.3 Roger Moore in John Glen's *Octopussy* (1983)

for the international trade and raised their financing by preselling new titles to local distributors in foreign markets. Cannon churned out as many as forty films a year that contained plenty of sex and action. Beginning in 1981, the company upgraded its product by hiring major stars and directors. Yablans signed up Golan and Globus in April 1983. The deal was for domestic distribution only. Cannon delivered eleven pictures before the deal collapsed in June 1984. Cannon delivered mostly flops, among them, Andrew McLaglen's *Sahara* (1983) starring Brooke Shields; Michael Winner's *The Wicked Lady* (1983) starring Faye Dunaway; Menahem Golan's *Over the Brooklyn Bridge* (1984) starring Elliott Gould and Margaux Hemingway; and John Derek's *Bolero* (1984) starring Bo Derek. (*Bolero* had received an X rating, and MGM/UA refused to release it.) But it was MGM/UA's handling of Joel Silberg's *Breakin'* (1984) that caused the rift. Globus maintained that MGM/UA 'had no idea' how to handle the picture, a musical about break dancing. The company thought the picture would appeal to black audiences only. 'It was the disagreement over the potential of *Breakin',*' reported Segers (1984: 28), 'which was the proverbial straw breaking the camel's back.' Cannon took over the release of *Breakin',* which became Cannon's biggest hit of the year.

Yablans signed up Dino De Laurentiis in May 1984. The deal was nonexclusive for domestic distribution. De Laurentiis had transferred his movie-making activities to the U.S. when the Italian film industry suffered a severe recession in the seventies. To produce a slate of ten or so pictures a year, he built a studio facility on sixteen acres in Wilmington, North Carolina, in 1983. Like Cannon, De Laurentiis relied on preselling to raise production financing. And like Cannon, his pictures lost money. They included Richard Fleischer's *Red Sonja* (1985) starring Brigitte Nielsen and Arnold Schwarzenegger; Roger Donaldson's *Marie* (1985) starring Sissy Spacek; Lewis Teague's *Cat's Eye* (1985) starring Drew Barrymore; and Michael Cimino's *Year of the Dragon* (1985) starring Mickey Rourke. *Year of the Dragon* was Cimino's first picture after the *Heaven's Gate* fiasco. Thinking that he could do a better job marketing his pictures on his own, De Laurentiis purchased Embassy Pictures with its twelve regional offices from Coca-Cola in October 1985.

Enter Alan Ladd Jr.

Yablans compiled a dismal production record. 'MGM/UA still hovered near the bottom of the list of companies with which important filmmakers would want to do business,' said Bart (1990: 214). The duds included Mel Brooks's remake of Ernst Lubitsch's *To Be or Not to Be* (1983), Sidney Lumet's *Garbo Talks* (1984), Robert Boris's *Oxford Blues* (1984), Arthur Hiller's *Teachers* (1984), James Foley's *Reckless* (1984), John Milius's *Red Dawn* (1984), and Gillian Armstrong's *Mrs. Soffel* (1984). Only Peter Hyams's *2010* (1984), a sequel to Kubrick's *2001*, earned any money, but it was not the blockbuster the company hoped for. Kerkorian was unhappy with the results, and in January 1985, Rothman split MGM/UA into two divisions to hedge his bets. Yablans was demoted and placed in charge of MGM Film. To head United Artists, Rothman brought in Alan Ladd Jr. in March 1985. Both would now be reporting to Rothman. As president of 20th Century Fox from 1976 to 1979, Ladd had greenlighted George Lucas's *Star Wars* (1977) and Ridley Scott's *Alien* (1979), among other hits. After resigning from the studio in 1979 over a dispute with Fox chair Dennis Stanfill, who refused to reward the members of Ladd's team with bonuses, Ladd formed the Ladd Company with two former Fox executives, Jay Kanter and Gareth Wigan, and linked up with Warner Bros. for distribution. The Ladd Company had a mixed record – it distributed Hugh Hudson's Oscar-winning *Chariots of Fire* (1981) and produced a few hits, including Lawrence Kasdan's *Body Heat* (1981) and Hugh Wilson's *Police Academy* (1984). But the company had more than its share of flops, including Ridley Scott's *Blade Runner* (1982), Philip Kaufman's *The Right Stuff* (1983), and Bob Fosse's *Star 80* (1983).

Two months after the reorganization, Yablans resigned under pressure in March 1985. The results for the last quarter had come in; MGM/UA posted a net loss of $82.2 million due mainly to poor box office (Harris 1985b). Rothman promoted Alan Ladd Jr. as president and CEO of MGM/UA. MGM Film and UA remained two separate divisions under Ladd. Rothman hired Jay Kanter to run MGM and Richard Berger, United Artists. Berger had also departed Fox with Ladd in 1979 and joined up with Disney, where he formed Touchstone Films in 1984. Touch-stone's pictures were designed to reach young adult audiences. Berger's single release was the Ron Howard hit *Splash* starring Daryl Hannah and Tom Hanks before he resigned to join MGM/UA.

Mysterious maneuvering

Kerkorian could not afford to stand pat. MGM/UA was a pure play company, which is to say that it focused on one area of the film business – motion picture production and distribution. Unlike Warner Communications, 20th Century Fox, or Universal, MGM/UA did not have numerous 'profit centers' to even out risks. Given the vagaries of the theatrical market and MGM/UA's pitiful track record, Kerkorian's investment was in jeopardy. He therefore pursued opportunities to protect it.

In December 1983, Kerkorian attempted to take MGM/UA Entertainment private. He owned 50.1 percent of the company's outstanding shares and was prepared to offer shareholders $17 a share, considerably more than the current $12 trading price. In total, he was prepared to pay $375 million for the 49.9 percent of the company he did not own (Salmans 1984).

Complete ownership would make it easier to sell the company, it was thought. Kerkorian withdrew the offer three weeks later; shareholders were not about to accept $17 a share when the previous spring the stock was being traded at a high of $22. They were likely to think the MGM and UA film libraries were being undervalued and would turn down Kerkorian's offer, it was thought.

In June 1984, Kerkorian joined forces with Saul P. Steinberg, a corporate raider, in a hostile takeover bid for the Walt Disney Company. Steinberg was adept at using junk bond financing through the New York–based Drexel Burnham Lambert investment bankers to acquire companies. Disney was experiencing an internecine battle for control led by Disney's nephew, Roy E. Disney, who wanted to oust the management headed by Ronald W. Miller, Disney's son-in-law. Disney's growth had leveled off, with little prospect of improving under the present management. Steinberg had earlier acquired an 11.1 percent stake in Disney and now wanted Kerkorian and others to invest $75 million each for a 20 percent stake in the proposed takeover bid (Sansweet 1984). As an incentive, Steinberg offered Kerkorian an option to buy Disney's movie studio and film library after the takeover. However, Disney's board decided to end the siege and get on with company business just hours before the tender announcement and agreed to buy back Steinberg's shares for $325.5 million in cash, which netted him a profit of $31.7 million. Industry analysts described Steinberg's bid as a form of 'greenmail' (ibid.). The takeover attempt led to Miller's ousting in September 1984 and the installation of a new management team headed by Michael Eisner. Kerkorian had only pledged to put up the $75 million for the takeover bid and had not purchased any Disney stock. Nonetheless, he was reputed to have received a hefty commitment fee for the pledge.

Also in June 1985, Kerkorian reacquired the 15 percent of MGM's Home Entertainment Group that he did not own. Kerkorian originally offered shareholders $22 a share but eventually paid $28 a share or $128 million to complete the transaction ('MGM/UA Merger' 1985: 42). Wall Street speculated that Kerkorian needed '100 percent ownership of the home video company in order to implement some other plan, such as selling part or all of the motion picture company,' said Harris (1985a). Kerkorian's financial maneuvering mystified many. As Delugach (1984) noted, the maneuvers were 'conducted with much planning and tight security, so that no one can safely presume to divine his ultimate strategy. He prefers it that way and, as his inner circle knows, he usually gets his way.'

It was hard to know where Kerkorian would go next. The company had survived the 1969 recession under James Aubrey, but at a cost. A downsized MGM had become a second-tier company, a position from which it never recovered. While other Hollywood studios either were diversifying or were being subsumed by outside conglomerates, Kerkorian spun off his hotels, leaving the studio a pure play company dependent mostly on the risky motion picture business. Acquiring United Artists signaled a potential comeback, but MGM's production chiefs had singularly bad luck in attracting new talent and in making pictures that made the grade. Kerkorian had to be looking for a way out.

9

KIRK KERKORIAN AND THE BUYING AND SELLING OF MGM, PART 2 (1985–2004)

Sale no. 1: Ted Turner

In August 1985, Ted Turner, the maverick Atlanta broadcaster and head of the Turner Broadcasting System, made a preemptive bid of $1.5 billion in cash for MGM/UA Entertainment Co. (Balio 1990b: 285–86). Turner had come a long way since 1976 when he transformed his fledgling Atlanta television station, WTBS, into a superstation that fed cable systems all over America. To provide a ready supply of inexpensive programming for his station, Turner bought the Atlanta Braves baseball team and the Atlanta Hawks basketball team in 1976. In 1980, he created the Cable News Network, the pioneering 24-hour news channel. He then stunned the industry by making a hostile, $5.41 billion offer for CBS in 1985 (ibid.). It was an outrageous move because in essence, Turner attempted to buy a company much larger than his own Turner Broadcasting without using any money, just junk bonds. CBS took him seriously, however, and killed the offer with a $954.8 million stock buyback. Undaunted, Turner went to Hollywood to expand his empire.

Kerkorian's buyback no. 1

Turner basically wanted the MGM film library to feed his cable system. Bidding on older films for programming had heated up as a result of the growth of independent stations and pay-TV services. The terms of the original deal called for him to buy the entire MGM/UA Entertainment Co. and then sell back the United Artists portion to Kirk Kerkorian's Tracinda Corp. for $470 million. To finance the acquisition, Turner turned to Drexel Burnham Lambert, the junk bond specialist. However, Drexel Burnham failed to arrange the necessary financing, and the terms of the deal were reduced by $200 million. Ultimately, Turner had to unload assets to complete the takeover. Turner took control of MGM/UA

Entertainment on 25 March 1986. Beginning in June 1986, he sold off MGM's remaining forty-four acres, including the Irving Thalberg Building and twenty-four sound stages, and MGM's Metrocolor Film Laboratory to Lorimar-Telepictures for $190 million. The Metrocolor Film Laboratory building was constructed in 1979, the first new permanent construction on the lot in more than twenty years. The facility, considered to be among the finest in the film industry, was designed to service MGM's motion picture print material and to house MGM's massive film library. Most of the 1,400 employees on the lot lost their jobs. Next, he sold back more assets to Kerkorian – the MGM studio, the Home Entertainment division, and the Leo the Lion trademark – which garnered him an additional $300 million (Fabricant 1986). The trademark was the third-most-recognized corporate symbol behind Coca-Cola and Disney, reported Frook (1990). At the conclusion of the deal, Turner was left with the MGM film library and the smaller pre-1948 Warner Bros. and RKO film libraries. In effect, Kerkorian sold the film libraries for $1.2 billion.

The residual assets comprising the MGM and United Artists film and television production companies and the United Artists film library Kerkorian bought back from Turner were subsumed under a new corporate umbrella, MGM/UA Communications Co., with 80 percent of its shares owned by Kerkorian's Tracinda Corp. Having sold its historic studio to Turner, MGM/UA had to find a new home. In October 1986, the company began moving its operations across the street to the new Filmland Corporate Center, where it leased four floors of the eight-storey building. In 1989, it moved its corporate headquarters to a four-storey structure on the northeast corner of Wilshire Boulevard and Crescent Drive in Beverly Hills. MGM/UA, with no film production facilities, now had to rent studio space from Lorimar and other rental studios to make its movies. Frank Rothman considered his job done at the conclusion of the sale and resigned on 22 January 1986 to return to private practice. Kerkorian replaced him with Lee Rich as the new chairman and chief executive on 28 April 1986. Rich had just parted ways with Merv Adelson, his long-time partner and cofounder of Lorimar Productions. Between 1969 and 1986, Lorimar placed more than thirty shows on the air, including *The Waltons* and *Dallas*, and produced a dozen feature films. Of the group, only Hal Ashby's *Being There* (1979) made any money. To complete the restructuring, Kerkorian appointed Stephen D. Silbert, Kerkorian's long-time legal counsel, to the new post of president and chief operating officer of the MGM/UA Communications Co. in October 1986.

Lee Rich management

Only two movies were in preparation when Rich took charge. Basically, he had to revamp MGM/UA's film and television operations from scratch. Rich kept the MGM and United Artists movie divisions separate. Alan Ladd Jr. continued to lead MGM. To head United Artists, Rich hired Anthony Thomopoulos, a former president of ABC Broadcast Group. Like Rich, Thomopoulos had no day-to-day experience running a movie studio. After the restructuring, MGM/UA fared no better than before. It posted a loss of $88 million for fiscal 1987 ('MGM/UA Loss' 1987). The company had released just two hits in 1987, John Glen's *The Living Daylights* (1987), the fifteenth James Bond, which starred Timothy Dalton in his first Bond role, and Norman Jewison's *Moonstruck* (1987), a romantic comedy starring Cher and Nicolas Cage. *The Living Daylights* received mixed reviews but did well at the box office per usual. *Moonstruck* was a surprise hit and the winner of three Academy Awards: they went to Cher as Best Actress, Olympia Dukakis as Best Supporting Actress, and John Patrick Shanley for Best Original Screenplay.

It was not long before Kerkorian was again looking around for buyers. In July 1988, the company announced that it was going to divide the MGM/UA into two separate companies and sell 25 percent of MGM to Barris Industries and to the Guber-Peters Co. for $96 million (Fabricant 1988). Barris Industries was headed by Burt Sugarman, a takeover specialist who specialized in producing game shows such as *The Dating Game, The Newlywed Game,* and *The Gong Show* for syndicated television. Peter Guber and Jon Peters were successful independent producers whose credits included Adrian Lyne's *Flashdance* (1983), Steven Spielberg's *The Color Purple* (1985), and George Miller's *The Witches of Eastwick* (1987). In January 1988, the two companies merged. The sale collapsed soon after it was announced with no public explanation given. Kerkorian had presented the deal to Rich and Ladd as a fait accompli. As reported in the *Wall Street Journal*

FIGURE 9.1 Cher and Nicolas Cage in Norman Jewison's *Moonstruck* (1987)

(Landro and Hughes 1988), Ladd 'was told in a Sunday meeting that his role in the new company hadn't been determined. But a friend called him at 7:30 a.m. the next morning and read him a press release announcing that Mr. Guber would become chairman and Mr. Peters president, effectively taking his job.' Lee Rich resigned in July 1988, a week after the announcement; he was followed by Ladd and Thomopoulos in September. Kerkorian named Stephen Silbert chairman and chief executive to replace Lee Rich. Silbert consolidated the two film divisions into a single unit, MGM/UA Film Group, and promoted Richard L. Berger as president and chief executive.

MGM/UA posted a loss of $48.7 million for fiscal 1988, an improvement over 1987 due, in part, to two big hits, Charles Crichton's *A Fish Called Wanda* (1988) and Barry Levinson's *Rain Man* (1988) (Stevenson 1988). They were in production when Rich and his team departed. *A Fish Called Wanda*, the British caper comedy, starred John Cleese, Jamie Lee Curtis, Kevin Kline, and Michael Palin. It was cowritten by Cleese and Crichton and produced by Michael Shamberg for MGM/UA after other studios rejected it. The low-budget picture was an unexpected box-office hit, while Kevin Kline won an Oscar for Best Supporting Actor. *Rain Man* (1988) was produced by Mark Johnson and starred Dustin Hoffman and Tom Cruise. It had been in development hell at MGM/UA since 1986. After rewrites and personnel changes, Thomopoulos finally convinced Silbert to put up the financing. *Rain Man* was a huge box-office sensation and the winner of four Academy Awards, including Best Picture.

FIGURE 9.2 Tom Cruise and Dustin Hoffman in Barry Levinson's *Rain Man* (1988)

Jeffrey C. Barbakow management

With MGM losing money and deep in debt, a more determined Kerkorian brought in a new management team headed by Jeffrey C. Barbakow, 42, a Merrill Lynch mergers and acquisitions specialist, in October 1988. Barbakow received a five-year contract at $1 million a year (Landro and Hughes 1988). As an extra incentive, he was to be given a bonus of 1.5 million shares currently valued at $20 million once a sale had closed. If he managed to sell the company at a premium, he stood to make even more. Barbakow replaced Silbert as chairman and CEO of the company. Silbert then took a position with Tracinda Corp. Barbakow abruptly halted production. Two hours after Donald Sutherland signed up to appear in Irwin Winkler's production of *Dessa Rose*, Barbakow pulled the plug on the picture, even though the company had already spent half of its $10 million budget. This was just a start. He canceled dozens of projects in development, dumped producers, and fired top executives. Two hundred regular employees also lost their jobs. 'It was a Saturday-night massacre,' said Winkler (Landro and Hughes 1988). Barbakow needed to rebuild MGM/UA's production roster to get top dollar for the company, but his team had no experience making movies. Knowing that the studio might soon be on the block, producers placed MGM/UA at the end of the line for the pitching of new projects.

Christopher Skase's bid

In March 1989, Christopher Skase and his Qintex Entertainment Inc. offered $1 billion in cash for the United Artists half of MGM/UA Communications, which is to say the United Artists studio and its film library (Stevenson 1989). Qintex Entertainment was an affiliate of the Qintex Group of Australia, one of the country's leading media companies and the owner of resorts in Australia and Hawaii. The company had a television production unit in Hollywood that financed the highly successful CBS mini-series, *Lonesome Dove*. Skase wanted United Artists because he needed a strong distribution and marketing arm in the U.S.

Had the deal gone through, it would have marked the second sale of a major Hollywood studio to an Australian media giant. The growing demand for filmed entertainment worldwide attracted foreign investment in Hollywood. Rupert Murdoch's News Corp. started the trend by acquiring 20th Century Fox in 1985. Murdoch's stated goal was 'to own every major form of programming – news, sports, films and children's shows – and beam them via satellite or TV stations to homes in the United States, Europe, Asia and South America' (Fabricant 1996b). Murdoch made a counteroffer of $1.35 billion for the entire company in September, but Kerkorian rebuffed it when Qintex agreed to sweeten its original bid by $850 million (Lev 1989). But the deal soon collapsed. Qintex was vastly overextended and had even failed to put up a $50 million letter of credit while the details of the purchase were worked out. MGM/UA terminated the deal in October 1989. A few weeks later, Qintex, in debt estimated at $1.3 billion, was placed in receivership.

Sale no. 2: Giancarlo Parretti

The next offer came from an Italian. In March 1990, Giancarlo Parretti and his Pathé Communications made a bid to buy all of MGM/UA Communications for $1.2 billion (Stevenson 1990). Parretti, a one-time waiter, was born in Orvieto, Italy. He claimed to have made his fortune 'by buying, restructuring and selling troubled companies in Europe' (Citron and Cieply 1990). Parretti's proxy filings with the Securities and Exchange Commission made at the time of the bid indicated that he and his associates owned real estate companies in France, Italy, Spain, and Panama; financial holding companies in Luxembourg and Switzerland; a charter airline in Los Angeles; and a posh disco and restaurant in Los Angeles. His media holdings included Pathé-Nordisk of Denmark, Pathé Communications of France, and Renta Inmobiliaria International of the Netherlands. Altogether, Parretti was involved in motion picture production, distribution, and exhibition throughout much of Europe.

Parretti made his foray into Hollywood in 1987 when he acquired a controlling interest in Golan-Globus's Cannon Group. After producing a string of failures, the company was nearly bankrupt. Moreover, the company had been charged by the SEC with making fraudulent financial statements. Cannon's principal backer was Crédit Lyonnais Nederland (CLN), the Dutch branch of the French state-owned Crédit Lyonnais, then the largest bank in Europe. During the eighties, CLN moved into Hollywood and had also financed such leading independents as Carolco, De Laurentiis, and Hemdale. CLN came through for Parretti by loaning him $250 million for the Cannon bid. After moving the base of his operations to Beverly Hills at the end of 1988, Parretti took over Dino De Laurentiis's lavish Wilshire Boulevard office. The De Laurentiis Entertainment Group had filed for bankruptcy. With Crédit Lyonnais money, Parretti purchased a $9 million mansion, a $200,000 Rolls-Royce, and $1 million in jewelry for three young Italian 'actresses' he had on the payroll (McClintick 1996). In March 1989, Parretti renamed the company Pathé Communications Group in anticipation of acquiring control of Pathé Cinema, one of France's leading film groups. But his moved was blocked by France's Finance Minister, Pierre Beregovoy, in June 1989. 'In blocking the takeover, Mr. Beregovoy said he was invoking his right to oppose any deal that threatened public order. The minister did not elaborate,' reported Fabricant (1990).

Parretti relaunched Cannon's dormant production activities in January 1989 by forming a new production company, Pathé Entertainment, and hiring Alan Ladd Jr. as chairman to head it. Paretti had been pursuing Ladd since the previous September when he resigned from MGM. Ladd was joined by Jay Kanter, who had also walked out of the company. With financing from CLN, Pathé planned on making up to ten films a year.

Parretti had been 'convicted seven times for passing bad checks from 1974 to 1980 and imprisoned 11 months in 1977 for making a separate "false representation"' (Wellman 1992). At the time Parretti made his bid for MGM, he was facing tax evasion charges in Rome and had been convicted of fraudulent bankruptcy in Naples. For the latter, he was sentenced in absentia to 3½ years in prison and appealed. He was also alleged to have ties with the Sicilian mafia and drug money laundering. Why the bank stuck by Parretti and why Kerkorian wanted to do business with the man were never satisfactorily answered. To seal the MGM/UA deal, Parretti put up a $50 million letter of credit to place the deal on hold while he arranged the financing. After missing the June deadline for the closing, Kerkorian extended the deadline to October after Parretti agreed to up his bid to $1.3 billion (Fleming 1990: 101). (This was 72 percent more than Kerkorian had paid for the studio four years earlier.)

Parretti was able to raise $325 million by preselling the home-video distribution rights to the United Artists films to Warner Home Video for $125 million and the domestic television broadcast rights to more than 800 films MGM made after 1986 as well as selected United Artists films to Turner Broadcasting for about $200 million. To close the funding gap, Parretti once again turn to CLN, which put up $1 billion (Fleming 1990: 1). The deal closed on 1 November 1990 and marked the third time a Hollywood studio had been taken over by a foreign company or investors. After successfully brokering the buyout and pocketing his bonus, Barbakow resigned. Having sold the ancillary rights to the film libraries, Parretti had essentially mortgaged the company, leaving few assets to generate revenue. In the process, the MGM Home Entertainment division became obsolete, and 110 employees lost their jobs.

Parretti merged Pathé's operations with MGM/UA's and named the new company MGM-Pathé Communications Company. Parretti took over as chairman and CEO, Yoram Globus, president and COO, and Florio Fiorini, Parretti's partner and financial brains behind the buyout, chairman of the board. Parretti 'pledged to make the studio a cornerstone of an international entertainment empire he was building' and picked Alan Ladd Jr. to run his company in May 1990. Parretti paid top dollar to obtain Ladd's services. He received a $2.5 million annual salary plus $750,000 in bonuses if targets were met (Citron and Cieply 1990). Ladd's team again included Jay Kanter, production head and chief operating officer, and Charles R. Meeker, president. Meeker, a former partner in the White & Case law firm, was brought in to oversee the financial and business affairs of the studio and to serve as a liaison with Crédit Lyonnaise.

In 1996, David McClintick (1996), the author of *Indecent Exposure: A True Story of Hollywood and Wall Street* (1982), published an in-depth investigation of Parretti's ill-fated takeover bid in *Fortune* under the title 'The Predator: How an Italian Thug Looted MGM, Brought Credit Lyonnais to Its Knees, and Made the Pope Cry.' 'Once MGM was his, almost without pause,' said McClintick, 'Parretti began looting the studio in earnest, firing most of the financial staff and naming his 21-year-old daughter, Valentina, to an important financial post. Parretti's many women were seen entering his office suite each afternoon. Sounds of sex could be heard from behind closed doors. Stories like this began to appear: 'Stuck with unpaid bills, labs refused to process MGM film. Advertising agencies wouldn't return artwork. . . . Every day as many as 70 creditors called begging for payment.' 'MGM had no cash,' it was learned. 'Actors, producers and suppliers fled. Parretti didn't help. He misled the press, harassed studio executives with memos and concocted fantasy schemes – such as building splashy new studio headquarters. Film production nearly ground to halt' ('Flea-Bitten' 1992). Several creditors, claiming that the company owed them $18 million, filed suit to force MGM-Pathé into liquidation.

To save its investment, Crédit Lyonnais stepped in and provided an emergency loan of $145 million with the stipulation that Parretti relinquish operating control to Alan Ladd Jr. (Stevenson 1991). At the same time, the bank appointed Dennis C. Stanfill, Ladd's old boss, as cochairman and cochief executive. The bank wanted to relieve Ladd of fiscal oversight so that he could focus exclusively on making movies. Stanfill was a Rhodes Scholar with extensive finance and management experience. Working under him at Fox, Ladd had remarked that he had been 'hamstrung by Mr. Stanfill's insistence on "systems analysis and going by the book," things incompatible with making movies' (Harmetz 1981). Parretti continued to hamper operations, and in June, the bank removed him from the board and instituted proceedings in the Chancery Court of Delaware charging him with breaking the loan agreement. The court ruled in Crédit Lyonnais's favor and turned over the studio to Ladd and the bank. While Parretti was fighting the Chancery Court battle, he was arrested in Rome on 27 December 1991 and sent to prison in Sicily, where he was placed in solitary confinement. He was charged 'with criminal association, tax evasion, destruction of fiscal records and falsifying the books of a number of Sicilian companies' (Young 1992: 69). Back in the United States, the deposed Parretti was indicted by a Delaware grand jury 'on two felony counts of perjury and of tampering with physical evidence' pertaining to the Chancery Court case (Eller 1992: 9). In addition, the Federal Bureau of Investigation and the SEC had begun probes into Parretti's activities. Parretti returned to the United States in 1995, where he faced criminal charges, but before he could be sentenced, he fled the country.

McClintick's *Fortune* article recounted Parretti's scams, but the real revelation was this: Paretti was able to secure his loans from Crédit Lyonnais by bribing three top executives in the bank. 'Far from being the unwitting victim of Parretti's deceptions and dirty dealings at MGM, Crédit Lyonnais, it turned out, was complicit in Parretti's exploits in several investments,' he said. The SEC now began a probe into Crédit Lyonnais as well, and as reported by Amdur (2003), 'In the years since Hollywood enjoyed the pleasure of Parretti's crooked company, the French bank and its government backers have been working overtime to subvert or at least disrupt the SEC's case against them.' As for Florio Fiorini, Parretti's partner and the financial brains behind his operations, he was convicted of fraud in Switzerland in 1995 and was sentenced to six years in prison.

Crédit Lyonnais foreclosure

Crédit Lyonnais foreclosed on MGM-Pathé after the Chancery Court decision and formally took possession in May 1992. The bank renamed the studio Metro-Goldwyn-Mayer Inc. and moved its 600 employees to new corporate headquarters at the Colorado Place office complex in Santa Monica. The complex was renamed Metro-Goldwyn-Mayer Plaza. MGM had reached its nadir under Parretti. To recoup its investment, Crédit Lyonnais intended to rebuild the studio and sell it. It had until 1997 to do it. Under U.S. law, a foreign bank that controls a non-banking American company in foreclosure must sell it within five years. During the first year of the takeover, the bank invested another $2 billion in the company. As *Variety* ('Will Lyonnais' 1995) observed, 'Crédit Lyonnais has always hoped that having inherited a near-defunct operation whose film library had been pillaged by successive owners, they could install a new management team, provide funds for production and then make pics that would breathe life into a moribund distribution division.' 'The studio could then be sold as a going concern rather than a piece of cinema history,' it was hoped.

Alan Ladd Jr. had hard going as production chief under Parretti. In 1990, MGM released John G. Avildsen's *Rocky V* (1990) starring Sylvester Stallone, which Irwin Winkler and Robert Chartoff had placed in production before the takeover. The picture was a hit but performed less well than expected at the box office. In 1991, the company had only one hit under its belt, Ridley Scott's *Thelma and Louise* (1991) starring Geena Davis and Susan Sarandon. MGM was losing an estimated $1 million a day in 1991. As Stevenson (1992) reported, 'Despite Mr. Ladd's reputation for nurturing and supporting top creative talent, MGM had been all but written off by many agents and industry executives, making it hard to attract the best writers, directors and actors.' In 1992, the company released eight pictures with not a single hit. The studio finished the year with a net loss of $271 million ('Company Reports' 1993).

FIGURE 9.3 Susan Sarandon and Geena Davis in Ridley Scott's *Thelma and Louise* (1991)

Frank Mancuso management

In a quandary, Crédit Lyonnaise hired Michael Ovitz in March 1993 to help set a course for the company. Ovitz was chairman of the Creative Artists Agency, the most powerful talent agency in Hollywood. Dennis Stanfill, seeing that his clout had diminished, resigned not long after. At Ovitz's recommendation, the bank recruited Frank Mancuso in July 1993 to shore up the studio. Ladd, who was stung by the hire, refused to share power with Mancuso and was dismissed by the bank. Jay Kanter and other members of Ladd's team were either dismissed or resigned. Mancuso had been top man at Paramount for seven years, from 1984 to 1991. During his tenure, Paramount released a string of hits like Tony Scott's *Top Gun* (1986) and *Beverly Hills Cop II* (1987), Peter Faiman's *Crocodile Dundee* (1986), Leonard Nimoy's *Star Trek IV* (1986), Brian DePalma's *The Untouchables* (1987), and Adrian Lyne's *Fatal Attraction* (1987), making it the most successful movie studio in Hollywood.

A revived United Artists

MGM's current box-office share was less than 3 percent. MGM needed 'at least 10 percent of the box office for Crédit Lyonnais to have any chance of selling the studio for more than a fire sale price,' Ginsberg (1993) reported. Ovitz, as a result, advised the bank to revive United Artists, which had been dormant since 1990. The plan was to emulate Disney, which was releasing movies under multiple labels, such as Touchstone, Hollywood, and Walt Disney Pictures, to increase the flow of films. Crédit Lyonnais agreed to the plan and increased its line of credit to support the expanded production program. To head United Artists, Mancuso lured John Calley out of retirement in August 1993. Calley had built his career at Warner Bros. during the seventies. 'Filmmakers loved and trusted him,' said Natale (2011), 'and over the years he developed close relationships with the likes of Mike Nichols, Stanley Kubrick and Clint Eastwood.' Some of the pictures Warner released under his watch included Stanley Kubrick's *A Clockwork Orange* (1971), Alan J. Pakula's *Klute* (1971), Don Siegel's *Dirty Harry* (1971), William Friedkin's *The Exorcist* (1973), and Alan J. Pakula's *All the President's Men* (1976). Feeling he'd had enough, Calley retired from the business in 1980 and retreated to rural Connecticut. To head MGM, Mancuso hired Michael Marcus, a former agent at Michael Ovitz's Creative Artists Agency. The plan was for each division to make ten to twelve pictures a year.

Under Marcus, MGM released its first hits since *Thelma and Louise*, among them *Stargate* (1994), Roland Emmerich's sci-fi adventure picture starring Kurt Russell and James Spader; *Species* (1995), Roger Donaldson's sci-fi horror picture starring Ben Kingsley, Michael Madsen, Alfred Molina, and Forest Whitaker, and *Get Shorty* (1995), Barry Sonnenfeld's crime comedy starring John Travolta, Gene Hackman, Rene Russo, and Danny DeVito. Still, MGM was in bad financial shape.

Taking the UA job, Calley said his charge was to 'put rouge on the corpse' to prepare the studio for sale (Barnes 2011). But first, he added some smudge in the form of Paul Verhoeven's *Showgirls* (1995), a Carolco production that UA released with an NC-17 rating. Mancuso and Calley were betting that this picture starring Elizabeth Berkley, which offered lap dancing and full frontal nudity, could bolster the bottom line. But the picture was universally reviled and openly mocked. Todd McCarthy said, 'The only positive thing there is to say about *Showgirls* is that the sensibility of the film perfectly matches that of its milieu. Impossibly vulgar, tawdry and coarse, this much-touted major studio splash into NC-17 waters is akin to being keel-hauled through a cesspool, with sharks swimming alongside' (*VFR*, 25 September 1995). The picture was a dud initially but went on to achieve cult status as a midnight movie and on DVD.

Calley redeemed himself by reviving the James Bond franchise. The franchise had been on hold since 1990, when Albert R. Broccoli and Danjaq filed a suit in federal court against Giancarlo Parretti's Pathé Communications in an attempt to block the sale of television rights to the first sixteen James Bonds at cut-rate prices in several major markets around the world. The sales were intended to help raise money for Parretti's buyout bid. Later, Danjaq amended its suit, petitioning the court to terminate its distribution deal with MGM/UA, and filed a restraining order to block the sale of the rights. Pathé countersued, and development of *GoldenEye*, the seventeenth James Bond, stopped. The lawsuits were settled after Parretti's ouster in December 1992; MGM agreed to pay Danjaq $13.5 million to release 'all claims against the studio and its former parent, Pathé Communications' (Bateman 1992: 4).

Timothy Dalton, who had starred in the previous two Bond pictures, *The Living Daylights* (1987) and *Licence To Kill* (1989), had decided that he no longer wished to play 007 after his contract with Danjaq expired in 1990. 'At the boxoffice, the series had been on a slow downward curve since *Moonraker* in 1979,' said Widdicombe (1995). 'The films were still making good money, but they were not the blockbusters of yore,' he said. 'The late 1980s vogue seemed to be for a different kind of hero, such as Bruce Willis in the *Die Hard* films a hero in need of a shave, who swore, bled, got frightened and made love without his clothes on.' 'In the age of cold-war thaw, real women and safe sex,' he concluded, 'Bond seemed like a man out of time.' Martin Campbell's *GoldenEye* (1995), the revamped James Bond starring Pierce Brosnan, premiered in the U.S. in November 1995. 'James Bond definitely is back in business with *GoldenEye*,' said Todd McCarthy. 'This first 007 adventure in six years breathes fresh creative and commercial life into the 33-year-old series. Pierce Brosnan makes a solid debut in the role . . . and Ian Fleming's very mid-century secret agent has been shrewdly repositioned in the '90s in ways that will amuse longtime fans.' 'The very definition of escapist fare, this should restore Bond's golden touch at the international box office,' he said (*VFR*, 20 November 1995). The film took in $350 million worldwide and, if nothing else, made MGM an attractive item. MGM reported a net loss of nearly $160 million (Fabricant 1996a). Although it was an improvement over the losses that the company was incurring when Paretti defaulted on loans, the chances of Crédit Lyonnais ever recovering all of its $2.5 billion investment were nil. Calley's

FIGURE 9.4 Pierce Brosnan in Martin Campbell's *GoldenEye* (1995)

other successes included Mike Figgis's *Leaving Las Vegas* (1995), which garnered a Best Actor Oscar for Nicolas Cage, and Mike Nichols's *The Birdcage* (1996), the American remake of *La Cage aux Folles* (1978) starring Robin Williams.

Kerkorian's buyback no. 2

On 12 March 1996, Crédit Lyonnais put Metro-Goldwyn-Mayer Inc. up for auction. The leading contenders included Rupert Murdoch's News Corp.; Poly-gram, a subsidiary of the Dutch conglomerate Royal Philips Electronics; Morgan Creek Productions; and an MGM management team headed by Frank Mancuso. The bank had hoped to reap $2 billion from the auction, but after the initial offers came in lower than expected, the bank opened a second round of bidding with a July deadline. At the last minute, Kerkorian joined the bidding by teaming up with Seven Network Group, Ltd., Kerry Stokes's Australian media conglomer-ate. Kerkorian's $1.3 billion bid won the prize (Weiner 1996). Kerkorian, through his Tracinda Corp., put up $650 million and Seven Network, $250 million. The remainder was secured from J. P. Morgan.

Crédit Lyonnais and Kerkorian had been involved in protracted litigation since the foreclosure. The bank had brought suit against Kerkorian in a Los Angeles court, contending that he sold the studio without fully disclosing its true financial problems. Kerkorian countersued, and the case was finally settled in 1995 with an out-of-court settlement. 'Bad blood between the two parties,' said Bannon (1996), didn't prevent the bank from selling the asset to Kerkorian and his partners.

Kerry Stokes, with aspirations to be a big-time media player, wanted a stake in MGM to gain access to its films for Seven Network's free-to-air TV network. Oddly enough, Seven Network's previous owner was Christopher Skase, who made an abortive attempt to acquire MGM in 1989. Skase was now a fugitive living on the Spanish island of Majorca, having fled Australia to escape his creditors and the Australian Securities Commission. Why Kerkorian wanted to acquire MGM for the third time was open to speculation. 'One banker said the acquisition is a way for Mr. Kerkorian to set the record straight with Hollywood about his commitment to the entertainment industry. He has been criticized frequently for his previous involvement in the studio and some say the 79-year-old financier would like to be remembered as a builder rather than an asset stripper.' Others said, 'his main agenda is more basic: He smells a good deal' (Bannon 1996).

Building the film library

Kerkorian, ever on the lookout for bargains, seized the opportunity to acquire the film libraries of Orion Pictures, Samuel Goldwyn Entertainment, and Motion Picture Corporation of America from billionaire John Kluge's Metromedia International Group in April 1997. Metromedia was changing course and wanted to unload its software businesses and focus on developing hardware to provide basic communications services for emerging economies. Kerkorian and Seven Networks paid $573 million for studios and their libraries ('Metromedia' 1997). The acquisition of more than 2,200 film and television titles made MGM's library the world's largest.

Kerkorian seized another opportunity to enlarge MGM's library by acquiring the Polygram Film Entertainment library from the Seagram Company for $250 million in 1998 ('MGM Says' 1998). Under the leadership of Edgar Bronfman Jr., a scion of the Bronfman family fortune, Seagram had branched out into entertainment and purchased MCA, the parent company of Universal Pictures, in 1995. But when Seagram's investment in the movie business turned sour, Bronfman decided to invest in the faster-growing music business and paid more than $10 billion to acquire Polygram, the world's largest recorded-music company, from Royal Philips Electronics in 1998. To offset the cost, Bronfman unloaded Polygram's film library, among other assets. The library, containing 1,300 titles, *The Graduate* and *Fargo* among them, increased MGM's library to 5,200 titles – 'more than half of all Hollywood films produced since 1948' ('MGM Says' 1998).

Kerkorian next proposed a public offering to raise $500 million in working capital and to pay down debt. Seven Network, however, was unwilling or unable to invest in the offering. Kerkorian, therefore, bought out Seven Network's stake in MGM for $389 million (Eller 1998). MGM went ahead with the public offering in 1999: participation in the offering raised his investment in MGM to $950 million, which made him 89 percent owner of the company ('MGM Planning to Sell' 1999).

Protecting Bond

John Calley resigned shortly after the takeover and became president and chief executive of Sony Pictures Entertainment. In October 1997, Sony announced that its Columbia Pictures division had reached an agreement with Kevin McClory to produce a new series of James Bond pictures. McClory's 'claim that he can create a James Bond franchise is delusional,' said Mancuso. 'We hope that Sony has not been duped by Mr. McClory's deception,' and he threatened the company would 'pursue all means to protect this valued franchise,' reported Sterngold (1997). McClory, a little-known Irish writer, had acquired the right to produce *Thunderball* in 1963 after a lengthy court battle in England with Ian Fleming, the James Bond author. McClory and his partner had written a treatment called *Thunderball*, which they had shown to Fleming, who then proceeded to turn it into a James Bond novel without crediting its origins. The court allowed Fleming to continue reaping the royalties from book sales but awarded the movie rights to McClory. Albert Broccoli and Harry Saltzman, who had earlier secured the exclusive motion picture rights from Ian Fleming for all the published James Bond novels, were anxious to include *Thunderball* as the fourth picture in its series and paid McClory a substantial sum to produce it and release it through United Artists. In return, McClory had to agree not to produce a remake of the picture for a period of ten years.

Ten years later, McClory planned on making the remake. He claimed that he had equal rights to the James Bond character and that he could produce a James Bond series on his own based on his screenplay. UA and Danjaq, Broccoli's and Saltzman's production company, took him to court, asserting that their common-law copyright protected the formula. The Bond formula consisted of the famous gun-barrel logo, which began every picture, followed by the distinctive James Bond theme, the precredits sequence, and then the main titles, the latter accompanied by a title tune. The plot consisted of a series of self-contained action sequences strung together as set pieces. Acknowledging that McClory could produce a picture based on the *Thunderball* story, UA and Danjaq contended that he could not infringe on the James Bond character and formula in the process. Hamstrung by the decision, McClory failed to produce a remake and eventually sold off his rights to Hollywood producer Jack Schwartzman. Schwartzman commissioned a script and lined up financing and distribution from Warner Bros. and a foreign distributor. Schwartzman then convinced the British courts that the film would essentially be a remake of the original and would not infringe on the James Bond formula. He went on to overcome numerous obstacles and even persuaded Sean Connery to come out of retirement to play James Bond. Released in 1983, *Never Say Never Again* differed in several significant respects from the novel and kept to a more realistic framework than its predecessor. The picture was well received but did not affect the Bond franchise. MGM obtained a temporary restraining order preventing Sony from moving ahead with its plan. It then filed a lawsuit against the company, which it won. Sony settled the suit in March 1999 and agreed to pay MGM $5 million; in return, MGM agreed to pay Sony $10 million for the rights to an early James Bond spoof, *Casino Royale*, which was produced by Columbia Pictures. 'The end of this case reaffirms that James Bond resides at one address – that of MGM and Danjaq, his constant home for the last 37 years,' said Frank Mancuso (Sterngold 1999).

Alex Yemenidjian management

In a management shakeup, Mancuso and Robert Pisano, the second in command, resigned in April 1999. The company had not made a profit for eleven years. Since MGM remained a second-tier company, top stars and directors snubbed it, and talent agents hesitated to shop scripts there. Kerkorian installed Alex Yemenidjian as chairman and chief executive and Christopher McGurk as vice chairman. Yemenidjian, 43, was a certified public accountant when Kerkorian hired him in 1990 to serve as the top financial officer of Tracinda's Grand Hotel, Inc. Yemenidjian also handled Kerkorian's personal business affairs and negotiated the sale of MGM/UA to Parretti's Pathé Communications. Yemenidjian had never worked in the movie business and lured McGurk, 42, from Universal Pictures. McGurk was president and CEO of the studio. Before that, he spent eight years at Disney rising to president, Motion Pictures Group. Their announced goal was to build a much bigger company. 'We came here to turn the company around and use it as a vehicle to make acquisitions,' Mr. Yemenidjian said. 'We want to grow the company, make it a big entertainment company' (Block 2004: 3).

MGM Worldwide Television

Taking charge, the new management announced that MGM would post a $250 million loss in the second quarter of 1999. It stemmed from a one-time charge of $225 million for the write-off of film projects and other expenses involved in the reorganization (Orwall 1999). Forty-five employees, or 5 percent of MGM's work force, lost their jobs as a result. Hardest hit was MGM's television division, MGM Worldwide Television. MGM Television at one time was a major supplier of original TV shows for network television. During the eighties, for example, it produced such long-running series as *thirtysomething* and *In the Heat of the Night*. During Parretti's reign, the division was closed in 1991. Parretti considered television production a drain on company resources and was unwilling to spend the money to support it. Frank Mancuso, who was looking to create new franchises, revived the television division in 1994 and brought in John Symes after a long run at Paramount Television to head it. Under Symes, MGM got out of network production entirely to sidestep the deficit financing gamble and focused on less risky pay-television and first-run syndication markets. By 1998, MGM had three successful hour-long sci-fi series running, *The Outer Limits*, *Poltergeist: The Legacy*, and *Stargate SG-1*. The shows premiered on the Showtime premium subscription channel, then eight months later they were released to first-run syndication. The setup generated two revenue streams in the domestic market, which covered production costs. Revenues from foreign distribution were 'gravy,' said Dempsey (1996: 137). Symes's TV division was MGM's most profitable sector, and MGM would continue with the current three series and others in development, but MGM's main focus would be on the film library.

Exploiting the film library

MGM owned the world's largest film library but did not control all the rights. Parretti sold the home-video distribution rights to the United Artists films to Warner Home Video for thirteen years for $125 million. He also sold the domestic television broadcast rights to more than 800 films MGM made after 1986 as well as selected United Artists films to Turner Broadcasting for about $200 million (Stevenson 1990). In March 1999, MGM paid $225 million to Warner Bros. to buy out the home-video contract (Bates 1999). MGM had been paying around $50 million a year in distribution fees, which meant it would have had to pay Warner Bros. only $150 million over the next three years, but MGM was anxious to reestablish its home-video business and was willing to pay a premium for the buyout (Peers 1999). In September 1999, MGM reacquired the broadcast rights to the 800 films previously licensed to TBS from Time Warner. It was a barter arrangement. MGM extended the broadcast rights to the films on Turner's WTBS network for two years beyond the expiration dates and enhanced the terms on 600 titles on Turner's sister network, Turner Classic Movies. In return, MGM received exclusive broadcast rights to 200 titles in the package and the nonexclusive rights to the remaining 600 titles on any MGM-owned and -operated network after September 2000 ('MGM Regains Rights' 1999). The second provision allowed MGM to use the films to create new revenue streams.

To strengthen MGM's worldwide distribution apparatus, the new management immediately formed an alliance with 20th Century Fox. MGM was withdrawing from United Pictures International (UPI), the joint venture with Universal and Paramount, at the conclusion of its contract. Because MGM had been releasing only a few pictures a year through UPI, it felt that it had been paying a disproportionate share of UPI's operating costs. The deal with Fox gave the company the worldwide distribution rights to MGM's theatrical and video titles for three years beginning in 2000. MGM Home Entertainment continued to handle the domestic distribution of MGM's video product. As a result of the growing DVD market, MGM's film library was soon generating $400 million a year in cash flow (Block 2004).

Unlike the other Hollywood studios that were parts of larger media conglomerates that owned cable channels, MGM lacked a dedicated outlet for its library. Yemenidjian, therefore, intended to develop branded channels, such as MGM Drama or MGM Comedy, and negotiate with cable operators for carriage. He also set his sights on Cablevision's American Movie Classics cable channel. In February 2001, MGM bought a 20 percent stake in Rainbow Media, the majority owner of Cablevision, for $825 million (Sperling 2003: 1). But this was a false start since MGM received 'no control, board representation or the guarantee that it will gain a wider distribution for its massive film library over Cablevision's networks.' In July 2003, MGM sold back its stake in Rainbow Media for $500 million and took a loss.

Restructuring film production

MGM had a new production chief, Michael Nathanson, who replaced Mike Marcus as president and CEO of MGM Pictures following his resignation in February 1997. He came to MGM from Arnon Milchan's New Regency Productions, where his production credits included Oliver Stone's *Natural Born Killers* (1994), Joel Schumacher's *A Time to Kill* (1996), two *Free Willy* installments, and Curtis Hanson's Oscar winner, *L.A. Confidential* (1997). Before that, he was in charge of worldwide production at Columbia Pictures. Nathanson's first big hit at MGM was Rupert Wainwright's *Stigmata* (1999), a supernatural thriller produced by Frank Mancuso Jr. and starring Patricia Arquette and Gabriel Byrne.

To replace John Calley at United Artists. Mancuso hired Lindsay Doran, production chief at Sydney Pollack's Mirage Enterprises, where she produced the Academy Award winner Ang Lee's *Sense and Sensibility* (1995), and such hits as Pollack's *The Firm* (1993) starring Tom Cruise and *Sabrina* (1995), a remake starring Harrison Ford and Julia Ormond. Before that, she worked with Mancuso at Paramount as senior vice president of production. Albert Broccoli, the producer of the James Bond pictures, died in 1996. Barbara Broccoli, his daughter, and Michel G. Wilson, his stepson, took over the franchise and worked with Doran to release the eighteenth and nineteenth James Bonds, Roger Spottiswoode's *Tomorrow Never Dies* (1997) and James Michael Apted's *The World Is Not Enough* (1999), both starring Pierce Brosnan. MGM opened the latter in 3,100 theaters on more than 5,000 screens backed by a massive promotion campaign, making it the most successful Bond film in the series. Under Doran's watch, UA released two other noteworthy pictures, Randall Wallace's *The Man in the Iron Mask* (1998), a remake starring Leonardo Di Caprio, and John McTiernan's *The Thomas Crown Affair* (1999) starring Pierce Brosnan and Rene Russo, a remake of Norman Jewison's 1968 caper film starring Steve McQueen and Faye Dunaway.

Having bulked up on content, Yemenidjian and McGurk intended to keep the film library fresh with around ten pictures a year. Their first move was to reposition United Artists as a specialty unit in June 1999. Both MGM and UA had been functioning side by side with the aim of producing mainstream movie fare. With the restructuring, the unit would produce or acquire films costing less than $10 million targeted at the international marketplace. 'We thought it was important to restructure the brands, whereby MGM is a major Hollywood motion pictures and UA a more artist-friendly unit for smaller pictures,' said McGurk (Goodridge 1999: 1). Lindsay Doran, UA president, stepped down to become an independent producer, and her ten-person staff was merged with MGM Pictures, run by Nathanson. Thereafter, MGM became the producer of the James Bond films. Doran's post went vacant while McGurk searched for a new management team.

Yemenidjian and McGurk planned on supporting a few 'tent pole' pictures, but they placed their bets mainly on low-budget, franchise-friendly movies that catered to teen and urban audiences. To counter the perception that MGM was a 'one-trick pony' totally dependent on the Bond franchise, they took it out of a two-year cycle and put it in a three-year cycle (Block 2004). Yemenidjian and McGurk wanted to prove to the industry and Wall Street that MGM could succeed without Bond.

In 2000, MGM released a series of critical and box-office failures that included Walter Hill's *Supernova* (2000), a sci-fic pic starring James Spader and Angela Basset; DJ Pooh's *3 Strikes* (2000), a screwball comedy starring Brian Hooks; Joan Chen's *Autumn in New York* (2000), a romantic drama costarring Richard Gere and Winona Ryder; Barry Levinson's *Bandits* (2001), a crime comedy starring Bruce Willis; and Peter Howitt's *Antitrust* (2001), a high-tech thriller starring Tim Robbins, who portrays a software-company founder reminiscent of Bill Gates. *Supernova* and *Autumn in New York* were so unpromising that the studio refused to screen them for critics.

MGM began 2001 with a huge hit, Ridley Scott's *Hannibal* (2001), a sequel to Jonathan Demme's *The Silence of the Lambs* (1991) starring Anthony Hopkins and Jodie Foster, which swept the top five Academy Awards. *Hannibal*, based on Thomas Harris's 1999 best seller, starred Anthony Hopkins and Julianne Moore. Dino De Laurentiis, who owned the rights to the Lecter character, originally pitched the project to Universal Pictures, which agreed to finance and distribute it, but when the budget approached $80 million, it looked for a coproducing partner. MGM agreed to sign on and supplied half the budget in return for the domestic rights. Although the picture set box-office records, MGM's half share was diluted; De Laurentiis participated in the profits and had struck gross participation deals with Harris, Hopkins, Scott, and writer Steven Zaillian to get the picture off the ground. *Hannibal*, nonetheless, spun off a successful prequel, *Red Dragon* (2002), coproduced by Universal and MGM.

MGM's low-budget production strategy kicked in with the release of Robert Luketic's *Legally Blonde* (2001), a 2001 summer release starring Reese Witherspoon. It was MGM's biggest comedy debut ever, taking in nearly $80 million in five weeks. MGM planned a sequel straight off, *Legally Blonde 2: Red, White & Blonde* (2003), and developed a Broadway musical and syndicated TV series based on the property. MGM had similar luck with Tim Story's *Barbershop* (2002) starring Ice

Cube, which struck it big with urban audiences. The sequel, *Barbershop 2: Back in Business* (2004), barely broke even.

Not until 2002 did MGM release another successful tent pole; Lee Tamahori's *Die Another Day* (2002), the twentieth James Bond, starring Pierce Brosnan. 'The story formula, meanwhile, remains numbingly familiar: a debonair Pierce Brosnan employs all manner of gadgets, unshaven villains plot all manner of mayhem, damsels pose in all manner of undress,' said Hayes (2002: 14). *Die Another Day* cost more than *The World Is Not Enough* and surpassed it at the box office. MGM needed the money, having released three blockbuster failures earlier in the year – John McTiernan's *Rollerball* (2002), a remake of Norman Jewison's 1975 sci-fi release; Gregory Hoblit's *Hart's War* (2002), a military drama starring Bruce Willis and Colin Farrell; and John Woo's *Windtalkers* (2002), an action film starring Nicolas Cage.

A repositioned United Artists

MGM found a replacement to run United Artists in September 2001, Bingham Ray. Ray cofounded October Films with Jeff Lipsky in 1991 and served as its president until 1999. October was one of the leading independent film distributors in the nineties, having released a series of award-winning art-house hits such as Mike Leigh's *Secrets & Lies* (1996), Lars von Trier's *Breaking the Waves* (1996), David Lynch's *Lost Highway* (1997), and Jafar Panahi's *The White Balloon* (1995), one of the first Iranian imports.

MGM had earlier entered the specialty market when it acquired the Samuel Goldwyn Co. from Metromedia in 1997. In 1999, MGM changed the name of the unit to G2 Films after Samuel Goldwyn Jr. filed a lawsuit alleging trademark infringement. G2 was based in London under Wendy Palmer and was to function as foreign film producer and distributor, but the goals were not fully realized. In any event, MGM was late in the game. Sony Pictures Classics, Disney's Miramax, Fox Searchlight, and Time Warner's Fine Line Features were long-time fixtures in the specialty market. Yemenidjian and McGurk perhaps saw gold in the specialty market. Sony Pictures Classics' *Howards End* (1992) earned more than $25 million and picked up the Best Actress Oscar. Miramax released a string of Oscar-winning crossover hits that included Quentin Tarantino's *Pulp Fiction* (1994), Anthony Minghella's *The English Patient* (1996), Gus Van Sant's *Good Will Hunting* (1997), and John Madden's *Shakespeare in Love* (1998). And Fox Searchlight struck it big by releasing *The Full Monty* (1997), a low-budget British comedy directed by Peter Cattaneo.

Ray insisted on operating out of New York to be in the center of art-house distribution. Under Ray, United Artists released Danis Tanovic's Balkan War drama *No Man's Land* (2001), which won the Academy Award for Best Foreign Language Film, and Michael Moore's musings on gun culture, *Bowling for Columbine* (2002), which won an Academy Award for Best Documentary Feature and became the highest-grossing documentary ever. UA, in addition, released a number of film festival favorites, such as Rebecca Miller's *Personal Velocity* (2002), Peter Hedges's *Pieces of April* (2003), and Michael Winterbottom's *24 Hour Party People* (2002). But 'Ray's sensibilities never seemed to mesh with those of his bosses at MGM,' said Harris (2004: 8). McGurk and Ray were at odds over the direction of the company. McGurk wanted more commercial fare; Ray wanted to take more creative risks. Ray departed in January 2004, after 28 months. 'The problem was that in the current Hollywood economy, even art movies have to make money,' added Harris. Ray was replaced by Danny Rosett, MGM's former head of international theatrical distribution. His team included Sara Rose, Mary Ann Hult, and Jack Turner. UA released an eclectic mix of pictures in 2004, among them Terry George's *Hotel Rwanda* (2004).

The urge to merge

From the beginning, Yemenidjian and McGurk intended to grow MGM into a major company equal to Time Warner, Viacom, or News Corp. As a pure play company, MGM was 'dependent on content, both new and library product,' as McGurk put it (Block 2004: 3). Time Warner and the two others had metamorphosed into completely integrated entertainment conglomerates with the distribution clout to tap every region of the world. Their cable and television systems were impressive. Time Warner, for example, the owner of Warner Bros., owned Home Box Office, the nation's biggest pay-television channel, the Turner Broadcasting System, the biggest cable network in the country, and Time Warner Cable, one of the largest cable operators in the country. Viacom, the owner of Paramount Pictures, had a near monopoly on the music television field, owning MTV and VH1 cable networks as well as the Nickelodeon and USA channels and its Showtime premium service. In 1994, Viacom strengthened its home video position by acquiring Blockbuster Entertainment, the world's largest video retailer with more than 3,500 video stores. News Corp., the parent of 20th Century Fox, controlled a full-blown fourth TV network, Fox Broadcasting Co., and the Sky satellite television network in Europe.

In 2003, MGM moved into new headquarters more befitting of Yemenidjian's grand design for the company. It was located in a high-profile skyscraper in Century City at 10250 Constellation Blvd. Yemenidjian planned the move in 2000 and 'spared no expense in building out the studio's space with such Las Vegas-style flourishes as towering marble pillars and a grand spiral staircase lined with a wall of awards. In the lobby of the 14th floor, which includes the executive suites, is a wall of floating Oscar statuettes for such Academy Award winners as *Silence of the Lambs*, *Rocky* and *West Side Story*.' MGM became the anchor tenant and the building was renamed MGM Tower, on top of which 'a massive sign with MGM's roaring lion logo . . . lights up at night' (Vincent and Eller 2010).

Yemenidjian and McGurk had held unsuccessful talks to merge with Sony Pictures Entertainment and the Walt Disney Company, but its big chance to become a major conglomerate occurred in 2003 when it entered a bidding war to acquire the ailing Vivendi Universal. Vivendi, the French telecommunications company, acquired Seagram's Universal Studios for $34 billion in stock in 1999 ('Jean-Marie' 2003). The deal was spearheaded by Vivendi chairman Jean-Marie Messier, who was aspiring to transform Vivendi from a French water utility into a global media conglomerate. But his effort was cut short by the dotcom bubble burst, decimating Vivendi's stock, which it had used to finance its expansion. And because Messier reputedly overpaid for his acquisitions, Vivendi posted a $14 billion loss at the close of 2001, 'the biggest loss in French corporate history' ('Jean-Marie' 2003). Following Messier's ouster as chairman, Jean-Rene Fourtou, his successor, put the Universal assets on the block in 2003.

MGM put in a cash bid of $10.5 billion specifically to acquire Universal's movie studio, film library, theme parks, television production group, and the USA Network and Sci-Fi cable channels (Sorkin 2003). To help finance the bid, Kerkorian's Tracinda Corp. lined up $2 billion in financing from a consortium of private equity investors that included Providence Equity Partners and Morgan Stanley Capital Partners. MGM's bid topped the list, which included offers from Comcast, Viacom, Cablevision, and Liberty Media. However, MGM withdrew from the auction when Vivendi established a floor of $14 billion. After a second round of bidding, Vivendi Universal was sold to General Electric in 2003. McGurk said, 'When that didn't happen we looked around and tried to acquire other studios.' 'There isn't much available and what is available is at very high multiples [high valuation],' he reported. 'We were at a point where if you can't grow, we certainly didn't want to watch grass grow. So we began for the first time to respond to inquiries and approaches [from potential buyers]' (quoted in Block 2004: 3).

Kerkorian had invested about $3 billion in MGM over the years, it was estimated. While management fielded inquiries from potential buyers, the board approved a one-time dividend to enable Kerkorian to realize some return on his investment in May 2004. The board essentially refinanced the company by borrowing the money at low interest from the banks to pay the dividend – $8 a share dividend payable to all MGM stockholders. Since Kerkorian and his Tracinda Corp. together owned 174 million shares, or 74 percent of the company, Kerkorian received $1.39 billion ('MGM's Directors' 2004). New buyers would have to assume the debt.

Kirk Kerkorian was 86. He had bought MGM three times and was looking for a buyer for a third time. It was obvious that Kerkorian was not a builder like Steve Ross at Time Warner or Lew Wasserman at MCA or Rupert Murdoch at News Corp.; he was primarily an investor and a shrewd one at that. 'A strategic speculator of the first order, Kerkorian has had the knack of almost always buying low and selling high, whether it's airlines, studios or casinos,' said Egan (2004: 5). Kerkorian bought MGM the first time in 1969 when the company was going downhill fast. James Aubrey turned it around using draconian methods that many found offensive. Aubrey sold off assets – Judy Garland's ruby-red slippers included – and retreated from distribution but left a functioning studio with a physical presence. It was Ted Turner who dismantled the famous MGM lair when he failed to come up with the money to complete his buyout in 1986. To acquire his prize – the MGM library – he sold the Irving Thalberg Building, the sound stages, the remaining portions of the backlot, and other assets. The studio was gone. MGM remained a second-tier company afterward, dependent on motion picture production for most of its income. Unlike the other majors, MGM did not or could not diversify to create 'profit centers' to even out the risks of motion picture production. The James Bond films righted the ship more than once. MGM was a revolving door of production chiefs who turned out far more misses than hits. But MGM still retained its allure and attracted some unsavory characters, chief among them Giancarlo Parretti. Kerkorian was happy to take his money, and in 1990, he sold MGM a second time to the Italian financier, only to buy it back later at a bargain price. Kerkorian then built the world's largest film vault by acquiring the Orion Pictures, Samuel Goldwyn Pictures, and Polygram Film Entertainment film libraries. He then held talks to acquire or merge with other companies, but when his bid to acquire Vivendi Universal fell short, he began to look for an exit strategy to cash out.

10

MGM HOLDINGS

The coda (2004–15)

Sale no. 3: Sony Corporation

Suitors were soon at the door. In April 2004, MGM entered into negotiations with a consortium led by Sony Corporation of America to buy out the company. The consortium included three buyout firms, Providence Equity Partners, Texas Pacific Group, and DLJ Merchant Banking Partners. Sony's bid of $4.8 billion in cash and the assumption of MGM's debt won out over a competing bid from Time Warner, and the deal was signed on 23 September 2004 (Sorkin 2004b). At the last moment, Comcast joined Sony's consortium as a strategic partner and put up $300 million to seal the deal. The deal was spearheaded by Howard Stringer, chairman and chief executive of Sony Corporation of America, and Robert S. Wiesenthal, Sony's chief financial officer and a former First Boston banker. Kerkorian netted more than $2 billion at the close of the deal. Yemenidjian and McGurk, for their part, were able to cash out millions in stock and stock options (Block 2004).

'The structure of Sony's offer is particularly ingenious in that it puts most of the financial burden on the shoulders of its partners,' said Sorkin (2004a). 'The acquisition strategy is this,' he explained: 'Sony, using Texas Pacific and Providence money and possibly some of its own, would buy MGM, shutter most of the movie studio operation and then license and distribute MGM's most valuable asset, the film library.' 'This way,' he said, 'not only do others wind up financing most of the deal, but Sony also basically takes control of the library without having to put the operation on its balance sheet.'

Sony wanted MGM's library to help its Blu-ray technology win the high-definition format war, which was being waged with the rival HD DVD group led by Toshiba and NEC. A lot was at stake. As Arnold (2004: 3) reported, 'Consumer spending on DVD has risen steadily each year, with last year's total for sales-only estimated at $11.8 billion. That's more than consumers ever spent on movies in the VHS era, and a record that's likely to be shattered this year, as spending on DVDs for the first half is already at $6.6 billion, according to *Video Store Magazine* Market Research.' Comcast, the nation's largest cable system operator, wanted access to both MGM's and Sony's film libraries for its contemplated premium cable channels and its video-on-demand platform. Texas Pacific and Providence were in it strictly as an investment.

Sony needed the win badly. The company had been in turmoil ever since the 'Sony shock' of 2003, when the company posted massive losses and eliminated much of its worldwide workforce, including 9,000 jobs in the U.S. Once known for creating elegant products like Walkman, Trinitron TV, and PlayStation, Sony was being outpaced by Apple's iPod and upstart manufacturers of flat-screen TVs in South Korea, Taiwan, and China. Should Sony win the DVD format war, it could also profit from the selling of a new generation of disc players for the new format and from exploiting MGM's films on Sony's PlayStation game consoles and other platforms.

MGM Holdings, Inc.

At the conclusion of the buyout in September, Metro-Goldwyn-Mayer became a private company. To take ownership of MGM, the consortium formed MGM Holdings, Inc. and committed a total of $1.6 billion in the leveraged buyout, giving the investors proportionate stakes in MGM Holdings as follows: Providence Equity Partners (29 percent), Texas Pacific Group (21 percent), Sony Corporation of America (20 percent), Comcast (20 percent), DLJ Merchant Banking Partners (7 percent) and Quadrangle Group (3 percent) (Sorkin 2004b). The remainder of the financing was supplied by a bank syndicate headed by JP Morgan Chase and loaded onto the studio as debt after the closing.

The owners dismantled MGM's movie business, and most of MGM's 1,400 employees lost their jobs. Those dismissed were given severance packages. Sony absorbed MGM's Home Entertainment division, dismissed most of its staff, and took over the home video and television distribution of the film catalog in the domestic market. Fox Home Entertainment continued handling distribution in foreign markets. To keep the library relevant to retailers, Sony intended to cofinance and coproduce new motion pictures for the company, in particular future installments of the James Bond, Pink Panther, and Rocky franchises and remakes of popular titles for international distribution.

During the first year, Sony mined the library and released Shawn Levy's *The Pink Panther* (2006) starring Steve Martin as Inspector Clouseau, a new iteration of the Peter Sellers Pink Panther pictures, and *Rocky Balboa* (2006), the sixth installment of the Rocky franchise, written, directed, and starring the 60-year old Sylvester Stallone. The Steve Martin picture was a modest success, but Stallone's defied expectations. It was 'an underdog of sorts,' said Arnold (2006), 'since no film franchise has ever successfully been revived after three decades with its original star.' The picture recouped its production cost the first week of its release in the

FIGURE 10.1 Daniel Craig in Martin Campbell's *Casino Royale* (2006)

U.S. and went on to earn nearly $156 million worldwide, twice as much as its predecessor *Rocky V* in 1990 (Box Office Mojo).

As a co-owner of MGM, Sony Pictures secured the rights from Danjaq to make two Bond pictures. The deal was negotiated with Barbara Broccoli and Michael G. Wilson, her half brother, who took over the franchise after the death of Albert Broccoli in 1996. Sony agreed to put up the production costs of the two pictures as well as the advertising costs in return for worldwide distribution rights. In addition to a fee for their work, Broccoli and Wilson were to receive a substantial share of the profits. They led off with *Casino Royale* (2006), the property MGM acquired from Sony in 1999. Ian Fleming's novel, *Casino Royale*, marked the start of James Bond's career as an MI6 agent. A young Daniel Craig, age 37, replaced Pierce Brosnan in the series and was the sixth actor to play the lead. Broccoli and Wilson, who retained creative control over the franchise, worked with Amy Pascal, Sony's production chief, and selected a relatively unknown Daniel Craig to make the series 'younger, darker and more hip' to attract a twenty-first-century audience (Waxman 2005). The revamping worked; *Casino Royale*, directed by Martin Campbell ,outperformed all the other Bonds and took in $558 million at the global box office (Box Office Mojo).

Harry Sloan management

During the transition, Sony, the only consortium partner with film industry experience, took over the management of the company, but 'diverse agendas clouded the picture,' reported Goldsmith and LaPorte (2006: 69). Sony, a minority investor in the venture, soon found itself sidelined. Providence Equity and Texas Pacific, which took most of the financial risk and together had a majority on the board, took effective control of the company and appointed Harry E. Sloan chairman and chief executive in October 2005. Jonathan Nelson, MGM board chairman and Providence Equity chief, made the appointment. The investors 'just wanted to make money,' said Goldsmith and LaPorte. 'The partners came to believe their new asset would be impaired by the general impression that MGM had been absorbed by Sony and was closed for business.'

Sloan, a lawyer and high-flying entrepreneur, had help build Lionsgate Entertainment into a mini-major as its chairman and largest shareholder. Earlier in the year, Sloan had received more than $200 million for his interest in the sale of the European broadcasting giant SBS Broadcasting Group to a German broadcaster for over $2 billion. Sloan founded SBS in 1990 on an investment of $5 million. Sloan resigned from Lions Gate's board in April 2005, 'possibly sensing a chance to replicate that vision under the esteemed MGM banner,' said Eller (2007), and persuaded Nelson to put him on MGM's board. 'That fall, when the investors were looking to hire a new chief executive, Sloan pitched himself. The owners bought it.' Sloan then invested $15 million of his own money in the studio, gambling that he could turn it around. To work alongside him as chief operating officer, Sloan hired Rick Sands, who had held similar positions at DreamWorks and Miramax Films.

Ensconced in MGM's fourteenth-floor headquarters in the MGM Tower, Sloan set out to reestablish MGM as a major player in the industry. To do that, he restarted MGM's theatrical and TV distribution operations. This required seventy new hires. His first move was to dump Sony as a distributor of MGM's film and television library. The DVD market, had softened and Sony was not meeting its targets, which allowed the board to contract with Fox Video in June 2006 to take over the distribution of MGM's DVDs worldwide. In addition, MGM ceased outsourcing the distribution of its film library to worldwide television via Sony and brought the business back in-house under the umbrella MGM Worldwide Television Distribution Group. The top TV shows in the library now included the Stargate SG-1 sci-fi series, containing more than 200 episodes on the Sci-Fi Channel, and *The L Word*, the immensely popular drama series which aired on Showtime.

To build an annual slate of films, MGM would eschew in-house production and function purely as a distribution and marketing outlet for independent producers under the supervision of Rick Sands. MGM intended to acquire pictures via pickups and cofinancing and charge a distribution fee for its marketing efforts. In return, MGM would also receive a profit participation for those pictures it cofinanced. To reduce costs and to play it safe, MGM would concentrate on cofinancing mid-range indie pics. MGM would market the pictures on its own in the U.S. and Canada and sell the distribution rights market by market overseas. Sands quickly signed distribution agreements with the Weinstein Co., Bauer Martinez Studios, Kimmel Entertainment, Lakeshore, and other production companies. It was a false start. Sloan quickly learned that mid-range pictures were a tough sell in a theatrical market dominated by blockbusters. Paul McGuigan's *Lucky Number Slevin* (2006) from the Weinstein Co. was its first release. By March 2007, MGM had released nearly twenty pictures. Most were box-office and critical failures. The few hits included Mikael Håfström's *1408* (2007) and Rob Zombie's

Halloween (2007), both from Weinstein's Dimension Films. On average, the others grossed just $12 million in ticket sales. 'Outsourcing production to independents has been a disaster for MGM's image and has done little for its bottom line,' said Halbfinger (2008).

A rebooted United Artists

On 2 November 2006, MGM announced that it had concluded a joint venture with Tom Cruise and Paula Wagner to reboot United Artists. This was Sloan's chance to burnish MGM's standing in the creative community and to secure quality pictures to refresh the film library, it was thought. As for Cruise, the deal gave him a chance to revive a damaged career. In August 2006, Sumner Redstone, the head of Viacom and Paramount's parent company, fired Cruise after fourteen years because the actor's erratic behavior over the last year was 'not acceptable' to Paramount. Redstone was referring 'to Cruise's couch-jumping on Oprah Winfrey's show, and his frequent mentions of his belief in Scientology,' reported Holson (2006). 'Mr. Redstone claimed that his behavior had cost the studio as much as $150 million in movie ticket sales for *Mission: Impossible III*.' Declining DVD sales and the recession forced studios to become increasingly tightfisted. Paramount was tired of paying out $10 million a year to carry Cruise's company.

Cruise and Wagner were given a minority stake in United Artists without having to put up any money of their own. Wagner was Cruise's agent at Creative Artists Agency before they joined forces in 1993 to form Cruise/Wagner Productions and produced the *Mission Impossible* franchise, Steven Spielberg's *Minority Report* (2002) and *War of the Worlds* (2005), and Edward Zwicks's *The Last Samurai* (2003), among others. At United Artists, Wagner was to oversee the business end of the new venture, with the authority to produce four or more pictures a year at an average cost of $50 million (Holson 2006). MGM secured a $500 million production fund from Merrill Lynch for a slate of twelve to eighteen films to be developed by Paula Wagner and Tom Cruise over five years. MGM was required to put up $75 million to seal the deal and cover costs above the $60 million mark on a picture (Halbfinger 2008). The financing was to be used exclusively for United Artists films.

United Artists' inaugural was *Lions for Lambs* (2007), Robert Redford's polemic against the Bush administration's handling of the war in Afghanistan. With a star-studded cast of Redford, Cruise, and Merryl Streep, '*Lions for Lambs* was expected to be one of the most prestigious films of the awards season' ('Cruise Studio' 2007), but the picture was lambasted by the critics and died at the box office. Manohla Dargis said, 'It's a long conversation, more soporific than Socratic, and brimming with parental chiding, generational conflict and invocations of Vietnam' (*NYTFR*, 9 November 2007). UA's second release was Bryan Singer's *Valkyrie* (2008), starring Tom Cruise as Count Claus Schenk von Stauffenberg, the disillusioned Nazi officer who planned to assassinate Hitler. *Valkyrie* was the most expensive picture produced under Sloan's watch, with the exception of the James Bond pictures. A lot was riding on the picture – United Artists' credibility as a serious contender, for one thing, and Tom Cruise's chance of a comeback. The picture was originally scheduled to open in July 2008, but the release date was moved several times because of production delays and while the company repositioned the picture as an action-thriller. Meanwhile, in August 2008, Paula Wagner was eased out of United Artists to return to full-time independent production. She was not greenlighting enough projects to suit MGM's needs was the story. She retained her stake in the company, and Cruise stayed put, which was crucial if UA wanted continued access to the Merrill Lynch financing. However, United Artists was left in limbo after Wagner's departure. *Valkyrie* was released in December 2008 and was a modest success, saving the day for all concerned.

MGM Motion Picture Group

Sloan had wanted tentpoles and franchises and hired Mary Parent as chairwoman of the new MGM Motion Picture Group in March 2008. Parent was previously production chief for Universal Pictures from 2003–05. She was credited with overseeing a string of hits that included Jay Roach's *Meet the Parents* (2000), Doug Liman's *The Bourne Identity* (2002), Gary Ross's *Seabiscuit* (2003), *American Pie* franchise, and the five-time Academy Award–winning *Gladiator* (2000), a coproduction with DreamWorks. After that she formed an independent production unit with Scott Stuber and produced a number of pictures for Universal release, among them Anthony and Joe Russo's *You, Me and Dupree* (2006) and Peter Berg's *The Kingdom* (2007). Parent's announced goal was to greenlight 'enough projects for MGM to roar into theaters with as many as 12 of its own movies in 2010.' Yet, as Halbfinger (2008) pointed out, 'Parent, who has never marketed or distributed her own films before, is being asked to turn MGM into a player, and do it quickly.' Soon after her hiring, Rick Sands, MGM's CEO since 2006, resigned. His future with the studio was not assured since Parent was to report directly to Sloan.

While Parent prepared her slate and Sloan attempted to line up the financing, MGM awaited the returns on the next installments of the James Bond and Pink Panther franchises from Sony. Marc Forster's *Quantum of Solace* (2008), the twenty-second James Bond picture, opened in the U.S. on 14 November 2008. The title was taken from an Ian Fleming short story and was the first true sequel in the franchise's forty-six-year history. Daniel Craig reprised his role as a gentleman predator to good effect. *Quantum of Solace*, with a combined marketing and production budget estimated at $400 million, became the second-highest-grossing film in the series worldwide (Barnes 2008). However, Harald Zwart's *Pink Panther 2* (2009) starring Steve Martin, which was released in February 2009, failed.

Stephen F. Cooper management

MGM's revival had stalled, and on 17 August 2009, Sloan stepped down as chief executive officer but remained on the board. He was immediately replaced by Stephen F. Cooper, a corporate turnaround specialist, who had overseen the restructuring of Enron in 2002 as vice chair and had righted the troubled Krispy Kreme as CEO from 2002–05. The situation Cooper faced was grim. The studio was hobbled by $3.5 billion in debt from the 2005 buyout. MGM had released only one film of its own since *Valkyrie* in December 2008 – Kevin Tancharoen's *Fame*, a teen musical coproduced with Lakeshore Entertainment, and that was a dismal failure. And DVD sales, the most profitable side of MGM's business, had plunged as consumers switched to new technologies. DVD sales and rentals nationwide had peaked at $24.1 billion in 2006. DVDs were the main engine of growth for the majors between 1999 and 2006. During that period, revenues from theatrical exhibition accounted for only around 25 percent of domestic studio revenues, with most of the rest coming from home video, including DVD rentals and sales, reported Caranicas (2010). Until 2008, MGM's film library had been generating more than $500 million in revenue annually, which was used mainly to service the interest on the debt (Barnes 2009). But by 2009, its DVD sales had declined by nearly half. MGM needed to restructure its debt to finance big franchise films like *The Hobbit* and other projects Mary Parent had in the works, but the aftermath of the global credit crisis made it hard to raise new money from hedge funds and foreign investors. Nor could Sloan look to MGM's current owners – Providence Equity, TPG Capital, Sony, Comcast, DLJ Merchant, and Quadrangle – for new money. They were not about to throw good money after bad.

At the owners' insistence, Cooper put MGM up for auction in November 2009 and arranged for Goldman Sachs to shop for potential buyers. If the exit strategy worked, the owners hoped to recoup most of their investment, and MGM's creditors could be assuaged. But MGM was not worth anything close to what they had paid for it. MGM was not a going motion picture concern and had lost much of its 'enterprise value.' Its primary assets remained its film library and rights to the James Bond film franchise. Time Warner, Lionsgate Entertainment, and smaller private companies showed interest. The best offer came from Time Warner, which bid a meager $1.5 billion for the company. The low bid was a shocker. Lattman (2009) reported that 'Providence Equity Partners has marked its equity investment at 10 cents on the dollar' afterward.

MGM's creditors rejected the Time Warner bid, and Cooper weighed other options to salvage the company. The best solution, it seemed, came from the creditors' committee in March 2010: a prepackaged bankruptcy, a move that would allow MGM's creditors to take control of the studio in exchange for debt forgiveness. To run it after it emerged from bankruptcy, the committee proposed Spyglass Entertainment, an independent production company founded in 1998 by veteran Hollywood producers Gary Barber and Roger Birnbaum. The company had coproduced more than fifty movies with Disney, Paramount, DreamWorks, and Universal, among them such hits as M. Night Shyamalan's *The Sixth Sense* (1999), Gary Ross's *Seabiscuit* (2003), and J. J. Abrams's *Star Trek* (2009).

In October 2010, activist investor Carl C. Icahn, who owned 10 percent of MGM's debt, proposed an alternative, a merger with Lionsgate Entertainment, the aspiring mini-major in which he held a one-third stake (Kaplan 2010). He offered to buy MGM's debt for 53 cents on the dollar if the creditors voted down the Spyglass deal. Overall, Icahn was prepared to spend $1 billion to accomplish this. His plan would give MGM creditors about a 55 percent stake in a new company. Assuming they held onto their stakes for five years, he argued, they stood a chance to get back what they were owed. The creditors voted for the Spyglass deal, which allowed them to exchange nearly $5 billion in debt for most of the equity in a new company. As DiOrio (2010) explained, 'Major debt holders are pushing Spyglass because the deal represents a longer-term play and, atypically, the hedge funds holding much of the debt like that. They're now "underwater," having bought debt at high prices during the failed MGM auction, so the prospect of raising MGM's value over time is more appealing than it might be otherwise.' Icahn endorsed the bankruptcy plan after winning certain concessions, including the right to elect a director to MGM's new board.

In November 2010, MGM filed for a prepackaged Chapter 11 bankruptcy in the Federal Bankruptcy Court in Manhattan, and on 2 December 2010, the court approved the reorganization plan. After investing $1.6 billion in the company in 2005, the consortium's stake was wiped out. Providence Equity Partners and the other hedge funds became the latest casualties of the buying and selling of MGM. However, Sony's gambit worked. The MGM titles Sony placed exclusively on Blu-ray helped it win the high-definition format war. Sony had also recouped most of its $300 million investment from the distribution fees collected from the two new Bond movies. MGM's creditors, which numbered more than 100, now owned the company. Anchorage Capital Group and Carl C. Icahn were among the largest shareholders. Gary Barber and Roger Birnbaum were named as cochairs and cochief executives of the company. (Mary Parent resigned from MGM in October 2010 to make way for the new management.) The new nine-member board was headed by Ann Mather, a former chief financial officer of Pixar; Kevin Ulrich of Anchorage Capital Group; Patrick H. Daugherty of Highland Capital Management; Christopher Pucillo of Solus Alternative; Jason O. Hirschhorn, MySpace copresident; and Frederic G. Reynolds, a former CBS chief financial officer in addition to Barber and Birnbaum.

The Barber–Birnbaum management

To fund operations and resume making movies, MGM had secured $500 million in exit financing from JPMorgan Chase ('MGM Gets Court Approval' 2010). Barber and Birnbaum set MGM on a new course. To reduce overhead, it streamlined operations by moving its headquarters from the opulent MGM Tower in Century City to a six-story building in a Beverly Hills retail strip and reduced staff to fewer than 300 from a high of 450. They then refashioned the company as a worldwide television-rights company and abandoned its domestic theatrical distribution operation. Although international television sales was the greatest source of revenue remaining in its film library, MGM still needed new product to freshen its catalog as before. To head the MGM Motion Picture Group, Barber and Birnbaum brought in Jonathan Glickman, a former Spyglass president, in February 2011. To head MGM's Television Group and Digital division, they recruited Roma Khanna from Comcast's NBCUniversal that June.

MGM renewed its agreement with Fox Home Entertainment to distribute its DVDs worldwide through 2016. The new deal allowed Fox for the first time to sell MGM titles on digital platforms, such as Apple's iTunes. Khanna set out to produce two to three new series a year by developing original concepts and mining source material from MGM's film library. By 2014, MGM's *Teen Wolf* was in its third season on MTV and went on to be renewed for six seasons. MGM also had *Paternity Court*, a 150-episode courtroom drama, on national syndication and was developing a ten-episode TV adaptation of *Fargo*, which was destined for FX. *Fargo* lasted for three seasons. In addition, MGM controlled the worldwide distribution rights for *The Vikings*, a Canadian-Irish historical drama series written and created by Michael Hirst, which was being shown on the History Channel in the U.S.

United Artists Media Group

In September 2014, MGM expanded its television business by acquiring a majority stake in One Three Media and LightWorkers Media, owned by Emmy winners Mark Burnett and Roma Downey and Hearst Productions, and consolidated the entities into a new venture called United Artists Media Group. This was the third time MGM resurrected the United Artists banner. One Three Media produced the hit network reality shows *The Voice*, *Survivor*, *The Apprentice*, and *Shark Tank*. LightWorkers Media, the smaller of the two, produced scripted religious programming such as *The Bible*, a History Channel miniseries. Burnett was named as CEO of the company with the charge to develop and produce scripted and nonscripted television shows and motion pictures. Barber (Miller 2014) said, 'It made sense to dust off the United Artists name for use in conjunction with Downey and Burnett because partnering with them offers the chance at another terrific success story to build value in the brand again.'

Production-distribution partnerships

MGM had no releases scheduled for 2011 when it emerged from bankruptcy and little funding for production. Becoming a pure-play motion picture company, MGM entered into coproduction-distribution partnerships with Sony, New Line Cinema and Paramount. MGM would typically put up a half of the financing and receive half of the profits, if any. In every case, MGM tried to get international television and home video rights. Dealing with Sony, MGM used the Bond franchise to leverage cofinancing rights to select Sony pictures, such as David Fincher's *The Girl With the Dragon Tattoo* (2011) starring Daniel Craig and Rooney Mara, a remake of the 2009 Swedish hit based on the Stieg Larrson novel; Phil Lord's and Christopher Miller's *21 Jump Street* (2012), a relatively inexpensive action-comedy starring Jonah Hill and Channing Tatum based on the Fox Network television series (1987–91); and David Frankel's *Hope Springs* (2012) starring Meryl Streep, Tommy Lee Jones, and Steve Carell.

But MGM pinned its hopes on the James Bond and *Hobbit* franchises. After *Quantum of Solace* in 2008, the motion picture rights to the Bond franchise reverted to MGM. Sony acquired the worldwide distribution rights to the next two Bond pictures, but MGM drove a hard bargain. Leaked information from a devastating cyberattack on Sony Pictures revealed that MGM was able to strike a 'one-sided deal' for the Bond pictures. MGM and Sony had been 50–50 partners on the first two Bonds. Under the terms of the new deal, Sony agreed to fund half of the production budgets as well as the advertising costs for the next two Bonds in return for 25 percent of the profits, while MGM kept the rest. Separately, Danjac was to receive 'a hefty portion of the films' revenues.' MGM insisted on a low distribution fee and retained the television and home video rights as well, reported Fritz (2015). *Skyfall*, the next in line, was put on hold in April 2010 while MGM was undergoing reorganization. There were fears that Sam Mendes, the director, and Craig might walk away from the production in the interim. But Barber and Birnbaum placed the production back on track when they successfully persuaded MGM's creditors to put up the financing for *Skyfall* and the twenty-fourth edition, *Spectre* (2015). *Skyfall* (2012) was a huge box-office success, grossing $1.1 billion worldwide, the highest ever for the series (Kilday 2015: 18). As a result of the 'one-sided deal,' Sony made just $57 million, while MGM made $175 million. Danjaq's share was $109 million. 'As far as MGM is concerned, Bond is the lifeblood of the company right now,' said Merrill Lynch analyst Hal Vogel (ibid.).

The Hobbit: An Unexpected Journey was a long time in gestation before principal photography began in February 2011 under Peter Jackson's direction in New Zealand. It was scheduled for release in December 2012. MGM inherited the distribution rights to *The Hobbit* films when Kerkorian bought United Artists in 1981. United Artists had acquired the film rights to the J.R.R. Tolkien book as well as Tolkien's *Lord of the Rings* trilogy in 1969. In 1976, UA sold the film rights to both properties to producer Saul Zaentz. Zaentz produced only one film, Ralph Bakshi's animated *Lord of the Rings* in 1978, which did poorly at the box office. Zaentz disputed UA's accounting of the proceeds, and after a long legal battle, Zaentz wound up with the rights to develop *Lord of the Rings* and UA with the rights to distribute *The Hobbit*. Zaentz sold the production rights to *The Hobbit* to New Line Cinema in the nineties. Warner Bros., which now owned New Line, wanted to develop a new franchise to fill the gap left by the winding down of the *Harry Potter* franchise and struck a deal with MGM in 2007 to produce the first two installments of the *Hobbit* franchise, which were to be shot back to back. *The Hobbit: The Desolation of Smaug*, the second installment, was scheduled for release in December 2013. Originally, Warner Bros. and MGM were to cofinance the two pictures, with Warner taking the U.S. distribution rights and MGM the foreign. How MGM would pull this off remained a problem. The issue was

FIGURE 10.2 Cate Blanchett in Peter Jackson's *The Hobbit: Battle of the Five Armies* (2014)

resolved when Warner agreed to advance all the financing for the two pictures, an estimated $200 million for each, in return for worldwide theatrical and home video distribution rights for both films, with MGM taking the international television rights. MGM was left off the hook and could use its money to invest in other projects. In July 2012, at the end of the shoot, New Line and MGM announced their intent to produce the third installment of the trilogy, *The Hobbit: The Battle of the Five Armies* (2014). *The Battle of the Five Armies* did not quite measure up to the previous installments, but by the end of the run, Peter Jackson's trilogy had grossed nearly $3 billion at the box office.

The die is set

By 2011, Barber and Birnbaum's overhaul was working. MGM reported net operating income of $38 million for the year ('MGM Books' 2012). As a result of the restructuring, 57 percent of the revenue came from international television distribution, 27 percent from DVD and Blu-ray sales, and the remainder from films. Earnings rose steadily afterward. In 2011, MGM acquired Tom Cruise's and Paula Wagner's minority stakes in United Artists. In 2012, the company bought out Carl C. Icahn's entire stake in the company, a move that allowed MGM to make a public offering, if necessary, without possible interference from the activist Icahn. In October 2012, Roger Birnbaum resigned as cochairman and co-CEO of MGM and entered into an exclusive producing deal with the studio. By 2013, MGM had eliminated most of its debt, using the proceeds from *The Hobbit* trilogy and *Skyfall*, each of which grossed more than $1 billion worldwide. In December 2015, MGM bought out Mark Burnett's, Roma Downey's, and Hearst Productions's minority interest in the United Artists Media Group and appointed Burnett president of MGM Television and Digital Group. At the end of 2015, MGM announced the third consecutive year of record profits.

The record net of $252 million for 2015 was generated in large measure by the release of Sam Mendes's *Spectre* (2015), the twenty-fourth James Bond, starring Daniel Craig, which shattered box-office records everywhere ('MGM Posts' 2016). Sony's distribution contract for the Bond films expired afterward, and MGM and Danjaq put the franchise out for bid. Which company would take over the distribution of the industry's longest-running franchise became the object of speculation. There was much to covet in the franchise. 'Sony's four-film distribution run of Bond movies was impressive, raking in $3.17 billion at the worldwide box office from 2006 through 2015,' reported Hughes (2016). 'Daniel Craig, a controversial choice at the time he was cast, has become a favorite of fans and critics, earning high praise for his complex, nuanced portrayal of the character.' 'The four-film outing has earned more than $400 million in domestic DVD and Blu-ray revenue, and close to $1 billion in DVD/Blu-ray/Digital-HD sales and rentals around the world since 2006,' he reported. Product placements and tie-ins, he said, 'bring roughly $100–200 million per film, while the box office and all merchandising revenue streams combine for an average of as much as $500+ million per year from 2006 through 2015, for Sony's Bond releases.' 'That's a hefty sum and sets the bar high for whoever winds up carrying the series forward in the future,' he said. The leading contenders for the franchise were Sony, Warner Bros., and 20th Century Fox. Complicating Bond's future, both Daniel Craig and director Sam Mendes resigned from the franchise. James Bond would have to be relaunched again with a new creative team.

MGM ended up a hybrid – a company with a historic brand that owns a treasure trove of films containing mostly non-MGM titles and earns the lion's share of its revenue distributing reality television shows. It took a prepackaged bankruptcy that wiped out a $1.6 billion investment to right the company after the Sony consortium buyout. MGM's business plan succeeded. MGM will remain a center of media attention because it holds the rights to the James Bond films, which originated with United Artists. Its film library will be recycled on all the emerging platforms. And its motion picture output will comprise mostly remakes of old favorites. Such is the coda of a great motion picture studio.

BIBLIOGRAPHY

'6 Top Loew-Metro Execs Received 31% of the Net Profits' (1938) *Variety*, 7 December.

'35 Years of Bond: History of a Franchise' (1997) *Screen International*, 5 December, p. 21.

'60 Top Grossers of 1946' (1947) *Variety*, 8 January, p. 8.

'All-Time Boxoffice Champs' (1970) *Variety*, 7 January.

Amdur, M. (2003) 'Inside Move: Bill Comes Due for Credit Lyonnais,' *Variety*, 30 November.

'Anna Karenina' (1935) *Hollywood Reporter*, 29 June, p. 3.

'Another Negro Film' (1929) *New York Times*, 2 June.

'Antonioni's Hypnotic Eye on a Frantic World' (1967) *Life*, 27 January, pp. 62–7.

Arnold, T. (2004) 'Sony's MGM Deal Hedges All Bets,' *Video Store Magazine*, 19–25 September.

Arnold, T. (2006) 'Lord of the Ring,' *Hollywood Reporter*, online, 12 December, www.hollywoodreporter.com/news/lord-ring-146196 (accessed 20 March 2017).

Bach, S. (1985) *Final Cut: Dreams and Disasters in the Making of Heaven's Gate*, New York: William Morrow.

Balio, T. (1976) *United Artists: The Company Built by the Stars*, Madison: University of Wisconsin Press.

Balio, T. (1987) *United Artists: The Company That Changed the Film Industry*, Madison: University of Wisconsin Press.

Balio, T. (1990a) 'Introduction to Part I,' in T. Balio (ed.) *Hollywood in the Age of Television*, London: Routledge, pp. 3–40.

Balio, T. (1990b) 'Introduction to Part II,' in T. Balio (ed.) *Hollywood in the Age of Television*, London: Routledge, pp. 259–95.

Balio, T. (1993) *Grand Design: Hollywood as a Modern Business Enterprise, 1930–1939*, New York: Charles Scribner's Sons.

Balio, T. (2010) *The Foreign Film Renaissance on American Screen: 1946–1973*, Madison: University of Wisconsin Press.

Bannon, L. (1996) 'Kerkorian Group Wins Bid for MGM,' *Wall Street Journal*, 17 July.

Barnes, B. (2008) 'James Bond, Armed with Record, Controls Box Office,' *New York Times*, 16 November.

Barnes, B. (2009) 'MGM Replaces Chief Executive,' *New York Times*, 18 August.

Barnes, B. (2011) 'John Calley, Hollywood Chief, Dies at 81,' *New York Times*, 14 September.

Barnes, H. (1937) 'Captains Courageous,' *New York Herald Tribune*, 12 May.

Barnes, H. (1938) 'The Citadel,' *New York Times Herald Tribune*, 4 November.

Barnes, H. (1945) 'They Were Expendable,' *New York Herald Tribune*, 21 December.

Bart, P. (1990) *Fade Out: The Calamitous Final Days of MGM*, New York: Morrow.

Barton, R. (2014) *Rex Ingram: Visionary Director of the Silent Screen*, Lexington: University of Kentucky Press.

Bateman, L. (1992) 'Bond Returns as Rights Deadlock Is Resolved,' *Screen International*, 18 December.

Bates, J. (1999) 'MGM Buys Its Way Out of Pact for $225 Million,' *Los Angeles Times*, 16 March.

Bedingfield, R. (1969) 'An Armenian with a Flying Carpet,' *New York Times*, 16 February.

'Begelman Furnishes UA with New Chair' (1981) *Variety*, 7 October.

'Big Stockholder in Loew's Seeks Resignation of Five Directors' (1956) *New York Times*, 20 December.

Bingen, S. (2011) *MGM: Hollywood's Greatest Backlot*, Salona Beach, CA: Santa Monica Press.

'Bioff, Browne Guilty; Facing 30-Year Terms' (1941) *New York Times*, 7 November.

'Biographical Cycle' (1934) *Variety*, 13 February, pp. 3, 25.

Block, A. (2004) 'Staying at MGM Until the End,' *Television Week*, 7 September.

'Booming the Feature Film' (1914) *Moving Picture World*, 17 January, p. 32.

Bosworth, P. (1969) 'Antonioni Discovers America,' *Holiday*, March.

Box Office Mojo, online, www.boxofficemojo.com

Brady, T. (1949) 'Hollywood Notes,' *New York Times*, 13 February.

Brady, T. (1951) 'L. B. Mayer Leaving Metro Film Studio,' *New York Times*, 23 June.

'Brando's "Bounty" Costliest Pic Ever; Near $19,000,000' (1962) *Variety*, 22 February.

'Bronfman as Chair, O'Brien Exits Metro' (1969) *Variety*, 28 May.

Byron, S. (1968) 'Showmen's Instant Folklore,' *Variety*, 11 December.

Byron, S. (1969) 'MGM Echo of Producers Past,' *Variety*, 19 May.

Canby, V. (1961) 'British-French in Sex Battle,' *Variety*, 8 February, p. 1.

Canby, V. (1967) 'MGM Critic Sells Shares to Time and Bronfman,' *New York Times*, 23 August.

Canby, V. (1973) 'Leo's Roar Becomes a Whimper,' *New York Times*, 30 September.

'Cantor to Confer with Roosevelt' (1933) *New York Times*, 14 November.

Caranicas, P. (2010) 'Studios Hit with Homevideo Slump,' *Variety*, online, 1 May, http://variety.com/2010/digital/features/studios-hit-with-homevideo-slump-1118018573/ (accessed 8 November 2016).

Carey, G. (1981) *All the Stars in Heaven: Louis B. Mayer's MGM*, New York: E. P. Dutton.

Carr, H. (1924) 'Harry Carr's Page,' *Los Angeles Times*, 3 December.

Chamberlin, W. (1930) 'Are They Versatile?,' *Picture Play Magazine*, January.

Champlin, C. (1966) 'Movie Magic Versus the Ledger Domain,' *Los Angeles Times*, 13 November.

Champlin, C. (1969) 'Brisk Winds of Change Rustle Hollywood,' *Los Angeles Times*, 23 February.

Champlin, C. (1970) 'The 1960s: A Revolution in Movie Audiences,' *Los Angeles Times*, 18 January.

Champlin, C. (1973) 'Muffling the Lion's Roar,' *Los Angeles Times*, 28 September.

Churchill, D. (1937) 'Hollywood Rediscovers the "Short",' *New York Times*, 18 July.

Churchill, D. (1941) 'Hollywood Wire,' *New York Times*, 27 July.

Citron, A. and Bernstein, S. (1991) 'Money Woes Make Script for MGM a Tragedy,' *Los Angeles Times*, 27 October.

Citron, A. and Cieply, M. (1990) 'Hollywood Mystery: Despite Giancarlo Parretti's Lavish Lifestyle and His Bid for MGM/UA, the Italian Financier Remains a Little-Known Outsider,' *Los Angeles Times*, 6 May.

Cole, R. (1979) 'Begelman to Be President of MGM Film Division,' *New York Times*, 19 December.

'Company Reports: Metro-Goldwyn-Mayer Inc' (1993) *New York Times*, 1 April.

Conant, M. (1976) 'The Impact of the *Paramount* Decrees,' in T. Balio (ed.) *The American Film Industry*, Madison: University of Wisconsin Press, pp. 346–70.

'Corporation Profits' (1928) *New York Times*, 18 December.

Crafton, D. (1997) *The Talkies: American Cinema's Transition to Sound: 1926–1931*, New York: Charles Scribner's Sons.

Crowther, B. (1942) 'Semi Annual Report,' *New York Times*, 28 June.

Crowther, B. (1943) 'So Long, Andy,' *New York Times*, 21 February.

Crowther, B. (1951) 'Whither Bound?,' *New York Times*, 18 November.

Crowther, B. (1956) 'Value of Stars,' *New York Times*, 12 August.

Crowther, B. (1957) *The Lion's Share: The Story of an Entertainment Empire*, New York: Dutton.

Crowther, B. (1960) *Hollywood Rajah*, New York: Holt, Reinhart and Winston.

Crowther, B. (1963) 'MGM Planning More Art Films,' *New York Times*, 2 March.

Crowther, B. (1965) 'Sensational Sob Stories on Screen,' *New York Times*, 25 July.

'Cruise Studio Struggles as Lions Fails to Roar' (2007) *The Guardian*, 9 November.

Dallos, R. and Delugach, A. (1971) 'MGM to Specialize and Diversify, Too,' *Los Angeles Times*, 24 October.

'David Bernstein, Loew's Aide, Dies' (1945) *New York Times*, 11 November.

Delugach, A. (1974) 'Grand Hotel Gamble Pays Off – MGM Has Best Year Ever,' *Los Angeles Times*, 10 December.

Delugach, A. (1984) 'Disney Bid Is Kerkorian's Latest High-Stakes Fling for a Studio,' *Los Angeles Times*, 9 June.

Dempsey, J. (1996) 'MGM's Solid TV Unit Pushes "Limit",' *Variety*, 24 June.

Dietz, H. (1925) 'Transcontinental Trip of First Trackless Train,' *Exhibitors Trade Review*, 25 April.

DiOrio, C. (2010) 'Why MGM Is Choosing Spyglass over Others,' *Hollywood Reporter*, online, 12 August, www.hollywoodreporter.com/news/why-mgm-choosing-spyglass-over-26627 (accessed 20 March 2017).

'The Dirty Dozen' (1967) *Boxoffice*, 26 June.

'Divestment Plan Voted for Loew's' (1958) *New York Times*, 30 October.

Dooley, R. (1979) *From Scarface to Scarlet: American Films in the 1930s*, New York: Harcourt, Brace.

'Dr. Kildare's Wedding Day' (1941) *Photoplay*, November 1941, p. 97.

Egan, J. (2004) '21st Century Mogul: Lion's Shareholder Kirk Kerkorian Driven by the Deal,' *Variety*, 19–25 April.

Eller, C. (1992) 'Parretti Indicted, Could Face 10 Years,' *Variety*, 27 July.

Eller, C. (1998) 'Seven Sells Is MGM Stake to Kerkorian,' *Los Angeles Times*, 20 August.

Eller, C. (2007) 'A Mogul Returns to Finish What He Started,' *Los Angeles Times*, 4 March.

Esterow, M. (1956) 'Schary Ousted as Chief as MGM,' *New York Times*, 29 November.

Everson, W. (1992) *The Hollywood Western*, Secaucus, NJ: Carol Publishing.

'Expansion of Small Time' (1919) *Variety*, 19 December.

Eyman, S. (2005) *Lion of Hollywood: The Life and Legend of Louis B. Mayer*, New York: Simon & Schuster.

Fabricant, G. (1986) 'Turner to Sell MGM Assets,' *New York Times*, 7 June.

Fabricant, G. (1988) 'Plan to Split MGM/UA Is Reported,' *New York Times*, 11 July.

Fabricant, G. (1990) 'Pathe again Extends Offer for MGM/UA,' *New York Times*, 16 June.

Fabricant, G. (1996a) 'Kerkorian Group to Buy Ailing MGM Film Studio,' *New York Times*, 17 July.

Fabricant, G. (1996b) 'Murdoch Bets Heavily on a Global Vision,' *New York Times*, 29 July.

'Facts about Marcus Loew' (1914) *Los Angeles Times*, 19 April.

'Film Quotas Eased in New British Act' (1938) *New York Times*, 3 April.

'Film Salaries Revealed by U.S' (1939) *Motion Picture Herald*, 15 April, pp. 44–7.

'Flea-Bitten MGM Lion Gets Ready to Roar again' (1992) *Toronto Star*, 6 January.

Fleming, C. (1990) 'Did Parretti Buy a Paper Lion?,' *Variety*, 5 November, pp. 1, 101.

Flint, P. B. (1977) 'Joan Crawford Dies at Home,' *New York Times*, 11 May.

Flint, P. B. (1992) 'Hal Roach Is Dead at 100,' *New York Times*, 3 November.

Flint, P. B. (1996) 'Greer Garson, 92, Actress, Dies,' *New York Times*, 7 April.

Fordin, H. (1975) *The World of Entertainment: Hollywood's Greatest Musicals*, New York: Doubleday.

'Fox and Warners Are Sued as Trusts; Dissolution Sought' (1929) *New York Times*, 28 November.

'Fox Out of Films' (1930) *New York Times*, 8 April.

Franklin, J. (1959) 'The Big Parade,' in *Classics of the Silent Screen*, New York: Citadel Press.

'Free and Easy' (1930) *Film Daily*, 20 April.

Fritz, B. (2015) 'Pursuit of James Bond Film Rights Kicks Into High Gear,' *Wall Street Journal*, 30 October.

Frook, J. (1990) 'MGM/UA Says to Heck With Movies, Let's Sell the Company again,' *Los Angeles Business Journal*, 2 April.

'Garbo's "Christina" Sets New Fashions' (1934) *Motion Picture Herald*, 6 January, p. 67.

Gent, G. (1972) 'Black Films Are In, So Are Profits,' *New York Times*, 18 July.

Ginsberg, S. (1993) 'Mancuso Takes on the Challenge of Giving MGM Lion Back Its Roar,' *Los Angeles Business Journal*, 2 August.

Gish, L. (1987) 'Memories of a Time When "The Wind" Blew Hot,' *New York Times*, 1 March.

Glancy, H. (1992) 'MGM Film Grosses, 1924–1948: The Eddie Mannix Ledger,' *Journal of Film Television & Radio*, Vol. 12, No. 2, pp. 127–44.

Glancy, H. (1999) *When Hollywood Loved Britain: The Hollywood 'British' Films 1939–45*, New York: Manchester University Press.

Goldsmith, J. and LaPorte, N. (2006) 'The MGM Saga: When Harry Met Leo,' *Variety*, 11–17 September.

Gomery, D. (1986) *The Hollywood Studio System*, New York: St. Martin's Press.

Goodridge, M. (1999) 'McGurk Sets UA as MGM Specials Arm,' *Screen International*, 11 June.

Gottfried, H. (1965) 'The Sandpiper,' *Women's Wear Daily*, 16 July.

Gottshalk, E. (1973) 'MGM's Aubrey Resigns as President and Chief,' *Wall Street Journal*, 1 November.

'"Grand Hotel" to Road Show at Many Cities' (1932) *New York Times*, 18 April.

Grant, L. (1976) 'Daniel Melnick Leaves MGM,' *Los Angeles Times*, 14 July.

Green, S. (1981) *Encyclopedia of the Musical Film*, New York: Oxford University Press.

Griffith, R. (1941) 'Hepburn's "Woman of the Year" Rated Satirical Triumph,' *Los Angeles Times*, 17 February.

Guernsey, O., Jr. (1954) 'The Long, Long Trailer,' *New York Herald Tribune*, 19 February.

Guiles, F. (1972) *Marion Davies: A Biography*, New York: McGraw-Hill.

Haber, J. (1973) 'James Aubrey Calls it "Quits" at MGM,' *Los Angeles Times*, 1 November.

Halbfinger, D. (2008) 'MGM: A Lion or a Lamb,' *New York Times*, 8 June.

Hall, M. (1927) 'The Screen,' *New York Times*, 29 May.

Hall, M. (1930) 'Three Fine Portrayals,' *New York Times*, 31 August.

Hall, M. (1932a) 'Blue-Ribbon Pictures of 1931,' *New York Times*, 3 January.

Hall, M. (1932b) 'The Hotel Parade,' *New York Times*, 17 April.

Harmetz, A. (1981) 'Battle for Control of Fox is Surfacing,' *New York Times*, 12 February.

Harmetz, A. (1982) 'Summer 82 Is Hollywood's Most Lucrative Year,' *New York Times*, 6 September.

Harmetz, A. (2001) 'Ann Sothern Is Dead at 92,' *New York Times*, 17 March.

Harmetz, A. (2014) 'Mickey Rooney, Master of Putting on a Show,' *New York Times*, 7 April.

Harris, D. (2004) 'Inside Moves: Ill-Suited Turn for Ray,' *Variety*, 12–18 January.

Harris, K. (1985a) 'MGM/UA Ups Bid for Rest of Video Holding,' *Los Angeles Times*, 3 April.

Harris, K. (1985b) 'MGM/UA Reports Loss of $82.2 Million in 3 Months,' *Los Angeles Times*, 5 April.

Hay, P. (1991) *MGM: When the Lion Roars*, Atlanta, GA: Turner Publishing.

Hayes, D. (2002) 'James Bond at 40: Martinis & Bikinis: If Bond Is Showing His Age, the 007 Label Is Vintage,' *Variety*, 11–17 November.

Hayes, T. (1982) 'Profit Surges at MGM/UA,' *New York Times*, 10 November.

Heisner, B. (1990) *Hollywood Art: Art Direction in the Days of the Great Studios*, Jefferson, NC: McFarland.

Hirschhorn, C. (1981) *The Hollywood Musical*, New York: Crown.

Holson, L. (2006) 'Mission: Rescue Operation,' *New York Times*, 3 November.

Howe, A. (1969) 'A Banker Looks at the Picture Business,' *Journal of the Screen Producers Guild*, March, pp. 15–22.

Hudgins, M. (1953) 'Logistics of a Bivouac on the Liffey River,' *New York Times*, 22 November.

Hughes, E. (1957) 'M.G.M.: War Among the Lion Tamers,' *Fortune*, August 1957, pp. 98–103, 206, 208, 210, 212, 214 and 216.

Hughes, M. (2016) 'How James Bond Could Head to Warner Bros with Christopher Nolan,' *Forbes*, 10 June.

'Inside Stuff' (1926) *Variety*, 1 September.

'Inside Stuff – Pictures' (1934) *Variety*, 30 January, p. 52.

'Jean-Marie Messier Himself: Where Did It All Go Wrong?' (2003) *Economist*, 12 June.

Judson, H. (1917) 'Marcus Loew, a Real Showman,' *Moving Picture World*, 6 October.

'Jupiter's Darling' (no date) *Turner Classic Movies*, online, www.tcm.com/this-month/article.html?id=382966%7C376552 (accessed 6 July 2016).

Kael, P. (1970) 'The Beauty of Destruction,' *New Yorker*, 21 February.

Kaplan, T. (2010) 'Bashing Spyglass Deal, Icahn Offers to Buy MGM Debt,' *New York Times*, 21 October.

Kasindorf, M. (1972) 'How Now, Dick Daring?,' *New York Times*, 10 September.

Kendall, J. (2015) 'Kirk Kerkorian Dies at 98; Shaped Hollywood and Las Vegas,' *International New York Times*, 18 June.

Kilday, G. (2015) 'What Now as James Bond Goes from Super Agent to Free Agent,' *Hollywood Reporter*, 30 October.

Koppes, C. and Black, G. (1987) *Hollywood Goes to War*, New York: Macmillan.

Koszarski, R. (1990) *An Evening's Entertainment: The Age of the Silent Feature Film*, New York: Charles Scribner's Sons.

Lafferty, W. (no date) 'Douglas Shearer – Writer,' *Film Reference*, online, www.filmreference.com/Writers-and-Production-Artists-Ro-She/Shearer-Douglas.html (accessed 23 January 2015).

Lambert, G. (1990) *Norma Shearer: A Life*, New York: Knopf.

Landro, L. and Hughes, K. (1988) 'MGM/UA, Burdened by Debt and Deficits, Is on the Block Again,' *Wall Street Journal*, 21 December.

'Last Rites Said at Bier of Loew' (1927) *Los Angeles Times*, 9 September.

Lattman, P. (2009) 'MGM Hires Crisis Expert – Burdened by Debt, Film Studio Removes Chief Executive Sloan,' *Wall Street Journal*, 19 August.

Lee, W. (1968) 'Scientist's Evaluation of "2001" Saga of Things to Come,' *Los Angeles Times*, 2 June.

'Leo's 20th Birthday' (1944) *Variety*, 21 June.

Lev, M. (1989) 'MGM/UA Accepts New Qintex Bid,' *New York Times*, 16 September.

Lev, P. (2003) *The Fifties: Transforming the Screen 1950–1959*, New York: Charles Scribner's Sons.

Lichtman, L. (1983) 'CBS Songs Grows with MGM/UA Deal,' *Billboard*, 8 January.

'Lillian Gish Film Sold as "Western"' (1928) *Variety*, 10 October.

'Loew Interests Completely Reorganized' (1919) *New York Clipper*, 15 October, p. 3.

'Loew's and MGM Set Profit Marks' (1967) *New York Times*, 9 November.

'Loew's Doubles Net in Four-Year Period' (1927) *Film Daily*, 24 June.

'Loew's in Black' (1959) *New York Times*, 9 January.

'Loew's Inc' (1939) *Fortune*, August, in T. Balio (ed.) (1976) *The American Film Industry*, Madison: University of Wisconsin Press, pp. 278–94.

'Loew's Stockholders Highly Critical' (1956) *New York Times*, 24 February.

'Loew's Stockholders' Suits Consolidated' (1938) *Motion Picture Daily*, 17 May, p. 2.

'Loew's Wins Stockholder Suit' (1939) *Variety*, 25 January.

'Lon Chaney's Five Voices' (1930) *New York Times*, 6 July.

Lusk, N. (1926) 'The Scarlet Letter,' *Picture-Play Magazine*, November.

Lusk, N. (1929) '"Mary Dugan" Brilliant Hit,' *Los Angeles Times*, 7 April.

Lusk, N. (1931) '"Susan Lenox" Smash in East,' *Los Angeles Times*, 25 October.

Lusk, N. (1932) 'Joan Now Bows to Garbo Only,' *Los Angeles Times*, 8 May.

Lusk, N. (1944) '"Velvet" Climaxes Season; Elizabeth Taylor Hailed,' *Los Angeles Times*, 22 December.

Maltby, R. (1995) 'The Production Code and the Hays Office,' in T. Balio, *Grand Design: Hollywood as a Modern Business Enterprise, 1930–1939*, New York: Charles Scribner's Sons, pp. 37–72.

Maltby, R. (2003) 'More Sinned against Than Sinning: The Fabrications of "Pre-Code Cinema",' *Senses of Cinema*, online, December, http://sensesofcinema.com/2003/feature-articles/pre_code_cinema/ (accessed 23 July 2015).

'Marcus Loew Dies' (1927) *New York Times*, 6 September.

'Marlon Brando's "Mutiny on the Bounty" Seen Depressing Metro Quotations' (1962) *Variety*, 28 May.

Marx, S. (1975) *Mayer and Thalberg: The Make-Believe Saints*, New York: Random House.

Maslin, J. (1991) 'Pre-Wedding Jitters, Mostly Dad's,' *New York Times*, 20 December.

McClintick, D. (1982) *Indecent Exposure: A True Story of Hollywood and Wall Street*, New York: Morrow.

McClintick, D. (1996) 'The Predator: How an Italian Thug Looted MGM, Brought Credit Lyonnais to Its Knees, and Made the Pope Cry,' *Fortune*, online, 8 July, http://archive.fortune.com/magazines/fortune/fortune_archive/1996/07/08/214344/index.htm (accessed 9 September 2016).

Merrick, M. (1931) 'Entente Hinges on Chatterton,' *Los Angeles Times*, 16 August.

'Metro Abandons Producer System' (1947) *New York Times*, 12 December.

'Metro-Goldwyn-Mayer' (1932) *Fortune*, December, in T. Balio (ed.) (1976) *The American Film Industry*, Madison: University of Wisconsin Press, pp. 256–70.

'Metro-Goldwyn Pictures' (1934) *Wall Street Journal*, 15 December, p. 5.

'Metromedia to Sell Film Units to MGM for $573 Million' (1997) *New York Times*, 29 April.

'Metro to Continue Lew Ayres Films' (1942) *New York Times*, 3 April.

'MGM Books Loss on *Dragon Tattoo*, Expects Profit on *21 Jump Street*' (2012) *Los Angeles Times*, online, 22 March, http://latimesblogs.latimes.com/entertainmentnews-buzz/2012/03/mgm-books-loss-on-dragon-tattoo-expects-profit-on-21-jump-street.html (accessed 20 March 2017).

'MGM Executive Scores Levin in Letter to Holders' (1967) *New York Times*, 30 January.

'MGM Gets Court Approval of Reorganization Plan' (2010) *Entertainment Close-Up*, 8 December.

'MGM Leases "Wizard" for CBS-TV Showings' (1956) *Broadcasting*, 30 July, p. 60.

'MGM Planning to Sell $750 Million in Its Stock' (1999) *New York Times*, 11 September.

'MGM Posts Record Financial Results Courtesy of "Spectre"' (2016) *Hollywood Reporter*, online, 24 March, www.hollywoodreporter.com/news/mgm-posts-record-financial-results-878050 (accessed 20 March 2017).

'MGM Regains Rights to Films' (1999) *New York Times*, 16 September.

'MGM Reports $17 Million Loss' (1963) *New York Times*, 30 November.

'MGM Says It Will Buy Polygram's Movie Library' (1998) *New York Times*, 23 October.

'MGM Scrams Theatre Distribution' (1973) *Variety*, 19 September.

'MGM's Directors Approve a One-Time Dividend' (2004) *New York Times*, 27 April.

'MGM Slashes Pay of Film Executives' (1952) *New York Times*, 10 July.

'MGM Struggle Near Showdown' (1967) *New York Times*, 20 February.

'MGM to Cut Activities in Film and Stress TV' (1973) *New York Times*, 18 September.

'MGM/UA Loss Grows' (1987) *New York Times*, 13 November.

'MGM/UA Merger Now Fait Accompli, Shares at $28 Per' (1985) *Variety*, 19 June, p. 42.

'M'Grath Approves Split-Up of Loew's' (1952) *New York Times*, 29 January.

'Michael Arlen, Novelist, Dead' (1956) *New York Times*, 24 June.

Miller, D. (2014) 'MGM Buys 55% Stake in Production Firms of Roma Downey and Mark Burnett,' *Los Angeles Times*, 23 September.

'Millions for Film Program' (1924) *Los Angeles Times*, 2 June.

Morgenstern, J. (1962) 'Wonderful World of the Brothers Grimm,' *New York Herald Tribune*, 8 August.

Morris, G. (1998) 'A Quickie Look at the Life & Career of Tex Avery,' *Bright Lights Film Journal*, online, 1 September, http://brightlightsfilm.com/quickie-look-life-career-tex-avery/#.WIh9oZWmk5s (accessed 28 October 2016).

Morris, R. (1931) 'Sinful Ladies Lead in 1931,' *Variety*, 29 December, p. 5.

'A Motion Picture Show Magnate' (1911) *The Nickelodeon*, 25 March.

'Movies to Out Ten Cited for Contempt of Congress' (1947) *New York Times*, 26 November.

'Music Records' (1972) *Variety*, 10 May, p. 69.

'"Mutiny" to Be MGM's 3rd Biggest Grosser' (1963) *Boxoffice*, 20 May, p. E2.

Natale, R. (2011) 'John Calley, Studio Lion, Dies at 81,' *Variety*, 13 September.

'Nelson Eddy, Baritone of the Movies, Dead at 65' (1967) *New York Times*, 7 May.

'News of the Screen' (1937) *New York Times*, 14 December.

'Niblo and *Ben-Hur*' (1925) *Variety*, 18 January.

'Nick Schenck, L. B. Mayer's Boss Dies Three Days after Vogel' (1969) *Variety*, 5 March.

Nugent, F. (1938) 'A Medical Trilogy Comes to Town,' *New York Times*, 6 November.

'O'Brien to Step Down as MGM President' (1968) *Wall Street Journal*, 16 October.

'Orders Election by Screen Writers' (1938) *New York Times*, 7 June.

Orwall, B. (1999) 'MGM to Take $225 Million of Charges on Reorganization and Film Cutbacks,' *Wall Street Journal*, 22 June.

'Our Blushing Brides' (1930) *Film Daily*, 3 August, p. 10.

Parish, J. R. (1971) *The Great Movie Series*, South Brunswick and New York: A. S. Barnes.

Peers, M. (1999) 'MGM Presses Stop on WB Homevid Deal,' *Variety*, 15 March.

Penn, S. (1967) 'Mad for the Movies,' *Wall Street Journal*, 20 February.

'Pictures and Players' (1931) *New York Times*, 8 March.

'The Picture Parade' (1926) *Motion Picture Magazine*, May.

'Proxy Battle-Scarred Joe Vogel, of Metro No-Fun Era, Is Dead' (1969) *Variety*, 5 March.

Pryor, T. (1952) 'The Bard's "Julius Caesar" Begins Production at MGM,' *New York Times*, 21 September.

Pryor, T. (1953) 'Hollywood Warning,' *New York Times*, 6 September.

Pryor, T. (1955) 'Metro, Goldwyn in Picture Deal,' *New York Times*, 9 March.

Pryor, T. (1957) 'Production and Other Problems Still Unsolved by Harried Loew's Chief,' *New York Times*, 21 July.

Quigley, M. (1938) 'Man-Power,' *Motion Picture Herald*, 8 January, p. 16.

'Radio Finally Links Motion Pictures' (1925) *Radio Age*, December.

Reckert, C. (1957) 'Lion's Roar at Loew's,' *New York Times*, 13 October.

'Regard Irving Thalberg's Passing as a World's Loss in Entertainment' (1936) *Variety*, 16 September, p. 1.

Reid, L. and Smith, A. (1926) 'The Picture Parade,' *Motion Picture Magazine*, May.

Ross, L. (1993) *Picture*, rev. ed., New York: Doubleday.

Rosten, L. (1941) *Hollywood: The Movie Colony, the Movie Makers*, New York: Harcourt, Brace.

'Rounding Up "Our Gang"' (1938) *New York Times*, 26 June.

Russell, W. (1929) 'Screen Setting New Song Records,' *Exhibitors Herald-World*, 2 November, pp. 55–6.

'Sale of MGM Urged' (1958) *New York Times*, 28 February.

Salmans, S. (1984) 'An About-Face for Kerkorian,' *New York Times*, 13 January.

Sansweet, S. (1981) 'MGM Film Assigns Begelman, Fischer to Run Recently Acquired United Artists,' *Wall Street Journal*, 2 October.

Sansweet, S. (1982) 'United Artists: Begelman Leaves 2 Posts,' *Wall Street Journal*, 13 July.

Sansweet, S. (1984) 'Disney Holder Appears to Have Lined Up,' *Wall Street Journal*, 8 June.

'The Scarlet Letter' (1926) *Motion Picture News*, 21 August, p. 681.

Schaffer, G. (1937) '"Maytime" Sets New Standard in Sound Film,' *Chicago Daily Tribune*, 8 March.

Schallert, E. (1924) 'Wife of the Centaur,' *Los Angeles Times*, 6 December.

Schallert, E. (1926) 'La Boheme,' *Los Angeles Times*, 15 May.

Schallert, E. (1927) 'The Student Prince,' *Los Angeles Times*, 11 December.

Schallert, E. (1932a) 'Rivals Menace Greta's Reign,' *Los Angeles Times*, 10 April.

Schallert, E. (1932b) 'Ideal Film Romance Wins Tear at Loew's,' *Los Angeles Times*, 15 October.

Schallert, E. (1937) '"Good Earth" Triumphs at Carthay Premiere,' *Los Angeles Times*, 30 January.

Schallert, E. (1938) '"Antoinette" Lustrous Film Event,' *Los Angeles Times*, 9 July.

Schallert, E. (1952) '"Ivanhoe" Cinema Spectacle of Medieval Combat, Romance,' *Los Angeles Times*, 10 October.

Schatz, T. (1997) *Boom and Bust: Hollywood in the 1940s*, New York: Charles Scribner's Sons.

Schenck, N. (1929) 'Changes in Industry Sweeping,' *Exhibitors Herald-World*, 29 June, p. 145.

'Schenck, Bernstein, Mayer Tell of Payments to Browne and Bioff' (1941) *Motion Picture Herald*, 18 October.

Scheuer, P. (1932) 'Jean Harlow Surprises,' *Los Angeles Times*, 25 June.

Scheuer, P. (1952a) 'The Merry Widow,' *Los Angeles Times*, 23 August.

Scheuer, P. (1952b) '"Bad and Beautiful" Hollywood Expose,' *Los Angeles Times*, 26 December.

Scheuer, P. (1958) 'Cat on a Hot Tin Roof,' *Los Angeles Times*, 30 August.

Scheuer, P. (1962) 'The Story behind an $18 Million Mutiny,' *Los Angeles Times*, 21 October.

Schmidt, J. (1982) 'On the Road to MGM: A History of Metro Pictures Corporation, 1915–1920,' *Velvet Light Trap*, No. 19, January, pp. 46–52.

Schumach, M. (1962a) 'Weitman of MGM Will Head Studio,' *New York Times*, 8 January.

Schumach, M. (1962b) 'Hollywood Shift,' *New York Times*, 14 January.

Schumach, M. (1962c) 'Hollywood at Sea,' *New York Times*, 25 March.

Segers, F. (1984) 'Cannon Breakup with MGM/UA Leaves Golan, Globus Furious,' *Variety*, 7 November.

Selznick, D. (1972) 'The Functions of a Producer,' *Journal of the Producers Guild of America*, December, pp. 24–6.

'The Shadow Stage' (1925) *Photoplay*, July, p. 50.

'The Shadow Stage' (1927) *Photoplay*, January, p. 55.

Shearer, L. (1947) 'GWTW: Supercolossal Saga of an Epic,' *New York Times*, 26 October.

'Shearer Gives Up Role of Scarlett' (1938) *New York Times*, 1 August.

Sherwood, R. E. (1928) 'The Silent Drama,' *Life*, 22 March.

'The Shock of Freedom in Films' (1967) *Time*, 8 December.

Skretvedt, R. (1987) *Laurel and Hardy: The Magic Behind the Movies*, Beverly Hills, CA: Moonstone Press.

Sloane, L. (1969a) 'MGM Says Loss in Year Could Rise to $19 Million,' *New York Times*, 27 May.

Sloane, L. (1969b) 'Some New Teeth for MGM Lion,' *New York Times*, 26 October.

Sloane, L. (1969c) 'New MGM Chief Trims Expenses,' *New York Times*, 12 December.

Smith, C. (1964) 'Runaway Films Tide Turns as Hollywood "Comes Home",' *Los Angeles Times*, 14 June.

'Some Statistics on Four Horsemen' (1923) *Los Angeles Times*, 27 January.

Sorkin, A. (2003) 'MGM Sets Conditions on Bid for Vivendi Units,' *New York Times*, 15 July.

Sorkin, A. (2004a) 'Will This Thriller End Up on the Cutting Room Floor?,' *New York Times*, 2 May.

Sorkin, A. (2004b) 'Sony-Led Group Makes a Late Bid to Wrest MGM from Time Warner,' *New York Times*, 14 September.

Sperling, N. (2003) 'Lion Disconnects Cable,' *Hollywood Reporter*, 1–7 July.

Spiro, J. (1950) 'Now It's for Sure,' *New York Times*, 7 May.

'Star System Folly, Says Rowland' (1919) *Moving Picture World*, 1 January.

Sterngold, J. (1997) 'A Dispute That's Worthy of the Title "Battle Royale",' *New York Times*, 14 October.

Sterngold, J. (1999) 'Advertising,' *New York Times*, 31 March.

Stevenson, R. (1988) 'Question Marks about MGM/UA,' *New York Times*, 9 December.

Stevenson, R. (1989) 'MGM/UA Assets Sold to Qintex,' *New York Times*, 1 April.

Stevenson, R. (1990) 'Pathe Finally Takes Over MGM/UA,' *New York Times*, 2 November.

Stevenson, R. (1991) 'Parretti Out as Chairman of Pathe,' *New York Times*, 17 April.

Stevenson, R. (1992) 'Making the Lion's Den Hospitable,' *New York Times*, 18 February.

'Summer Parks' (1906) *Variety*, 28 July.

Summers, J. (1983) 'Octopussy,' *Boxoffice*, 11 August.

Tazelaar, M. (1929) 'The Kiss,' *New York Herald Tribune*, 16 November.

Tazelaar, M. (1937) 'Way Out West,' *New York Herald Tribune*, 4 May.

'"The Temptress" with Greta Garbo Fulfills Title' (1926) *Los Angeles Times*, 3 October, p. 16.

Thomas, B. (1961) 'Brando Gives His Side of "Bounty" Trouble,' *Los Angeles Times*, 3 November.

Thomas, B. (1978) *Joan Crawford: A Biography*, New York: Simon & Schuster.

Thomas, B. (2000) *Thalberg: Life and Legend*, Los Angeles: New Millennium Press.

Thomas, K. (1971) 'MGM's Sound Expert Shearer – in Memoriam,' *Los Angeles Times*, 17 January.

Thompson, M. (1938) 'Hollywood Is a Uniontown,' *The Nation*, 2 April.

'Time and Bronfman Buy Out Levin's Interest in MGM' (1967) *Boxoffice*, 28 August.

Turk, E. (1998) *Hollywood Diva: A Biography of Jeanette MacDonald*, Berkeley: University of California Press.

'Two Lions May Roar for Separate MGM's' (1979) *Variety*, 21 November.

'Two Producers Quit Hays Group' (1933) *New York Times*, 24 October.

'UA's "Gone with Wind" Release' (1937) *Variety*, 31 March, p. 7.

Underhill, H. (1924) 'Tess of the d'Ubervilles,' *New York Herald Tribune*, 28 July, p. 6.

Underhill, H. (1926) 'Valencia,' *New York Herald Tribune*, 27 December, p. 9.

'Updated All-Time Film Champs' (1975) *Variety*, 8 January, p. 9.

'Valencia' (1927) *Film Daily*, 2 January, p. 9.

Vidor, K. (1935) 'From a Vidor Notebook,' *New York Times*, 10 March.

Vieira, M. (2009) *Irving Thalberg: Boy Wonder to Producer Prince*, Berkeley: University of California Press.

Vincent, R. and Eller, C. (2010) 'MGM to Move from Luxurious Century City Offices,' *Los Angeles Times*, 30 December.

'Vogel Praises Brando for "Mutiny" Acting' (1962) *Boxoffice*, 2 July.

Walker, A. (1980) *Garbo: A Portrait*, New York: Macmillan.

Walker, A. (1983) *Joan Crawford: The Ultimate Star*, New York: Harper & Row.

Waller, T. (1930) 'Year in Pictures,' *Variety*, 8 January.

Ward, R. (2003) 'Extra Added Attractions: The Short Subjects of MGM, Warner Bros. and Universal,' *Media History*, Vol. 9, No. 3, pp. 221–44.

Ward, R. (2005) *A History of the Hal Roach Studios*, Carbondale: Southern Illinois University Press.

Warga, W. (1969) 'Herbert Solow Strives to Leave His Mark at MGM,' *Los Angeles Times*, 31 August.

Warga, W. (1971) 'What's Going on in the Lion's Den at MGM,' *Los Angeles Times*, 26 December.

Watts, R., Jr. (1927) 'Flesh and the Devil,' *New York Herald Tribune*, 16 January, p. E3.

Watts, R., Jr. (1930) 'Comment on Favorite Topics: The Triumph of Greta Garbo,' *New York Herald Tribune*, 23 May.

Watts, R., Jr. (1932a) 'Grand Hotel,' *New York Herald Tribune*, 13 April.

Watts, R., Jr. (1932b) 'Letty Lynton,' *New York Herald Tribune*, 30 April.

Watts, R., Jr. (1933) 'Rasputin and the Empress,' *New York Herald Tribune*, 8 January.

Watts, R., Jr. (1934) 'The Merry Widow,' *New York Herald Tribune*, 12 October.

Watts, R., Jr. (1935) 'Naughty Marietta,' *New York Herald Tribune*, 23 March.

Watts, R., Jr. (1937) 'Good Earth,' *New York Herald Tribune*, 3 February.

Watts, S. (1966) 'London, In and Out of Focus,' *New York Times*, 31 July, p. 3.

Waxman, S. (2005) 'Bond Franchise Is Shaken and Stirred,' *New York Times*, 15 October.

Weiner, R. (1996) 'Kerkorian: Lion King Once again,' *Variety*, 22–28 July, pp. 1, 65.

Weinraub, B. (1993) 'Chief Dismissed in MGM Shake-Up,' *New York Times*, 26 July.

Welles, C. (1969) 'Bo Polk and B School Moviemaking,' *Los Angeles Times*, 3 August.

Wellman, D. (1992) 'New Excesses Found in Parretti's MGM Tenure,' *Los Angeles Times*, 10 April.

Widdicombe, R. (1995) 'James Bond,' *The Times*, 5 November.

'Willie Bioff Defense Accepts the Action but Changes the Script' (1941) *Motion Picture Herald*, 1 November, p. 16.

'Will Lyonnais Liberate Leo?' (1995) *Variety*, 5 November.

Wright, R. (1973) 'MGM Opens Its 2,000 Room Hotel in Las Vegas,' *New York Times*, 6 December.

'Yields to Protests Over Garbo Film' (1941) *New York Times*, 7 December.

York, C. (1927) 'What's the Matter with Greta Garbo?,' *Photoplay*, April, p. 29.

Young, D. (1992) 'Parretti Rings in 92 Behind Bars,' *Variety*, 6 January.

Zinsser, W. (1956) 'Forever Darling,' *New York Herald Tribune*, 10 February.

GENERAL INDEX

producer credit 95; production supervisor 55, 67; profit-sharing agreement 97, 196

Weinstein Co. 277

Weissmuller, Johnnie 84

Weitman, Robert M. 7, 213, 216

Welles, Orson 185, 186, 202, 209

Wellman, William 167

West, Claudine 112, 114, 135, 147

Western Air Lines 228, 232

Western Electric 59, 60, 61

Westerns 51

Whitney, Jock 131

Wilder, Billy 121, 185, 224, 245

William Morris vaudeville circuit 15

Williams, Esther 140, 153, 154, 159, 165, 177, 179

Willis, Bruce 262, 269, 270

Willis, Ed 115

Wilson, Carey 31, 35, 36

Wilson, Michael G. 268, 276

Winkler, Irwin 234, 244, 246, 256, 260

Winters, Shelley 186, 221

Wise, Robert 185, 224

woman's film 5, 63–6, 85, 120; Greta Garbo 47–9, 51–2, 65–6, 85, 120–2; Jean Harlow 89; Joan Crawford 56–7, 85–8, 123–4; Norma Shearer 63, 85–6, 122–3

Wood, Sam 54, 89–90, 125, 134, 136, 165

Writers Guild of America 214

WTBS 252, 267

Wurtzel, Sol 25

Wyler, William 6, 7, 128, 147, 148, 200, 201

Wyman, Jane 157, 158

Yablans, Frank 246–9

Yemenidjian, Alex 8, 266, 268, 269–70, 271, 274

Young, Robert 124, 145, 146

Young, Roland 62, 106

youthpix 234

Zaentz, Saul 244, 283

Zanra Productions 192

Zanuck, Darryl F. 25, 111, 171, 230

Zanuck, Richard D. 225, 231

Zeffirelli, Franco 233, 242

Zimbalist, Sam 137, 150, 168, 169

Zuckor, Adolph 4, 10, 12, 15–16, 18, 24, 97

Zugsmith, Albert 202, 207

INDEX OF FILM AND TELEVISION TITLES